THE CONSTITUTION

AND THE SUPREME COURT

THE

CONSTITUTION

AND THE

SUPREME COURT

A Documentary History

VOLUME II

Edited by

LOUIS H. POLLAK

Introduction by
GEORGE F. SCHEER

THE WORLD PUBLISHING COMPANY

Cleveland and New York

Published by The World Publishing Company
2231 West 110th Street, Cleveland 2, Ohio

Library of Congress Catalog Card Number: 63–12324

First Edition

Printed in the United States of America

CONTENTS

NOTE: *The documents, or excerpts of documents, that are listed above are set in italics, and the editor's commentary is set in roman type.*

PREFACE

THE AMERICAN PENCHANT FOR CONSTITUTIONAL DISCOURSE is an integral part of our national character. As Alexis de Tocqueville observed, "Scarcely any question arises in the United States which does not become, sooner or later, a subject of judicial debate. . . ." The wise French traveler was writing more than a century ago, but his perception is no less apt today. And it is that perception which is the *raison d'être* of these two volumes. They are volumes of documents, and of attendant commentary, designed to convey, in broad outline, the constitutional development of the United States.

The first volume begins with the Declaration of Independence, for the obvious reason that the act of denying continued British dominion forced the American states to develop new political relationships among themselves and with other nations. To formulate—to *constitute*—these new relationships was a two-phased process.

The first phase—the drawing up and ratification of Articles of Confederation which "shall be inviolably observed" by states constituting a "Union [which] shall be perpetual"—in retrospect seems abortive. For the Articles of Confederation were superseded within a decade. But if the Articles were not "inviolably observed," the union nonetheless has continued in being to this day.

In short, the states' unsuccessful attempt to live together under the Articles of Confederation was the necessary historic precondition of the second phase of America's political development: the negotiation and adoption of the Constitution.

The adoption of the Constitution is only the preface to America's constitutional history. The history itself has been the development of institutions—primarily, the United States Supreme Court—capable of giving continuity and contemporary force to generalizations about the politics of freedom which were crystallized in the eighteenth century.

To make this history meaningful (and, simultaneously, to convey some sense of the actual workings of the judicial process) a considerable portion of the first volume is devoted to the Supreme Court's early and fundamental assertions of authority:

First, there is the history of *Marbury v. Madison,* which gave John Marshall a platform for claiming vast judicial power while eschewing the hazards of its immediate and almost assuredly unsuccessful exercise.

Second, there is the history of the Bank of the United States: a constitutional debate which began with the first Congress; a constitutional debate in which Alexander Hamilton, James Madison, Thomas Jefferson, George Washington, Daniel Webster, Andrew Jackson, and Roger B. Taney all played major roles; a constitutional debate in which, nevertheless, as our national myths have evolved, Marshall occupies the center of the stage alone. It is a history which began to shape the concurrent responsibilities of Congress, the President, and the federal courts, for declaring the nation's fundamental law. And it is a history which largely settled the supremacy of federal over state law, and the correlative authority of the Supreme Court as the ultimate arbiter between them.

Third, there is the history of *Gibbons v. Ogden,* in which the Supreme Court, again speaking through Marshall, put itself into the business of reviewing state economic policies assertedly inconsistent with the national free market embodied in the Constitution. The later history of the case shows the compliance of state judicial authority with the Supreme Court's mandate, a compliance which has been customary (though not invariable) and for lack of which the American constitutional experiment would long since have been liquidated. Cases subsequent to *Gibbons v. Ogden,* under both the commerce clause and the Fourteenth Amendment, show something of the Court's periodic wisdom, and something of the Court's periodic folly, as reviser of state economic policy and hence as shaper of national economic policy.

Next, the first volume considers the role of the Supreme Court in relation to the slow-in-coming, but ultimately massive, assertion by Congress and the President of the power to govern the whole United States, internally and as a nation in the world. Here, the limits of judicial competence—especially as illustrated by the Supreme Court's calamitous war with Franklin D. Roosevelt—are etched most sharply.

The first volume closes with a brief look at the United Nations and the International Court of Justice—supranational institutions which have thus far acquired very little real authority but which may, in the long future, become the instrumentalities of a viable and world-wide constitutionalism.

The second volume then concentrates on those phases of America's constitutional development in which claims to personal freedom have been juxtaposed against the powers to govern. Here, in accommodating democratic aspirations with one another and with the pragmatic demands of effective government, the Constitution and the Supreme Court have perhaps achieved their most considerable successes. The materials canvass familiar and currently compelling issues—issues of free speech; issues of freedom of religion and its correlative separation of church and state; and, at considerable length, issues of racial equality and of legislative reapportionment which are today the first order of judicial business. Also, the materials consider, in some detail, cases raising questions as to the procedures constitutionally required in order to assure a fair trial for one charged with crime. Underlying this extended treatment of due-process questions are the recognition that the criminal process has direct impact on hundreds of thousands of Americans every year, and the cognate hope that ruminating about these questions will yield some rudimentary understanding of what is at once the law's most threatening and most familiar face.

The Constitution, more modest in program than the Articles of Confederation, sought only to build "a more perfect Union." This it has done and is doing; not without lapses, but with an over-all success far beyond the most spacious hopes of the men who met in Philadelphia in 1787, in constitutional convention assembled. And—barring a holocaust which would end all experiments in civilization—there seems reason to believe that the Constitution can continue into an indefinite future the enterprise launched by the Articles of Confederation: a "Union [which] shall be perpetual." Indeed, it may well be that the Constitution, and the supporting energies of the American people, can in decades still remote assist in the building of a wider international union dedicated to the principles of freedom that have made the American experience man's noblest adventure.

July, 1965

LOUIS H. POLLAK

Grateful acknowledgment is made to the following for permission to reprint from copyrighted works:

ACADEMIC REPRINTS, Stanford, California, for material from *Mr. Dooley: Now and Forever*, by Finley Peter Dunne; selected, with commentary and introduction by Louis Filler (1954).

APPLETON-CENTURY, DUELL, SLOAN & PEARCE, for material from *The Complete Jefferson*, edited by Saul K. Padover (1943); and for material from *Documents of American History*, edited by Henry Steele Commager, 4th edition (1948).

ASSOCIATION OF AMERICAN LAW SCHOOLS, for material from "Sociological Factors in the Effectiveness of Projected Legal Remedies," by Arnold M. Rose, 11 *Journal of Legal Education* (1959).

ATHENEUM PUBLISHERS, for material from *The Making of the President, 1960*, by Theodore White (1961).

BEACON PRESS, for material from *Church, State and Freedom*, by Leo Pfeffer (1953).

THE BOBBS-MERRILL COMPANY, INC., for material from *Alexander Hamilton's Papers on Public Credit, Commerce and Finance*, edited by Samuel McKee, Jr., copyright, 1934, by Columbia University Press, © 1957, by The Liberal Arts Press, Inc., reprinted by permission of the Liberal Arts Press Division of The Bobbs-Merrill Company, Inc.; for material from *James Madison: The Nationalist, 1780–1787*, by Irving Brant, copyright © 1948, by The Bobbs-Merrill Company, Inc., reprinted by permission of the publishers; for material from *James Madison: Father of the Constitution, 1787–1800*, by Irving Brant, copyright © 1950, by The Bobbs-Merrill Company, Inc., reprinted by permission of the publishers; for material from *The Least Dangerous Branch: The Supreme Court at the Bar of Politics*, by Alexander M. Bickel, copyright © 1962, by The Bobbs-Merrill Company, Inc., reprinted by permission of the publishers; and for material from *Justice Rutledge and the Bright Constellation*, by Fowler V. Harper, copyright © 1965, by The Bobbs-Merrill Company, Inc., reprinted by permission of the publishers.

CENTER FOR THE STUDY OF DEMOCRATIC INSTITUTIONS, for material from *The Rule of Law in World Affairs*, by William O. Douglas (1961).

COLUMBIA LAW REVIEW, for material from "Free Speech in War Time," by James Parker Hall, 21 *Columbia Law Review* (1921).

COLUMBIA UNIVERSITY PRESS, for material from *Vagaries and Varieties in Constitutional Interpretation*, by Thomas Reed Powell (1956); and for material from *Race Relations and American Law*, by Jack Greenberg (1959).

DOUBLEDAY & COMPANY, INC., for material from *The 168 Days*, by Joseph Alsop and Turner Catledge. Copyright 1937, 1938 by Joseph Alsop and Turner Catledge. Reprinted by permission of Doubleday & Company, Inc.; and for material from *Crisis of the House Divided*, by Harry V.

Jaffe. Copyright © 1959 by Harry V. Jaffe. Reprinted by permission of Doubleday & Company, Inc.

E. P. DUTTON & CO., INC., and Everyman's Library, for material from *Two Treatises of Government*, by John Locke (1924).

ENCYCLOPAEDIA BRITANNICA, INC., for material from Volume III of *The Encyclopaedia Britannica*.

FOUNDATION PRESS, for material from "The Still Small Voice of the Commerce Clause," *Selected Essays on Constitutional Law*, by Thomas Reed Powell (1938); for material from *The Federal Courts and the Federal System*, by Henry M. Hart and Herbert Wechsler (1953); and for material from *Cases on Constitutional Law*, by Noel T. Dowling, 6th edition (1959).

FUND FOR THE REPUBLIC, for material from *The United States and Revolution*, by Kenneth Boulding (1961).

HARCOURT, BRACE & WORLD, INC., for material from *Law and Politics: Occasional Papers of Felix Frankfurter, 1913–1938*, edited by Archibald MacLeish and E. F. Prichard, Jr. (1939); and for material from *Of Law and Men: Papers and Addresses of Felix Frankfurter, 1939–1956*, edited by Philip Elman (1956).

HARPER & ROW, PUBLISHERS, INC., for material from "The Case of the Louisiana Traveler," by C. Vann Woodward, in *Quarrels That Have Shaped the Constitution*, edited by John A. Garraty (1964); and for material from *Congress: The Sapless Branch*, by Joseph S. Clark (1964).

HARRISON-BLAINE OF NEW JERSEY, INC., for material from "Felix Frankfurter, 1882–1965," by Alexander M. Bickel, in *The New Republic*, March 6, 1965.

HARVARD LAW REVIEW, for material from "Mr. Justice Brandeis and the Constitution," by Felix Frankfurter, 45 *Harvard Law Review* (1931), copyright © 1931 by The Harvard Law Review Association; for material from "The Original Understanding and the Segregation Decision," by Alexander M. Bickel, 69 *Harvard Law Review* (1955), copyright © 1955 by The Harvard Law Review Association; for material from "Foreword: The Reapportionment Case," by Robert G. McCloskey, 76 *Harvard Law Review* (1962), copyright © 1962 by The Harvard Law Review Association; and for material from "The Supreme Court 1962 Term Foreword: Public Prayers in Public Schools," by Louis H. Pollak, 77 *Harvard Law Review* (1963), copyright © 1963 by The Harvard Law Review Association.

HARVARD UNIVERSITY PRESS, for material from *Free Speech in the United States*, by Zechariah Chafee, Jr. (1946); for material from *The Supreme Court in the American System of Government*, by Robert H. Jackson (1955); for material from *The Unpublished Opinions of Mr. Justice Brandeis*, edited by Alexander M. Bickel (1957); and for material from *The Bill of Rights*, by Learned Hand (1958).

ALFRED A. KNOPF, INC., for material from *The Struggle for Judicial Supremacy*, by Robert H. Jackson (1941); for material from *Liberty and Justice: A Historical Record of American Constitutional Development*, edited by James Morton Smith and Paul L. Murphy (1958); and for material from *The Spirit of Liberty: Papers and Address of Learned Hand,* collected and with an introduction and notes by Irving Dilliard, 3rd edition (1960).

LAW AND CONTEMPORARY PROBLEMS, for material from "Law or Prepossessions?" by John Courtney Murray, reprinted from a symposium *Religion and the State,* Vol. 14, No. 1 (Winter 1949), by permission from Father Courtney and from *Law and Contemporary Problems,* published by the Duke University School of Law, Durham, N.C. Copyright © 1949, by Duke University.

LIFE magazine, for material from "Adams Papers," edited by L. H. Butterfield, *Life,* June 30, 1961.

LITTLE, BROWN AND COMPANY, for material from *The Supreme Court in United States History,* by Charles Warren. Copyright 1922, 1926, by Little, Brown and Company. Reprinted by permission of Little, Brown and Company; for material from *On Understanding the Supreme Court,* by Paul A. Freund. Copyright 1951, by Little, Brown and Company. Reprinted by permission of Little, Brown and Company; and for material from *Constitutional Law: Cases and Other Problems,* by Paul A. Freund and others, 2nd edition, Copyright 1961 by Little, Brown and Company. Reprinted by permission of Little, Brown and Company.

THE MACMILLAN COMPANY, for material from *An Economic Interpretation of the Constitution of the United States,* by Charles A. Beard (1913). Reprinted by permission of the publisher; for material from *Encyclopedia of the Social Sciences,* edited by Edwin R. A. Seligman (1930). Reprinted by permission of the publisher; for material from *The Information Please Almanac* (1956). Reprinted by permission of the publisher; and for material from *Morrison R. Waite: The Triumph of Character,* by C. Peter Magrath (1963). Reprinted by permission of the publisher.

NEW HAVEN REGISTER, for material from the issues of December 12, 1962, and July 21, 1964.

NEW YORK TIMES, for material from the issues of September 26, 1957; March 3, June 23, 1960; July 2, December 19, 1961; January 29, February 1, June 27, 28, July 1, 11, 1962; June 12, 17, 18, July 27, September 17, November 28, 1963; May 24, July 3, 12, 19, 23, August 6, 10, 11, 13, October 6, December 11, 15, 20, 1964; March 2, May 16, June 27, July 7, 17, 18, 1965. © 1957, 1960, 1961, 1962, 1963, 1964, 1965 by The New York Times Company. Reprinted by permission.

NEW YORK UNIVERSITY, for material from "The Bill of Rights and the States," by William J. Brennan, Jr., 36 *New York University Law Review* (1961). 1961 James Madison Lecture delivered at New York University School of Law. Reprinted with permission of New York University, copyright owner; and for material from "Equality and Governmental Action," by Arthur Goldberg, 39 *New York University Law Review* (1964). 1964 James Madison Lecture delivered at New York University School of Law. Reprinted with permission of New York University, copyright owner.

OCEANA PUBLICATIONS, INC., for material from *The Tradition of Freedom: Selections from the Writers Who Shaped the Traditional Concepts of Freedom and Justice in America*, edited by M. Mayer (1957).

OXFORD UNIVERSITY PRESS, for material from *Sources and Documents Illustrating the American Revolution*, edited by Samuel E. Morison (1923); for material from *The Growth of the American Republic*, by Samuel E. Morison and Henry S. Commager (1956–1957); and for material from *The Strange Career of Jim Crow*, by C. Vann Woodward (1957).

RANDOM HOUSE, INC., for material from *The Public Papers and Addresses of Franklin D. Roosevelt*, edited by Samuel I. Rosenman. Copyright 1938 by Franklin Delano Roosevelt. Reprinted by permission of Random House, Inc.; and for material from *Gideon's Trumpet*, by Anthony Lewis (1964). Reprinted by permission of Random House, Inc.

SIMON AND SCHUSTER, INC., for material from *Law as Large as Life*, by Charles Pelham Curtis (1959).

SOUTHERN EDUCATION REPORTING SERVICE, for material from *Southern School News* (October 1962); and for material from *Statistical Summary of School Segregation-Desegregation in the Southern and Border States, 1963–1964*.

STANFORD UNIVERSITY PRESS, for material from *Origins of the American Revolution*, by John C. Miller (1959).

UNIVERSITY OF CHICAGO LAW REVIEW, for material from "An Introduction to Legal Reasoning," by Edward H. Levi, 15 *University of Chicago Law Review* (1948).

UNIVERSITY OF CHICAGO PRESS, for material reprinted from *Created Equal?* by Paul Angle, by permission of The University of Chicago Press. Copyright 1958 by the University of Chicago; and for material reprinted from *We the People*, by Forrest McDonald, by permission of The University of Chicago Press. Copyright 1958 by the University of Chicago.

UNIVERSITY OF KANSAS PRESS, for material from *A Declaration of Legal Faith*, by Wiley B. Rutledge (1947).

UNIVERSITY OF NORTH CAROLINA PRESS, for material from *The Commerce Clause under Marshall, Taney and Waite*, by Felix Frankfurter (1937).

UNIVERSITY OF SOUTH CAROLINA PRESS, for material from *Justice William Johnson, the First Dissenter*, by Donald G. Morgan (1954).

VANDERBILT UNIVERSITY, for material from 2 *Race Relations Law Reporter* (1957); and for material from "The Waite Court and the Fourteenth Amendment," by Howard Jay Graham, 17 *Vanderbilt Law Review* (1964).

JOHN WILEY & SONS, for material from *Basic Writings*, by Thomas Paine (1942).

YALE LAW JOURNAL, for material from "William Cushing," by Arthur P. Rugg, 30 *Yale Law Journal* (1920); for material from "The 'Conspiracy' Theory of the Fourteenth Amendment," by Howard Jay Graham, 47 *Yale Law Journal* (1938); for material from "Treaties and Executive Agreement—A Reply," by Edwin M. Borchard, 54 *Yale Law Journal*

(1945); for material from "The Proposed Amendment of Article V: A Threatened Disaster," by Charles L. Black, Jr., 72 *Yale Law Journal* (1963); and for material from "Toward a General Theory of the First Amendment," by Thomas Emerson, 72 *Yale Law Journal* (1963). Reprinted by permission of the Yale Law Journal Company and Fred B. Rothman & Company.

YALE REVIEW, for material from "The Supreme Court and Democracy," by Charles L. Black, Jr., 50 *Yale Review* (1961).

YALE UNIVERSITY PRESS, for material from *The Nature of the Judicial Process*, by Benjamin N. Cardozo (1932); for material from *The Records of the Federal Convention of 1787*, edited by Max Farrand (1937); for material from *The Twilight of the Supreme Court: A History of Our Constitutional Theory*, by Edward S. Corwin (1934); and for material from *The Framing of the Constitution of the United States*, by Max Farrand (1962).

Grateful acknowledgment is made also to Paul A. Freund for permission to reprint excerpts from his address before the American Jewish Committee on November 11, 1962.

A careful effort has been made to trace the ownership of selections included in these volumes in order to secure permission to reprint copyrighted material and to make full acknowledgment of its use. If any error or omission has occurred, it is purely inadvertent and will be corrected in subsequent editions.

IV

Democratic Restraints
on the
Power to Govern

IV

Democratic Restraints
on the
Power to Govern

THE COMPLEX FEDERALISM contemplated by the Constitution was to be more than just an effective instrument for the government of a vast new domain. The United States was to be a republic—or, in today's coinage, a democracy. The United States, Lincoln said in the Gettysburg Address, was "a new nation, conceived in liberty, and dedicated to the proposition that all men are created equal." What follows is an attempt to identify, rather than to survey in detail, the chief restraints that a commitment to democracy—to liberty and to equality—imposes on the power to govern.

A. THE FIRST AMENDMENT

THE FIRST AMENDMENT provides:

> Congress shall make no law respecting an establishment of religion, or prohibiting the free exercise thereof; or abridging the freedom of speech, or of the press; or the right of the people peaceably to assemble, and to petition the Government for a redress of grievances.

Embodied in the amendment are two kinds of guarantees: One is a comprehensive injunction that government keep hands off the people's right to worship, think, talk, and write. The second, which is a corollary of the freedom of *religious* thought and expression, is the injunction that government and religion steer wholly clear of one another.

Much recent constitutional mythology has rotated about questions of relative orders of importance to be ascribed to various of the liberties that the Constitution protects. One may venture a mild skepticism about the worth, or indeed the feasibility, of working out a very exact table of constitutional valences. The ultimate purpose to be served by the Constitution is the creation of a cohesive community, endowed with a congeries of liberal values, and the withdrawal of any important value seriously impairs the worth of the community. Nevertheless, there is a well-founded consensus that the values of free thought and expression are crucial for a community which fosters the dignity and personal fulfillment of each individual. What underlies this consensus is the conviction, expressed by Justice Benjamin N. Cardozo, that "freedom of thought, and speech . . . is the matrix, the indispensable condition, of nearly every other form of freedom. With rare aberrations a pervasive recognition of that truth can be traced in our history, political and legal."[1]

The political processes of a democratic community of course depend on free thought and free expression. But the freedoms cut deeper still. Science, religion, art, poetry—all the aspects of man's reaching out for wider horizons—depend upon free inquiry and free intellectual exchange. This, at bottom, is the lesson of John Milton's *Areopagitica*, his speech to Parliament in 1644 "for the Liberty of Unlicenc'd Printing":

. . . Good and evill we know in the field of this World grow up together almost inseparably; and the knowledge of good is so involv'd and interwoven with the knowledge of evill, and in so many cunning resemblances hardly to be discern'd, that those confused seeds which were impos'd on Psyche as an incessant labour to cull out, and sort asunder, were not more intermixt. It was from out the rinde of one apple tasted, that the knowledge of good and evill as two twins cleaving together leapt forth into the World. And perhaps this is that doom which Adam fell into of knowing good and evill, that is to say of knowing good by evill. As therefore the state of man now is; what wisdome can there be to choose, what continence to forbeare without the knowledge of evill? He that can apprehend and consider vice with all her baits and seeming pleasures, and yet abstain, and yet distinguish, and yet prefer that which is truly better, he is the true wayfaring Christian. I cannot praise a fugitive and cloister'd vertue, unexercis'd and unbreath'd, that never sallies out and sees her adversary, but slinks out of the race, where that immortall garland is to be run for, not without dust and heat. Assuredly we bring not innocence into the world, we bring impurity much rather: that which purifies us is triall, and triall is by what is contrary. That vertue therefore which is but a youngling in the contemplation of evill, and knows not the utmost that vice promises to her followers, and rejects it, is but a blank vertue, not a pure. . . . Since therefore the knowledge and survay of

vice is in this world so necessary to the constituting of human vertue, and the scanning of error to the confirmation of truth, how can we more safely, and with lesse danger scout into the regions of sin and falsity then by reading all manner of tractats, and hearing all manner of reason? And this is the benefit which may be had of books promiscuously read.[2]

1. Freedom of speech and of the press

In 1819, writing to Virginia's Judge Spencer Roane, Thomas Jefferson described the triumph of his Republicans over the Federalists as "the revolution of 1800, for that was as real a revolution in the principles of our government as that of 1776 was in its form; not effected indeed by the sword, as that, but by the rational and peaceable instrument of reform, the suffrage of the people."[3] In his first inaugural address, on March 4, 1801, Jefferson spoke in pacific terms about the "revolution" which had just taken place:

During the contest of opinion through which we have passed, the animation of discussion and of exertions has sometimes worn an aspect which might impose on strangers unused to think freely and to speak and to write what they think; but this being now decided by the voice of the nation, announced according to the rules of the constitution, all will, of course, arrange themselves under the will of the law, and unite in common efforts for the common good. All, too, will bear in mind this sacred principle, that though the will of the majority is in all cases to prevail, that will, to be rightful, must be reasonable; that the minority possess their equal rights, which equal laws must protect, and to violate which would be oppression. Let us, then, fellow-citizens, unite with one heart and one mind. Let us restore to social intercourse that harmony and affection without which liberty and even life itself are but dreary things. And let us reflect that having banished from our land that religious intolerance under which mankind has so long bled and suffered, we have yet gained little if we countenance a political intolerance as despotic, as wicked, and capable of as bitter and bloody persecutions. During the throes and convulsions of the ancient world, during the

*agonizing spasms of infuriated man, seeking through blood and
slaughter his long-lost liberty, it was not wonderful that the
agitation of the billows should reach even this distant and peaceful shore; that this should be more felt and feared by some and
less by others; that this should divide opinions as to measures of
safety. But every difference of opinion is not a difference of
principle. We have called by different names brethren of the
same principle. We are all republicans—we are all federalists. If
there be any among us who would wish to dissolve this Union or
to change its republican form, let them stand undisturbed as
monuments of the safety with which error of opinion may be
tolerated where reason is left free to combat it. I know, indeed,
that some honest men fear that a republican government cannot
be strong; that this government is not strong enough. But would
the honest patriot, in the full tide of successful experiment,
abandon a government which has so far kept us free and firm, on
the theoretic and visionary fear that this government, the world's
best hope, may by possibility want energy to preserve itself? I
trust not. I believe this, on the contrary, the strongest government
on earth. I believe it is the only one where every man, at the call
of the laws, would fly to the standard of the law, and would meet
invasions of the public order as his own personal concern. Sometimes it is said that man cannot be trusted with the government
of himself. Can he, then, be trusted with the government of
others? Or have we found angels in the forms of kings to govern
him? Let history answer this question.*[4]

Doubtless Jefferson was remembering the late and unla-
mented Sedition Act, which had expired the day before, when he
spoke of those enemies of the nation "who would wish to dissolve
this Union or to change its republican form" and urged that they
be permitted to "stand undisturbed as monuments of the safety
with which error of opinion may be tolerated where reason is left
free to combat it." Doubtless Jefferson was recalling also how the
Adams administration had made partisan use of the Sedition Act
to pillory newspaper editors who supported the Republican
cause. And doubtless Jefferson had in mind his and Madison's
joint efforts, through the Kentucky and Virginia Resolutions, to
declare the Sedition Act invalid—efforts which, like Franklin
Roosevelt's "court packing" plan, were abortive in technique but

led to a radical change in the dominant principles of constitutional law.

At all events, during the more than a century from the demise of the Sedition Act to the adoption of the Espionage Acts in World War I, only the Civil War provoked massive national repression of free speech. And then the repression was not fashioned by Congress. Professor James Parker Hall, writing just after World War I, provided a succinct summary of the withering of free speech during the Civil War:

> *Those who have criticised the recent Espionage Acts have sometimes referred to the lack of similar legislation in the Civil War as proof that such laws were unnecessary and unwise. But there is more than one way to skin a cat—or, in the more dignified language of political science, a powerful government in war time can find other means of dealing with disloyalty than through the courts. During the Civil War it was deemed politically inexpedient to legislate against disloyal utterances in general. In the earlier stages of the contest Lincoln earnestly sought to hold the border slave states in the Union. He was represented as praying: "Oh, Lord, we earnestly hope that Thou will favor our cause, but we must have Kentucky." Men not irreconcilably of Southern sympathies were to be won over, if possible, by the methods of persuasion. Many utterances that in Massachusetts would have been treated as clearly indicative of disloyalty, in Kentucky were the natural expressions of men sorely perplexed and reluctant to make a decision that either way was fraught with such sorrow. Legislation applying to all alike would have been unjust and alienating to the border state doubters, and would have been widely criticized as an illustration of the despotism so often charged again[st] Lincoln by his opponents. But, without the sanction of legislation, the federal government arrested by the thousand men whom it knew or suspected to be dangerous or disaffected, and confined them without charges and without trial in military prisons as long as it saw fit,—and public opinion generally acquiesced in this as a fairly necessary measure of war-time precaution. The number of such executive arrests has been variously estimated up to as high as 38,000. The War Department records, confessedly very incomplete, show over 13,000. Our recent record of about 2,000 prosecutions under the Espionage*

Acts, with perhaps half as many convictions, compares very favorably with this, and gives no ground for saying that freedom of any sort was more interfered with in the war with Germany than in the war between the states.[5]

The World War I Espionage Acts were not, in terms, aimed at speech. They were aimed at actions interfering with the war effort. Quite obviously, a nation at war is fully entitled to protect itself against actual or attempted espionage, sabotage, and the like. The problem presented by the Espionage Acts was that certain of their provisions ran, or were construed to run, farther afield—making it criminal, for example, to obstruct recruiting; cause insubordination in the armed forces; say anything abusive about the American form of government, or the flag, or the military uniform; urge the curtailment of military production with intent to hinder prosecution of the war, etc. Such provisions were clearly susceptible of use as weapons against those who held, and expressed, honest misgivings about the nation's participation in the war.

In *Schenck v. United States,* the first of the World War I cases involving free speech to reach the Supreme Court, a conviction for attempting to cause insubordination in the armed forces was unanimously sustained. The defendants were two Socialists who printed and distributed to draftees pamphlets that contained the text of the Thirteenth Amendment (abolishing slavery) plus a harangue on why young men should not submit to the involuntary servitude of army life just to benefit Wall Street. Justice Oliver Wendell Holmes, the author of the Court's opinion, dismissed the constitutional issue in the following words, which are the genesis of the ever-since-incanted "clear and present danger" test:

. . . It well may be that the prohibition of laws abridging the freedom of speech is not confined to previous restraints, although to prevent them may have been the main purpose, as intimated in Patterson v. Colorado, 205 U.S. 454, 462. We admit *that in many places and in ordinary times the defendants in saying all that was said in the circular would have been within their constitutional rights. But the character of every act depends upon the circumstances in which it is done.* Aikens v. Wisconsin, 195 U.S. 194, 205, 206. The most stringent protection of free *speech would not protect a man in falsely shouting fire in a*

theatre and causing a panic. It does not even protect a man from an injunction against uttering words that may have all the effect of force. Gompers v. Bucks Stove & Range Co., 221 U.S. 418, 439. *The question in every case is whether the words used are used in such circumstances and are of such a nature as to create a clear and present danger that they will bring about the substantive evils that Congress has a right to prevent. It is a question of proximity and degree. When a nation is at war many things that might be said in time of peace are such a hindrance to its effort that their utterance will not be endured so long as men fight and that no Court could regard them as protected by any constitutional right.*[6]

Several months later the Supreme Court reviewed an Espionage Act conviction which Holmes (and his great colleague, Justice Louis D. Brandeis) found could not be squared with the First Amendment. This time the defendants had printed and distributed leaflets that attacked the Wilson administration for its "hypocrisy" in sending an American expeditionary force to intervene in the Russian Revolution, and that urged workers to halt production—by a general strike, if necessary—of weapons to be used in Russia. In *Abrams v. United States,* the Court affirmed the convictions and twenty-year prison sentences. Holmes explained at length why he and Brandeis disagreed:

. . . I do not doubt for a moment that by the same reasoning that would justify punishing persuasion to murder, the United States constitutionally may punish speech that produces or is intended to produce a clear and imminent danger that it will bring about forthwith certain substantive evils that the United States constitutionally may seek to prevent. The power undoubtedly is greater in time of war than in time of peace because war opens dangers that do not exist at other times.

But as against dangers peculiar to war, as against others, the principle of the right to free speech is always the same. It is only the present danger of immediate evil or an intent to bring it about that warrants Congress in setting a limit to the expression of opinion where private rights are not concerned. Congress certainly cannot forbid all effort to change the mind of the country. Now nobody can suppose that the surreptitious publishing of a silly leaflet by an unknown man, without more, would present any immediate danger that its opinions would hinder the success of the government arms or have any appreciable tendency to do so. Publishing those opinions for the very purpose of obstructing however, might indicate a greater danger and at any rate would have the quality of an attempt. . . . But it seems pretty clear to me that nothing less than that would bring these papers within the scope of this law.

.   .   .   .   .

In this case sentences of twenty years imprisonment have been imposed for the publishing of two leaflets that I believe the defendants had as much right to publish as the Government has to publish the Constitution of the United States now vainly invoked by them. Even if I am technically wrong and enough can be squeezed from these poor and puny anonymities to turn the color of legal litmus paper; I will add, even if what I think the necessary intent were shown; the most nominal punishment seems to me all that possibly could be inflicted, unless the defendants are to be made to suffer not for what the indictment alleges but for the creed that they avow—a creed that I believe to be the creed of ignorance and immaturity when honestly held, as I see no reason to doubt that it was held here, but which, although made the subject of examination at the trial, no one has a right even to consider in dealing with the charges before the Court.

Persecution for the expression of opinions seems to me perfectly logical. If you have no doubt of your premises or your power and want a certain result with all your heart you naturally express your wishes in law and sweep away all opposition. To allow opposition by speech seems to indicate that you think the speech impotent, as when a man says that he has squared the circle, or that you do not care wholeheartedly for the result, or that you doubt either your power or your premises. But when men have realized that time has upset many fighting faiths, they may come to believe even more than they believe the very foundations of their own conduct that the ultimate good desired is better reached by free trade in ideas—that the best test of truth is the power of the thought to get itself accepted in the competition of the market, and that truth is the only ground upon which their wishes safely can be carried out. That at any rate is the theory of our Constitution. It is an experiment, as all life is cn experiment. Every year if not every day we have to wager our salvation upon some prophecy based upon imperfect knowledge. While that experiment is part of our system I think that we should be eternally vigilant against attempts to check the expression of opinions that we loathe and believe to be fraught with death, unless they so imminently threaten immediate interference with the lawful and pressing purposes of the law that an immediate check is required to save the country. I wholly disagree with the argument of the Government that the First Amendment left the common law as to seditious libel in force. History seems to me against the notion. I had conceived that the United States through many years had shown its repentance for the Sedition Act of 1798, by repaying fines that it imposed. Only the emergency that makes it immediately dangerous to leave the correction of evil counsels to time warrants making any exception to the sweeping command, "Congress shall make no law . . . abridging the freedom of speech." Of course I am speaking only of expressions of opinion and exhortations, which were all that were uttered here, but I regret that I cannot put into more impressive words my belief that in their conviction upon this indictment the defendants were deprived of their rights under the Constitution of the United States.[7]

But these were dissenting views. The Court uniformly sustained the statute in the few prosecutions which came before it, a tiny fraction of the approximately one thousand convictions which the government achieved.[8] "It became criminal," reported Professor Zechariah Chafee, Jr., the great student of American free speech,

to advocate heavier taxation instead of bond issues, to state that conscription was unconstitutional though the Supreme Court had not yet held it valid, to say that the sinking of merchant vessels was legal, to urge that a referendum should have preceded our declaration of war, to say that war was contrary to the teachings of Christ.[9]

The next major free speech case to come to the Supreme Court was the 1925 case of *Gitlow v. New York,* a criminal conviction based on a state statute making the teaching of "criminal anarchy" a felony. Benjamin Gitlow, a leader of the dissident Left Wing of the Socialist Party, was prosecuted for publishing thousands of copies of a characteristically turgid proletarian

"Manifesto." The general tenor of the "Manifesto" can be gleaned from the following passages:

The bourgeois parliamentary state is the organ of the bourgeoisie for the coercion of the proletariat. The revolutionary proletariat must, accordingly, destroy this state. . . . It is therefore necessary that the proletariat organize its own state for the coercion and suppression of the bourgeoisie. *. . . Proletarian dictatorship is a recognition of the necessity for a revolutionary state to coerce and suppress the bourgeoisie; it is equally a recognition of the fact that, in the Communist reconstruction of society, the proletariat as a class alone counts. . . . The old machinery of the state cannot be used by the revolutionary proletariat. It must be destroyed. . . . It is not a problem of immediate revolution. It is a problem of the immediate revolutionary struggle. The revolutionary epoch of the final struggle against Capitalism may last for years and tens of years; but the Communist International offers a policy and program immediate and ultimate in scope, that provides for the immediate class struggle against Capitalism, in its revolutionary implications, and for the final act of the conquest of power. The old order is in decay. Civilization is in collapse. The proletarian revolution and the Communist reconstruction of society—the struggle for these— is now indispensable. This is the message of the Communist International to the workers of the world. The Communist International calls the proletariat of the world to the final struggle!*[10]

Because his was a state prosecution, Gitlow could not stand on the First Amendment. That amendment—indeed, the entire Bill of Rights—binds only the national government.[11] (Madison, when he presented his draft Bill of Rights to Congress, also proposed amendments which would have bound the states; but Congress took no action on these.)

Thus, Gitlow could rely only on the Fourteenth Amendment—specifically on the "liberty" which is not to be taken without "due process of law." When it was adopted, in 1868, the due process clause of the Fourteenth Amendment was presumably thought to be simply a requirement of procedural fair play. But by the mid-1920s the Supreme Court had long since endowed the due process clause with substantive content, reading into its "liberty" a charter of economic freedom. The enormous importance of the *Gitlow* decision was that Benjamin Gitlow's attorneys prevailed upon the entire Supreme Court to enlarge that "liberty": "For present purposes," wrote the majority, "we may and do assume that freedom of speech and of the press—which are protected by the First Amendment from abridgment by Congress—are among the fundamental personal rights and 'liberties' protected by the due process clause of the Fourteenth Amendment from impairment by the States."[12] Having made this assumption, the majority, speaking through Justice Edward T. Sanford, went on to sustain Gitlow's conviction:

By enacting the present statute the State has determined, through its legislative body, that utterances advocating the overthrow of organized government by force, violence and unlawful means, are so inimical to the general welfare and involve such danger of substantive evil that they may be penalized in the exercise of its police power. That determination must be given great weight. Every presumption is to be indulged in favor of the validity of the statute. . . . That utterances inciting to the overthrow of organized government by unlawful means, present a sufficient danger of substantive evil to bring their punishment within the range of legislative discretion, is clear. Such utterances, by their very nature, involve danger to the public peace and to the security of the State. They threaten breaches of the peace and ultimate revolution. And the immediate danger is none the less real and substantial, because the effect of a given utterance cannot be accurately foreseen. The State cannot reasonably be required to measure the danger from every such utterance in the nice balance of a jeweler's scale. A single revolutionary spark may kindle a fire that, smoldering for a time, may burst into a sweeping and destructive conflagration. It cannot be said that the State is acting arbitrarily or unreasonably when in the exercise of its judgment as to the measures necessary to protect the public peace and safety, it seeks to extinguish the spark without waiting until it has enkindled the flame or blazed into the conflagration. It cannot reasonably be required to defer the adoption of measures for its own peace and safety until the revolutionary utterances lead to actual disturbances of the public peace or imminent and immediate danger of its own destruction; but it may, in the exercise of its judgment, suppress the threatened danger in its incipiency. . . .[13]

Holmes and Brandeis once again dissented. Like their brethren of the majority, they found free speech a part of the Fourteenth Amendment's liberty, "in view of the scope that has been given to the word 'liberty' as there used." And on this premise, they felt the conviction could not stand:

Mr. Justice Brandeis and I are of opinion that this judgment should be reversed. The general principle of free speech, it seems to me, must be taken to be included in the Fourteenth Amendment, in view of the scope that has been given to the word "liberty" as there used, although perhaps it may be accepted with a somewhat larger latitude of interpretation than is allowed to Congress by the sweeping language that governs, or ought to govern, the laws of the United States. If I am right, then I think that the criterion sanctioned by the full Court in Schenck v. United States, *249 U.S. 47, 52 applies: "The question in every case is whether the words used are used in such circumstances and are of such a nature as to create a clear and present danger that they will bring about the substantive evils that [the State] has a right to prevent." It is true that in my opinion this criterion was departed from in* Abrams v. United States, *250 U.S. 616, but the convictions that I expressed in that case are too deep for it to be possible for me as yet to believe that it and* Schaefer v. United States, *251 U.S. 466, have settled the law. If what I think the correct test is applied, it is manifest that there was no present danger of an attempt to overthrow the government by force on the part of the admittedly small minority who shared the defendant's views. It is said that this manifesto was more than a theory, that it was an incitement. Every idea is an incitement. It offers itself for belief, and if believed it is acted on unless some other belief outweighs it, or some failure of energy stifles the movement at its birth. The only difference between the expression of an opinion and an incitement in the narrower sense is the speaker's enthusiasm for the result. Eloquence may set fire to reason. But whatever may be thought of the redundant discourse before us it had no chance of starting a present conflagration. If in the long run the beliefs expressed in proletarian dictatorship are destined to be accepted by the dominant forces of the community, the only meaning of free speech is that they should be given their chance and have their way.*

If the publication of this document had been laid as an

attempt to induce an uprising against government at once and not at some indefinite time in the future it would have presented a different question. The object would have been one with which the law might deal, subject to the doubt whether there was any danger that the publication could produce any result, or in other words, whether it was not futile and too remote from possible consequences. But the indictment alleges the publication and nothing more.[14]

After the Supreme Court's decision, New York's Governor Alfred E. Smith freed Gitlow.[14a] But, more important, ever since that decision, the Supreme Court has held states to substantially the same standard the First Amendment imposes on the United States (some might say a stricter standard, since the Court has frequently invalidated state laws, but only once a federal law,[14b] on free speech grounds). And with the *Gitlow* case began the slow process of "incorporating" into the due process clause those of the other personal liberties in the Bill of Rights—such as freedom of worship, or the right of one accused of crime to be represented by counsel—which the Court regards as "fundamental." From one perspective this constitutional evolution may seem anachronistic: The beginning point for this judicial expansion of the "due process" clause was the Court's unwarranted exercise of the clause as a grant of authority to censor state laws regulating economic affairs. Having accustomed itself to this usurped power, the Court became receptive to taking on a further kind of censorship of legislation—in the field of personal liberty. But, when the Court finally forsook doctrines of "liberty of contract," it did not abandon its new role. It continued, and continues to this day, to give the "due process" clause substantive content in the field of personal liberty. Yet there is ample reason for the Court to persist in the new role after shucking off the old one. The economic liberties, once enforced, had behind them only the transient momentum of a single era's devotion to doctrines of *laissez faire*—doctrines not contained in the Constitution except as particular Justices chose to place them there. By contrast, the basic personal liberties, including freedom of speech and thought, are a permanent and central element of our nation's democratic commitment. They were—as *laissez faire* economics was not—written into the Bill of Rights. And though the Bill of Rights did then, and does now, limit only the national government, it furnishes a philosophically valid, if not an exclusive, guide to the definition of the non-self-defining word "liberty" in the Fourteenth Amendment.

The third, and perhaps the most powerful, of the trio of Holmes-Brandeis expositions of the principles underlying the First Amendment, was their concurring opinion in *Whitney v. California*. Anita Whitney, a social worker of great dedication and high repute (and also, incidentally, a niece of Justice Stephen J. Field, one of the Supreme Court's leading conservatives from the Civil War to the end of the century), was prosecuted under California's "criminal syndicalism" law for having, in 1919, attended an organizing convention of the Communist Labor Party of California. Her conviction was sustained by the Supreme Court. Holmes and Brandeis, in an opinion by the latter, joined in affirmance on the ground that Miss Whitney's lawyers had not undertaken, in the trial court, to demonstrate that in California, in 1919, there was no such "clear and present danger" of insurrection as would justify the enforcement of the statute. Absent such a showing by the defendant, the statute, as applied to Miss Whitney, was entitled to the presumption of validity with which all challenged legislation is generally clothed. Especially so where, as in *Whitney*, there was some evidence in the record which tended to support the California legislature's apparent fear that an armed Left-Wing conspiracy was in the making. Defendant's failure to counter this evidence was, according to Brandeis, beyond the Court's power to remedy. On reviewing a state conviction, the Supreme Court "is limited . . . to the particular claims duly made below, and denied. . . ."[15]

Brandeis' and Holmes' insistence on what may seem to the layman a "technical" point was really an acknowledgment of the sensitivity of the Supreme Court's role in reviewing the laws and judicial decisions of a state. As Felix Frankfurter once put it, in an essay on Justice Brandeis, "In view of our federalism and the Court's peculiar function, questions of jurisdiction in constitutional adjudication imply questions of political power."[16]

The degree to which these "questions of political power" weighed with Brandeis and Holmes can be inferred from the strong intimation in Brandeis' opinion in *Whitney* that, had he and Holmes been furnished with relevant materials in the record enabling them to weigh the California statute on an accurate judicial scale, the two Justices would have found the statute wanting. Brandeis' opinion is political philosophy of the highest order: succinctly and in plain words he explores the genesis and the character of America's commitment to free speech, and the overlapping responsibilities of legislators and judges to honor that commitment. But Brandeis' opinion is also marked by an eloquence which he normally eschewed. In combination, the power of the opinion and the magic of its language stamp it as an enduring contribution to the literature of freedom:

Despite arguments to the contrary which had seemed to me persuasive, it is settled that the due process clause of the 14th Amendment applies to matters of substantive law as well as to matters of procedure. Thus all fundamental rights comprised within the term liberty are protected by the Federal Constitution from invasion by the States. The right of free speech, the right to teach and the right of assembly are, of course, fundamental rights. . . . These may not be denied or abridged. But, although the rights of free speech and assembly are fundamental, they are not in their nature absolute. Their exercise is subject to restriction, if the particular restriction proposed is required in order to protect the State from destruction or from serious injury, political, economic or moral. That the necessity which is essential to a valid restriction does not exist unless speech would produce, or is intended to produce, a clear and imminent danger of some substantive evil which the state constitutionally may seek to prevent has been settled. See Schenck v. United States, 249 U.S. 47, 52. . . .

It is said to be the function of the legislature to determine whether at a particular time and under the particular circumstances the formation of, or assembly with, a society organized to advocate criminal syndicalism constitutes a clear and present danger of substantive evil; and that by enacting the law here in question the legislature of California determined that question in the affirmative. . . . The legislature must obviously decide, in the first instance, whether a danger exists which calls for a particular protective measure. But where a statute is valid only in case certain conditions exist, the enactment of the statute cannot alone establish the facts which are essential to its validity. Prohibitory legislation has repeatedly been held invalid, because unnecessary, where the denial of liberty involved was that of engaging in a particular business. The power of the courts to strike down an offending law is no less when the interests involved are not property rights, but the fundamental personal rights of free speech and assembly.

This Court has not yet fixed the standard by which to determine when a danger shall be deemed clear; how remote the danger may be and yet be deemed present; and what degree of evil shall be deemed sufficiently substantial to justify resort to abridgment of free speech and assembly as the means of protection. To reach sound conclusions on these matters, we must bear in mind why a State is, ordinarily, denied the power to prohibit dissemination of social, economic and political doctrine which a vast majority of its citizens believes to be false and fraught with evil consequence.

Those who won our independence believed that the final end of the State was to make men free to develop their faculties; and that in its government the deliberative forces should prevail over the arbitrary. They valued liberty both as an end and as a means. They believed liberty to be the secret of happiness and courage to be the secret of liberty. They believed that freedom to think as you will and to speak as you think are means indispensable to the discovery and spread of political truth; that without free speech and assembly discussion would be futile; that with them, discussion affords ordinarily adequate protection against the dissemination of noxious doctrine; that the greatest menace to freedom is an inert people; that public discussion is a political duty; and that this should be a fundamental principle of the American government. They recognized the risks to which all human institutions are subject. But they knew that order cannot be secured merely through fear of punishment for its infraction; that it is hazardous to discourage thought, hope and imagination; that fear breeds repression; that repression breeds hate; that hate menaces stable government; that the path of safety lies in the opportunity to discuss freely supposed grievances and proposed remedies; and that the fitting remedy for evil counsels is good ones. Believing in the power of reason as applied through public discussion, they eschewed silence coerced by law—the argument of force in its worst form. Recognizing the occasional tyrannies of governing majorities, they amended the Constitution so that free speech and assembly should be guaranteed.

Fear of serious injury cannot alone justify suppression of free speech and assembly. Men feared witches and burned women. It is the function of speech to free men from the bondage of irrational fears. To justify suppression of free speech there must be reasonable ground to fear that serious evil will result if free speech is practiced. There must be reasonable ground to believe that the danger apprehended is imminent. There must be reasonable ground to believe that the evil to be prevented is a serious one. Every denunciation of existing law tends in some measure to increase the probability that there will be a violation of it. Condonation of a breach enhances the probability. Expressions of approval add to the probability. Propagation of the criminal state of mind by teaching syndicalism increases it. Advocacy of lawbreaking heightens it still further. But even advocacy of violation, however reprehensible morally, is not a justification for denying free speech where the advocacy falls short of incitement and there is nothing to indicate that the advocacy would be immediately acted on. The wide difference between advocacy and incitement, between preparation and attempt, between assembling and conspiracy, must be borne in mind. In order to support a finding of clear and present danger it must be shown either that immediate serious violence was to be expected or was advocated, or that the past conduct furnished reason to believe that such advocacy was then contemplated.

Those who won our independence by revolution were not cowards. They did not fear political change. They did not exalt order at the cost of liberty. To courageous, self-reliant men, with confidence in the power of free and fearless reasoning applied through the processes of popular government, no danger flowing from speech can be deemed clear and present, unless the incidence of the evil apprehended is so imminent that it may befall before there is opportunity for full discussion. If there be time to expose through discussion the falsehood and fallacies, to avert the evil by the processes of education, the remedy to be applied is more speech, not enforced silence. Only an emergency can justify repression. Such must be the rule if authority is to be reconciled with freedom. Such, in my opinion, is the command of the Constitution. It is therefore always open to Americans to challenge a law abridging free speech and assembly by showing that there was no emergency justifying it.[17]

In the three decades that have passed since *Whitney* was decided, the Holmes-Brandeis latitudinarian view of free speech has become generally accepted by the later judicial majorities— just as the two Justices' criticism of their colleagues' solicitude for economic freedom has also won subsequent acceptance. But, while their general concern for free speech seems to have evoked a sympathetic response among their successors, the curious fact is that the Holmes-Brandeis view turned out to have only a narrowly semantic impact on the Supreme Court's subsequent treatment of the very kind of problem with which *Abrams, Gitlow,* and *Whitney* were concerned.

In 1940, Congress adopted the Smith Act, which is closely akin to the New York "criminal anarchy" and the California "criminal syndicalism" acts. During World War II, the Smith Act was invoked twice: once, with success, against a small group of Trotskyites, whose conviction the Supreme Court did not review;[18] and once, without success, against a motley group of alleged Nazi sympathizers.[19] After World War II, as the era of "cold war" got under way, eleven top Communist leaders were convicted under the Smith Act for having led a political party directed at violent overthrow of the government. Their convictions were sustained by the Supreme Court, which, over dissents by Justices Hugo L. Black and William O. Douglas, concluded, in *Dennis v. United States,* that the Communist Party did present a real enough hazard to justify prosecution of those who organized it.[20]

Actually, most of the free speech cases which have come to the Court since Justice Brandeis' retirement in 1939 have not been couched in the classic pattern of prosecutions of those who allegedly threaten armed overthrow of the state. Free speech has turned up in a variety of contexts—e.g., picketing; the claimed right of a witness before a legislative investigation to refuse to discuss his political views and associations; the administration of governmental (and indeed of quasi-private) "loyalty" programs; the authority of the postal authorities, and of state and local regulatory agencies, to bar the distribution of "obscene" books and movies; the power of judges to punish vigorous criticism as contempt of court; the power of the United States to deport, and otherwise penalize, aliens for present and even long-past political activity; the law of libel, etc.[20a]

To characterize the judicial process as it has acted in all, or even several, of these areas would be impossible within the confines of these volumes. Any comprehensive study would have to consider the great shifts in national mood, which have largely paralleled the shifts in judicial mood. What is called for is, first, a study of the know-nothing, anti-alien, anti-Catholic, anti-intellectual climate of the 1920s (the *Sacco-Vanzetti Case*, the Palmer Raids after World War I, the *Scopes* prosecution for teaching evolution, the rebirth of the Ku Klux Klan, etc.). Such a study would then turn to the doubtings, the beginnings of restless inquiry, of greater tolerance of dissent, of greater hospitality toward foreign ideas and peoples, which characterized the Depression-ridden 1930s and (with the demise of isolationism) our involvement in World War II. And then, following the war, the slide into fear, "cold war," and the calamitous epoch of the junior Senator from Wisconsin, Joseph R. McCarthy. And, since then, a thaw.

Throughout, the judicial record has been spotty. There is much that lends credence to the late Judge Learned Hand's doubts as to the efficacy of judicial checks on invasions of liberty. These doubts were felicitously expressed in a speech Judge Hand gave in celebration of I Am an American Day, in the relatively hopeful year of 1944:

. . . *What do we mean when we say that first of all we seek liberty? I often wonder whether we do not rest our hopes too much upon constitutions, upon laws and upon courts. These are false hopes; believe me, these are false hopes. Liberty lies in the hearts of men and women; when it dies there, no constitution, no law, no court, can save it; no constitution, no law, no court can even do much to help it. While it lies there it needs no constitution, no law, no court to save it.*[21]

It is proper to note that Judge Hand's views partake of the nature of a self-fulfilling pessimism. He was a stalwart doubter not only of the efficacy but of the *propriety* of judicial review. And it was his opinion sustaining the first Communist prosecution under the Smith Act which Chief Justice Vinson affirmed and, in its crucial part, adopted verbatim in *Dennis v. United States.* Yet it should be remembered that even Madison—who wrote the Bill of Rights and publicly assured Congress that judges "will consider themselves in a peculiar manner the guardians of those rights [and] will be an impenetrable bulwark"—privately wrote

Jefferson that "experience proves the inefficacy of a bill of rights on those occasions when its controul is most needed."[22]

The generality of constitutional litigation does not, however, consist of great landmark cases which search the judicial institution to its foundations. Most cases concern more or less isolated aspects of a general theme—aspects which turn, in large part, on a particular judge's evaluation of a particular factual narrative played out against a particular social setting. The raw stuff of which litigation is made, in the free speech area as elsewhere, is illustrated by a news item which appeared in *The New York Times* in the summer of 1960. The item describes the decision of New York City officials to turn down an application for permission to hold a Fourth of July rally in a city park. Ordinarily such an application would have interested no one, and would have been granted as a matter of course. What made this situation unusual—what made it front-page news at a time when most Americans had their minds on baseball, summer vacations, or the forthcoming Democratic Convention—was that the man who had been told not to hold a public meeting was George Lincoln Rockwell, the "Commander" of the minuscule American Nazi Party. This was the item that appeared in *The Times:*

The American Nazi party yesterday was denied the right to hold a rally in Union Square on July 4.

The decision was made by Mayor Wagner, who said the organization's purpose was to incite a riot by preaching "race hatred and violence."

The Mayor made the statement at City Hall shortly after George Lincoln Rockwell of Arlington, Va., and Washington, D.C., the party's leader, had been mobbed in the rotunda of the State Supreme Court Building in Foley Square.

Mr. Rockwell had appeared at a hearing before Justice Vincent A. Lupiano to defend his application for a permit to hold the July 4 meeting. The disorder, nearly reaching the proportions of a riot, occurred during a five-minute recess when Mr. Rockwell showed up in the rotunda for television interviews.

He was greeted by shouts and curses from about 150 persons, some of them wearing veterans' overseas caps. Television cameras were tipped over and several persons were knocked to the ground as members of the crowd tried to hit the Nazi party leader. A riot call to Police Headquarters soon brought sixteen patrolmen and two sergeants to the scene.

However, court security guards crowded around Mr. Rockwell and he was hustled into "protective custody" in a room off the rotunda. Later, he was whisked off under a police escort into a taxicab after appearing briefly when the court resumed. It was reported later that a special detail of detectives escorted him to La Guardia Airport where he left for Washington at 1:10 P.M.

It was almost precisely at that moment that Newbold Morris, the recently appointed Commissioner of Parks, arrived at City Hall for a conference with Mayor Wagner. Mr. Morris had indicated several days ago that he would grant a permit for the Nazi meeting unless the Police Department advised against it. Mr. Morris had taken his stand on Constitutional provisions of freedom of speech.

More than 100 patrolmen were guarding City Hall when Mr. Morris entered into a closed conference with the Mayor. Also present at the meeting were Abe Stark, president of the City Council; Charles H. Tenney, the Corporation Counsel; Acting Police Commissioner James R. Kennedy and Warren Moscow, assistant to the Mayor.

The conference lasted for about fifteen minutes. When it was over, Mayor Wagner held a press conference in his office. Declaring that he was speaking as the Mayor and chief magistrate of the city, Mr. Wagner then read the following statement:

> *I have the primary and overwhelming obligation to the people of the city for the maintenance of law and order. A man named George Rockwell of Washington, D.C., has applied for a permit to speak in Union Square on July 4. Information supplied to me by qualified sources shows clearly that Mr. Rockwell's intent is to incite a riot by preaching in a city where people of all races live peacefully together, [a] philosophy of race hatred and extermination by violence.*
>
> *Left to their own devices, the people of the city will stone Rockwell out of town. There is not a decent responsible citizen in the city who would follow him in his preaching. There are millions who have friends and relatives who died because of this race hatred either as unarmed victims or soldiers fighting for freedom.*
>
> *We have in this city the largest and best police force of any municipality. It can quell any riot; but no police force in*

the world can stop a riot from starting. In this case, every fact we have shows Rockwell's presence as a preacher of race hatred will cause a riot the police will have to quell.

This is an invitation to riot and disorder from a half-penny Hitler. The invitation is declined. Mr. Rockwell will not speak here on the Fourth of July or any other time in terms of race hatred and race extermination.

As the Mayor spoke, 150 county and post commanders of the Jewish War Veterans from all parts of the state marched on Park Row east of City Hall Park. Several were in his office when he read his statement, and when he finished they shook his hand and congratulated him enthusiastically.

.   .   .   .   .

Justice Lupiano adjourned the hearing until 10 A.M. today. However, as a result of the Mayor's subsequent decision to ban the meeting, Mr. Rockwell's only legal recourse may be to seek a court order rescinding the ban.[23]

Rockwell did "seek a court order rescinding the ban." He was represented by a lawyer for the American Civil Liberties Union, an organization which has for over forty years sought to vindicate the constitutional rights—and especially the free speech rights—of every American, no matter how obnoxious. The trial judge sustained the denial of the permit. But a New York appellate court reversed. Justice Charles D. Breitel, an extremely able state judge, spoke for his court:

Now, there is no question that government, in each of its branches—executive, legislative, and judicial—faces here one of its gravest domestic problems. . . .

A community need not wait to be subverted by street riots and stormtroopers; but, also, it cannot, by its policemen or commissioners, suppress a speaker, in prior restraint, on the basis of news reports, hysteria, or inference that what he did yesterday, he will do today. Thus, too, if the speaker incites others to immediate unlawful action he may be punished—in a proper case, stopped when disorder actually impends; but this is not to be confused with unlawful action from others who seek unlawfully to suppress or punish the speaker.

So, the unpopularity of views, their shocking quality, their obnoxiousness, and even their alarming impact is not enough. Otherwise, the preacher of any strange doctrine could be stopped;

the anti-racist himself could be suppressed, if he undertakes to speak in "restricted" areas; and one who asks that public schools be open indiscriminately to all ethnic groups could be lawfully suppressed, if only he choose to speak where persuasion is needed most.

.   .   .   .   .

Only if Rockwell speaks criminally (or, perhaps, if it is established on a proper record, in that very rare case, that he will speak criminally, not because he once did, but that he will this time, and irreparable harm will ensue) can his right to speak be cut off. If he does not speak criminally, then, of course, his right to speak may not be cut off, no matter how offensive his speech may be to others. Instead, his right, and that of those who wish to listen to him, must be protected, no matter how unpleasant the assignment.[24]

One judge (Justice Samuel W. Eager) dissented:

. . . I fully agree that it should be and is the policy of the courts to exercise discretion in favor of complete freedom of speech rather than in restriction thereof. A court should not, and may not prohibit any person from speaking merely upon the premise that it disagrees or is displeased with or even abhors the doctrine to be proclaimed in his proposed utterances. Nor should fear of an anticipated breach of peace or other consequences influence any court to silence a political zealot, however abominable his doctrine may be. But it is one thing for a court to restrain a person absolutely from speaking in a community and quite another for the court, in the interest of public peace and order, merely to refuse to affirmatively act to enable him to speak in a public park in the community. (Here, it should be noted that petitioner concedes that he is not silenced—that he is not being restrained in speaking in the public street or in private hall in the City.)

.   .   .   .   .

The granting of relief to the petitioner Rockwell amounts to an invitation for a display of disgraceful mob action as is fully indicated by his prior speech-making incidents. We abhor mob action—for the havoc, the destruction, the injury and the misery it causes. We seek to guard against it, for, as history teaches us, mob action gnaws at the very heart of liberty and can be to free citizens the forerunner of the loss of most precious rights.

Where, as here, it clearly appears that the protecting of one individual in unrestrained freedom of speech is incompatible with public policy and order, the latter should prevail. In holding otherwise, this court would relinquish its role as a true guardian of the proper rights of all our people.[25]

Justice Breitel's decision was affirmed, without opinion, by the highest court of New York. And the Supreme Court declined to review the case. This final nonaction of the Supreme Court came on November 12, 1961. No judge could restore to Rockwell the opportunity to speak on July 4, 1960. But, under Justice Breitel's ruling, Rockwell could at least reapply for a new permit. Not long after Rockwell won his legal victory, he did decide to make another attempt to speak in New York City. An editorial in *The New York Times*, entitled "Free Speech on Hitler," deals with this postscript to litigation:

We know of no public demand for celebrating the birthday of the execrable Adolf Hitler. But since George Lincoln Rockwell, leader of the so-called American Nazi party, wants to publicize himself by holding a rally in Union Square on that day, April 20, the city has no grounds in law or principle to deny him a permit. Rockwell's right to speak has been tested to the highest court in the land, and upheld. Determined to be offensively obnoxious, he nevertheless has the same constitutional protection as people we agree with. How else can speech be free?[26]

As *The New York Times* observed, New York City had "no grounds in law or principle to deny . . . [Rockwell] a permit" to preach Nazism, notwithstanding the likelihood that his preachments would provoke an enormously bitter response. The outcome of Rockwell's case seemed to mark a swing back in the New York courts from a more restrictive view which had prevailed— and which had been sustained by the United States Supreme Court—a decade before in *Feiner v. New York.*[27] In 1949, Irving Feiner addressed some seventy-five whites and Negroes gathered on a street-corner in Syracuse. Feiner "gave the impression that he was endeavoring to arouse the Negro people against the whites, urging that they rise up in arms and fight for equal rights."[28] In the course of his remarks Feiner said that "Mayor Costello [of Syracuse] is a champagne-sipping bum; he does not speak for the negro people"; that "President Truman is a bum"; that "Mayor O'Dwyer [of New York City] is a bum"; and that "the American Legion is a Nazi Gestapo."[29] Feiner's audience, containing sympathizers and opponents, began to get "restless."[30] After Feiner had gone on in this vein for "about 20 minutes a man said to the police officers, 'If you don't get that son of a bitch off, I will go over and get him off there myself.' It was then that the police ordered Feiner to stop speaking; when he refused, they arrested him."[31] Feiner was convicted of disorderly conduct and sentenced to thirty days' imprisonment. His conviction was sustained by the New York appellate courts and ultimately (1951) affirmed by a six-to-three margin in the Supreme Court. The majority rejected the dissenting view—expressed by Justices Black, Douglas, and Sherman Minton—that, short of an imminent outbreak of violence not disclosed by the record, the function of the police was to protect the unpopular speaker, not to arrest him.

The need to rethink *Feiner* became more apparent when, in the 1960s, the rising tide of Negro protest throughout the South precipitated many instances in which public demonstrations were impeded or broken up by police action. One of these—a demonstration by a large number of high-school and college students on the grounds of South Carolina's state capitol—took place in the spring of 1961, while Rockwell's case was still being litigated. The mass arrests and convictions that ensued were reviewed by the Supreme Court two years later. The case was *Edwards v. South Carolina:*

MR. JUSTICE [POTTER] STEWART *delivered the opinion of the Court.*

The petitioners, 187 in number, were convicted in a magistrate's court in Columbia, South Carolina, of the common-law crime of breach of the peace. Their convictions were ultimately affirmed by the South Carolina Supreme Court, 239 S.C. 339, 123 S.E. 2d 247. We granted certiorari, 369 U.S. 870, to consider the claim that these convictions cannot be squared with the Fourteenth Amendment of the United States Constitution.

There was no substantial conflict in the trial evidence. Late in the morning of March 2, 1961, the petitioners, high school and college students of the Negro race, met at the Zion Baptist Church in Columbia. From there, at about noon, they walked in separate groups of about 15 to the South Carolina State House grounds, an area of two city blocks open to the general public. Their purpose was "to submit a protest to the citizens of South Carolina, along with the Legislative Bodies of South Carolina, our feelings and our dissatisfaction with the present condition of discriminatory actions against Negroes, in general, and to let them know that we were dissatisfied and that we would like for the laws which prohibited Negro privileges in this State to be removed."

Already on the State House grounds when the petitioners arrived were 30 or more law enforcement officers, who had advance knowledge that the petitioners were coming. Each group of petitioners entered the grounds through a driveway and parking area known in the record as the "horseshoe." As they entered, they were told by the law enforcement officials that "they had a right, as a citizen, to go through the State House grounds, as any other citizen has, as long as they were peaceful." During the next half hour or 45 minutes, the petitioners, in the same small groups, walked single file or two abreast in an orderly way through the grounds, each group carrying placards bearing such messages as "I am proud to be a Negro" and "Down with segregation."

During this time a crowd of some 200 to 300 onlookers had collected in the horseshoe area and on the adjacent sidewalks. There was no evidence to suggest that these onlookers were anything but curious, and no evidence at all of any threatening remarks, hostile gestures, or offensive language on the part of any member of the crowd. The City Manager testified that he recognized some of the onlookers, whom he did not identify, as "possible trouble makers," but his subsequent testimony made clear that nobody among the crowd actually caused or threatened any trouble. There was no obstruction of pedestrian or vehicular traffic within the State House grounds. No vehicle was prevented from entering or leaving the horseshoe area. Although vehicular traffic at a nearby street intersection was slowed down somewhat, an officer was dispatched to keep traffic moving. There were a number of bystanders on the public sidewalks adjacent to the State House grounds, but they all moved on when asked to do so, and there was no impediment of pedestrian traffic. Police protection at the scene was at all times sufficient to meet any foreseeable possibility of disorder.

In the situation and under the circumstances thus described, the police authorities advised the petitioners that they would be arrested if they did not disperse within 15 minutes. Instead of dispersing, the petitioners engaged in what the City Manager described as "boisterous," "loud," and "flamboyant" conduct, which, as his later testimony made clear, consisted of listening to a "religious harangue" by one of their leaders, and loudly singing "The Star Spangled Banner" and other patriotic and religious songs, while stamping their feet and clapping their hands. After 15 minutes had passed, the police arrested the petitioners and marched them off to jail.

Upon this evidence the state trial court convicted the petitioners of breach of the peace, and imposed sentences ranging from a $10 fine or five days in jail, to a $100 fine or 30 days in jail. In affirming the judgments, the Supreme Court of South Carolina said that under the law of that State the offense of breach of the peace "is not susceptible of exact definition," but that the "general definition of the offense" is as follows:

> *In general terms, a breach of the peace is a violation of public order, a disturbance of the public tranquility, by any act or conduct inciting to violence . . . , it includes any violation of any law enacted to preserve peace and good order. It may consist of an act of violence or an act likely to produce violence. It is not necessary that the peace be actually broken to lay the foundation for a prosecution for this offense. If what is done is unjustifiable and unlawful, tending with sufficient directness to break the peace, no more is required. Nor is actual personal violence an essential element in the offense. . . .*
>
> *By "peace," as used in the law in this connection, is meant the tranquility enjoyed by citizens of a municipality where good order reigns among its members, which is the natural right of all persons in political society. 239 S.C., at 343–344, 123 S.E. 2d, at 249.*

The petitioners contend that there was a complete absence of any evidence of the commission of this offense, and that they were thus denied one of the most basic elements of due process of law. Thompson v. Louisville, 362 U.S. 199; *see* Garner v.

Louisiana, 368 U.S. 157; Taylor v. Louisiana, 370 U.S. 154. *Whatever the merits of this contention, we need not pass upon it in the present case. The state courts have held that the petitioners' conduct constituted breach of the peace under state law, and we may accept their decision as binding upon us to that extent. But it nevertheless remains our duty in a case such as this to make an independent examination of the whole record.* Blackburn v. Alabama, 361 U.S. 199, 205, n. 5; Pennekamp v. Florida, 328 U.S. 331, 335; Fiske v. Kansas, 274 U.S. 380, 385–386. *And it is clear to us that in arresting, convicting, and punishing the petitioners under the circumstances disclosed by this record, South Carolina infringed the petitioners' constitutionally protected rights of free speech, free assembly, and freedom to petition for redress of their grievances.*

It has long been established that these First Amendment freedoms are protected by the Fourteenth Amendment from invasion by the States. Gitlow v. New York, 268 U.S. 652; Whitney v. California, 274 U.S. 357; Stromberg v. California, 283 U.S. 359; De Jonge v. Oregon, 299 U.S. 353; Cantwell v. Connecticut, 310 U.S. 296. *The circumstances in this case reflect an exercise of these basic constitutional rights in their most pristine and classic form. The petitioners felt aggrieved by laws of South Carolina which allegedly "prohibited Negro privileges in this State." They peaceably assembled at the site of the State Government and there peaceably expressed their grievances "to the citizens of South Carolina, along with the Legislative Bodies of South Carolina." Not until they were told by police officials that they must disperse on pain of arrest did they do more. Even then, they but sang patriotic and religious songs after one of their leaders had delivered a "religious harangue." There was no violence or threat of violence on their part, or on the part of any member of the crowd watching them. Police protection was "ample."*

This, therefore, was a far cry from the situation in Feiner v. New York, 340 U.S. 315, *where two policemen were faced with a crowd which was "pushing, shoving and milling around," id., at 317, where at least one member of the crowd "threatened violence if the police did not act," id., at 317, where "the crowd was pressing closer around petitioner and the officer," id., at 318, and where "the speaker passes the bounds of argument or persuasion and undertakes incitement to riot." Id., at 321. And the record is*

barren of any evidence of "fighting words." See Chaplinsky v.
New Hampshire, 315 *U.S. 568.*

*We do not review in this case criminal convictions resulting
from the evenhanded application of a precise and narrowly drawn
regulatory statute evincing a legislative judgment that certain
specific conduct be limited or proscribed. If, for example, the
petitioners had been convicted upon evidence that they had
violated a law regulating traffic, or had disobeyed a law reasonably limiting the periods during which the State House grounds
were open to the public, this would be a different case. See*
Cantwell v. Connecticut, 310 *U.S. 296, 307–308;* Garner v.
Louisiana, 368 *U.S. 157, 202 (concurring opinion). These petitioners were convicted of an offense so generalized as to be, in the
words of the South Carolina Supreme Court, "not susceptible of
exact definition." And they were convicted upon evidence which
showed no more than that the opinions which they were peaceably expressing were sufficiently opposed to the views of the
majority of the community to attract a crowd and necessitate
police protection.*

*The Fourteenth Amendment does not permit a State to make
criminal the peaceful expression of unpopular views. "[A]
function of free speech under our system of government is to invite
dispute. It may indeed best serve its high purpose when it induces
a condition of unrest, creates dissatisfaction with conditions as
they are, or even stirs people to anger. Speech is often provocative
and challenging. It may strike at prejudices and preconceptions
and have profound unsettling effects as it presses for acceptance
of an idea. That is why freedom of speech . . . is . . . protected
against censorship or punishment, unless shown likely to produce
a clear and present danger of a serious substantive evil that rises
far above public inconvenience, annoyance, or unrest. . . . There
is no room under our Constitution for a more restrictive view.
For the alternative would lead to standardization of ideas either
by legislatures, courts, or dominant political or community
groups."* Terminiello v. Chicago, 337 *U.S. 1, 4–5. As in the*
Terminiello *case the courts of South Carolina have defined a
criminal offense so as to permit conviction of the petitioners if
their speech "stirred people to anger, invited public dispute, or
brought about a condition of unrest. A conviction resting on any
of those grounds may not stand." Id., at 5.*

As Chief Justice Hughes wrote in Stromberg v. California, "The maintenance of the opportunity for free political discussion to the end that government may be responsive to the will of the people and that changes may be obtained by lawful means, an opportunity essential to the security of the Republic, is a fundamental principle of our constitutional system. A statute which upon its face, and as authoritatively construed, is so vague and indefinite as to permit the punishment of the fair use of this opportunity is repugnant to the guaranty of liberty contained in the Fourteenth Amendment. . . ." 283 U.S. 359, 369.

For these reasons we conclude that these criminal convictions cannot stand.

Reversed.

MR. JUSTICE [TOM C.] CLARK, dissenting.

The convictions of the petitioners, Negro high school and college students, for breach of the peace under South Carolina law are accepted by the Court "as binding upon us to that extent" but are held violative of "petitioners' constitutionally protected rights of free speech, free assembly, and freedom to petition for redress of their grievances." Petitioners, of course, had a right to peaceable assembly, to espouse their cause and to petition, but in my view the manner in which they exercised those rights was by no means the passive demonstration which this Court relates; rather, as the City Manager of Columbia testified, "a dangerous situation was really building up" which South Carolina's courts expressly found had created "an actual interference with traffic and an imminently threatened disturbance of the peace of the community." . . .

. . . It is undisputed that the city officials specifically granted petitioners permission to assemble, imposing only the requirement that they be "peaceful." Petitioners then gathered on the State House grounds, during a General Assembly session, in a large number of almost 200, marching and carrying placards with slogans such as "Down with segregation" and "You may jail our bodies but not our souls." Some of them were singing.

The activity continued for approximately 45 minutes, during the busy noon-hour period, while a crowd of some 300 persons congregated in front of the State House and around the area directly in front of its entrance, known as the "horseshoe," which *was used for vehicular as well as pedestrian ingress and egress. During this time there were no efforts made by the city officials to hinder the petitioners in their rights of free speech and assembly; rather, the police directed their efforts to the traffic problems resulting from petitioners' activities. It was only after the large crowd had gathered, among which the City Manager and Chief of Police recognized potential trouble-makers, and which together with the students had become massed on and around the "horseshoe" so closely that vehicular and pedestrian traffic was materially impeded, that any action against the petitioners was taken. Then the City Manager, in what both the state intermediate and Supreme Court found to be the utmost good faith, decided that danger to peace and safety was imminent. Even at this juncture no orders were issued by the City Manager for the police to break up the crowd, now about 500 persons, and no arrests were made. Instead, he approached the recognized leader of the petitioners and requested him to tell the various groups of petitioners to disperse within 15 minutes, failing which they would be arrested. Even though the City Manager might have been honestly mistaken as to the imminence of danger, this was certainly a reasonable request by the city's top executive officer in an effort to avoid a public brawl. But the response of petitioners and their leader was defiance rather than cooperation. . . .*

. . . The question thus seems to me whether a State is constitutionally prohibited from enforcing laws to prevent breach of the peace in a situation where city officials in good faith believe, and the record shows, that disorder and violence are imminent, merely because the activities constituting that breach contain claimed elements of constitutionally protected speech and assembly. To me the answer under our cases is clearly in the negative.

.   .   .   .   .   .

In Cantwell v. Connecticut, *supra, at 308, this Court recognized that "[w]hen clear and present danger of riot, disorder, interference with traffic upon the public streets, or other immediate threat to public safety, peace, or order, appears, the power of the State to prevent or punish is obvious." And in* Feiner v. New York, *340 U.S. 315 (1951), we upheld a conviction for breach of the peace in a situation no more dangerous than that found here.*

There the demonstration was conducted by only one person and the crowd was limited to approximately 80, as compared with the present lineup of some 200 demonstrators and 300 onlookers. There the petitioner was "endeavoring to arouse the Negro people against the whites, urging that they rise up in arms and fight for equal rights." Id., at 317. Only one person—in a city having an entirely different historical background—was exhorting adults. Here 200 youthful Negro demonstrators were being aroused to a "fever pitch" before a crowd of some 300 people who undoubtedly were hostile. Perhaps their speech was not so animated but in this setting their actions, their placards reading "You may jail our bodies but not our souls" and their chanting of "I Shall Not Be Moved," accompanied by stamping feet and clapping hands, created a much greater danger of riot and disorder. It is my belief that anyone conversant with the almost spontaneous combustion in some Southern communities in such a situation will agree that the City Manager's action may well have averted a major catastrophe.[32]

Proponents of civil rights are not the only people whose rights of speech and assembly are subject to restraints imposed by local southern officials. In 1961 the authorities in Fairfield, Alabama—a town of some 15,000 people—tried to stop an arch-racist outfit called the National States Rights Party from holding a public meeting. The setting, as it was later described by the Alabama Supreme Court, was as follows:

Petitioners were distributing handbills in the City of Fairfield, which read:

WHITE WORKERS
MEETING
* NIGGERS ARE TAKING OVER UNIONS!
* NIGGERS WANT OUR PARKS AND POOLS!
* NIGGERS DEMAND MIXED SCHOOLS!

Communists in NAACP *and in* WASHINGTON *say*
Whites HAVE NO RIGHTS!
The Nigger gets everything he DEMANDS!
White Supremacy CAN *be saved!*
Whites CAN STOP *this second Reconstruction!*
Hear Important Speakers from 4 States

Time — 8 P.M.   Date — Wed. Oct. 11
Place — 5329 Valley Road
In Downtown Fairfield, Alabama
ABOVE THE CAR WASH
THUNDERBOLT *Mobile Unit Will Be Parked Out Front!*
Sponsored by National States Rights Party
Box 783, Birmingham, Alabama

PUBLIC INVITED
Come And Bring Your Friends!

The attorney for the city sought a temporary injunction to enjoin petitioners from holding the advertised meeting because they had not complied with an ordinance of the City Code which provided "It shall be unlawful for any person or persons to hold a public meeting in the city or police jurisdiction without first having obtained a permit from the mayor to do so." The judge issued the temporary injunction and a copy was served on Fields at Noon, Wednesday, October 11th. Lyons also had notice of the temporary injunction which enjoined them "from holding a public meeting at 8 P.M. on Wednesday, October 11, 1961, at 5329 Valley Road, Fairfield, Alabama, as announced, and from distributing further in the City of Fairfield, handbills announcing such meeting such as were distributed in the City of Fairfield, Alabama, on October 10, 1961, until further orders from this Court; and this you will in no wise omit under penalty, etc."[33]

Up to this point the problem looked very much like that presented by the *Rockwell* litigation. But then the form of the problem changed: Fields and Lyons did not go to court to get the injunction dissolved. Instead, on the evening of October 11th, they appeared "across the street from the advertised place of the meeting,"[34] and handed out copies of *The Thunderbolt*—the newspaper of the National States Rights Party—to the assembled crowd. They were promptly arrested, charged with contempt of court for violating the injunction, found guilty, and sentenced to five days in jail and fines of $50 apiece. On appeal, Fields and Lyons argued (1) that there was no evidence that they had violated the injunction because they had not conducted the proscribed meeting and they had not distributed any more announcements of the proscribed meeting, and (2) that the injunction invaded their constitutional rights of free speech and assembly. The Alabama Supreme Court, rejecting both arguments, affirmed the convictions. First, the court asserted that there was some evidence that appellants had violated the injunction. Second, the court said that appellants could not challenge the constitutionality of the injunction by violating it. Relying on a Supreme Court decision in a major post-World-War-II labor injunction case (*United States v. United Mine Workers*),[35] the state court said that Fields and Lyons should have appealed the injunction rather than defied it.

The second half of the Alabama court's holding obviously presented a major constitutional issue, since to force a person to appeal from a hypothetically invalid restraint on speech or assembly or the distribution of literature as the only means of presenting a constitutional claim would mean that in the vast majority of cases the occasion for exercising one's rights would have disappeared months or years before one won an empty judicial victory. Fields and Lyons took their case to the Supreme Court. They were represented by Melvin Wulf, legal director of the American Civil Liberties Union, and Charles Morgan, one of the handful of white lawyers in the South ready to assert in court the constitutional rights of Negroes as well as whites. And briefs supporting Fields and Lyons were filed by two *amici curiae* (friends of the court): one of these was the United States; the other was the NAACP Legal Defense and Educational Fund. The Supreme Court reversed the convictions.[36] The one-sentence opinion cited two cases, *Thompson v. Louisville*,[37] and *Garner v. Louisiana*,[38] which stand for the proposition that a criminal conviction unsupported by any evidence is a denial of due process of law. Evidently, therefore, the Supreme Court did not feel that Fields and Lyons, in distributing their party newspaper, could on any reasonable reading of the injunction be regarded as having committed acts which fell within the injunction's ambit. Just as evidently, the Supreme Court was not anxious to reach the more ticklish First Amendment questions presented by the case: (1) whether in this instance the likelihood of violence ensuing from the proposed meeting was, demonstrably, so great as to justify a prior ban on the meeting; and (2) whether, if the answer to the first question was in the negative, those enjoined could challenge the ban by violating it or only by appealing from it.

Even though the *Fields* case was not decided on First

Amendment grounds, the judgment of reversal can fairly be taken to reflect the unanimous insistence of the Justices that avenues of public communication be kept open for the ventilation of every point of view—including the claptrap of the racist zealots who are doing their best to undercut the Court's efforts to vindicate the Negro's constitutional right to full participation in the American community. However, just as hostility to civil rights does not deprive the speaker of the First Amendment's protection, so too a speaker derives no special title to the amendment's protection merely because he claims to be a proponent of civil rights. This truism is illustrated by an episode which may, in due course, ripen into a criminal conviction reviewable by the Supreme Court:

On July 16, 1964, a fifteen-year-old Negro youth was shot to death in Harlem by a New York City police lieutenant. The turbulence which began that day swelled into the massive Harlem riots of July 18 and July 19—riots which, in ensuing weeks, were to repeat themselves in predominantly Negro sections of Brooklyn, Rochester, Jersey City, and other northern urban centers. On July 18 a speech was made on a Harlem street-corner by William Epton, an official of a militant Left-Wing group called the Progressive Labor Movement. Epton, who reportedly characterizes himself as "a disciple of the Chinese Communists," was charged by police with having said the following in the course of his speech on July 18:

> *We're going to have a demonstration and we don't say that it is going to be peaceful because the cops have declared war on the people of Harlem and . . . no country or peoples in the world that have had war declared on them have not declared war on their enemy. They declared war on us and we should declare war on them and every time they kill one of us, damn it, we'll kill one of them and we should start thinking that way right now . . . preaching violence because we had better stop talking about violence as a dirty word.*
> *. . . [I]f we're going to be free, we will not be fully free until we smash this state completely and totally. Destroy and set up a new state of our own choosing and our own liking. . . .*
> *And in that process of smashing this state we're going to have to kill a lot of these cops, a lot of these judges, and we'll have to*

*go up against their army. We'll organize our own militia and our
own army.*

*If we don't do it, brothers, you'll be subjugated. We'll be
kept in chains for another 200 or 300 years. Think about it because no people in this world have ever achieved independence
and freedom through the ballot or having it legislated to them.
All people in this world who are free got their freedom through
struggle and through revolution. That's the only way to gain
freedom.*[39]

For having allegedly said this, Epton was indicted under New
York's "criminal anarchy" statute. He appears to have been the
first person charged under the statute since the arrest, in 1919, of
Benjamin Gitlow, in the prosecution which ultimately came before the Supreme Court in *Gitlow v. New York.*[40]

Against the *Rockwell, Feiner, Edwards, Fields,* and *Epton*
cases may be balanced a case which, while lacking the drama of
those five, may be regarded as presenting even more difficult
First Amendment questions. The case was *Marsh v. Alabama.*
The problem was whether Mrs. Marsh, a Jehovah's Witness,
could exercise her freedom of speech and worship through the
peaceful distribution of religious tracts. What made the problem
difficult was that Mrs. Marsh distributed the tracts *not* on public
property but on the streets of a so-called "company town"—the
town of Chickasaw, Alabama, which belonged to the Gulf Shipbuilding Corporation. The corporation had apparently wanted to
curtail the common practice of salesmen and of do-gooders alike
of peddling their wares and/or their ideas on street-corners and
from door to door. What the corporation had done was to put up
signs announcing that all solicitation was forbidden in Chickasaw
except by those persons who had permits to solicit issued by the
corporation. Mrs. Marsh had no such permit; and therefore, when
she persisted in distributing her tracts on the streets of Chickasaw, she was arrested and prosecuted for trespass.

Thus, Mrs. Marsh's conviction presented to the Supreme
Court a major conflict between the personal liberty of Mrs. Marsh
and the proprietary rights of the corporation. And (though probably none foresaw it in 1946, when *Marsh v. Alabama* was
decided) substantially that conflict was to repeat itself in a
different context nearly two decades later, when the "sit-ins" of

the sixties were to juxtapose the claims of southern Negroes to be served a hamburger and coffee and the claims of lunch-counter proprietors to be able to pick and choose their customers as they saw fit. The opinions in *Marsh v. Alabama* were as follows:

MR. JUSTICE BLACK *delivered the opinion of the Court.*

In this case we are asked to decide whether a State, consistently with the First and Fourteenth Amendments, can impose criminal punishment on a person who undertakes to distribute religious literature on the premises of a company-owned town contrary to the wishes of the town's management. The town, a suburb of Mobile, Alabama, known as Chickasaw, is owned by the Gulf Shipbuilding Corporation. Except for that it has all the characteristics of any other American town. The property consists of residential buildings, streets, a system of sewers, a sewage disposal plant and a "business block" on which business places are situated. A deputy of the Mobile County Sheriff, paid by the company, serves as the town's policeman. Merchants and service establishments have rented the stores and business places on the business block and the United States uses one of the places as a post office from which six carriers deliver mail to the people of Chickasaw and the adjacent area. The town and the surrounding neighborhood, which cannot be distinguished from the Gulf property by anyone not familiar with the property lines, are thickly settled, and according to all indications the residents use the business block as their regular shopping center. To do so, they now, as they have for many years, make use of a company-owned paved street and sidewalk located alongside the store fronts in order to enter and leave the stores and the post office. Intersecting company-owned roads at each end of the business block lead into a four-lane public highway which runs parallel to the business block at a distance of thirty feet. There is nothing to stop highway traffic from coming onto the business block and upon arrival a traveler may make free use of the facilities available there. In short the town and its shopping district are accessible to and freely used by the public in general and there is nothing to distinguish them from any other town and shopping center except the fact that the title to the property belongs to a private corporation.

Appellant, a Jehovah's Witness, came onto the sidewalk we have just described, stood near the post office and undertook to distribute religious literature. In the stores the corporation had posted a notice which read as follows: "This Is Private Property, and Without Written Permission, No Street, or House Vendor, Agent or Solicitation of any Kind Will Be Permitted." Appellant was warned that she could not distribute the literature without a permit and told that no permit would be issued to her. She protested that the company rule could not be constitutionally applied so as to prohibit her from distributing religious writings. When she was asked to leave the sidewalk and Chickasaw she declined. The deputy sheriff arrested her and she was charged in the state court with violating Title 14, § 426 of the 1940 Alabama Code which makes it a crime to enter or remain on the premises of another after having been warned not to do so. Appellant contended that to construe the state statute as applicable to her activities would abridge her right to freedom of press and religion contrary to the First and Fourteenth Amendments to the Constitution. This contention was rejected and she was convicted. The Alabama Court of Appeals affirmed the conviction, holding that the statute as applied was constitutional because the title to the sidewalk was in the corporation and because the public use of the sidewalk had not been such as to give rise to a presumption under Alabama law of its irrevocable dedication to the public. 21 So.2d 558. The State Supreme Court denied certiorari, 246 Ala. 539, 21 So.2d 564, and the case is here on appeal under § 237 (a) of the Judicial Code, 28 U.S.C. § 344 (a).

Had the title to Chickasaw belonged not to a private but to a municipal corporation and had appellant been arrested for violating a municipal ordinance rather than a ruling by those appointed by the corporation to manage a company town it would have been clear that appellant's conviction must be reversed. . . . [N]either a State nor a municipality can completely bar the distribution of literature containing religious or political ideas on its streets, sidewalks and public places or make the right to distribute dependent on a flat license tax or permit to be issued by an official who could deny it at will. . . . And we have recognized that the preservation of a free society is so far dependent upon the right of each individual citizen to receive such literature as he himself might desire that a municipality could not, without jeopardizing

*that vital individual freedom, prohibit door to door distribution
of literature.* Martin v. Struthers, 319 U.S. 141, 146, 147. *From
these decisions it is clear that had the people of Chickasaw owned
all the homes, and all the stores, and all the streets, and all the
sidewalks, all those owners together could not have set up a
municipal government with sufficient power to pass an ordinance
completely barring the distribution of religious literature. Our
question then narrows down to this: Can those people who live in
or come to Chickasaw be denied freedom of press and religion
simply because a single company has legal title to all the town?
For it is the State's contention that the mere fact that all the
property interests in the town are held by a single company is
enough to give that company power, enforceable by a state
statute, to abridge these freedoms.*

*We do not agree that the corporation's property interests
settle the question. The State urges in effect that the corporation's
right to control the inhabitants of Chickasaw is coextensive with
the right of a homeowner to regulate the conduct of his guests.
We cannot accept that contention. Ownership does not always
mean absolute dominion. The more an owner, for his advantage,
opens up his property for use by the public in general, the more
do his rights become circumscribed by the statutory and constitutional rights of those who use it. . . . Thus, the owners of
privately held bridges, ferries, turnpikes and railroads may not
operate them as freely as a farmer does his farm. Since these
facilities are built and operated primarily to benefit the public
and since their operation is essentially a public function, it is
subject to state regulation. And, though the issue is not directly
analogous to the one before us, we do want to point out by way
of illustration that such regulation may not result in an operation
of these facilities, even by privately owned companies, which unconstitutionally interferes with and discriminates against interstate
commerce. . . . Had the corporation here owned the segment
of the four-lane highway which runs parallel to the "business
block" and operated the same under a state franchise, doubtless no one would have seriously contended that the corporation's
property interest in the highway gave it power to obstruct
through traffic or to discriminate against interstate commerce. . . .*

*We do not think it makes any significant constitutional differ-
ence as to the relationship between the rights of the owner and*

those of the public that here the State, instead of permitting the corporation to operate a highway, permitted it to use its property as a town, operate a "business block" in the town and a street and sidewalk on that business block. Cf. Barney v. Keokuk, 94 U.S. 324, 340. *Whether a corporation or a municipality owns or possesses the town the public in either case has an identical interest in the functioning of the community in such manner that the channels of communication remain free. As we have heretofore stated, the town of Chickasaw does not function differently from any other town. The "business block" serves as the community shopping center and is freely accessible and open to the people in the area and those passing through. The managers appointed by the corporation cannot curtail the liberty of press and religion of these people consistently with the purposes of the Constitutional guarantees, and a state statute, as the one here involved, which enforces such action by criminally punishing those who attempt to distribute religious literature clearly violates the First and Fourteenth Amendments to the Constitution.*

Many people in the United States live in company-owned towns. [The Court, in a footnote, recited the following facts: "In the bituminous coal industry alone, approximately one-half of the miners in the United States lived in company-owned houses in the period from 1922–23. The percentage varied from 9 per cent in Illinois and Indiana and 64 per cent in Kentucky, to almost 80 per cent in West Virginia. U. S. Coal Commission, Report, 1925, Part III, pp. 1467, 1469 summarized in Morris, The Plight of the Coal Miner, Philadelphia 1934, Ch. VI, p. 86. The most recent statistics we found available are in Magnusson, Housing by Employers in the United States, Bureau of Labor Statistics Bulletin No. 263 (Misc. Ser.) p. 11. See also United States Department of Labor, Wage and Hour Division, Data on Pay Roll Deductions, Union Manufacturing Company, Union Point, Georgia, June 1941; Rhyne, Some Southern Cotton Mill Workers and Their Villages, Chapel Hill, 1930 (Study completed under the direction of the Institute for Research in Social Science at the University of North Carolina); Comment, Urban Redevelopment, 54 Yale L.J. 116."] These people, just as residents of municipalities, are free citizens of their State and country. Just as all other citizens they must make decisions which affect the welfare of community and nation. To act as good citizens they must be informed. In order to enable them to be properly informed their information must be uncensored. There is no more reason for depriving these people of the liberties guaranteed by the First and Fourteenth Amendments than there is for curtailing these freedoms with respect to any other citizen.

When we balance the Constitutional rights of owners of property against those of the people to enjoy freedom of press and religion, as we must here, we remain mindful of the fact that the latter occupy a preferred position. As we have stated before, the right to exercise the liberties safeguarded by the First Amendment "lies at the foundation of free government by free men" and we must in all cases "weigh the circumstances and . . . appraise the . . . reasons . . . in support of the regulation . . . of the rights." Schneider v. State, 308 U.S. 147, 161. *In our view the circumstance that the property rights to the premises where the deprivation of liberty, here involved, took place, were held by others than the public, is not sufficient to justify the State's permitting a corporation to govern a community of citizens so as to restrict their fundamental liberties and the enforcement of such restraint by the application of a state statute. Insofar as the State has attempted to impose criminal punishment on appellant for undertaking to distribute religious literature in a company town, its action cannot stand. The case is reversed and the cause remanded for further proceedings not inconsistent with this opinion.*

Reversed and remanded.

MR. JUSTICE [ROBERT H.] JACKSON *took no part in the consideration or decision of this case.*

MR. JUSTICE FRANKFURTER, *concurring.*

So long as the views which prevailed in Jones v. Opelika, 319 U.S. 103, *in connection with* 316 U.S. 584, 600; Murdock v. Pennsylvania, 319 U.S. 105; Martin v. Struthers, 319 U.S. 141, *express the law of the Constitution, I am unable to find legal significance in the fact that a town in which the Constitutional freedoms of religion and speech are invoked happens to be company-owned. These decisions accorded the purveyors of ideas, religious or otherwise, "a preferred position,"* Murdock v. Pennsylvania, supra *at* 115, *even to the extent of relieving them from an unhampering and non-discriminatory duty of bearing their share of the cost of maintaining the peace and the other amenities of a civilized society. Constitutional privileges having such a reach ought not to depend upon a State court's notion of the extent of "dedication" of private property to public purposes. Local determinations of such technical matters govern controversies affecting property. But when decisions by State courts involving local matters are so interwoven with the decision of the question of Constitutional rights that one necessarily involves the other, State determination of local questions cannot control the Federal Constitutional right.*

A company-owned town gives rise to a network of property relations. As to these, the judicial organ of a State has the final say. But a company-owned town is a town. In its community aspects it does not differ from other towns. These community aspects are decisive in adjusting the relations now before us, and more particularly in adjudicating the clash of freedoms which the Bill of Rights was designed to resolve—the freedom of the community to regulate its life and the freedom of the individual to exercise his religion and to disseminate his ideas. Title to property as defined by State law controls property relations; it cannot control issues of civil liberties which arise precisely because a company town is a town as well as a congeries of property relations. And similarly the technical distinctions on which a finding of "trespass" so often depends are too tenuous to control decision regarding the scope of the vital liberties guaranteed by the Constitution.

Accordingly, as I have already indicated, so long as the scope of the guarantees of the Due Process Clause of the Fourteenth Amendment by absorption of the First remains that which the Court gave to it in the series of cases in the October Term, 1942, the circumstances of the present case seem to me clearly to fall within it. And so I agree with the opinion of the Court, except that portion of it which relies on arguments drawn from the restrictions which the Commerce Clause imposes on State regulation of commerce. It does not seem to me to further Constitutional analysis to seek help for the solution of the delicate problems arising under the First Amendment from the very different order of problems which the Commerce Clause presents. The latter involves an accommodation between National and State powers operating in the same field. Where the First Amendment applies, it is a denial of all governmental power in our Federal system.

MR. JUSTICE [STANLEY F.] REED, *dissenting.*

Former decisions of this Court have interpreted generously the Constitutional rights of people in this Land to exercise freedom of religion, of speech and of the press. It has never been held and is not now by this opinion of the Court that these rights are absolute and unlimited either in respect to the manner or the place of their exercise. What the present decision establishes as a principle is that one may remain on private property against the will of the owner and contrary to the law of the state so long as the only objection to his presence is that he is exercising an asserted right to spread there his religious views. See Marrone v. Washington Jockey Club, 227 U.S. 633. This is the first case to extend by law the privilege of religious exercises beyond public places or to private places without the assent of the owner. Compare Martin v. Struthers, 319 U.S. 141.

As the rule now announced permits this intrusion, without possibility of protection of the property by law, and apparently is equally applicable to the freedom of speech and the press, it seems appropriate to express a dissent to this, to us, novel Constitutional doctrine. Of course, such principle may subsequently be restricted by this Court to the precise facts of this case—that is to private property in a company town where the owner for his own advantage has permitted a restricted public use by his licensees and invitees. Such distinctions are of degree and require new arbitrary lines, judicially drawn, instead of those hitherto established by legislation and precedent. While the power of this Court, as the interpreter of the Constitution to determine what use of real property by the owner makes that property subject, at will, to the reasonable practice of religious exercises by strangers, cannot be doubted, we find nothing in the principles of the First Amendment, adopted now into the Fourteenth, which justifies their application to the facts of this case. . . .

Our Constitution guarantees to every man the right to express his views in an orderly fashion. An essential element of "orderly" is that the man shall also have a right to use the place he chooses for his exposition. The rights of the owner, which the Constitution protects as well as the right of free speech, are not outweighed by the interests of the trespasser, even though he trespasses in behalf of religion or free speech. We cannot say that Jehovah's Witnesses can claim the privilege of a license, which has never been granted, to hold their meetings in other private places, merely because the *owner has admitted the public to them for other limited purposes. Even though we have reached the point where this Court is required to force private owners to open their property for the practice there of religious activities or propaganda distasteful to the owner, because of the public interest in freedom of speech and religion, there is no need for the application of such a doctrine here. Appellant, as we have said, was free to engage in such practices on the public highways, without becoming a trespasser on the company's property.*

The CHIEF JUSTICE [HARLAN F. STONE] *and* MR. JUSTICE [HAROLD H.] BURTON *join in this dissent.*[41]

The overriding question in the *Marsh* case was whether the exclusionary rules laid down by a "company town" should be analogized to the ordinances of an ordinary municipality or to the whims of privacy that each individual can indulge in his own home. For the Fourteenth Amendment comes into play only against *state* (or city, or town) action. But identifying what is "state" and what is "private" becomes increasingly hard as (1) the range and power of "private" groups (corporations, labor unions, foundations, etc.) extend, and (2) the sweep of routine governmental activity takes it deeper and deeper into realms of traditionally "private" responsibility. The problem of distinguishing between private and public action bears directly on Justice Frankfurter's rebuke to Justice Black for analogizing the *Marsh* case to a hypothetical situation in which a corporation which owned and, pursuant to state authority of some sort, operated a segment of an interstate highway, chose to interfere with or close off traffic on the highway. Such an eventuality would raise commerce clause, not Fourteenth Amendment, problems; and the commerce clause is supreme over *any* interference, whether of public or private origin. In a way, Justice Black's use of the inapposite commerce analogy to support his result in *Marsh* is the obverse of his technique in dissent in *Southern Pacific v. Arizona*,[42] (the case invalidating the Arizona Long Train Law). There, *in a commerce clause context*, Justice Black censured the Court for acting as a "super-legislature"; but the phrase of censure that Black employed derived from what Brandeis and Holmes had said *in a Fourteenth Amendment setting*, objecting to the majority's use of the due process clause to strike down state economic regulations.

The Black-Frankfurter disagreement, aired in passing in *Marsh*, over whether free speech has a "preferred position," suggests—but does not begin to describe—the polarity of the views of these two Justices on free speech questions.

The late Justice Frankfurter tended to regard free speech issues—like other due process issues—as ones of reasonableness (or, to use Holmes' language in *Schenck*, "of proximity and degree"). Solution of the issues depended on inquiry into the urgency of the state's need to regulate and the competing urgency of the individual's need to stay unregulated. Frankfurter's presumption that the legislative process is a responsible one—and his conviction that judicial inquiry is incomplete, episodic, and unbound by an anchoring in the needs of the electorate—led him in most cases (though not all: see his concurrence in *Sweezy v. New Hampshire*[43]) to sustain the authority the state exercises. Justice Frankfurter frequently seemed to belong to the class of judges who, as Professor Paul Freund put it, "have allowed themselves to be repelled too strongly away from their private bent and the advances of their brethren. If anything more is needed to assure a disinterested judgment than a bias against bias, it is perhaps a bias against bias against bias. For balance may be lost by leaning backwards as well as forwards."[44]

Justice Black, on the other hand, has moved beyond the view that First Amendment rights are "preferred" to other constitutional rights, such as rights of property. He now talks of these limitations as "absolute."[45] In part this is bottomed on the fact that the First Amendment—"Congress shall make no law . . ."—is written "in no equivocal language."[46] (This cannot be said for the Fourteenth Amendment, whether it is "privileges or immunities" or the "liberty" of the due process clause which incorporates the First Amendment as a limitation on the states.) And Black also calls to witness Madison's prophecy to Congress that courts would be "impenetrable bulwarks against every assumption of power" foreclosed by the Bill of Rights.[47] But absolutism as a judicial virtue has its limitations, not least of which is the difficulty of determining, without some inquiry into the context of a particular exercise of state authority and a particular challenge to that authority, whether the "absolute" constitutional provision applies or not. Also to be kept in mind is the pragmatic skepticism which Madison, in his letter to Jefferson of October 17, 1788, privately expressed: "I am inclined to think that *absolute* restrictions in cases that are doubtful or where emergencies may overrule them, ought to be avoided."[48]

The Supreme Court's apparent inability to develop a comprehensive approach to the multifarious questions of freedom of expression has periodically generated grave doubts both as to the basic rationale of these First Amendment guarantees and as to the effectiveness of legal institutions in implementing them. Professor Thomas I. Emerson, a leading student of the Court's work in the field of civil liberties, has suggested that these doubts necessitate the formulation of a new "general theory of the First Amendment." As a predicate to the formulation of such a theory, Professor Emerson has sought to demonstrate that legal institutions are fit instruments for developing and enforcing workable guarantees of freedom of expression:

No one concerned with freedom of expression in the United States today can fail to be alarmed by the unsatisfactory state of first amendment doctrine. Despite the mounting number of decisions and an even greater volume of comment, no really adequate or comprehensive theory of the first amendment has been enunciated, much less agreed upon. Proponents of the "absolute" or "literal" interpretation of the first amendment have failed to define the bounds of their position or to account for such apparent exceptions to the absolute test as the law of libel, the application of child labor laws to the distribution of literature, and the regulation of election campaigns. Their views have therefore been dismissed as impractical or illogical, or both. At the other end of the spectrum, the "balancing" test has tended to reduce the first amendment, especially when a legislative judgment is weighed in the balance, to a limp and lifeless formality. Among intermediate positions, the "clear and present danger" test is the best known; yet not only has this formula often been ignored, but it was discarded in Dennis *and at any rate is hardly applicable to many of the issues which now arise, such as the extent of the protection afforded by the first amendment from the legislative investigating power. Other efforts to formulate an overall theory have not met outstanding success. Nor has doctrine been evolved to deal with some of the newer problems, where the issue is not pure restraint on government interference but rather the use of governmental power to encourage freedom of expression or the actual participation by government itself in the realm of expression.*

This failure to develop a satisfactory theory of the first amendment is hardly surprising. The issues are controversial and the problems complex. The Supreme Court did not seriously commence the task of interpretation until a few decades ago, beginning with the Schenck *case in 1919. And rapidly changing conditions in the country have presented the issues in new and more difficult forms. Irrespective of the causes, however, there is grave danger in the present situation. Not only are courts and the legal profession in sharp conflict but the public is seriously confused and the first amendment is threatened with disintegration. . . .*

The American people have frequently been warned that they must not count too heavily upon the legal system for the preservation of democratic liberties. Judge Learned Hand, one of the most eloquent exponents of this view, has made the point in the strongest language:

> *I often wonder whether we do not rest our hopes too much upon constitutions, upon laws and upon courts. These are false hopes; believe me, these are false hopes. Liberty lies in the hearts of men and women; when it dies there, no constitution, no law, no court can save it; no constitution, no law, no court can even do much to help it. While it lies there it needs no constitution, no law, no court to save it.*

Certainly this admonition must be taken to heart. Obviously a perfect set of legal rules and an ideal array of judicial institutions could not by themselves assure an effective system of free expression. Many other factors are critical. There must be a substantial consensus on the values and goals of the society—some minimum area of agreement or acquiescence. The economic structure must provide a certain standard of material welfare, shared broadly by all elements of the population. Political institutions must have some basis in the traditions of the people, must receive some degree of acceptance, must prove reasonably effective in meeting the problems of the society, and must remain capable of adjustment and change. Other institutions, such as private corporations and labor organizations, must permit communication on a diverse scale in important areas of decision-making. There must be some feeling of security in relation to other nations or societies. The educational system, the media of communication, and similar institutions moulding public opinion must have some capacity to produce mature and independent members of the local and national community. The general philosophy, attitudes and mental health of the citizenry must be favorable. In short, basic conditions for a viable democratic society must be present.

Yet surely Judge Hand has overstated the case. The legal system is not so peripheral to the maintenance of free expression as his words imply. The experience of mankind demonstrates the contrary. Wherever the principles of free expression have prevailed in a society they have been closely supported by law and legal institutions. This is particularly true, of course, in the United States. . . .

The legal system is, of course, one of the most effective instruments available to a society for controlling the behavior of its members so as to realize the values and goals sought by that society. Because of certain characteristics of a system of free expression, the role of law is of peculiar significance in any social effort to maintain such a system.

First, a system of free expression is designed to encourage a necessary degree of conflict within a society. To be sure, it attempts to avoid resort to force or violence by channelling this conflict into the area of expression and persuasion. And it contemplates that a longer-range consensus will ultimately be achieved. Yet, because it recognizes the right of the citizen to disagree with, arouse, antagonize and shock his fellow citizens and the government, such an arrangement of human affairs is hardly likely to be self-operating. In its short-term effects it may indeed be highly volatile. Hence the system needs the legitimizing and harmonizing influence of the legal process to keep it in successful balance.

Other features of a system of free expression likewise demonstrate the need for buttressing it through law and legal institutions. The full benefits of the system can be realized only when the individual knows the extent of his rights and has some assurance of protection in exercising them. Thus the governing prin-

*ciples of such a system need to be articulated with some precision
and clarity. Doubt or uncertainty negates the process. Furthermore, the theory rests upon subordination of immediate interests
in favor of long-term benefits. This can be achieved only through
the application of principle, not by ad hoc resolution of individual
cases. And it requires procedures adequate to relieve immediate
pressures and facilitate objective consideration. All these elements
a legal system is equipped to supply.*

*Further . . . the theory of freedom of expression is a sophis-
ticated and even complex one. It does not come naturally to the
ordinary citizen, but needs to be learned. It must be restated and
reiterated not only for each generation but for each new situation.
It leans heavily upon understanding and education, both for the
individual and the community as a whole. The legal process is
one of the most effective methods for providing the kind of social
comprehension essential for the attainment of society's higher
and more remote ideals.*

*Finally, the principles of the system must be constantly re-
shaped and expanded to meet new conditions and new threats to
its existence. This requires the deliberate attention of an institution entrusted with that specific obligation and possessing the expertise to perform such a function.*

*The function of the legal process is not only to provide a
means whereby a society shapes and controls the behavior of its
individual members in the interests of the whole. It also supplies
one of the principal methods by which a society controls itself,
limiting its own powers in the interests of the individual. The role
of law here is to mark and guard the line between the sphere of
social power, organized in the form of the state, and the area of
private right. The legal problems involved in maintaining a system of free expression fall largely into this realm. In essence,
legal support for such a system involves the protection of individual rights against interference or unwarranted control by the
government. More specifically the legal structure must provide:*

*(1) Protection of the individual's right to freedom of expres-
sion against interference by the government in its efforts to
achieve other social objectives or to advance its own interests.
This has been in the past the main area of legal concern, and it
remains so, although other phases of the problem are assuming increasing importance.*

(2) *The use, and simultaneous restriction, of government in regulating conflicts between individuals or groups within the system of free expression itself; in protecting individuals or groups from non-governmental interference in the exercise of their rights; and in eliminating obstacles to the effective functioning of the system.*

(3) *Restriction of the government in so far as the government itself participates in the system of expression.*

All these requirements involve control over the state. The use of law to achieve this kind of control has been one of the central concerns of freedom-seeking societies over the ages. Legal recognition of individual rights, enforced through the legal process, has become the core of free society.

One must recognize, of course, that the legal system can be used to undermine or destroy freedom of expression. Often in the past, and still in the present, the judicial process has served the function of legitimizing action that is wholly contrary to the elemental principles of free expression. Indeed, even in the police state, infringements of political freedom are normally accomplished in the name of the law. Yet this fact does not lessen, but rather emphasizes, the power of law and legal institutions as an instrument of social persuasion and control. It underlines the warning that the legal system is not by itself sufficient to guarantee free expression. But it also furnishes evidence that without the support of the legal structure the values of such a system are not likely to prevail in the community.[49]

2. Freedom of worship and the separation of church and state

One of the most important and perplexing constitutional problems to bedevil the American community was a political-legal controversy of major dimension before the Constitution was adopted. And it remains so today. The problem is to define the place of religion in American public life. It is a problem which, even more than most other profound constitutional dilemmas, cannot seem to escape its history. The materials that follow tell something of the history of the problem. They also suggest something of the present impact of the problem upon an enterprise of the highest national importance—the job of education. These materials are likely to raise, in the reader's mind, questions as to the utility of history as a guide to the judicial solution of current social issues. Or, to put it another way, these materials may force the reader to re-examine what he means by "history" and what he means by "law."

a. The background of the First Amendment

The Constitution as originally adopted mentioned religion only once, and its command was clear:

> . . . [N]o religious test shall ever be required as a qualification to any office or public trust under the United States.

In fewer words, the First Amendment added two far more important, and far less precise, injunctions:

> Congress shall make no law respecting an establishment of religion, or prohibiting the free exercise thereof. . . .

More than a century and a half after the adoption of the amendment, the late Justice Wiley B. Rutledge (in a case in which he dissented from a Supreme Court holding that states could finance the bus travel of children attending parochial schools) put heavy stress on the amendment's roots in the past:

> *No provision of the Constitution is more closely tied to or given content by its generating history than the religious clause of the First Amendment.*[50]

That "generating history" began with American's beginnings. A brilliant journalist, Theodore H. White, has recently recalled those beginnings:

> *America as a civilization began with religion. The first and earliest immigrants from Europe, those who shaped America's culture, law, tradition and ethics, were those who came from England—and they came when English civilization was in torment over the manner in which Englishmen might worship Christ. All through the seventeenth century, as the settlers arrived from the downs, the moors, and the villages of England, they came scarred with the bitterness and intensity of the religious wars of that era, wars no less bloody and ferocious for the fact that they were fought between Protestant sects, Protestant*

against Protestant. The harshness of Cromwell, that somber fig-
ure, was a reflection of the harshness with which Protestants
assailed each other, as well as Catholics, over sect and dogma.

It was with this remembered bitterness that the English mi-
grants began the building of a new society in a new world; and
out of this bitterness they distilled, though not without a struggle,
that first great landmark in America's unique civilization, that first
of the creative American compromises that was to set America
apart from the old world: freedom of worship, the decision that
government should have no right to make inquiry into the faith
of its citizens and that the state should remain forever divorced
from any religious establishment. Never in civilization, since the
earliest ziggurats and temples went up in the mud-walled villages
of prehistoric Mesopotamia, had there been any state that left
each individual to find his way to God without the guidance of
the state. In retrospect, this is probably the greatest historic deci-
sion enshrined in the American Constitution.[51]

The Bill of Rights, including the First Amendment, was
added to propitiate those who felt that the Constitution as originally drawn did not fully secure individual liberty. It was James
Madison who was chiefly responsible for presenting, and securing
adoption of, the Bill of Rights. And the "generating history"
directly antedating the "religious clause" of the amendment was
the fight waged by Jefferson and Madison, from 1776 to 1786, to
secure religious toleration in Virginia.

On the eve of the American Revolution, the Anglican (i.e.,
Episcopalian) Church was the "established" church in Virginia.
This meant, according to Leo Pfeffer, a noted student of the
separation of church and state, that the laws of Virginia

. . . provided for: religious services according to the laws and
orders of the Church of England; a ministry conformable to the
canons; compulsory attendance at religious services; the regula-
tion of nonconformists; glebe lands for the support of the clergy;
closed, corporate and nonresponsible vestries empowered to levy
tithes for ministers' salaries, upkeep of the church, and support of
the poor, and occupied by vestrymen subscribing to the doctrine
and discipline of the church and bound by the oath of suprem-
acy.[52]

In June 1776 the Virginia legislature adopted a Bill of Rights As we have seen, the opening paragraphs of the Virginia enactment were clearly echoed a month later in those "self-evident" propositions of equality and of government-by-consent-of-the-governed which were contained in the Declaration of Independence. But the last paragraph of Virginia's Bill of Rights dealt with a matter mentioned only tangentially in the Declaration—man's relation to God. And it announced principles which, at least on a rhetorical level, were inconsistent with the then prevailing concept of an official "established" creed:

That religion, or the duty which we owe to our Creator, and the manner of discharging it, can be directed only by reason and conviction, not by force or violence; and therefore all men are equally entitled to the free exercise of religion, according to the dictates of conscience; and that it is the mutual duty of all to practice Christian forbearance, love, and charity towards each other.[53]

During the next decade, most of the Virginia laws giving official preference to the Anglican Church were modified or repealed. In 1776 non-Anglicans were exempted from paying the hitherto compulsory tithes for the support of the Anglican Church, and three years later Anglicans themselves were removed from legal coercion to support their own church. Then the issue became generalized: Should the state tax everyone to help support *all* (Christian) churches? Patrick Henry sponsored a bill which would have exacted from each taxpayer a sum "for the support of Christian teachers," but which would have given the taxpayer the right to designate the particular "society of Christians" which should benefit from his assessment.[54] The draft bill recited its allegiance to "the liberal principle heretofore adopted and intended to be preserved by abolishing all distinctions of pre-eminence amongst the different societies or communities of Christians."[55] But this equality of treatment of all Christian sects did not pacify Madison and Jefferson and their adherents, most of whom were Deists, Baptists, and Presbyterians. Relying on Virgina's Bill of Rights, they challenged the basic concept of governmental support of religion. In this vein Madison, in 1785, penned the historic *Memorial and Remonstrance against Re-*

ligious Assessments, which denounced the policy of the proposed assessment bill *and denied the legislature's authority to enact it:*

> *We, the subscribers, citizens of the . . . Commonwealth, . . . remonstrate against the said Bill,*
>
> *1. Because we hold it for a fundamental and undeniable truth, "that Religion or the duty which we owe to our Creator and the Manner of discharging it, can be directed only by reason and conviction, not by force or violence." The Religion then of every man must be left to the conviction and conscience of every man; and it is the right of every man to exercise it as these may dictate. This right is in its nature an unalienable right. It is unalienable; because the opinions of men, depending only on the evidence contemplated by their own minds, cannot follow the dictates of other men: It is unalienable also; because what is here a right towards men, is a duty towards the Creator. It is the duty of every man to render to the Creator such homage, and such only, as he believes to be acceptable to him. This duty is precedent both in order of time and degree of obligation, to the claims of Civil Society. Before any man can be considered as a member of Civil Society, he must be considered as a subject of the Governor of the Universe: And if a member of Civil Society, who enters into any subordinate Association, must always do it with a reservation of his duty to the general authority; much more must every man who becomes a member of any particular Civil Society, do it with a saving of his allegiance to the Universal Sovereign. We maintain therefore that in matters of Religion, no man's right is abridged by the institution of Civil Society, and that Religion is wholly exempt from its cognizance. True it is, that no other rule exists, by which any question which may divide a Society, can be ultimately determined, but the will of the majority; but it is also true, that the majority may trespass on the rights of the minority.*
>
> *2. Because if religion be exempt from the authority of the Society at large, still less can it be subject to that of the Legislative Body. The latter are but the creatures and vicegerents of the former. Their jurisdiction is both derivative and limited: it is limited with regard to the coordinate departments, more necessarily is it limited with regard to the constituents. The preservation of a free government requires not merely, that the metes and bounds which separate each department of power may be in-*

variably maintained; but more especially, that neither of them be suffered to overleap the great Barrier which defends the rights of the people. The Rulers who are guilty of such an encroachment, exceed the commission from which they derive their authority, and are Tyrants. The People who submit to it are governed by laws made neither by themselves, nor by an authority derived from them, and are slaves.

3. Because, it is proper to take alarm at the first experiment on our liberties. We hold this prudent jealousy to be the first duty of citizens, and one of [the] noblest characteristics of the late Revolution. The freemen of America did not wait till usurped power had strengthened itself by exercise, and entangled the question in precedents. They saw all the consequences in the principle, and they avoided the consequences by denying the principle. We revere this lesson too much, soon to forget it. Who does not see that the same authority which can establish Christianity, in exclusion of all other Religions, may establish with the same ease any particular sect of Christians, in exclusion of all other Sects? That the same authority which can force a citizen to contribute three pence only of his property for the support of any one establishment, may force him to conform to any other establishment in all cases whatsoever?

.   .   .   .   .

5. Because the bill implies either that the Civil Magistrate is a competent Judge of Religious truth; or that he may employ Religion as an engine of Civil policy. The first is an arrogant pretension falsified by the contradictory opinions of Rulers in all ages, and throughout the world: The second an unhallowed perversion of the means of salvation.

6. Because the establishment proposed by the Bill is not requisite for the support of the Christian Religion. To say that it is, is a contradiction to the Christian Religion itself; for every page of it disavows a dependence on the powers of this world. . . . It is moreover to weaken in those who profess this Religion a pious confidence in its innate excellence, and the patronage of its Author; and to foster in those who still reject it, a suspicion that its friends are too conscious of its fallacies, to trust it to its own merits.

.   .   .   .   .

9. *Because the proposed establishment is a departure from that generous policy, which, offering an asylum to the persecuted and oppressed of every Nation and Religion, promised a lustre to our country, and an accession to the number of its citizens. What a melancholy mark is the Bill of sudden degeneracy? Instead of holding forth an asylum to the persecuted, it is itself a signal of persecution. It degrades from the equal rank of Citizens all those whose opinions in Religion do not bend to those of the Legislative authority. Distant as it may be, in its present form, from the Inquisition it differs from it only in degree. The one is the first step, the other the last in the career of intolerance. The magnanimous sufferer under this cruel scourge in foreign Regions, must view the Bill as a Beacon on our Coast, warning him to seek some other haven, where liberty and philanthropy in their due extent may offer a more certain repose from his troubles.*

.   .   .   .   .

11. *Because, it will destroy that moderation and harmony which the forbearance of our laws to intermeddle with Religion, has produced amongst its several sects. Torrents of blood have been spilt in the old world, by vain attempts of the secular arm to extinguish Religious discord, by proscribing all difference in Religious opinions. Time has at length revealed the true remedy. Every relaxation of narrow and rigorous policy, wherever it has been tried, has been found to assuage the disease. The American Theatre has exhibited proofs, that equal and compleat liberty, if it does not wholly eradicate it, sufficiently destroys its malignant influence on the health and prosperity of the State. . . .*

.   .   .   .   .

13. *Because attempts to enforce by legal sanctions, acts obnoxious to so great a proportion of Citizens, tend to enervate the laws in general, and to slacken the bands of Society. . . .*

.   .   .   .   .

15. *Because, finally, "the equal rights of every citizen to the free exercise of his Religion according to the dictates of conscience" is held by the same tenure with all our other rights. If we recur to its origin, it is equally the gift of nature; if we weigh its importance, it cannot be less dear to us; if we consult the Declaration of those rights which pertain to the good people of Virginia, as the "basis and foundation of Government," it is*

enumerated with equal solemnity, or rather studied emphasis. Either then, we must say, that the will of the Legislature is the only measure of their authority; and that in the plenitude of this authority, they may sweep away all our fundamental rights; or, that they are bound to leave this particular right untouched and sacred: Either we must say, that they may controul the freedom of the press, may abolish the trial by jury, may swallow up the Executive and Judiciary Powers of the State; nay that they may despoil us of our very right of suffrage, and erect themselves into an independent and hereditary assembly: or we must say, that they have no authority to enact into law the Bill under consideration. . . .[56]

The *Memorial and Remonstrance* stopped the assessment bill. More than that, it set the stage for the enactment, in 1786, a year before the Constitutional Convention, of Virginia's Statute of Religious Liberty. The Statute was guided through the legislature by Madison, but it was drafted by Jefferson. Indeed, as Jefferson's tombstone bears witness, it was one of the three achievements for which he wished chiefly to be remembered. The Statute follows:

An Act for establishing Religious Freedom.

I. WHEREAS Almighty God hath created the mind free; that all attempts to influence it by temporal punishments or burthens, or by civil incapacitations, tend only to beget habits of hypocrisy and meanness, and are a departure from the plan of the Holy author of our religion, who being Lord both of body and mind, yet chose not to propagate it by coercions on either, as was in his Almighty power to do; that the impious presumption of legislators and rulers, civil as well as ecclesiastical, who being themselves but fallible and uninspired men, have assumed dominion over the faith of others, setting up their own opinions and modes of thinking as the only true and infallible, and as such endeavouring to impose them on others, hath established and maintained false religions over the greatest part of the world, and through all time; that to compel a man to furnish contributions of money for the propagation of opinions which he disbelieves, is sinful and tyrannical; that even the forcing him to support this or that teacher of his own religious persuasion, is depriving him of the comfortable liberty of giving his contributions to the par-

ticular pastor whose morals he would make his pattern, and whose powers he feels most persuasive to righteousness, and is withdrawing from the ministry those temporary rewards, which proceeding from an approbation of their personal conduct, are an additional incitement to earnest and unremitting labours for the instruction of mankind; that our civil rights have no dependence on our religious opinions, any more than our opinions in physics or geometry; that therefore the proscribing any citizen as unworthy the public confidence by laying upon him an incapacity of being called to offices of trust and emolument, unless he profess or renounce this or that religious opinion, is depriving him injuriously of those privileges and advantages to which in common with his fellow-citizens he has a natural right; that it tends only to corrupt the principles of that religion it is meant to encourage, by bribing with a monopoly of worldly honours and emoluments, those who will externally profess and conform to it; that though indeed these are criminal who do not withstand such temptation, yet neither are those innocent who lay the bait in their way; that to suffer the civil magistrate to intrude his powers into the field of opinion, and to restrain the profession or propagation of principles on supposition of their ill tendency, is a dangerous fallacy, which at once destroys all religious liberty, because he being of course judge of that tendency will make his opinions the rule of judgment, and approve or condemn the sentiments of others only as they shall square with or differ from his own; that it is time enough for the rightful purposes of civil government, for its officers to interfere when principles break out into overt acts against peace and good order; and finally, that truth is great and will prevail if left to herself, that she is the proper and sufficient antagonist to error, and has nothing to fear from the conflict, unless by human interposition disarmed of her natural weapons, free argument and debate, errors ceasing to be dangerous when it is permitted freely to contradict them.

II. Be it enacted by the General Assembly, *that no man shall be compelled to frequent or support any religious worship, place or ministry whatsoever, nor shall be enforced, restrained, molested, or burthened in his body or goods, nor shall otherwise suffer on account of his religious opinions or belief; but that all men shall be free to profess, and by argument to maintain, their opinion in matters of religion, and that the same shall in no wise diminish, enlarge or affect their civil capacities.*

III. *And though we well know that this assembly, elected by the people for the ordinary purposes of legislation only, have no power to restrain the acts of succeeding assemblies, constituted with powers equal to our own, and that therefore to declare this act to be irrevocable would be of no effect in law; yet as we are free to declare, and do declare, that the rights hereby asserted are of the natural rights of mankind, and that if any act shall hereafter be passed to repeal the present, or to narrow its operation, such act will be an infringement of natural right.*[57]

Supported by this "generating history" which they themselves had chiefly made, Jefferson and Madison must have regarded the "religious clause" of the First Amendment as essentially a succinct statement of their own views. In fact, Jefferson himself interpreted the amendment as "building a wall of separation between church and State." He used the metaphor, whose descriptive accuracy has since become a bone of bitter constitutional contention, in a letter written on New Year's Day, 1802. Jefferson was President, and he was acknowledging a communication from "a Committee of the Danbury Baptist Association, in the State of Connecticut":

GENTLEMEN: *The affectionate sentiments of esteem and approbation which you are so good as to express towards me, on behalf of the Danbury Baptist Association, give me the highest satisfaction. My duties dictate a faithful and zealous pursuit of the interests of my constituents, and in proportion as they are persuaded of my fidelity to those duties, the discharge of them becomes more and more pleasing.*

Believing with you that religion is a matter which lies solely between man and his God, that he owes account to none other for his faith or his worship, that the legislative powers of government reach actions only, and not opinions, I contemplate with sovereign reverence that act of the whole American people which declared that their legislature should "make no law respecting an establishment of religion, or prohibiting the free exercise thereof," thus building a wall of separation between church and State. Adhering to this expression of the supreme will of the nation in be-

*half of the rights of conscience, I shall see with sincere satisfac-
tion the progress of those sentiments which tend to restore to
man all his natural rights, convinced he has no natural right in
opposition to his social duties.*

*I reciprocate your kind prayers for the protection and bless-
ing of the common Father and Creator of man, and tender you for
yourselves and your religious association, assurances of my high
respect and esteem.*[58]

Jefferson's "wall of separation" metaphor has been heavily
relied on, in recent constitutional litigation, to support the argument that the amendment's ban on "an establishment of religion"
foreclosed any sort of state assistance to, or cooperation with,
religion. Justice Black and the late Justices Frankfurter, Rutledge,
and Robert H. Jackson, in varying accents and with varying em-
phases, identified themselves with this general position. But
others—notably former Justice Reed, and (with some ambivalence)
Justice Douglas—have not agreed that the historical materials warrant reading the First Amendment as an unqualified endorsement
of the rigorous Jefferson-Madison position.

Sometimes the point is made that the two great Virginians
were not themselves inflexible on these matters. Justice Reed
made such an argument in the first "released time" case to reach
the Supreme Court. ("Released time" is a system whereby public
schools give up some of their class hours so that students can go
to religious classes: In the first "released time" case, the religious
classes were conducted in the public schools, and the Court, over
Justice Reed's dissent, held the system, in that form, unconstitutional.[59]) Justice Reed recalled that Jefferson had proposed, and
Madison endorsed, a scheme whereby students at the state-con-
trolled University of Virginia would, each morning before class,
"be . . . expected to attend religious worship at the establishment of their religious sects. . . ."[60] Concrete evidence of a
particular incident so similar to the case in hand seems compelling. But it has to be borne in mind that Jefferson's proposal
was made at a time (almost half a century before the adoption of the Fourteenth Amendment) when there was no thought
that the First Amendment applied to the states. Moreover, even
men as thoughtful and concerned as Jefferson and Madison
probably do not test their every action or attitude in terms of

broad constitutional principle. So, one can reasonably doubt whether such an incident throws much light on what the First Amendment meant to those who drafted and adopted it at the time (thirty years before the incident) of its adoption.

What may be more significant for one attempting to estimate the original meaning of the constitutional provision is some recognition that the adoption of the First Amendment was a *national* act, not merely the private accomplishment of Jefferson and Madison. This perspective prompts the student of history to remember that Virginia was not the only part of the United States in which the relationship between religion and government was being thrashed out in the years leading up to the Constitution. Thus, South Carolina and Massachusetts subscribed to political arrangements quite unlike those reflected in Virginia's Bill of Rights and Statute of Religious Liberty. And, in general, "separation of Church and State . . . [was] the exception rather than the rule in American revolutionary constitutions."[61] Moreover, it is sometimes recalled that the Northwest Ordinance of 1787 (with which Jefferson and Madison were deeply concerned, but in which others also had a major hand) recites:

> *Religion, morality, and knowledge, being necessary to good government and the happiness of mankind, schools and the means of education shall forever be encouraged.*

On the other hand, although the Land Ordinance of 1785 (a precursor of the Northwest Ordinance) contained a reservation of one lot (a thirty-sixth share) of every square mile of the territories "for the maintenance of public schools," Congress (much to Madison's delight) declined to include in that Ordinance a further proviso reserving one lot for religious purposes.[62]

But opponents of the "wall of separation" view also argue that the history of the debates in the Virginia ratifying convention, and later in Congress, shows that the "establishment" clause of the First Amendment was not expected to do more than prevent a national legislative preference for one religious sect as against all others. A succinct statement of this historical analysis was formulated, in 1949, by the distinguished Jesuit theologian, Father John Courtney Murray, to demonstrate that the Supreme Court majority had fallen into historical error in endorsing Jefferson's "wall of separation" in two recent decisions. The gist of Father Murray's "Historical Note" runs as follows:

The following notes may serve to clarify the original historical meaning of the First Amendment, as conceived by Madison and the first Congress. In the Virginia ratifying convention that met in June, 1788, when the elimination of religious tests was being discussed, Madison said: "I confess to you, sir, were uniformity of religion to be introduced by this system, it would, in my opinion, be ineligible; but I have no reason to conclude that uniformity of government will produce that of religion. This subject is, for the honor of America, perfectly free and unshackled. The government has no jurisdiction over it: the least reflection will convince us there is no danger to be feared on this ground." *The [words in roman] indicate the basic problem of the time: a national government must not mean a national religion made obligatory on all by federal law; for this would be a violation at once of the sovereignty of the states and of the individual conscience. In Madison's consistent view the danger was removed by the sheer fact that the Federal Government was one of delegated powers; and "no jurisdiction" over religion was committed to Congress. Congress has no legal power to legislate as to what the religious beliefs or practices of the American people shall be, imposing on them a national religion. Madison maintained, therefore, that no further explication on the point was necessary. However, he accepted the decision of the committee on amendments (twenty members, chairmanned by George Wythe) to submit the following amendment (its twentieth):* "That religion, or the duty which we owe to our Creator, and the manner of discharging it, can be directed only by reason and conviction, not by force or violence; and therefore all men have an equal, natural and inalienable right to the free exercise of religion, according to the dictates of conscience, and that no particular religious sect or society ought to be favored or established, by law, in preference to others." *Nothing could be clearer than this statement. First, the concept of "no establishment" is subordinated to the concept of "free exercise" as means to end; second, "no establishment" means "no favor, no preference in law."*

While maintaining his position that a bill of rights was not "essential" but likewise "neither improper nor altogether useless,"

Madison assembled and presented to the first Congress the follow-ing text embodying the wishes of the states which had either explicitly (by submitting an amendment: New Hampshire, Vir-ginia, South Carolina) or implicitly (in their ratifying resolutions: New York, North Carolina) demanded an amendment: "Fourthly. That in article 1st, section 9, between clauses 3 and 4, be inserted these clauses, to wit: The civil rights of none shall be abridged on account of religious belief or worship, nor shall any national religion be established, nor shall the full and equal rights of conscience be in any manner, or on any pretext, infringed." Again the idea is clear: political equality regardless of religion, no one national religion, equality before the law of all consciences or religions.

This draft was committed to a committee of eleven, Madison among them, by which it was reported out in this form: "No religion shall be established by law, nor shall the equal rights of conscience be infringed." The brief debate turned on two points. First, was the amendment necessary? Roger Sherman of Con-necticut and others thought it was not, "inasmuch as Congress had no authority whatever delegated to them by the Constitution to make religious establishments." I would note that everywhere in the recorded debate "establishment of religion" was used uni-formly in its proper technical sense, "to favor or prefer." The second question was, Was the amendment too radical? Peter Sylvester of New York "had some doubts about the propriety of the mode of expression used in this paragraph. He apprehended that it was liable to a construction different from what had been made by the committee. He feared it might be thought to have a tendency to abolish religion altogether." Benjamin Huntington of Rhode Island agreed "that the words might be taken in such latitude as to be extremely hurtful to the cause of religion." . . . Here I pause to remark how right these gentlemen were. . . . Elbridge Gerry of Massachusetts wanted the intended sense made clearer: "that no religious doctrine shall be established by law."

Whereupon Madison, to calm their fears, explained the narrow and exact sense: "Mr. Madison said, he apprehended the meaning of the words to be, that Congress should not establish *a* religion, *and* enforce *the legal observation of it by law, nor* compel *men to worship God in any manner contrary to their* conscience. *Whether the words are necessary or not, he did not mean to say, but they had been required by some of the State Conventions, who seemed to entertain an opinion that under the clause of the Constitution, which gave power to Congress to make all laws necessary and proper to carry into execution the Constitution, and the laws made under it, enabled them (sic) to make laws of such a nature as might* infringe the rights of conscience *and establish* a national *religion; to prevent* these effects *he presumed the amendment was intended, and he thought it was as well expressed as the nature of the language would admit." Notice that here we have not Justice Rutledge's Madison, the fiery, implacable doctrinaire denouncing three-pence levies, but Madison the statesman. The operative words are* [*in roman*]: *the* "*effects*" *barred are* (1) *compulsion of conscience, by* (2) *the establishment of,* i.e., *preference in law accorded to, a national religion. . . . Again Madison patiently explained the precise narrow sense of the words: "Mr. Madison thought, if the word 'national' was inserted before religion, it would satisfy the minds of* [the] *honorable gentlemen. He believed that the people feared one sect might obtain a preeminence, or two combine together, and establish a religion to which they would compel others to conform. He thought if the word 'national' was introduced, it would point the amendment directly to* the object *it was intended to prevent." . . . Again we are very, very far from Mr. Rutledge's Madison. . . . And again the sense of the Amendment is luminously not the sense attributed to it by Justice Black.*

There is no need here to comment on the other three versions through which the text passed in the House, nor on the original Senate version: "Congress shall make no law establishing articles of faith or a mode of worship or prohibiting the free exercise of religion. . . ." This was reconciled with the final House version by a conference committee, by a linguistic compromise that issued in the present version. The essential point is that from the beginning to end of the debate the legislative intent was perfectly clear and unanimously agreed on: the primary thing was that these were to be no legal constraints on freedom of conscience and on the free exercise of religion; secondly, to this end there was to be no one national religion endowed with legal privilege for its beliefs. It is utterly impossible to get out of the legislative history of the Amendment that construction which Justice Black and Justice Rutledge, supposedly under appeal to history, attempted to put upon it.[63]

b. The impact of the First Amendment

The adoption of the First Amendment did not automatically usher in an era of complete religious toleration. The tribulations of the Mormons, the Know-Nothing Party's anti-Catholicism, the Ku Klux Klan's virulent campaigns against Catholics and Jews alike—each of these unhappy episodes reminds us of deep religious animosities which have by no means entirely abated even today. Nonetheless, the broad thrust of the amendment—disestablishing every church, and making religious affiliation and activity totally a matter of individual election—has been to encourage the growth in the United States of a uniquely flourishing religious pluralism. By 1833, every state government had abandoned taxes in aid of religion, thereby finally conforming to the federal constitutional example (an example which was not *constitutionally* binding on the *states* until, many decades later, the Supreme Court held that the First Amendment had been incorporated into the Fourteenth Amendment). It was at just this time, in the early 1830s, that Alexis de Tocqueville journeyed across the Atlantic and made the extraordinarily perceptive observations he recorded in *Democracy in America:*

Upon my arrival in the United States, the religious aspect of the country was the first thing that struck my attention; and the longer I stayed there, the more did I perceive the great political consequences resulting from this state of things, to which I was unaccustomed. In France I had almost always seen the spirit of religion and the spirit of freedom pursuing courses diametrically opposed to each other; but in America I found that they were intimately united, and that they reigned in common over the same country. My desire to discover the causes of this phenomenon increased from day to day. In order to satisfy it, I questioned the members of all the different sects; and I more especially sought the society of the clergy, who are the depositaries of the different persuasions, and who are more especially interested in their duration. As a member of the Roman catholic church I was more particularly brought into contact with several

*of its priests, with whom I became intimately acquainted. To
each of these men I expressed my astonishment and I explained
my doubts: I found that they differed upon matters of detail
alone; and that they mainly attributed the peaceful dominion of
religion in their country, to the separation of church and state. I
do not hesitate to affirm that during my stay in America, I did
not meet with a single individual, of the clergy or of the laity,
who was not of the same opinion upon this point.*[64]

In retrospect, Tocqueville's appraisal seems almost too bland.
No landscape inhabited by human beings could have been quite
that serene. This, at least, is an almost instinctive reaction when
one looks back from the perspective of the mid-twentieth century,
at a time when the problem of separation of church and state has
again become a political and a legal issue of first importance. It is
an issue of many ramifications, involving, for example, the validity of "Sunday closing" laws,[65] or of a law requiring a notary
public to avow a belief in God.[66] But the issue's most important
current impact is in the field of education. There it concerns (1)
the role of religion in public schools, and (2) the proper relationship between the state and private, avowedly religious, parochial
schools.

If we look back to pre-Civil-War America, we find a consensus as to the particular relationship between religion and
public education much like that which Tocqueville sensed in his
generalized view of the relationship between American churches
and civil authority. Justice Frankfurter, in his 1948 concurring
opinion in *McCollum v. Board of Education,* the first "released
time" case, sought to reconstruct that consensus:

*The evolution of colonial education, largely in the service of
religion, into the public school system of today is the story of
changing conceptions regarding the American democratic society, of the functions of State-maintained education in such a
society, and of the role therein of the free exercise of religion by
the people. The modern public school derived from a philosophy
of freedom reflected in the First Amendment. It is appropriate
to recall that the Remonstrance of James Madison, an event basic
in the history of religious liberty, was called forth by a proposal
which involved support to religious education. . . . As the momentum for popular education increased and in turn evoked
strong claims for State support of religious education, contests*

not unlike that which in Virginia had produced Madison's Remonstrance appeared in various forms in other States. New York and Masachusetts provide famous chapters in the history that established dissociation of religious teaching from State-maintained schools. In New York, the rise of the common schools led, despite fierce sectarian opposition, to the barring of tax funds to church schools, and later to any school in which sectarian doctrine was taught. In Massachusetts, largely through the efforts of Horace Mann, all sectarian teachings were barred from the common school to save it from being rent by denominational conflict. The upshot of these controversies, often long and fierce, is fairly summarized by saying that long before the Fourteenth Amendment subjected the States to new limitations, the prohibition of furtherance by the State of religious instruction became the guiding principle, in law and feeling, of the American people. . . .

Separation in the field of education, then, was not imposed upon unwilling States by force of superior law. In this respect the Fourteenth Amendment merely reflected a principle then dominant in our national life. To the extent that the Constitution thus made it binding upon the States, the basis of the restriction is the whole experience of our people. Zealous watchfulness against fusion of secular and religious activities by Government itself, through any of its instruments but especially through its educational agencies, was the democratic response of the American community to the particular needs of a young and growing nation, unique in the composition of its people. A totally different situation elsewhere, as illustrated for instance by the English provisions for religious education in State-maintained schools, only serves to illustrate that free societies are not cast in one mould. See the Education Act of 1944, 7 and 8 Geo. VI, c. 31. Different institutions evolve from different historic circumstances.[67]

In 1875, eight years after the adoption of the Fourteenth Amendment, President Ulysses S. Grant echoed this consensus in a notable speech to the Convention of the Army of the Tennessee:

Encourage free schools, and resolve that not one dollar appropriated for their support shall be appropriated to the support of any sectarian schools. Resolve that neither the State nor nation, nor both combined, shall support institutions of learning other than those sufficient to afford every child growing up in the land the opportunity of a good common-school education, unmixed with sectarian, pagan, or atheistical dogmas. Leave the matter of religion to the family altar, the church, and the private school, supported entirely by private contributions. Keep the church and the state forever separate. . . .[68]

The Supreme Court's first great test of the application of the "religious clause" to education was not, however, a matter of the vulnerability of public schools to religious teaching. The question in *Pierce v. Society of Sisters,* decided in 1925, was the validity of an Oregon compulsory education statute which forbade children between the ages of eight and sixteen to attend *private* schools. This post-World-War-I statute was enacted by popular referendum, when "the people of Oregon were largely under the influence of Ku Klux Klan elements"; its "effect—and purpose—was to outlaw private and parochial schools."[69] But a unanimous Supreme Court, in an opinion by Justice James C. McReynolds, held the statute unconstitutional:

The fundamental theory of liberty upon which all governments in this Union repose excludes any general power of the State to standardize its children by forcing them to accept instruction from public teachers only. The child is not the mere creature of the State; those who nurture him and direct his destiny have the right, coupled with the high duty, to recognize and prepare him for additional obligations.[70]

Justice McReynolds' opinion was the first Supreme Court opinion which apparently, if not explicitly, read into the Fourteenth Amendment, as limitations on the states, the limitations on national power contained in the First Amendment. As the materials on free speech have indicated, the Court's formal pronouncement of this fundamental constitutional doctrine came a few weeks later, in *Gitlow v. New York.* At all events, from 1925 on, the Supreme Court has entertained, in the context of education and otherwise, complaints that state governments have infringed on religious freedom or violated the "no establishment" principle.

For the next two decades, the education cases that came to

the Supreme Court were few in number and, though dramatic at the time, not really of surpassing importance. In 1934, in *Hamilton v. Regents,*[71] the Court unanimously rejected a claim that students of a pacifist religious persuasion had a constitutional right to exemption from required military training courses at a state university. And in 1940, the Court, in an opinion by Justice Frankfurter, over the lone dissent of Justice Harlan F. Stone, held that Jehovah's Witness children enrolled in compulsory public schools could be required to salute the flag, notwithstanding their faith's insistence that obeisance to a national flag violated the command of Exodus "not [to] bow down thyself" to "any graven image."[72] But three years later, after two new justices had joined the Court (and three others had changed their minds), the Court, in *Board of Education v. Barnette,* overruled its flag-salute decision.

Justice Jackson's opinion in the second flag-salute case is memorable for its rhetoric:

If there is any fixed star in our constitutional constellation, it is that no official, high or petty, can prescribe what shall be orthodox in politics, nationalism, religion, or other matters of opinion or force citizens to confess by word or act their faith therein.[73]

But of greater intrinsic interest, as we look back two decades later, is Justice Frankfurter's dissent, in the course of which he canvassed the unresolved issues that he feared might be thrust upon the Court:

Consider the controversial issue of compulsory Bible-reading in public schools. The educational policies of the states are in great conflict over this, and the state courts are divided in their decisions on the issue whether the requirement of Bible-reading offends constitutional provisions dealing with religious freedom. The requirement of Bible-reading has been justified by various state courts as an appropriate means of inculcating ethical precepts and familiarizing pupils with the most lasting expression of great English literature. Is this Court to overthrow such variant state educational policies by denying states the right to entertain such convictions in regard to their school systems, because of a belief that the King James version is in fact a sectarian text to which parents of the Catholic and Jewish faiths and of some

Protestant persuasions may rightly object to having their children exposed? On the other hand the religious consciences of some parents may rebel at the absence of any Bible-reading in the schools. See Washington ex rel. Clithero v. Showalter, 284 U.S. 573. *Or is this Court to enter the old controversy between science and religion by unduly defining the limits within which a state may experiment with its school curricula? The religious consciences of some parents may be offended by subjecting their children to the Biblical account of creation, while another state may offend parents by prohibiting a teaching of biology that contradicts such Biblical account. Compare* Scopes v. State, 154 Tenn. 105, 289 S.W. 363. *What of conscientious objections to what is devoutly felt by parents to be the poisoning of impressionable minds of children by chauvinistic teaching of history? This is very far from a fanciful suggestion for in the belief of many thoughtful people nationalism is the seed-bed of war.*

There are other issues in the offing which admonish us of the difficulties and complexities that confront states in the duty of administering their local school systems. All citizens are taxed for the support of public schools although this Court has denied the right of a state to compel all children to go to such schools and has recognized the right of parents to send children to privately maintained schools. Parents who are dissatisfied with the public schools thus carry a double educational burden. Children who go to public school enjoy in many states derivative advantages such as free textbooks, free lunch, and free transportation in going to and from school. What of the claims for equality of treatment of those parents who, because of religious scruples, cannot send their children to public schools? What of the claim that if the right to send children to privately maintained schools is partly an exercise of religious conviction, to render effective this right it should be accompanied by equality of treatment by the state in supplying free textbooks, free lunch, and free transportation to children who go to private schools? What of the claim that such grants are offensive to the cardinal constitutional doctrine of separation of church and state?

These questions assume increasing importance in view of the steady growth of parochial schools both in number and in population. I am not borrowing trouble by adumbrating these issues nor am I parading horrible examples of the consequences of today's decision. I am aware that we must decide the case before us and not some other case. But that does not mean that a case is dissociated from the past and unrelated to the future. We must decide this case with due regard for what went before and no less regard for what may come after. . . .[74]

Four years later, in *Everson v. Board of Education,* the Supreme Court considered a New Jersey statute authorizing local school districts to pay for the bus transportation of children attending parochial schools. The majority opinion, written by Justice Black, adopted Jefferson's "wall of separation" formula, and acknowledged that a state may not constitutionally "contribute tax-raised funds to the support of an institution which teaches the tenets and faith of any church."[75] But the majority concluded that this expenditure did not come within the ban. It was, so Justice Black said, comparable with an expenditure for "state-paid policemen, detailed to protect children going to and from church schools. . . ."[76]

Justices Frankfurter, Jackson, Rutledge, and Harold H. Burton disagreed. They felt the expenditure was an unconstitutional subsidy. Justice Rutledge supported his dissent with an extensive survey of the Jefferson-Madison campaign to uproot Virginia's Anglican "establishment" and enact the Statute of Religious Liberty. With this history as his premise, Justice Rutledge put, and answered, what seemed to him the central question:

Does New Jersey's action furnish support for religion by use of the taxing power? Certainly it does, if the test remains undiluted as Jefferson and Madison made it, that money taken by taxation from one is not to be used or given to support another's religious training or belief, or indeed one's own. . . .

. . . .

Believers of all faiths, and others who do not express their feeling toward ultimate issues of existence in any creedal form, pay the New Jersey tax. When the money so raised is used to pay for transportation to religious schools, the Catholic taxpayer to the extent of his proportionate share pays for the transportation of Lutheran, Jewish and otherwise religiously affiliated children to receive their non-Catholic religious instruction. Their parents likewise pay proportionately for the transportation of Catholic children to receive Catholic instruction. . . .

New Jersey's action therefore exactly fits the type of exaction and the kind of evil at which Madison and Jefferson struck. Under the test they framed it cannot be said that the cost of transportation is no part of the cost of education or of the religious instruction given. That it is a substantial and a necessary element is shown most plainly by the continuing and increasing demand for the state to assume it. Nor is there pretense that it relates only to the secular instruction given in religious schools or that any attempt is or could be made toward allocating proportional shares as between the secular and the religious instruction. It is precisely because the instruction is religious and relates to a particular faith, whether one or another, that parents send their children to religious schools under the Pierce *doctrine. And the very purpose of the state's contribution is to defray the cost of conveying the pupil to the place where he will receive not simply secular, but also and primarily religious, teaching and guidance.*[77]

At the close of his dissent, Justice Rutledge generalized the problem:

Two great drives are constantly in motion to abridge, in the name of education, the complete division of religion and civil authority which our forefathers made. One is to introduce religious education and observances into the public schools. The other, to obtain public funds for the aid and support of various private religious schools. . . . In my opinion both avenues were closed by the Constitution. Neither should be opened by this Court. The matter is not one of quantity, to be measured by the amount of money expended. Now as in Madison's day it is one of principle, to keep separate the separate spheres as the First Amendment drew them; to prevent the first experiment upon our liberties; and to keep the question from becoming entangled in corrosive precedents. We should not be less strict to keep strong and untarnished the one side of the shield of religious freedom than we have been of the other.[78]

A year later, in the 1948 case of *McCollum v. Board of Education,* the Supreme Court struck down the "released time" program adopted in the public schools of Champaign, Illinois. Under that program, "religious teachers employed by private religious groups, were permitted to come weekly into the school buildings during the regular hours set apart for secular teaching, and then and there for a period of thirty minutes substitute their religious teaching for the secular education provided under the compulsory education law."[79] Justice Black, again speaking for the Court, explained what was wrong in Champaign:

Pupils compelled by law to go to school for secular education are released in part from their legal duty upon the condition that they attend the religious classes. . . . This is beyond all question a utilization of the tax-established and tax-supported public school system to aid religious groups to spread their faith. And it falls squarely under the ban of the First Amendment (made applicable to the States by the Fourteenth). . . .[80]

Justice Reed, relying in part on Jefferson's proposal for the religious education of students at the University of Virginia, dissented.

As Justice Rutledge had indicated in the bus case, there is wide popular interest in utilizing some public funds to help support the thousands of religious schools—Catholic, Lutheran, Jewish, etc.—which carry out a vital societal function of educating millions of American children. Also, as Justice Rutledge likewise indicated, many religious groups are anxious to inject some awareness of religion into the public school curriculum. Because these are issues of such broad, and potentially divisive, public impact, the various opinions of the Justices in the bus case and the Champaign "released time" case provoked widespread and searching comment.[81]

In 1952, after four years of furious public discussion of the Supreme Court's role in matters of religious and educational policy, the Court had a further opportunity to think through the problems involved. The opportunity was presented by the 1952 case of *Zorach v. Clauson,* which was a challenge to the New York City "released time" program. This program was quite different in structure from Champaign's unsuccessful prototype. The majority of the Supreme Court, in an opinion by Justice Douglas, found the differences so striking that they sustained the New York plan. But Justice Black, Justice Frankfurter, and

Justice Jackson each filed a strenuous dissent. (Justice Rutledge, who died in 1949, would doubtless also have dissented had he still been on the Court.) The opinions in *Zorach v. Clauson* follow:

MR. JUSTICE DOUGLAS *delivered the opinion of the Court.*

New York City has a program which permits its public schools to release students during the school day so that they may leave the school buildings and school grounds and go to religious centers for religious instruction or devotional exercises. A student is released on written request of his parents. Those not released stay in the classrooms. The churches make weekly reports to the schools, sending a list of children who have been released from public school but who have not reported for religious instruction.

This "released time" program involves neither religious instruction in public school classrooms nor the expenditure of public funds. All costs, including the application blanks, are paid by the religious organizations. The case is therefore unlike McCollum v. Board of Education, 333 U.S. 203, *which involved a "released time" program from Illinois. In that case the classrooms were turned over to religious instructors. We accordingly held that the program violated the First Amendment which (by reason of the Fourteenth Amendment) prohibits the states from establishing religion or prohibiting its free exercise.*

Appellants, who are taxpayers and residents of New York City and whose children attend its public schools, challenge the present law, contending it is in essence not different from the one involved in the McCollum *case. Their argument, stated elaborately in various ways, reduces itself to this: the weight and influence of the school is put behind a program for religious instruction; public school teachers police it, keeping tab on students who are released; the classroom activities come to a halt while the students who are released for religious instruction are on leave; the school is a crutch on which the churches are leaning for support in their religious training; without the cooperation of the schools this "released time" program, like the one in the* McCollum *case, would be futile and ineffective. The New York Court of Appeals sustained the law against this claim of unconstitutionality. 303 N.Y. 161. . . .*

It takes obtuse reasoning to inject any issue of the "free exercise" of religion into the present case. No one is forced to go to the religious classroom and no religious exercise or instruction is brought to the classrooms of the public schools. A student need not take religious instruction. He is left to his own desires as to the manner or time of his religious devotions, if any.

There is a suggestion that the system involves the use of coercion to get public school students into religious classrooms. There is no evidence in the record before us that supports that conclusion. The present record indeed tells us that the school authorities are neutral in this regard and do no more than release students whose parents so request. If in fact coercion were used, if it were established that any one or more teachers were using their office to persuade or force students to take the religious instruction, a wholly different case would be presented. Hence we put aside that claim of coercion both as respects the "free exercise" of religion and "an establishment of religion" within the meaning of the First Amendment.

. . . There cannot be the slightest doubt that the First Amendment reflects the philosophy that Church and State should be separated. And so far as interference with the "free exercise" of religion and an "establishment" of religion are concerned, the separation must be complete and unequivocal. The First Amendment within the scope of its coverage permits no exception; the prohibition is absolute. The First Amendment, however, does not say that in every and all respects there shall be a separation of Church and State. Rather, it studiously defines the manner, the specific ways, in which there shall be no concert or union or dependency one on the other. That is the common sense of the matter. Otherwise the state and religion would be aliens to each other—hostile, suspicious, and even unfriendly. Churches could not be required to pay even property taxes. Municipalities would not be permitted to render police or fire protection to religious groups. Policemen who helped parishioners into their places of worship would violate the Constitution. Prayers in our legislative halls; the appeals to the Almighty in the messages of the Chief Executive; the proclamations making Thanksgiving Day a holiday; "so help me God" in our courtroom oaths—these and all other references to the Almighty that run through our laws, our public rituals, our ceremonies would be flouting the First Amendment. *A fastidious atheist or agnostic could even object to the supplication with which the Court opens each session: "God save the United States and this Honorable Court."*

We would have to press the concept of separation of Church and State to these extremes to condemn the present law on constitutional grounds. The nullification of this law would have wide and profound effects. A Catholic student applies to his teacher for permission to leave the school during hours on a Holy Day of Obligation to attend a mass. A Jewish student asks his teacher for permission to be excused for Yom Kippur. A Protestant wants the afternoon off for a family baptismal ceremony. In each case the teacher requires parental consent in writing. In each case the teacher, in order to make sure the student is not a truant, goes further and requires a report from the priest, the rabbi, or the minister. The teacher in other words cooperates in a religious program to the extent of making it possible for her students to participate in it. Whether she does it occasionally for a few students, regularly for one, or pursuant to a systemized program designed to further the religious needs of all the students does not alter the character of the act.

We are a religious people whose institutions presuppose a Supreme Being. We guarantee the freedom to worship as one chooses. We make room for as wide a variety of beliefs and creeds as the spiritual needs of man deem necessary. We sponsor an attitude on the part of government that shows no partiality to any one group and that lets each flourish according to the zeal of its adherents and the appeal of its dogma. When the state encourages religious instruction or cooperates with religious authorities by adjusting the schedule of public events to sectarian needs, it follows the best of our traditions. For it then respects the religious nature of our people and accommodates the public service to their spiritual needs. To hold that it may not would be to find in the Constitution a requirement that the government show a callous indifference to religious groups. That would be preferring those who believe in no religion over those who do believe. Government may not finance religious groups nor undertake religious instruction nor blend secular and sectarian education nor use secular institutions to force one or some religion on any person. But we find no constitutional requirement which makes it necessary for government to be hostile to religion and to throw its weight against efforts to widen the effective scope of religious influence. The government must be neutral when it comes to competition between sects. It may not thrust any sect on any person. It may not make a religious observance compulsory. It may not coerce anyone to attend church, to observe a religious holiday, or to take religious instruction. But it can close its doors or suspend its operations as to those who want to repair to their religious sanctuary for worship or instruction. No more than that is undertaken here.

．　　　　．　　　　．　　　　．　　　　．

MR. JUSTICE BLACK, *dissenting.*

Illinois ex rel. McCollum v. Board of Education, 333 U.S. 203, *held invalid as an "establishment of religion" an Illinois system under which school children, compelled by law to go to public schools, were freed from some hours of required school work on condition that they attend special religious classes held in the school buildings. Although the classes were taught by sectarian teachers neither employed nor paid by the state, the state did use its power to further the program by releasing some of the children from regular class work, insisting that those released attend the religious classes, and requiring that those who remained behind do some kind of academic work while the others received their religious training. We said this about the Illinois system:*

> *Pupils compelled by law to go to school for secular education are released in part from their legal duty upon the condition that they attend the religious classes. This is beyond all question a utilization of the tax-established and tax-supported public school system to aid religious groups to spread their faith. And it falls squarely under the ban of the First Amendment.* . . . McCollum v. Board of Education, supra, *at pp. 209–210.*

I see no significant difference between the invalid Illinois system and that of New York here sustained. Except for the use of the school buildings in Illinois, there is no difference between the systems which I consider even worthy of mention. In the New York program, as in that of Illinois, the school authorities release some of the children on the condition that they attend the religious classes, get reports on whether they attend, and hold the other children in the school building until the religious hour is over. As we attempted to make categorically clear, the McCollum decision would have been the same if the religious classes had not been held in the school buildings. We said:

> *Here not only are the State's tax-supported public school buildings used for the dissemination of religious doctrines. The State also affords sectarian groups an invaluable aid in that it helps to provide pupils for their religious classes through use of the State's compulsory public school machinery. This is not separation of Church and State. (Emphasis supplied.) McCollum v. Board of Education, supra, at p. 212.*

McCollum thus held that Illinois could not constitutionally manipulate the compelled classroom hours of its compulsory school machinery so as to channel children into sectarian classes. Yet that is exactly what the Court holds New York can do.

I am aware that our McCollum decision on separation of Church and State has been subjected to a most searching examination throughout the country. Probably few opinions from this Court in recent years have attracted more attention or stirred wider debate. Our insistence on "a wall between Church and State which must be kept high and impregnable" has seemed to some a correct exposition of the philosophy and a true interpretation of the language of the First Amendment to which we should strictly adhere. With equal conviction and sincerity, others have thought the McCollum decision fundamentally wrong and have pledged continuous warfare against it. The opinions in the court below and the briefs here reflect these diverse viewpoints. In dissenting today, I mean to do more than give routine approval to our McCollum decision. I mean also to reaffirm my faith in the fundamental philosophy expressed in McCollum and Everson v. Board of Education, 330 U.S. 1. That reaffirmance can be brief because of the exhaustive opinions in those recent cases.

Difficulty of decision in the hypothetical situations mentioned by the Court, but not now before us, should not confuse the issues in this case. Here the sole question is whether New York can use its compulsory education laws to help religious sects get attendants presumably too unenthusiastic to go unless moved to do so by the pressure of this state machinery. That this is the plan, purpose, design and consequence of the New York program cannot be denied. The state thus makes religious sects bene-

ficiaries of its power to compel children to attend secular schools. Any use of such coercive power by the state to help or hinder some religious sects or to prefer all religious sects over non-believers or vice versa is just what I think the First Amendment forbids. In considering whether a state has entered this forbidden field the question is not whether it has entered too far but whether it has entered at all. New York is manipulating its compulsory education laws to help religious sects get pupils. This is not separation but combination of Church and State.

The Court's validation of the New York system rests in part on its statement that Americans are "a religious people whose institutions presuppose a Supreme Being." This was at least as true when the First Amendment was adopted; and it was just as true when eight Justices of this Court invalidated the released time system in McCollum on the premise that a state can no more "aid all religions" than it can aid one. It was precisely because Eighteenth Century Americans were a religious people divided into many fighting sects that we were given the constitutional mandate to keep Church and State completely separate. Colonial history had already shown that, here as elsewhere zealous sectarians entrusted with governmental power to further their causes would sometimes torture, maim and kill those they branded "heretics," "atheists" or "agnostics." The First Amendment was therefore to insure that no one powerful sect or combination of sects could use political or governmental power to punish dissenters whom they could not convert to their faith. Now as then, it is only by wholly isolating the state from the religious sphere and compelling it to be completely neutral, that the freedom of each and every denomination and of all non-believers can be maintained. It is this neutrality the Court abandons today when it treats New York's coercive system as a program which merely "encourages religious instruction or cooperates with religious authorities." The abandonment is all the more dangerous to liberty because of the Court's legal exaltation of the orthodox and its derogation of unbelievers.

Under our system of religious freedom, people have gone to their religious sanctuaries not because they feared the law but because they loved their God. The choice of all has been as free as the choice of those who answered the call to worship moved only by the music of the old Sunday morning church bells. The spiritual mind of man has thus been free to believe, disbelieve, or doubt, without repression, great or small, by the heavy hand of government. Statutes authorizing such repression have been stricken. Before today, our judicial opinions have refrained from drawing invidious distinctions between those who believe in no religion and those who do believe. The First Amendment has lost much if the religious follower and the atheist are no longer to be judicially regarded as entitled to equal justice under law.

State help to religion injects political and party prejudices into a holy field. It too often substitutes force for prayer, hate for love, and persecution for persuasion. Government should not be allowed, under cover of the soft euphemism of "co-operation," to steal into the sacred area of religious choice.

Mr. Justice Frankfurter, *dissenting.*

By way of emphasizing my agreement with Mr. Justice Jackson's dissent, I add a few words.

The Court tells us that in the maintenance of its public schools, "[The State government] can close its doors or suspend its operations" so that its citizens may be free for religious devotions or instruction. If that were the issue, it would not rise to the dignity of a constitutional controversy. Of course, a State may provide that the classes in its schools shall be dismissed, for any reason, or no reason, on fixed days, or for special occasions. The essence of this case is that the school system did not "close its doors" and did not "suspend its operations." There is all the difference in the world between letting the children out of school and letting some of them out of school into religious classes. If every one is free to make what use he will of time wholly unconnected from schooling required by law—those who wish sectarian instruction devoting it to that purpose, those who have ethical instruction at home, to that, those who study music, to that—then of course there is no conflict with the Fourteenth Amendment.

The pith of the case is that formalized religious instruction is substituted for other school activity which those who do not participate in the released-time program are compelled to attend. The school system is very much in operation during this kind of released time. If its doors are closed, they are closed upon those students who do not attend the religious instruction, in order to keep them within the school. That is the very thing which raises the constitutional issue. It is not met by disregarding it. Failure to discuss this issue does not take it out of the case.

Again, the Court relies upon the absence from the record of evidence of coercion in the operation of the system. . . . But the Court disregards the fact that as the case comes to us, there could be no proof of coercion, for the appellants were not allowed to make proof of it. Appellants alleged that "The operation of the released time program has resulted and inevitably results in the exercise of pressure and coercion upon parents and children to secure attendance by the children for religious instruction." This allegation—that coercion was in fact present and is inherent in the system, no matter what disavowals might be made in the operating regulations—was denied by appellees. Thus were drawn issues of fact which cannot be determined, on any conceivable view of judicial notice, by judges out of their own knowledge or experience. Appellants sought an opportunity to adduce evidence in support of these allegations at an appropriate trial. And though the courts below cited the concurring opinion in McCollum v. Board of Education, 303 U.S. 203, 226, *to "emphasize the importance of detailed analysis of the facts to which the Constitutional test of Separation is to be applied," they denied that opportunity on the ground that such proof was irrelevant to the issue of constitutionality. . . .*

When constitutional issues turn on facts, it is a strange procedure indeed not to permit the facts to be established. When such is the case, there are weighty considerations for us to require the State court to make its determination only after a thorough canvass of all the circumstances and not to bar them from consideration. . . . If we are to decide this case on the present record, however, a strict adherence to the usage of courts in ruling on the sufficiency of pleadings would require us to take as admitted the facts pleaded in the appellants' complaint, including the fact of coercion, actual and inherent. See Judge Fuld, dissenting below, 303 N.Y., at 185. . . .

.   .   .   .   .

The deeply divisive controversy aroused by the attempts to secure public school pupils for sectarian instruction would promptly end if the advocates of such instruction were content to have the school "close its doors or suspend its operations"—that is, dismiss classes in their entirety, without discrimination—instead of seeking to use the public schools as the instrument for securing attendance at denominational classes. The unwillingness of the promoters of this movement to dispense with such use of the public schools betrays a surprising want of confidence in the inherent power of the various faiths to draw children to outside sectarian classes—an attitude that hardly reflects the faith of the greatest religious spirits.

MR. JUSTICE JACKSON, *dissenting.*

This released time program is founded upon a use of the State's power of coercion, which, for me, determines its unconstitutionality. Stripped to its essentials, the plan has two stages: first, that the State compel each student to yield a large part of his time for public secular education; and, second, that some of it be "released" to him on condition that he devote it to sectarian religious purposes.

No one suggests that the Constitution would permit the State directly to require this "released" time to be spent "under the control of a duly constituted religious body." This program accomplishes that forbidden result by indirection. If public education were taking so much of the pupils' time as to injure the public or the students' welfare by encroaching upon their religious opportunity, simply shortening everyone's school day would facilitate voluntary and optional attendance at Church classes. But that suggestion is rejected upon the ground that if they are made free many students will not go to the Church. Hence, they must be deprived of freedom for this period, with Church attendance put to them as one of the two permissible ways of using it.

The greater effectiveness of this system over voluntary attendance after school hours is due to the truant officer who, if the youngster fails to go to the Church school, dogs him back to the public schoolroom. Here schooling is more or less suspended during the "released time" so the nonreligious attendants will not forge ahead of the churchgoing absentees. But it serves as a temporary jail for a pupil who will not go to Church. It takes more subtlety of mind than I possess to deny that this is governmental constraint in support of religion. It is as unconstitutional, in my view, when exerted by indirection as when exercised forthrightly.

As one whose children, as a matter of free choice, have been sent to privately supported Church schools, I may challenge the Court's suggestion that opposition to this plan can only be anti-religious, atheistic, or agnostic. My evangelistic brethren confuse an objection to compulsion with an objection to religion. It is possible to hold a faith with enough confidence to believe that what should be rendered to God does not need to be decided and collected by Caesar.

The day that this country ceases to be free for irreligion it will cease to be free for religion—except for the sect that can win political power. The same epithetical jurisprudence used by the Court today to beat down those who oppose pressuring children into some religion can devise as good epithets tomorrow against those who object to pressuring them into a favored religion. And, after all, if we concede to the State power and wisdom to single out "duly constituted religious" bodies as exclusive alternatives for compulsory secular instruction, it would be logical to also uphold the power and wisdom to choose the true faith among those "duly constituted." We start down a rough road when we begin to mix compulsory public education with compulsory godliness.

A number of Justices just short of a majority of the majority that promulgates today's passionate dialectics joined in answering them in Illinois ex rel. McCollum v. Board of Education, 333 U.S. 203. *The distinction attempted between that case and this is trivial, almost to the point of cynicism, magnifying its non-essential details and disparaging compulsion which was the underlying reason for invalidity. A reading of the Court's opinion in that case along with its opinion in this case will show such difference of overtones and undertones as to make clear that the* McCollum *case has passed like a storm in a teacup. The wall which the Court was professing to erect between Church and State has become even more warped and twisted than I expected. Today's judgment will be more interesting to students of psychology and of the judicial processes than to students of constitutional law.*[82]

As if exhausted by its own fulminations, the Supreme Court waited ten years before it again ventured into these hazardous constitutional realms. In June of 1962, on the last day of the judicial term, the Court, by a six-to-one vote, invalidated the nondenominational voluntary prayer formulated by the New York State Regents for daily recital in public schools. The case was *Engel v. Vitale:*

MR. JUSTICE BLACK *delivered the opinion of the Court.*

The respondent Board of Education of Union Free School District No. 9, New Hyde Park, New York, acting in its official capacity under state law, directed the School District's principal to cause the following prayer to be said aloud by each class in the presence of a teacher at the beginning of each school day:

> *Almighty God, we acknowledge our dependence upon Thee, and we beg Thy blessings upon us, our parents, our teachers and our Country.*

This daily procedure was adopted on the recommendation of the State Board of Regents, a governmental agency created by the State Constitution to which the New York Legislature has granted broad supervisory, executive, and legislative powers over the State's public school system. These state officials composed the prayer which they recommended and published as a part of their "Statement on Moral and Spiritual Training in the Schools," saying: "We believe that this Statement will be subscribed to by all men and women of good will, and we call upon all of them to aid in giving life to our program."

Shortly after the practice of reciting the Regents' prayer was adopted by the School District, the parents of ten pupils brought this action in a New York State Court insisting that use of this official prayer in the public schools was contrary to the beliefs, religions, or religious practices of both themselves and their children. . . . The New York Court of Appeals, over the dissents of Judges Dye and Fuld, sustained an order of the lower state courts which had upheld the power of New York to use the Regents' prayer as a part of the daily procedures of its public schools so long as the schools did not compel any pupil to join in the prayer over his or his parents' objection. We granted certiorari to review this important decision involving rights protected by the First and Fourteenth Amendments. . . .

There can be no doubt that New York's state prayer program officially establishes the religious beliefs embodied in the Regents' prayer. The respondents' argument to the contrary, which is largely based upon the contention that the Regents' prayer is "non-denominational" and the fact that the program, as modified and approved by state courts, does not require all pupils to recite the prayer but permits those who wish to do so to remain silent or be excused from the room, ignores the essential nature of the program's constitutional defects. Neither the fact that the prayer may be denominationally neutral nor the fact that its observance on the part of the students is voluntary can serve to free it from the limitations of the Establishment Clause, as it might from the Free Exercise Clause, of the First Amendment, both of which are operative against the States by virtue of the Fourteenth Amendment. Although these two clauses may in certain instances overlap, they forbid two quite different kinds of governmental encroachment upon religious freedom. The Establishment Clause, unlike the Free Exercise Clause, does not depend upon any showing of direct governmental compulsion and is violated by the enactment of laws which establish an official religion whether those laws operate directly to coerce nonobserving individuals or not. This is not to say, of course, that laws officially prescribing a particular form of religious worship do not involve coercion of such individuals. When the power, prestige and financial support of government is placed behind a particular religious belief, the indirect coercive pressure upon religious minorities to conform to the prevailing officially approved religion is plain. But the purposes underlying the Establishment Clause go much further than that. Its first and most immediate purpose rested on the belief that a union of government and religion tends to destroy government and to degrade religion. The history of governmentally established religion, both in England and in this country, showed that whenever government had allied itself with one particular form of religion, the inevitable result had been that it had incurred the hatred, disrespect and even contempt of those who held contrary beliefs. That same history showed that many people had lost their respect for any religion that had relied upon the support of government to spread its faith. The Establishment Clause thus stands as an expression of principle on the part of the Founders of our Constitution that religion is too personal, too sacred, too holy, to permit its "unhallowed perversion" by a civil magistrate. Another purpose of the Establishment Clause rested upon an awareness of the historical fact that governmentally established religions and religious persecutions go hand in hand.

The Founders knew that only a few years after the Book of Common Prayer became the only accepted form of religious services in the established Church of England, an Act of Uniformity was passed to compel all Englishmen to attend those services and to make it a criminal offense to conduct or attend religious gatherings of any other kind—a law which was consistently flouted by dissenting religious groups in England and which contributed to widespread persecutions of people like John Bunyan who persisted in holding "unlawful [religious] meetings . . . to the great disturbance and distraction of the good subjects of this kingdom. . . ." And they knew that similar persecutions had received the sanction of law in several of the colonies in this country soon after the establishment of official religions in those colonies. It was in large part to get completely away from this sort of systematic religious persecution that the Founders brought into being our Nation, our Constitution, and our Bill of Rights with its prohibition against any governmental establishment of religion. The New York laws officially prescribing the Regents' prayer are inconsistent with both the purposes of the Establishment Clause and with the Establishment Clause itself.

It has been argued that to apply the Constitution in such a way as to prohibit state laws respecting an establishment of religious services in public schools is to indicate a hostility toward religion or toward prayer. Nothing, of course, could be more wrong. The history of man is inseparable from the history of religion. And perhaps it is not too much to say that since the beginning of that history many people have devoutly believed that "More things are wrought by prayer than this world dreams of." It was doubtless largely due to men who believed this that there grew up a sentiment that caused men to leave the crosscurrents of officially established state religions and religious persecution in Europe and come to this country filled with the hope that they could find a place in which they could pray when they pleased to the God of their faith in the language they chose. And there were men of this same faith in the power of prayer who led the fight for adoption of our Constitution and also for our Bill of Rights with the very guarantees of religious freedom that forbid the sort of governmental activity which New York has attempted here. These men knew that the First Amendment, which tried to put an end to governmental control of religion and of prayer, was not written to destroy either. They knew rather that it was written to quiet well-justified fears which nearly all of them felt arising out of an awareness that governments of the past had shackled men's tongues to make them speak only the religious thoughts that government wanted them to speak and to pray only to the God that government wanted them to pray to. It is neither sacrilegious nor antireligious to say that each separate government in this country should stay out of the business of writing or sanctioning official prayers and leave that purely religious function to the people themselves and to those the people choose to look to for religious guidance.

It is true that New York's establishment of its Regents' prayer as an officially approved religious doctrine of that State does not amount to a total establishment of one particular religious sect to the exclusion of all others—that, indeed, the governmental endorsement of that prayer seems relatively insignificant when compared to the governmental encroachments upon religion which were commonplace 200 years ago. To those who may subscribe to the view that because the Regents' official prayer is so brief and general there can be no danger to religious freedom in its governmental establishment, however, it may be appropriate to say in the words of James Madison, the author of the First Amendment:

[I]t is proper to take alarm at the first experiment on our liberties. . . . Who does not see that the same authority which can establish Christianity, in exclusion of all other Religions, may establish with the same ease any particular sect of Christians, in exclusion of all other Sects? That the same authority which can force a citizen to contribute three pence only of his property for the support of any one establishment, may force him to conform to any other establishment in all cases whatsoever?

The judgment of the Court of Appeals of New York is reversed and the cause remanded for further proceedings not inconsistent with this opinion.[83]

Justice Frankfurter, who had recently suffered the stroke which was in late summer to lead to his retirement from the bench, did not participate in the decision of *Engel v. Vitale*. Nor did Justice Byron R. White, who had replaced Justice Charles E. Whittaker subsequent to the argument of the case. Of the seven participating Justices, five signed Justice Black's opinion; one (Justice Douglas) agreed that the New York prayer was invalid but filed a concurring opinion articulating different reasons for so holding; and one (Justice Stewart) dissented. Justice Douglas differed with his brethren in that he could not "say that to authorize this prayer is to establish a religion in the strictly historic meaning of those words. A religion is not established in the usual sense merely by letting those who chose to do so say the prayer that the public school teacher leads.[84] What was decisive for Justice Douglas was that the prayer, however brief, was conducted by the teacher as part of the teacher's job and was, therefore, a religious exercise subsidized by government. Justice Douglas felt that "once government finances a religious exercise it inserts a divisive influence into our communities."[85] But this view apparently brought the Justice into conflict with an earlier decision he had joined—that in *Everson v. Board of Education,* where the Court, by a five-to-four vote, had upheld the expenditure of public funds to transport children to parochial schools. Justice Douglas, in *Engel v. Vitale,* resolved his dilemma by concluding that *Everson* had been "out of line with the First Amendment."[86] Since *Everson* has been a principal source of doctrinal strength for those who urge the constitutionality of federal and state appropriations in aid of parochial schools, Justice Douglas' repudiation of the bare-majority *Everson* opinion gave his concurrence in *Engel v. Vitale* a significance far beyond the school-prayer issue.[87]

Justice Stewart's dissent in *Engel v. Vitale* charged that:

. . . *I think the Court has misapplied a great constitutional principle. I cannot see how an "official religion" is established by letting those who want to say a prayer say it. On the contrary, I think that to deny the wish of these school children to join in reciting this prayer is to deny them the opportunity of sharing in the spiritual heritage of our Nation.*

The Court's historical review of the quarrels over the Book of Common Prayer in England throws no light for me on the issue before us in this case. England had then and has now an established church. Equally unenlightening, I think, is the history of the early establishment and later rejection of an official church in our own States. For we deal here not with the establishment of a state church, which would, of course, be constitutionally impermissible, but with whether school children who want to begin their day by joining in prayer must be prohibited from doing so. Moreover, I think that the Court's task, in this as in all areas of constitutional adjudication, is not responsibly aided by the uncritical invocation of metaphors like the "wall of separation," a phrase nowhere to be found in the Constitution. What is relevant to the issue here is not the history of an established church in sixteenth century England or in eighteenth century America, but the history of the religious traditions of our people, reflected in countless practices of the institutions and officials of our government.

At the opening of each day's Session of this Court we stand, while one of our officials invokes the protection of God. Since the days of John Marshall our Crier has said, "God save the United States and this Honorable Court." Both the Senate and the House of Representatives open their daily Sessions with prayer. Each of our Presidents, from George Washington to John F. Kennedy, has upon assuming his Office asked the protection and help of God.

The Court today says that the state and federal governments are without constitutional power to prescribe any particular form of words to be recited by any group of the American people on any subject touching religion. The third stanza of "The Star-Spangled Banner," made our National Anthem by Act of Congress in 1931, contains these verses:

> *Blest with victory and peace, may the heav'n*
> *rescued land*
> *Praise the Pow'r that hath made and preserved*
> *us a nation!*
> *Then conquer we must, when our cause it is just,*
> *And this be our motto "In God is our Trust."*

In 1954 Congress added a phrase to the Pledge of Allegiance to the Flag so that it now contains the words "one Nation under God, indivisible, with liberty and justice for all." In 1952 Congress enacted legislation calling upon the President each year to proclaim a National Day of Prayer. Since 1865 the words "IN GOD WE TRUST" have been impressed on our coins.

Countless similar examples could be listed, but there is no need to belabor the obvious. It was all summed up by this Court just ten years ago in a single sentence: "We are a religious people whose institutions presuppose a Supreme Being." Zorach v. Clauson, 343 U.S. 306, 313.

I do not believe that this Court, or the Congress, or the President has by the actions and practices I have mentioned established an "official religion" in violation of the Constitution. And I do not believe the State of New York has done so in this case. What each has done has been to recognize and to follow the deeply entrenched and highly cherished spiritual traditions of our Nation—traditions which come down to us from those who almost two hundred years ago avowed their "firm reliance on the Protection of Divine Providence" when they proclaimed the freedom and independence of this brave new world.

I dissent.[88]

Justice Douglas, in his concurring opinion, seemingly acquiesced in one of the points apparently made by Justice Stewart —that to hold the Regents' prayer invalid required a like holding as to the invocations of divine assistance which are the first order of business at each daily session of the House of Representatives, the Senate, and the Supreme Court. Justice Douglas at least indicated that these rituals could not constitutionally be conducted by paid government functionaries as part of their official duties. The majority of the Justices, however, seemed to feel that these and other official invocations of a deity were quite unlike the school prayer before the Court. In a footnote to their opinion, the majority observed:

There is of course nothing in the decision here that is inconsistent with the fact that school children and others are officially encouraged to express love for our country by reciting historical documents such as the Declaration of Independence which contain references to the Deity or by singing officially espoused anthems which include the composer's professions of faith in a Supreme Being, or with the fact that there are many manifestations in our public life of belief in God. Such patriotic or ceremonial occasions bear no true resemblance to the unquestioned religious exercise that the State of New York has sponsored in this instance.[89]

Not too surprisingly, the Supreme Court's decision in *Engel v. Vitale* provoked immediate and widespread controversy. On a political level, the most intemperate criticism came from southern segregationists who felt they had found a new stick to beat the Court with. One South Carolina Congressman announced that the Court had "now officially stated its disbelief in God Almighty"; the Court, he said, was "legislating—they never adjudicate—with one eye on the Kremlin and the other on the National Association for the Advancement of Colored People."[90] Alabama Congressman George W. Andrews said of the Court: "They put the Negroes in the schools, and now they've driven God out."[91] But the political criticism was not all southern, and not all Democratic. A Republican Senator from Connecticut, Prescott Bush, called *Engel v. Vitale* "most unfortunate," "divisive," and "quite unnecessary"; and a Republican Congressman from New York, Frank J. Becker, said the decision was "the most tragic in the history of the United States."[92]

Herbert Hoover, in one of his last public utterances on contemporary controversies, said that the Court's decision constituted "a disintegration of a sacred American heritage."[93] But John F. Kennedy took a more charitable view of the decision. At a press conference, the late President observed:

. . . The Supreme Court has made its judgment. A good many people obviously will disagree with it; others will agree with it. But I think that it is important for us, if we're going to maintain our constitutional principle, that we support Supreme Court decisions even when we may not agree with them.

In addition, we have in this case a very easy remedy, and that is to pray ourselves. And I would think that it would be a welcome reminder to every American family that we can pray a good deal more at home, we can attend our churches with a good deal more fidelity, and we can make the true meaning of prayer much more important in the lives of all of our children. That power is very much open to us. And I would hope that, as a result of this decision, that all American parents will intensify their efforts at home.

And the rest of us will support the Constitution and the responsibility of the Supreme Court in interpreting it, which is theirs and given to them . . . by the Constitution.[94]

The clerical reaction was divided. The top leadership of the Catholic Church promptly denounced the decision.[95] But one diocesan newspaper observed that "one can easily imagine the confusion, the violence of conscience which would result from the attempt of governmental agencies to compose prayers."[96] Leaders of the major Jewish groupings on the whole approved the decision.[97] But some highly orthodox rabbis had a very different view: "America has been blessed with hundreds of thousands of children, Jewish and gentile, who daily raise their voices to pray. Can anyone raise his hand to silence this vast body of American youth, saying 'Stop praising God! It is forbidden to do so in the American public school!'?"[98] Many leaders of the various Protestant denominations were very critical of the decision; but a strong minority of Protestant leadership voiced approval.[99]

The legal community was also divided, albeit not so stridently, in its response to *Engel v. Vitale*.[100] The thought that the Court reached the right result, but for the wrong reasons, was advanced in characteristically persuasive fashion by Professor Paul A. Freund, in a speech delivered before the American Jewish Committee on November 11, 1962:

The issues which we do expect our courts to decide are difficult and delicate enough; indeed they are often of a character that causes deep political cleavage and social disorder in other countries. I am referring to such issues as the meaning of separation of church and state as exemplified in the case of public school prayers. The issue of secularism versus sectarianism was responsible in India for bloody riots, partition, and relocation of populations; in Israel it has been an important factor impeding the adoption of a constitution. In our own country more than a hundred years ago the issue of the Bible in the public schools precipitated street fighting over the selection of scriptural texts.

The principle of separation is found in the two clauses of the First Amendment provision: Congress shall make no law respecting an establishment of religion or prohibiting the free exercise thereof. This guarantee has been absorbed into the Fourteenth Amendment due-process clause applicable to the states. Although the non-establishment and the free exercise clauses are in a sense complementary, at times they present a conflict bordering on a dilemma. If the voluntary recitation of prayers in the public schools looks like establishment of religion to one group, to another group it may appear to be simply a free exercise of religion. In the actual case of last year the Supreme Court treated the problem as one of establishment and thus stirred many issues that are very much in the public consciousness though hardly in the particular case—issues such as financial aid to parochial schools, the use of chaplains in governmental assemblies, religious texts on coins, tax exemption for churches, draft exemption only for religiously motivated conscientious objectors, and all the rest. . . .

The problem seems to me not so much one of establishment, not one that could be avoided by having the prayer composed and the expense of the ceremony borne by private groups, but rather an issue of free exercise of religion. Although the ceremony is in form voluntary, the atmosphere of the school room and the conformist psychology of school children are such that in a meaningful and realistic sense such exercises are in fact coercive. They are thus calculated to chill the free exercise or non-exercise of religion on the part of non-conformist groups. To view the cases in this way is to put to one side all the problems of state aid on which feelings are now running high, and to limit the decision to the context of the school room.

For those who insist that the public school should foster an atmosphere of reverence for the beauty of knowledge, of solemn humility in the presence of the unknown, and of awe in the face of the unknowable, there are several answers. There is nothing in the decision, so far as I can see, that would preclude a period of silent devotion or meditation, without the divisive element of a single spoken prayer. In any case, the more bland and diluted the spoken prayer, the less significant and meaningful it would become. Surely it is superficial and deluding to think that a few watered-down words spoken routinely are more important in creating an atmosphere of reverence, humility and awe than the character and quality of the teaching. I recall an account of Willard Gibbs, the Yale scientist, standing before a blackboard on which he had worked out an abstruse equation, tears streaming down his face, and the students looking up, his biographer writes, with the eyes of one who had just seen angels. I remember too some lines of Wordsworth:

> *Dear child, dear girl, who walkest with me here,*
> *If thou appear unmoved by solemn thought,*
> *Thy nature is not therefore less divine;*
> *Thou liest in Abraham's bosom all the year*
> *And worshipst at the temple's inner shrine,*
> *God being with thee when we know it not.*[101]

In the judicial term following *Engel v. Vitale*, the Supreme Court considered two cases, arising in Maryland and Pennsylvania, which raised questions as to the validity of school-opening exercises consisting of a voluntary recital of the Lord's Prayer and/or a voluntary reading of passages from the Bible. While the cases were pending before the Court, public debate continued over what had just been decided and what was about to be decided. In some quarters, for example, it was argued that all the Court had condemned in *Engel v. Vitale* was an "official" prayer composed by school authorities. But others contended that if an "official" nondenominational prayer offended the Establishment Clause, the use of an avowedly sectarian version of the Bible or of the Lord's Prayer was surely far more vulnerable to constitutional attack. In the spring of 1963, before the Court's decision, two major Protestant bodies, the National Council of Churches and the United Presbyterian Church, condemned Bible-reading in the schools. The National Council of Churches stated that "neither true religion nor good education is dependent upon the devotional use of the Bible in the public school program."[102]

In June of 1963, one year after *Engel v. Vitale*, the Court, in a single opinion disposing of the two consolidated cases, gave the constitutional *coup de grâce* to Bible-reading and the Lord's Prayer. Crucial to the Court's decision in *Abington School District v. Schempp* was its finding that in each instance the exercise itself was "religious" in character. The Court, in Justice Clark's majority opinion, made it clear that academic instruction *about* religion was entirely permissible:

The wholesome "neutrality" [of government in relation to religion] of which this Court's cases speak . . . stems from a recognition of the teachings of history that powerful sects or groups might bring about a fusion of governmental and religious func-

tions or a concert or dependency of one upon the other to the end that official support of the State or Federal Government would be placed behind the tenets of one or of all orthodoxies. This the Establishment Clause prohibits. And a further reason for neutrality is found in the Free Exercise Clause, which recognizes the value of religious training, teaching and observance and, more particularly, the right of every person to freely choose his own course with reference thereto, free of any compulsion from the state. This the Free Exercise Clause guarantees. Thus, as we have seen, the two clauses may overlap. As we have indicated, the Establishment Clause has been directly considered by this Court eight times in the past score of years and, with only one Justice dissenting on the point, it has consistently held that the clause withdrew all legislative power respecting religious belief or the expression thereof. The test may be stated as follows: what are the purpose and the primary effect of the enactment? If either is the advancement or inhibition of religion then the enactment exceeds the scope of legislative power as circumscribed by the Constitution. That is to say that to withstand the strictures of the Establishment Clause there must be a secular legislative purpose and a primary effect that neither advances nor inhibits religion. Everson v. Board of Education, *supra;* McGowan v. Maryland, *supra, at 442. The Free Exercise Clause, likewise considered many times here, withdraws from legislative power, state and federal, the exertion of any restraint on the free exercise of religion. Its purpose is to secure religious liberty in the individual by prohibiting any invasions thereof by civil authority. Hence it is necessary in a free exercise case for one to show the coercive effect of the enactment as it operates against him in the practice of his religion. The distinction between the two clauses is apparent—a violation of the Free Exercise Clause is predicated on coercion while the Establishment Clause violation need not be so attended.*

Applying the Establishment Clause principles to the cases at bar we find that the States are requiring the selection and reading at the opening of the school day of verses from the Holy Bible and the recitation of the Lord's Prayer by the students in unison. These exercises are prescribed as part of the curricular activities of students who are required by law to attend school. They are held in the school buildings under the supervision and with the participation of teachers employed in those schools. None of these factors, other than compulsory school attendance, was present in the program upheld in Zorach v. Clauson. The trial court in [the Pennsylvania case] has found that such an opening exercise is a religious ceremony and was intended by the State to be so. We agree with the trial court's finding as to the religious character of the exercises. Given that finding, the exercises and the law requiring them are in violation of the Establishment Clause.

There is no such specific finding as to the religious character of the exercises in [the Maryland case], and the State contends (as does the State in [the Pennsylvania case]) that the program is an effort to extend its benefits to all public school children without regard to their religious belief. Included within its secular purposes, it says, are the promotion of moral values, the contradiction to the materialistic trends of our times, the perpetuation of our institutions and the teaching of literature. The case came up on demurrer, of course, to a petition which alleged that the uniform practice under the rule had been to read from the King James version of the Bible and that the exercise was sectarian. The short answer, therefore, is that the religious character of the exercise was admitted by the State. But even if its purpose is not strictly religious, it is sought to be accomplished through readings, without comment, from the Bible. Surely the place of the Bible as an instrument of religion cannot be gainsaid, and the State's recognition of the pervading religious character of the ceremony is evident from the rule's specific permission of the alternative use of the Catholic Douay version as well as the recent amendment permitting nonattendance at the exercises. None of these factors is consistent with the contention that the Bible is here used either as an instrument for nonreligious moral inspiration or as a reference for the teaching of secular subjects.

The conclusion follows that in both cases the laws require religious exercises and such exercises are being conducted in direct violation of the rights of the appellees and petitioners. Nor are these required exercises mitigated by the fact that individual students may absent themselves upon parental request, for that fact furnishes no defense to a claim of unconstitutionality under the Establishment Clause. See Engel v. Vitale, *supra, at*

430. *Further, it is no defense to urge that the religious practices here may be relatively minor encroachments on the First Amendment. The breach of neutrality that is today a trickling stream may all too soon become a raging torrent and, in the words of Madison, "it is proper to take alarm at the first experiment on our liberties." Memorial and Remonstrance Against Religious Assessments, quoted in* Everson, *supra, at* 65.

It is insisted that unless these religious exercises are permitted a "religion of secularism" is established in the schools. We agree of course that the State may not establish a "religion of secularism" in the sense of affirmatively opposing or showing hostility to religion, thus "preferring those who believe in no religion over those who do believe." Zorach v. Clauson, *supra, at* 314. *We do not agree, however, that this decision in any sense has that effect. In addition, it might well be said that one's education is not complete without a study of comparative religion or the history of religion and its relationship to the advancement of civilization. It certainly may be said that the Bible is worthy of study for its literary and historic qualities. Nothing we have said here indicates that such study of the Bible or of religion, when represented objectively as part of a secular program of education, may not be effected consistently with the First Amendment. But the exercises here do not fall into those categories. They are religious exercises, required by the States in violation of the command of the First Amendment that the Government maintain strict neutrality, neither aiding nor opposing religion.*

Finally, we cannot accept that the concept of neutrality, which does not permit a State to require a religious exercise even with the consent of the majority of those affected, collides with the majority's right to free exercise of religion. While the Free Exercise Clause clearly prohibits the use of state action to deny the rights of free exercise to anyone, *it has never meant that a majority could use the machinery of the State to practice its beliefs. Such a contention was effectively answered by Mr. Justice Jackson for the Court in* West Virginia Board of Education v. Barnette, 319 U.S. 624, 638 (1943):

> *The very purpose of a Bill of Rights was to withdraw certain subjects from the vicissitudes of political controversy, to place them beyond the reach of majorities and*

officials and to establish them as legal principles to be applied by the courts. One's right to . . . freedom of worship . . . and other fundamental rights may not be submitted to vote; they depend on the outcome of no elections.

The place of religion in our society is an exalted one, achieved through a long tradition of reliance on the home, the church and the inviolable citadel of the individual heart and mind. We have come to recognize through bitter experience that it is not within the power of government to invade that citadel, whether its purpose or effect be to aid or oppose, to advance or retard. In the relationship between man and religion, the State is firmly committed to a position of neutrality. . . .[103]

Justice Douglas, Justice William J. Brennan, Jr., and former Justice Arthur J. Goldberg filed concurring opinions, and Justice Stewart dissented. Justice Brennan's opinion re-examined at length the development of the Court's jurisprudence in the intersecting fields of freedom of worship and establishment of religion. By way of preface, Justice Brennan discussed the way in which, in his judgment, the Court should use history in resolving constitutional controversies of this kind:

In sum, the history which our prior decisions have summoned to aid interpretation of the Establishment Clause permits little doubt that its prohibition was designed comprehensively to prevent those official involvements of religion which would tend to foster or discourage religious worship or belief.

But an awareness of history and an appreciation of the aims of the Founding Fathers do not always resolve concrete problems. The specific question before us has, for example, aroused vigorous dispute whether the architects of the First Amendment—James Madison and Thomas Jefferson particularly—understood the prohibition against any "law respecting an establishment of religion" to reach devotional exercises in the public schools. It may be that Jefferson and Madison would have held such exercises to be permissible—although even in Jefferson's case serious doubt is suggested by his admonition against "putting the Bible and Testament into the hands of the children at an age when their judgments are not sufficiently matured for religious inquiries. . . ." But I doubt that their view, even if perfectly clear one way or the other, would supply a dispositive answer to the question presented by these cases. A more fruitful inquiry, it seems to me, is whether the practices here challenged threaten those consequences which the Framers deeply feared; whether, in short, they tend to promote that type of interdependence between religion and state which the First Amendment was designed to prevent. Our task is to translate "the majestic generalities of the Bill of Rights, conceived as part of the pattern of liberal government in the eighteenth century, into concrete restraints on officials dealing with the problems of the twentieth century. . . ." West Virginia State Board of Education v. Barnette, 319 U.S. 624, 639.

A too literal quest for the advice of the Founding Fathers upon the issues of these cases seems to me futile and misdirected for several reasons: First, on our precise problem the historical record is at best ambiguous, and statements can readily be found to support either side of the proposition. The ambiguity of history is understandable if we recall the nature of the problems uppermost in the thinking of the statesmen who fashioned the religious guarantees; they were concerned with far more flagrant intrusions of government into the realm of religion than any that our century has witnessed. While it is clear to me that the Framers meant the Establishment Clause to prohibit more than the creation of an established federal church such as existed in England, I have no doubt that, in their preoccupation with the imminent question of established churches, they gave no distinct consideration to the particular question whether the clause also forbade devotional exercises in public institutions.

Second, the structure of American education has greatly changed since the First Amendment was adopted. In the context of our modern emphasis upon public education available to all citizens, any views of the eighteenth century as to whether the exercises at bar are an "establishment" offer little aid to decision. Education, as the Framers knew it, was in the main confined to private schools more often than not under strictly sectarian supervision. Only gradually did control of education pass largely to public officials. It would, therefore, hardly be significant if the fact was that the nearly universal devotional exercises in the schools of the young Republic did not provoke criticism; even today religious ceremonies in church-supported private schools are constitutionally unobjectionable.

Third, our religious composition makes us a vastly more diverse people than were our forefathers. They knew differences chiefly among Protestant sects. Today the Nation is far more heterogeneous religiously, including as it does substantial minorities not only of Catholics and Jews but as well of those who worship according to no version of the Bible and those who worship no God at all. See Torcaso v. Watkins, 367 U.S. 488, 495. *In the face of such profound changes, practices which may have been objectionable to no one in the time of Jefferson and Madison may today be highly offensive to many persons, the deeply devout and the nonbelievers alike.*

Whatever Jefferson or Madison would have thought of Bible reading or the recital of the Lord's Prayer in what few public schools existed in their day, our use of the history of their time must limit itself to broad purposes, not specific practices. By such a standard, I am persuaded, as is the Court, that the devotional exercises carried on in the Baltimore and Abington schools offend the First Amendment because they sufficiently threaten in our day those substantive evils the fear of which called forth the Establishment Clause of the First Amendment. It is "a constitution we are expounding," and our interpretation of the First Amendment must necessarily be responsive to the much more highly charged nature of religious questions in contemporary society.

Fourth, the American experiment in free public education available to all children has been guided in large measure by the dramatic evolution of the religious diversity among the population which our public schools serve. The interaction of these two important forces in our national life has placed in bold relief certain positive values in the consistent application to public institutions generally, and public schools particularly, of the constitutional decree against official involvements of religion which might produce the evils the Framers meant the Establishment Clause to forestall. The public schools are supported entirely, in most communities, by public funds—funds exacted not only from parents, nor alone from those who hold particular religious views, nor indeed from those who subscribe to any creed at all. It is implicit in the history and character of American public education that the public schools serve a uniquely public *function: the training of American citizens in an atmosphere free of parochial, divisive, or separatist influences of any sort— an atmosphere in which children may assimilate a heritage common to all American groups and religions. See Illinois ex rel. McCollum v. Board of Education, 333 U.S. 203. This is a heritage neither theistic nor atheistic, but simply civic and patriotic. See Meyer v. Nebraska, 262 U.S. 390, 400–403.*

Attendance at the public schools has never been compulsory; parents remain morally and constitutionally free to choose the academic environment in which they wish their children to be educated. The relationship of the Establishment Clause of the First Amendment to the public school system is preeminently that of reserving such a choice to the individual parent, rather than vesting it in the majority of voters of each State or school district. The choice which is thus preserved is between a public secular education with its uniquely democratic values, and some form of private or sectarian education, which offers values of its own. In my judgment the First Amendment forbids the State to inhibit that freedom of choice by diminishing the attractiveness of either alternative—either by restricting the liberty of the private schools to inculcate whatever values they wish, or by jeopardizing the freedom of the public schools from private or sectarian pressures. The choice between these very different forms of education is one—very much like the choice of whether or not to worship—which our Constitution leaves to the individual parent. It is no proper function of the state or local government to influence or restrict that election. The lesson of history —drawn more from the experiences of other countries than from our own—is that a system of free public education forfeits its unique contribution to the growth of democratic citizenship when that choice ceases to be freely available to each parent.[104]

Justice Stewart's dissent charged that the Court was not upholding governmental "neutrality" in matters of religion, but was weighing the scales against religion:

That the central value embodied in the First Amendment— and, more particularly, in the guarantee of "liberty" contained in the Fourteenth—is the safeguarding of an individual's right to free exercise of his religion has been consistently recognized.

Thus, in the case of Hamilton v. Regents, *293 U.S. 245, 265, Mr. Justice Cardozo, concurring, assumed that it was ". . . the religious liberty protected by the First Amendment against invasion by the nation [which] is protected by the Fourteenth Amendment against invasion by the states." (Emphasis added.) And in* Cantwell v. Connecticut, supra, *the purpose of those guarantees was described in the following terms: "On the one hand, it forestalls compulsion by law of the acceptance of any creed or the practice of any form of worship. Freedom of conscience and freedom to adhere to such religious organization or form of worship as the individual may choose cannot be restricted by law. On the other hand, it safeguards the free exercise of the chosen form of religion." 310 U.S. at 303.*

It is this concept of constitutional protection embodied in our decisions which makes the cases before us such difficult ones for me. For there is involved in these cases a substantial free exercise claim on the part of those who affirmatively desire to have their children's school day open with the reading of passages from the Bible.

It has become accepted that the decision in Pierce v. Society of Sisters, *268 U.S. 510, upholding the right of parents to send their children to nonpublic schools, was ultimately based upon the recognition of the validity of the free exercise claim involved in that situation. It might be argued here that parents who wanted their children to be exposed to religious influences in school could, under* Pierce, *send their children to private or parochial schools. But the consideration which renders this contention too facile to be determinative has already been recognized by the Court: "Freedom of speech, freedom of the press, freedom of religion are available to all, not merely to those who can pay their own way."* Murdock v. Pennsylvania, *319 U.S. 105, 111.*

It might also be argued that parents who want their children exposed to religious influences can adequately fulfill that wish off school property and outside school time. With all its surface persuasiveness, however, this argument seriously misconceives the basic constitutional justification for permitting the exercises at issue in these cases. For a compulsory state educational system so structures a child's life that if religious exercises are held to be an impermissible activity in schools, religion is placed at an artificial and state-created disadvantage. Viewed in this light, permission of such exercises for those who want them is necessary if the schools are truly to be neutral in the matter of religion. And a refusal to permit religious exercises thus is seen, not as the realization of state neutrality, but rather as the establishment of a religion of secularism, or at the least, as government support of the beliefs of those who think that religious exercises should be conducted only in private.[105]

Justice Stewart concluded that the central question was whether, notwithstanding their theoretically voluntary character, the religious exercises were so administered as in fact to impose substantial pressure on children to participate in forms of religious observance which were uncongenial to their beliefs or lack thereof. Thus, Justice Stewart regarded as crucial an issue of coercion which the majority thought irrelevant. Feeling that the records in the two cases did not adequately answer these factual questions on the issue of coercion, Justice Stewart would have remanded the cases for further proceedings. But just why, in Justice Stewart's view, a finding of noncoercion would validate the religious exercises remains unclear:

Behind Justice Stewart's "constitutional justification" for school prayers apparently lies the idea that a prayerless compulsory school, like a chaplain-less draft army, is an institution in which the free exercise and establishment clauses inevitably collide. But, assuming that it is constitutionally permissible for the United States to employ army chaplains, the "constitutional justification" for this government program is that otherwise the draftee would have no effective opportunity whatsoever to satisfy his religious needs, a situation which does not, of course, obtain for the schoolchild. Moreover, the availability of the chaplain to a religiously oriented draftee need not, and presumably does not, operate to suffuse the army experience of all draftees with an officially sponsored program of religious activity. But a school prayer program, whether or not participation is characterized as voluntary, operates through and on the pupil group and each of its members. If as to a particular schoolchild a particular prayerless public school really operates to restrain his religious faith, this surely suggests not that such a religious establishment should be tolerated, but that the child would be constitutionally exempt from compliance with the compulsory school laws.[106]

"The most unusual thing about the recent decision of the Supreme Court on the constitutionality of the use of the Lord's Prayer and the Bible reading in the schools was the mildness of the public reaction to it." These were the opening words of the sermon delivered by Rev. Charles L. Ives, a Protestant minister in New Haven, on the Sunday following the *Schempp* decision. To be sure, there was widespread criticism of the decision, but it was far more moderate in tone than that triggered by *Engel v. Vitale*. Moreover, there was substantially more public support for the decision than for its predecessor. In Indianapolis, for example, Catholic, Protestant, and Jewish leaders joined in a public statement approving the Court's holding.[107]

Not too surprisingly, however, there were, throughout the country, pockets of extreme hostility to *Schempp*. And, as the summer of 1963 progressed, there seemed fair reason for supposing that a number of public school systems would not comply with the principles announced in Schempp unless and until they were judicially directed to do so in lawsuits in which they were directly involved. In Florida, for instance, the state legislature made Bible reading and kindred practices a matter of local school board option, with the avowed object of forcing objectors to challenge religious exercises in each of the state's sixty-seven school districts.[108] And Alabama's Governor George Wallace persuaded his state board of education to require Bible reading throughout the state's public schools, announcing that if necessary he himself would read the Bible to Alabama's schoolchildren.[109] This grandstand play echoed Governor Wallace's previously announced intention to "stand in the school-house door" to resist integration of Alabama's public schools and colleges, a pledge which had collapsed two months before in a comic-opera confrontation with the Deputy Attorney General of the United States, when, over Governor Wallace's highly rhetorical protests, two Negroes were enrolled in the University of Alabama.[110]

In 1964, efforts to initiate a constitutional amendment overturning *Schempp* and *Engel v. Vitale* fizzled out when, in hearings before the House Judiciary Committee, numerous religious leaders opposed tampering with the First Amendment.

c. The "religious clause" today

Although the First Amendment was enacted as a limitation on the national government, most of the constitutional litigation involving the "religious clause" of the Amendment has (via the Fourteenth Amendment) tested state action. Today the focus has, in part, shifted back to the national arena. This is especially true in the field of education. Now that the financing of education has largely outstripped local capacities, attention has turned to the availability of federal revenues to help support parochial, as well as public, school systems. In his first year as President, the late John F. Kennedy declared his opposition, on constitutional grounds, to federal grants for parochial schools. Whether the President's doubts were justified was widely questioned.[111] However, President Kennedy's constitutional position was strengthened, in 1962, by the apparent implications of Justice Douglas' concurring opinion in *Engel v. Vitale.*[112]

Perhaps the most important measure of the present vitality of the "religious clause" is to be found not in the currently reported decisions of the Supreme Court but in the election, in 1960, of a Catholic as President of the United States. John F. Kennedy, speaking as a candidate, expressed his views about the "religious clause" in memorable terms. The following is the speech he made to a group of Protestant ministers in Texas on September 12, 1960:

> *I am grateful for your generous invitation to state my views.*
> *While the so-called religious issue is necessarily and properly the chief topic here tonight, I want to emphasize from the outset that I believe that we have far more critical issues in the 1960 election; the spread of Communist influence until it now festers only ninety miles off the coast of Florida—the humiliating treatment of our President and Vice-President by those who no longer respect our power—the hungry children I saw in West Virginia, the old people who cannot pay their doctor's bills, the families forced to give up their farms—an America with too many slums, with too few schools, and too late to the moon and outer space.*
> *These are the real issues which should decide this campaign. And they are not religious issues—for war and hunger and ignorance and despair know no religious barrier.*

But because I am a Catholic, and no Catholic has ever been elected President, the real issues in this campaign have been obscured—perhaps deliberately in some quarters less responsible than this. So it is apparently necessary for me to state once again—not what kind of church I believe in, for that should be important only to me, but what kind of America I believe in.

I believe in an America where the separation of church and state is absolute—where no Catholic prelate would tell the President (should he be a Catholic) how to act and no Protestant minister would tell his parishioners for whom to vote—where no church or church school is granted any public funds or political preference—and where no man is denied public office merely because his religion differs from the President who might appoint him or the people who might elect him.

I believe in an America that is officially neither Catholic, Protestant nor Jewish—where no public official either requests or accepts instructions on public policy from the Pope, the National Council of Churches or any other ecclesiastical source —where no religious body seeks to impose its will directly or indirectly upon the general populace or the public acts of its officials—and where religious liberty is so indivisible that an act against one church is treated as an act against all.

For while this year it may be a Catholic against whom the finger of suspicion is pointed, in other years it has been, and may someday be again, a Jew—or a Quaker—or a Unitarian—or a Baptist. It was Virginia's harassment of Baptist preachers, for example, that led to Jefferson's statute of religious freedom. Today, I may be the victim—but tomorrow it may be you—until the whole fabric of our harmonious society is ripped apart at a time of great national peril.

Finally, I believe in an America where religious intolerance will some day end—where all men and all churches are treated as equal—where every man has the same right to attend or not to attend the church of his choice—where there is no Catholic vote, no antiCatholic vote, no bloc voting of any kind—and where Catholics, Protestants and Jews, both the lay and the pastoral level, will refrain from those attitudes of disdain and division which have so often marred their works in the past, and promote instead the American ideal of brotherhood.

This is the kind of America in which I believe. And it represents the kind of Presidency in which I believe—a great office that must be neither humbled by making it the instrument of any religious group, nor tarnished by arbitrarily withholding it, its occupancy, from the members of any religious group. I believe in a President whose views on religion are his own private affair, neither imposed upon him by the nation or imposed by the nation upon him as a condition to holding that office.

I would not look with favor upon a President working to subvert the First Amendment's guarantees of religious liberty (nor would our system of checks and balances permit him to do so). And neither do I look with favor upon those who would work to subvert Article VI of the Constitution by requiring a religious test—even by indirection—for if they disagree with that safeguard, they should be openly working to repeal it.

I want a Chief Executive whose public acts are responsible to all and obligated to none—who can attend any ceremony, service or dinner his office may appropriately require him to fulfill—and whose fulfillment of his Presidential office is not limited or conditioned by any religious oath, ritual or obligation.

This is the kind of America I believe in—and this is the kind of America I fought for in the South Pacific and the kind my brother died for in Europe. No one suggested then that we might have a "divided loyalty," that we did "not believe in liberty" or that we belonged to a disloyal group that threatened "the freedoms for which our forefathers died."

And in fact this is the kind of America for which our forefathers did die when they fled here to escape religious test oaths, that denied office to members of less favored churches, when they fought for the Constitution, the Bill of Rights, the Virginia Statute of Religious Freedom—and when they fought at the shrine I visited today—the Alamo. For side by side with Bowie and Crockett died Fuentes and McCafferty and Bailey and Bedillio and Carey—but no one knows whether they were Catholics or not. For there was no religious test there.

I ask you tonight to follow in that tradition, to judge me on the basis of fourteen years in the congress—on my declared stands against an ambassador to the Vatican, against unconstitutional aid to parochial schools, and against any boycott of the public schools (which I attended myself)—instead of judging me on the basis of these pamphlets and publications we have *all seen that carefully select quotations out of context from the statements of Catholic Church leaders, usually in other countries, frequently in other centuries, and rarely relevant to any situation here—and always omitting, of course, that statement of the American bishops in 1948 which strongly endorsed church-state separation.*

I do not consider these other quotations binding upon my public acts—why should you? But let me say, with respect to other countries, that I am wholly opposed to the state being used by any religious group, Catholic or Protestant, to compel, prohibit or persecute the free exercise of any other religion. And that goes for any persecution at any time, by anyone, in any country.

And I hope that you and I condemn with equal fervor those nations which deny their Presidency to Protestants and those which deny it to Catholics. And rather than cite the misdeeds of those who differ, I would also cite the record of the Catholic Church in such nations as France and Ireland—and the independence of such statesmen as de Gaulle and Adenauer.

But let me stress again that those are my views—for, contrary to common newspaper usage, I am not the Catholic candidate for President. I am the Democratic Party's candidate for President, who happens also to be a Catholic.

I do not speak for any church on public matters—and the church does not speak for me.

Whatever issue may come before me as President, if I should be elected—on birth control, divorce, censorship, gambling, or any other subject—I will make my decision in accordance with these views, in accordance with what my conscience tells me to be in the national interest, and without regard to outside religious pressure or dictate. And no power or threat of punishment could cause me to decide otherwise.

But if the time should ever come—and I do not concede any conflict to be remotely possible—when my office would require me to either violate my conscience or violate the national interest, then I would resign the office, and I hope any other conscientious public servant would do likewise.

But I do not intend to apologize for these views to my critics of either Catholic or Protestant faith, nor do I intend to disavow either my views or my church in order to win this

*election. If I should lose on the real issues, I shall return to my
seat in the Senate, satisfied that I tried my best and was fairly
judged.*

*But if this election is decided on the basis that 40,000,000
Americans lost their chance of being President on the day they
were baptized, then it is the whole nation that will be the loser
in the eyes of Catholics and nonCatholics around the world, in
the eyes of history, and in the eyes of our own people.*

*But if, on the other hand, I should win this election, I shall
devote every effort of mind and spirit to fulfilling the oath of
the Presidency—practically identical, I might add, with the oath
I have taken for fourteen years in the Congress. For without
reservation, I can, and I quote, "solemnly swear that I will
faithfully execute the office of President of the United States and
will to the best of my ability preserve, protect and defend the
Constitution, so help me God."*[113]

The nation can take pride in the fact that John F. Kennedy's
Catholicism did not bar him from the Presidency. The nation also
can take pride in the twin facts that, four years later, (a) the
Republican Party put a Catholic (Congressman William Miller,
the Vice Presidential candidate) on its national ticket, and (b) the
Democratic Party did not feel bound to "balance" its ticket in
similar fashion. And one of the great gifts made by President
Kennedy to his countrymen during his tragically foreshortened
term was his exemplary demonstration of the irrelevance of particular sectarian commitment to the performance of public responsibilities. His skepticism about proposals for federal grants
to aid private, including parochial, schools was a conspicuous
illustration of this.

The lesson which Kennedy preached as a candidate and
practiced as President has had its recent counterparts in the
judicial and legislative branches of government. In 1965 the one
Catholic member of the Supreme Court, Justice Brennan, was
one of the seven-man majority which struck down the Connecticut
law forbidding the use of contraceptives.[114] And in the same year
a far more dramatic assertion of independence from theological
claims took place on Capitol Hill. In this instance an American
religious group actually made a formal claim upon the consciences of congregants in high office. The group was the Mormon

Church. The congregants were eleven Mormon Senators and Representatives. The story of the Mormon claim, and how it was answered, was told by John Cogley in *The New York Times:*

> There are "right-to-work" laws on the books in 19 of the 50 states. These laws make it illegal to enforce labor contracts that require membership in a union as a condition of employment. Section 14-b of the Taft-Hartley Act permits the states to pass such laws. It is President Johnson's wish that this section of the controversial law be repealed.
>
> The issue has revived the old question of religiously based conscientious objection, for certain religious groups—notably the Church of Jesus Christ of Latter-day Saints (Mormons)—are opposed to the closed shop on grounds of theological doctrine.
>
> The Mormon doctrine is called "free agency"—a belief that men are free to choose between good and evil and thereby to influence the condition of their souls in life after death. Civil laws that narrow the area of choice are consequently regarded with disfavor.
>
> It was learned last week that on June 22, the three top leaders of the Mormon church wrote to three Senators and eight members of the House of Representatives who have links with the church and urged them to oppose the repeal of Section 14-b.
>
> The church leaders—David O. McKay, 91 years of age, President; Hugh B. Brown, 81, First Counselor, and N. Eldon Tanner, 67, Second Counselor—form a body called the First Presidency of the church. . . .
>
> The First Presidency's objections were grounded in theology. "At the very basis of all our doctrine," Mr. McKay wrote, "stands the right to free agency of man. We are in favor of maintaining this free agency to the greatest extent possible." Repeal of the Taft-Hartley section backing up "right-to-work" legislation, he indicated, "would interfere with the God-given rights of men to exercise free agency in seeking and maintaining work privilege."
>
> The legislators, some of whom intend to vote against the proposed [repeal], politely rejected any indication that their votes would be determined by ecclesiastical directives. Five of the Democrats among them replied that while they respected the office of the First Presidency, they could not "delegate their own free agency to any but ourselves."

Still, the problem of conscience remains. A number of religious groups share the Mormons' objections to enforced union membership. If the Taft-Hartley section is repealed, they will insist on some provision for conscientious objectors. Some of them have indicated that, to meet the charge that they will be benefiting from union membership without paying union dues should their conscientious claim be recognized, they would be willing to pay an amount equivalent to union assessments to the Federal Government, to be used for general purposes.[115]

B. DUE PROCESS OF LAW
IN CRIMINAL TRIALS

". . . [I]N THE DEVELOPMENT of our liberty," wrote Brandeis, "insistence upon procedural regularity has been a large factor."[1] And this is especially true in the realm of criminal justice, where loss of liberty, or loss of life itself, may turn on the integrity of the inquiry made into the charges preferred against the accused. Nor is the accused's general bad character, or even his probable guilt, an acceptable excuse for the shoddy administration of justice. "Although," as Judge Cuthbert Pound of the New York Court of Appeals once put it, "the defendant may be the worst of men . . . [t]he rights of the best of men are secure only as the rights of the vilest and most abhorrent are protected."[2] The community that fails to insist on scrupulous observance of high standards by its police, by its prosecutors, and by its judges and juries, has surrendered responsibility for its own most awesome institutions. Such a community has lost track of the purposes that brought it into existence.

For the American community, the Constitution recites—as limitations on federal officials and courts—the familiar principles that surround the prosecution and trial of the civilian: freedom from unreasonable search and seizure; the right to counsel; the right to bail; indictment by a grand jury; "speedy and public trial" by a petit jury; the right to confront hostile witnesses; the right to have the court compel the attendance of "witnesses in the [accused's] favor"; no double jeopardy; no compulsory self-incrimination; no cruel and unusual punishment. And, beyond all this, the Fifth Amendment's right to due process of law, and the overriding right of habeas corpus to challenge unlawful detention.

As against the states, the constitutional limitation is the generic one, repeated in the Fourteenth Amendment—"due process of law"—and its companion, "equal protection of the laws."

A community with a strong enough sense of its traditions and responsibilities may not have to formulate a written code of procedural guarantees. It has been said by Felix Frankfurter that these procedural rights "are even more securely bedded in the texture of English feeling than they are secured through the written words in our Constitution."[3] Perhaps this is so. Yet writing them into the Constitution—and, by and large, enforcing them—has perhaps helped to inculcate into the heterogeneous American community the crucial importance of this English heritage.

1. The right to due process in times of crisis

The one mass breakdown of our conventional form of criminal trial took place during the Civil War. Thousands of civilians were then imprisoned under military order: some were tried by military commissions; some were not tried at all. The sure remedy of habeas corpus failed its high office. It had been suspended on April 27, 1861, by the President of the United States, Abraham Lincoln.

The legality of all this did not reach the Supreme Court during the Civil War. But one application for habeas corpus was, notwithstanding the President's asserted suspension of the writ, heard by Chief Justice Taney. The case came about in the following fashion:

John Merryman was seized in his own home, in Baltimore, on May 25, 1861, by soldiers acting under the orders of General Cadwalader. To secure Merryman's release, Merryman's lawyers went to the nearest federal trial court. There on the bench sat Maryland's most distinguished son, Roger B. Taney. By his own presence, the aging Chief Justice undermined the linked assertions that civil courts could not function in wartime, and that, therefore, unrestricted military apprehension of civilians was justified. Within four days of Merryman's arrest, Taney had ordered General Cadwalader to release Merryman and Taney's order had been defied.[4] Thereupon, in the first week of June, 1861, the Chief Justice prepared and filed the opinion that follows. Taney's opinion, denying that Lincoln had constitutional or inherent power to suspend the writ of habeas corpus, is a memorable statement of the permanent supremacy of the procedures marked out by the Constitution:

TANEY, *Circuit Justice. The application in this case for a writ of habeas corpus is made to me under the 14th section of the judiciary act of 1789 [1 Stat. 81], which renders effectual for the citizen the constitutional privilege of the writ of habeas corpus. . . .*

The petition presents the following case: The petitioner resides in Maryland, in Baltimore county; while peaceably in his own house, with his family, it was at two o'clock on the morning of the 25th of May 1861, entered by an armed force, professing to act under military orders; he was then compelled to rise from his bed, taken into custody, and conveyed to Fort McHenry, where he is imprisoned by the commanding officer, without warrant from any lawful authority.

The commander of the fort, General George Cadwalader, by whom he is detained in confinement, in his return to the writ, does not deny any of the facts alleged in the petition. He states that the prisoner was arrested by order of General Keim, of Pennsylvania, and conducted as aforesaid to Fort McHenry, by his order, and placed in his (General Cadwalader's) custody, to be there detained by him as a prisoner.

A copy of the warrant or order under which the prisoner was arrested was demanded by his counsel, and refused: and it is not alleged in the return, that any specific act, constituting any offence against the laws of the United States, has been charged against him upon oath, but he appears to have been arrested upon general charges of treason and rebellion, without proof, and without giving the names of the witnesses, or specifying the acts which, in the judgment of the military officer, constituted these crimes. Having the prisoner thus in custody upon these vague and unsupported accusations, he refuses to obey the writ of habeas corpus, upon the ground that he is duly authorized by the president to suspend it.

.   .   .   .   .

As the case comes before me, therefore, I understand that the president not only claims the right to suspend the writ of habeas corpus himself, at his discretion, but to delegate that discretionary power to a military officer, and to leave it to him to determine whether he will or will not obey judicial process that may be served upon him. No official notice has been given to the courts of justice, or to the public, by proclamation or otherwise, that the president claimed this power, and had exercised it in the manner stated in the return. And I certainly listened to it with some surprise, for I had supposed it to be one of those points of constitutional law upon which there was no difference of opinion, and that it was admitted on all hands, that the privilege of the writ could not be suspended, except by act of congress.

When the conspiracy of which Aaron Burr was the head, became so formidable, and was so extensively ramified, as to justify, in Mr. Jefferson's opinion, the suspension of the writ, he claimed, on his part, no power to suspend it, but communicated his opinion to congress, with all the proofs in his possession, in order that congress might exercise its discretion upon the subject, and determine whether the public safety required it. And in the debate which took place upon the subject, no one suggested that Mr. Jefferson might exercise the power himself, if, in his opinion, the public safety demanded it.

. . . .

The clause of the constitution, which authorizes the suspension of the privilege of the writ of habeas corpus, is in the 9th section of the first article. This article is devoted to the legislative department of the United States, and has not the slightest reference to the executive department. . . .

. . . The great importance which the framers of the constitution attached to the privilege of the writ of habeas corpus, to protect the liberty of the citizen, is proved by the fact, that its suspension, except in cases of invasion or rebellion, is first in the list of prohibited powers; and even in these cases the power is denied, and its exercise prohibited, unless the public safety shall require it.

It is true, that in the cases mentioned, congress is, of necessity, the judge of whether the public safety does or does not require it; and their judgment is conclusive. But the introduction of these words is a standing admonition to the legisla-

tive body of the danger of suspending it, and of the extreme caution they should exercise, before they give the government of the United States such power over the liberty of a citizen.

. . . . .

With such provisions in the constitution, expressed in language too clear to be misunderstood by any one, I can see no ground whatever for supposing that the president, in any emergency, or in any state of things, can authorize the suspension of the privileges of the writ of habeas corpus, or the arrest of a citizen, except in aid of the judicial power. He certainly does not faithfully execute the laws, if he takes upon himself legislative power, by suspending the writ of habeas corpus, and the judicial power also, by arresting and imprisoning a person without due process of law.

Nor can any argument be drawn from the nature of sovereignty, or the necessity of government, for self-defence in times of tumult and danger. The government of the United States is one of delegated and limited powers; it derives its existence and authority altogether from the constitution, and neither of its branches, executive, legislative or judicial, can exercise any of the powers of government beyond those specified and granted. . . .

. . . . .

The right of the subject to the benefit of the writ of habeas corpus, it must be recollected, was one of the great points in controversy, during the long struggle in England between arbitrary government and free institutions, and must therefore have strongly attracted the attention of the statesmen in framing a new and, as they supposed, a freer government than the one which they had thrown off by the revolution. From the earliest history of the common law, if a person were imprisoned, no matter by what authority, he had a right to the writ of habeas corpus, to bring his case before the king's bench; if no specific offence were charged against him in the warrant of commitment, he was entitled to be forthwith discharged; and if an offence were charged which was bailable in its character, the court was bound to set him at liberty on bail. The most exciting contests between the crown and the people of England, from the time of Magna Charta, were in relation to the privilege of this writ, and they continued until the passage of the statute of 31 Car. II., commonly known as the great habeas corpus act.

This statute put an end to the struggle, and finally and firmly secured the liberty of the subject against the usurpation and oppression of the executive branch of the government. . . .

.   .   .   .   .

. . . Accordingly, no power in England short of that of parliament can suspend or authorize the suspension of the writ of habeas corpus. I quote . . . from Blackstone (1 Bl. Comm. 136): "But the happiness of our constitution is, that it is not left to the executive power to determine when the danger of the state is so great as to render this measure expedient. It is the parliament only or legislative power that, whenever it sees proper, can authorize the crown by suspending the habeas corpus for a short and limited time, to imprison suspected persons without giving any reason for so doing." If the president of the United States may suspend the writ, then the constitution of the United States has conferred upon him more regal and absolute power over the liberty of the citizen, than the people of England have thought it safe to entrust to the crown; a power which the queen of England cannot exercise at this day, and which could not have been lawfully exercised by the sovereign even in the reign of Charles the First.

But I am not left to form my judgment upon this great question, from analogies between the English government and our own, or the commentaries of English jurists, or the decisions of English courts, . . .

[Chief Justice Taney then quotes from Justice Story's Commentaries on the Constitution and from an opinion by Chief Justice Marshall.]

But the documents before me show that the military authority in this case has gone far beyond the mere suspension of the privilege of the writ of habeas corpus. It has, by force of arms, thrust aside the judicial authorities and officers to whom the constitution has confided the power and duty of interpreting and administering the laws, and substituted a military government in its place, to be administered and executed by military officers. For, at the time these proceedings were had against John Merryman, the district judge of Maryland, the commis-

sioner appointed under the act of congress, the district attorney and the marshal, all resided in the city of Baltimore, a few miles only from the home of the prisoner. Up to that time, there had never been the slightest resistance or obstruction to the process of any court or judicial officer of the United States, in Maryland, except by the military authority. And if a military officer, or any other person, had reason to believe that the prisoner had committed any offence against the laws of the United States, it was his duty to give information of the fact and the evidence to support it, to the district attorney; it would then have become the duty of that officer to bring the matter before the district judge or commissioner, and if there was sufficient legal evidence to justify his arrest, the judge or commissioner would have issued his warrant to the marshal to arrest him; and upon the hearing of the case, would have held him to bail, or committed him for trial, according to the character of the offence, as it appeared in the testimony, or would have discharged him immediately, if there was not sufficient evidence to support the accusation. There was no danger of any obstruction or resistance to the action of the civil authorities, and therefore no reason whatever for the interposition of the military.

Yet, under these circumstances, a military officer, stationed in Pennsylvania, without giving any information to the district attorney, and without any application to the judicial authorities, assumes to himself the judicial power in the district of Maryland; undertakes to decide what constitutes the crime of treason or rebellion; what evidence (if indeed he required any) is sufficient to support the accusation and justify the commitment; and commits the party, without a hearing, even before himself, to close custody, in a strongly garrisoned fort, to be there held, it would seem, during the pleasure of those who committed him.

The constitution provides . . . that "no person shall be deprived of life, liberty or property, without due process of law." It declares that "the right of the people to be secure in their persons, houses, papers and effects, against unreasonable searches and seizures, shall not be violated; and no warrant shall issue, but upon probable cause, supported by oath or affirmation, and particularly describing the place to be searched, and the persons or things to be seized." It provides that the party accused shall be entitled to a speedy trial in a court of justice.

These great and fundamental laws, which congress itself could not suspend, have been disregarded and suspended, like the writ of habeas corpus, by a military order, supported by force of arms. Such is the case now before me, and I can only say that if the authority which the constitution has confided to the judiciary department and judicial officers, may thus, upon any pretext or under any circumstances, be usurped by the military power, at its discretion, the people of the United States are no longer living under a government of laws, but every citizen holds life, liberty and property at the will and pleasure of the army officer in whose military district he may happen to be found.

In such a case, my duty was too plain to be mistaken. I have exercised all the power which the constitution and laws confer upon me, but that power has been resisted by a force too strong for me to overcome. It is possible that the officer who has incurred this grave responsibility may have misunderstood his instructions, and exceeded the authority intended to be given him; I shall, therefore, order all the proceedings in this case, with my opinion, to be filed and recorded in the circuit court of the United States for the district of Maryland, and direct the clerk to transmit a copy, under seal, to the president of the United States. It will then remain for that high officer, in fulfillment of his constitutional obligation to "take care that the laws be faithfully executed," to determine what measures he will take to cause the civil process of the United States to be respected and enforced.[5]

To Attorney General Robert H. Jackson (writing in 1941, just before President Roosevelt elevated him to the Supreme Court), Taney's impotence in *Ex parte Merryman* was the fruit of Taney's own earlier judicial overreaching: Taney, in 1857, had held in the *Dred Scott* case that Congress was without power to limit the spread of slavery.[6] This decision had so narrowed the field of political maneuver as to make the ensuing Civil War almost inevitable. So Jackson saw Taney's opinions in *Dred Scott* and *Ex parte Merryman*, taken together, as an object lesson in judicial restraint which members of the Supreme Court should take to heart. This was why, in the passage that follows, Jackson dwelt upon the twilight image of the aged judge seeking to lecture President Lincoln on the obligation of "that high officer" to carry out the orders of the Court:

The [President's] answer, if any, was drowned out by the measured tread of marching feet. Judicial power was all but extinct. Nothing but the indispensable necessity for its function could bid it rise again.

Did the lonely and frustrated Chief Justice recall the tragic part that he, more than any other, had played in starting that march? Only four years before he had read the opinion in the Dred Scott case, in which his Court had held the Missouri Compromise to be unconstitutional. The Missouri Compromise itself had ceased to be important. But there was still hope that American forbearance and statesmanship would prove equal to finding some compromise between the angry forces that were being aroused by the slave issue. That hope vanished when the Supreme Court held that the Constitution would allow no compromise about the existence of slavery in the territories. Taney had attempted to forestall the anticipated verdict of coming elections—the verdict that came with the election of 1860. Now the weary and weatherbeaten old Chief Justice was overmastered by the violence of forces that he had himself turned away from compromise in legislative halls and had hurried toward war.[7]

Jackson was a brilliant advocate, but perhaps in this instance he overargued his case. For it is not quite true that Lincoln never answered Taney. He seems never to have answered Taney *directly*. But, without mentioning the Chief Justice by name, Lincoln took his own side of the constitutional issue to the country. In his special message to Congress, on July 4, 1861, Lincoln summarized the opening months of the war. And he devoted a long paragraph to defending his suspension of habeas corpus:

Soon after the first call for militia it was considered a duty to authorize the Commanding General in proper cases, according to his discretion, to suspend the privilege of the writ of habeas corpus, or, in other words, to arrest and detain without resort to the ordinary processes and forms of law such individuals as he might deem dangerous to the public safety. This authority has purposely been exercised but very sparingly. Nevertheless, the legality and propriety of what has been done under it are questioned, and the attention of the country has been called to the proposition that one who is sworn to "take care that the laws be faithfully executed" should not himself violate them. Of course some consideration was given to the questions of power and propriety before this matter was acted upon. The whole of the laws which were required to be faithfully executed were being resisted and failing of execution in nearly one-third of the States. Must they be allowed to finally fail of execution, even had it been perfectly clear that by the use of the means necessary to their execution some single law, made in such extreme tenderness of the citizen's liberty that practically it relieves more of the guilty than of the innocent, should to a very limited extent be violated? To state the question more directly, Are all the laws but one to go unexecuted, and the Government itself go to pieces lest that one be violated? Even in such a case, would not the official oath be broken if the Government should be overthrown when it was believed that disregarding the single law would tend to preserve it? But it was not believed that this question was presented. It was not believed that any law was violated. The provision of the Constitution that "the privilege of the writ of habeas corpus shall not be suspended unless when, in cases of rebellion or invasion, the public safety may require it" is equivalent to a provision—is a provision—that such privilege may be suspended when, in cases of rebellion or invasion, the public safety does require it. It was decided that we have a case of rebellion and that the public safety does require the qualified suspension of the privilege of the writ which was authorized to be made. Now it is insisted that Congress, and not the Executive, is vested with this power; but the Constitution itself is silent as to which or who is to exercise the power; and as the provision was plainly made for a dangerous emergency, it can not be believed the framers of the instrument intended that in every case the danger should run its course until Congress could be called together, the very assembling of which might be prevented, as was intended in this case, by the rebellion.[8]

Thus, Lincoln, without naming his adversary, challenged Taney *rhetorically* on the constitutional issues presented. And Lincoln never retreated from the broad ground he claimed. On the other hand, Lincoln did not permanently flout Taney's *judgment* in the particular litigated case: Not too long after Taney announced his decision, John Merryman was remanded to civil custody. He was then indicted for treason; but, he was not brought to trial.[9] In short, Lincoln never acknowledged that he and his generals were traveling beyond the law. But he also avoided placing his own "high office" in flat contempt of a direct judicial order. He was a master politician, as well as a remarkably shrewd lawyer. He must have sensed that ultimate constitutional showdowns, however dramatic, are not necessarily good medicine for the body politic.

Yet Justice Jackson's basic point about the *Merryman* case— that courts which enter the lists against the President and Congress have only their prestige as armament—is certainly well taken. And he was certainly right in regarding *Dred Scott* as a glaring instance of judicial self-assertion which squandered judicial prestige.[10]

After the war, and after Taney's death, the Court consolidated the ground that the late Chief Justice, in *Ex parte Merryman*, had patrolled as a lone sentinel. In *Ex parte Milligan*, the Court concluded that even Congress could not authorize the trial of civilians by military commissions so long as civil courts remained open; yet the decision was far from unanimous.[11]

But *Milligan*, in the prevailing opinion of Justice David Davis (whom Lincoln had appointed), also stated categorically a more general proposition from which there was no dissent:

. . . *Those great and good men [who launched the republic] foresaw that troublous times would arise, when rulers and people would become restive under restraint, and seek by sharp and decisive measures to accomplish ends deemed just and proper; and that the principles of constitutional liberty would be in peril, unless established by irrepealable law. The history of the world had taught them that what was done in the past might be attempted in the future. The Constitution of the United States is a law for rulers and people, equally in war and in peace, and covers with the shield of its protection all classes of* men, at all times, and under all circumstances. No doctrine, involving more pernicious consequences, was ever invented by the wit of man than that any of its provisions can be suspended during any of the great exigencies of government. Such a doctrine leads directly to anarchy or despotism, but the theory of necessity on which it is based is false; for the government, within the Constitution, has all the powers granted to it which are necessary to preserve its existence; as has been happily proved by the result of the great effort to throw off its just authority.[12]

2. What is due process?

For those federal offenses tried in federal courts—rather than by some form of military tribunal—the basic modes of trial are those specified in the Constitution. The cases clarifying those specifics—when is a search unreasonable, and what are its consequences? when is the privilege against self-incrimination available? what is double jeopardy?—are important, but need not be canvassed here.

What is worth sampling, however, are cases in which the Court has tried to identify those elements of a criminal trial and subsequent punishment that are essential ingredients of the "due process of law" that federal and state courts alike must accord the accused. Sometimes the Court's attempts to give content to due process are merely perplexing. But much of the time—and especially within the past thirty years—the Court here operates at its creative best. And so it should, for this is a field in which the Justices are making constitutional policy on matters which are peculiarly within their professional expertise—the processes of the law.

One might expect that the Supreme Court's major contributions to the definition of due process would generally have been made in very celebrated criminal cases. For the most part, however, the criminal defendants who have acquired a measure of constitutional immortality are people dwelling on the shadowed edges of society, whose lives and trials and tribulations are quite obscure. This is true, for example, of Frank Palko, Admiral Dewey Adamson, Willie Francis, Sam Thompson, Dr. Julius A.

Wolf, Antonio Rochin, Patrick Irvine, and Doll Ree Mapp, whose cases we will turn to shortly.

There have of course been American *causes célèbres*, criminal cases that have profoundly disturbed the American community for many years. Since World War II there have been three of these:

1. There was the case of Alger Hiss, a prominent public official, who, after two trials, was found guilty of perjury in denying that he had copied and disclosed secret government documents. Although there was enough evidence of guilt to lead the jury at the second trial to convict, there was enough conflicting evidence so that the jury at the first trial was unable to reach a verdict one way or another. Perhaps the full story of this strange and sad case has not yet, and may never, come to light.[13] At all events, the Supreme Court seems to have found no procedural problems serious enough to require review.[14]

2. There was the case of Julius and Ethel Rosenberg, who were convicted of stealing atomic secrets. Although there was widespread concern both here and abroad about whether the death sentence should have been imposed, there seems to be no real doubt that the defendants were guilty of the grave offense charged. Here again—although with rather more difficulty—the Supreme Court found no issue that required review.[15]

3. There was the case of Caryl Chessman, an habitual criminal sentenced to death for assault with intent to rape. Here again there was probably no real doubt about the defendant's guilt, but there were major procedural problems which prolonged the case for many years.[16] During these years of appellate litigation, Chessman wrote a number of books which brought his case— and, through it, the whole question of the propriety and utility of capital punishment—to national, and even international, attention. Chessman was finally executed. But the question of capital punishment continues to agitate the American conscience.[17]

a. Three American tragedies

These cases evoked widespread concern. But none, so far as is now known, was a plainly demonstrable miscarriage of justice. There are, however, three earlier American criminal cases that deserve more extended comment. These earlier cases arose, and stirred the nation, in the period running from World War I to the Depression. It is a fair guess that those who are concerned with the law's integrity will ponder these cases long after Chessman, the Rosenbergs, and even Hiss, are forgotten. For these are cases in which, for bigotry's sake, several men were wantonly convicted and sentenced to death—and, in one instance, executed—for crimes they probably did not commit. As will be seen hereafter, the Supreme Court played only a small role in the first of the cases, and virtually no role in the second, but, on two occasions, it played a decisive role in the third. That third case is the effective starting point for the Court's present vigilance in supervising the ground rules of American criminal justice. Taken together the three cases are a grim inventory of corruptions the Constitution no longer tolerates.

(1). *The Mooney-Billings Case*

Mooney and Billings were convicted of murder, on charges growing out of a bombing that killed nine people during a parade in San Francisco in 1916. Mooney, the principal defendant, was sentenced to death (a sentence that was later commuted to life imprisonment). Billings received a life term. There was considerable feeling that, because Mooney was a very militant California labor leader, powerful antilabor forces took charge of the investigation and prosecution in a deliberate attempt to find, and if necessary fabricate, evidence connecting Mooney with the crime. Mooney's case swiftly became a matter of international concern. President Woodrow Wilson asked his Mediation Commission, of which the Secretary of Labor was chairman and Felix Frankfurter was counsel, to inquire into the case. The Commission felt that it was not its province "to establish the guilt or innocence of Mooney and his associates," but did urge the President to request the Governor of California to seek "a new trial . . . for Mooney whereby guilt or innocence may be put to the test of unquestionable justice."[18] Although the case remained a center of controversy, and of appellate litigation, for two decades, Mooney was never retried. The Supreme Court, in 1935, acknowledged that Mooney's conviction was a denial of due process if, as he claimed, the prosecution had knowingly employed perjured testimony against him.[19] But the Supreme Court felt that it was up to the California courts to determine whether the facts supported Mooney's claim. After a few more years of fruit-less litigation, Governor Olson of California pardoned Mooney.[20]

(2). *The Sacco-Vanzetti Case*

The *Sacco-Vanzetti Case* arose in Massachusetts shortly after World War I. The defendants were two humble Italian working-men, of radical political persuasion. They were charged with, and found guilty of, a murder occurring in the course of a payroll robbery. They were sentenced to death, and appeals embroiled the courts of Massachusetts for many years. But the convictions were never reviewed by the Supreme Court, although last-ditch applications were made to some of the Justices. Meanwhile, a known gang leader confessed his complicity in the crime and exonerated the defendants. Nevertheless, in 1927, Sacco and Vanzetti were electrocuted. Some still argue that the two men did commit the holdup and the murder;[21] but the general consensus of those who have studied the facts with care is that Sacco and Vanzetti were guilty only of being Italians and radicals and were quite innocent of the crime charged.[22]

(3). *The Scottsboro Case*

The *Scottsboro Case* draws its name from the town of Scottsboro, Alabama. There, in 1931, nine Negro youths (two of them boys of thirteen and fourteen) were charged with raping two white prostitutes, fellow passengers on a freight train. Eight of the youths were found guilty and sentenced to death. One conviction was set aside by the Alabama Supreme Court. The seven remain-ing convictions were reviewed by the United States Supreme Court, which reversed on the ground that the defendants had not been adequately represented by counsel at their mass trial.[23] Two of the defendants were then retried and the Supreme Court reviewed the ensuing death sentences. The Court once again reversed, this time on the ground that Negroes had been sys-tematically excluded from the grand and petit juries.[24] Subse-quently, Alabama dropped the rape charges against five of the nine (one of these pleaded guilty to stabbing a sheriff). But, in 1936 and 1937, the other four were retried and convicted. Three of the four received long jail sentences and the fourth a death sentence which was later commuted to life imprisonment. Three of the four were later paroled. The fourth, Hayward Patterson, escaped, and in 1952 died in a Michigan prison, where he was under sentence for manslaughter.[25] There seems good reason to believe that in the *Scottsboro Case*, as in the *Sacco-Vanzetti Case*, the defendants were guilty only of being members of a mistreated minority, not of the offenses charged.[26]

The trio of cases just summarized reflect local criminal justice at its desperate worst. They should not be taken as representative of the way American criminal procedure works in the ordinary criminal case. At the same time, these cases are symptomatic of what can happen when constitutional limitations break down. And one of the Supreme Court's great accomplishments, in the three decades since those cases caused national and international concern, has been to move forward aggressively, in a long series of relatively unnoticed criminal cases, to promulgate new and more rigorous constitutional standards. The following cases sample the Court's method. The first is the Court's initial intervention in the *Scottsboro* Case. This may be taken as the starting point for the Court's new vigilance in vindicating the guarantee of "due process of law."

b. Due process as adversary process: the right to counsel

The first time the *Scottsboro Case* reached the Supreme Court, the dominant question was whether the lawyers assigned to represent the defendants at trial had furnished their young and unlettered clients anything more than token legal representation. The Supreme Court, in an opinion written by the deeply conservative and deeply conscientious Justice George Sutherland, examined with minute lawyerly concern the question of whether the defendants were represented by counsel in any meaningful sense. Finding the answer to be in the negative, Justice Sutherland then addressed himself to the question of whether, at least in some circumstances, the due process clause of the Fourteenth Amendment requires the state to furnish counsel. The verbal fact that the federal Bill of Rights requires the *federal* government to accord due process and also specifically guarantees the accused a lawyer in a *federal* criminal trial did not deter Justice Sutherland from reading "due process" in the Fourteenth Amendment *to include*, at least in capital cases, the assistance of counsel.

Thereby the Court took another step on the path which started with *Gitlow* and free speech[27] of "incorporating" fundamental rights into the Fourteenth Amendment:

MR. JUSTICE SUTHERLAND *delivered the opinion of the Court.*

These cases were argued together and submitted for decision as one case.

The petitioners, hereinafter referred to as defendants, are negroes charged with the crime of rape, committed upon the persons of two white girls. The crime is said to have been committed on March 25, 1931. . . .

. . . [T]he defendants were tried in three . . . groups. . . . Each of the three trials was completed within a single day. Under the Alabama statute the punishment for rape is to be fixed by the jury, and in its discretion may be from ten years imprisonment to death. The juries found defendants guilty and imposed the death penalty upon all. . . .

In this court the judgments are assailed upon the grounds that the defendants, and each of them, were denied due process of law and the equal protection of the laws, in contravention of the Fourteenth Amendment, specifically as follows: (1) they were not given a fair, impartial and deliberate trial; (2) they were denied the right of counsel, with the accustomed incidents of consultation and opportunity of preparation for trial; and (3) they were tried before juries from which qualified members of their own race were systematically excluded. These questions were properly raised and saved in the courts below.

The only one of the assignments which we shall consider is the second, in respect of the denial of counsel; and it becomes unnecessary to discuss the facts of the case or the circumstances surrounding the prosecution except in so far as they reflect light upon that question.

The record shows that on the day when the offense is said to have been committed, these defendants, together with a number of other negroes, were upon a freight train on its way through Alabama. On the same train were seven white boys and the two white girls. A fight took place between the negroes and the white boys, in the course of which the white boys, with the exception of one named Gilley, were thrown off the train. A message was sent ahead, reporting the fight and asking that every negro be gotten off the train. The participants in the fight, and the two girls, were in an open gondola car. The two girls testified that each of them was assaulted by six different negroes in turn, and they identified the seven defendants as having been among the number. None of the white boys was called to testify, with the exception of Gilley, who was called in rebuttal.

Before the train reached Scottsboro, Alabama, a sheriff's posse seized the defendants and two other negroes. Both girls and the negroes then were taken to Scottsboro, the county seat. Word of their coming and of the alleged assault had preceded them, and they were met at Scottsboro by a large crowd. It does not sufficiently appear that the defendants were seriously threatened with, or that they were actually in danger of, mob violence; but it does appear that the attitude of the community was one of great hostility. The sheriff thought it necessary to call for the militia to assist in safeguarding the prisoners. . . . Soldiers took the defendants to Gadsden for safekeeping, brought them back to Scottsboro for arraignment, returned them to Gadsden for safekeeping while awaiting trial, escorted them to Scottsboro for trial a few days later, and guarded the court house and grounds at every stage of the proceedings. It is perfectly apparent that the proceedings, from beginning to end, took place in an atmosphere of tense, hostile and excited public sentiment. During the entire time, the defendants were closely confined or were under military guard. The record does not disclose their ages, except that one of them was nineteen; but the record clearly indicates that most, if not all, of them were youthful, and they are constantly referred to as "the boys." They were ignorant and illiterate. All of them were residents of other states, where alone members of their families or friends resided.

However guilty defendants, upon due inquiry, might prove to have been, they were, until convicted, presumed to be innocent. It was the duty of the court having their cases in charge to see that they were denied no necessary incident of a fair trial. . . .

First: the record shows that immediately upon the return of the indictment defendants were arraigned and pleaded not guilty. Apparently they were not asked whether they had, or were able to employ, counsel, or wished to have counsel appointed; or whether they had friends or relatives who might assist in that regard if communicated with. . . .

. . . . .

April 6, six days after indictment, the trials began. When the first case was called, the court inquired whether the parties were ready for trial. The state's attorney replied that he was ready to proceed. No one answered for the defendants or appeared to represent or defend them. Mr. Roddy, a Tennessee lawyer not a member of the local bar, addressed the court, saying that he had not been employed, but that people who were interested had spoken to him about the case. He was asked by the court whether he intended to appear for the defendants, and answered that he would like to appear along with counsel that the court might appoint. The record then proceeds:

"The Court: If you appear for these defendants, then I will not appoint counsel; if local counsel are willing to appear and assist you under the circumstances all right, but I will not appoint them.

"Mr. Roddy: Your Honor has appointed counsel, is that correct?

"The Court: I appointed all the members of the bar for the purpose of arraigning the defendants and then of course I anticipated them to continue to help them if no counsel appears.

"Mr. Roddy: Then I don't appear then as counsel but I do want to stay in and not be ruled out in this case.

"The Court: Of course I would not do that—

"Mr. Roddy: I just appear here through the courtesy of Your Honor.

"The Court: Of course I give you that right; . . ."

And then, apparently addressing all the lawyers present, the court inquired:

". . . well are you all willing to assist?

"Mr. Moody: Your Honor appointed us all and we have been proceeding along every line we know about it under Your Honor's appointment.

"The Court: The only thing I am trying to do is, if counsel appears for these defendants I don't want to impose on you all, but if you feel like counsel from Chattanooga—

"*Mr. Moody: I see his situation of course and I have not run out of anything yet. Of course, if Your Honor purposes to appoint us, Mr. Parks, I am willing to go on with it. Most of the bar have been down and conferred with these defendants in this case; they did not know what else to do.*

"*The Court: The thing, I did not want to impose on the members of the bar if counsel unqualifiedly appears; if you all feel like Mr. Roddy is only interested in a limited way to assist, then I don't care to appoint—*

"*Mr. Parks: Your Honor, I don't feel like you ought to impose on any member of the local bar if the defendants are represented by counsel.*

"*The Court: That is what I was trying to ascertain, Mr. Parks.*

"*Mr. Parks: Of course if they have counsel, I don't see the necessity of the Court appointing anybody; if they haven't counsel, of course I think it is up to the Court to appoint counsel to represent them.*

"*The Court: I think you are right about it Mr. Parks and that is the reason I am trying to get an impression from Mr. Roddy.*

"*Mr. Roddy: I think Mr. Parks is entirely right about it, if I was paid down here and employed, it would be a different thing, but I have not prepared this case for trial and have only been called into it by people who are interested in these boys from Chattanooga. Now, they have not given me an opportunity to prepare the case and I am not familiar with the procedure in Alabama, but I merely came down here as a friend of the people who are interested and not as paid counsel, and certainly I haven't any money to pay them and nobody I am interested in had me to come down here has put up any fund of money to come down here and pay counsel. If they should do it I would be glad to turn it over—a counsel but I am merely here at the solicitation of people who have become interested in this case without any payment of fee and without any preparation for trial and I think the boys would be better off if I step entirely out of the case according to my way of looking at it and according to my lack of preparation of it and not being familiar with the procedure in Alabama. . . .*"

Mr. Roddy later observed:

"*If there is anything I can do to be of help to them, I will be glad to do it; I am interested to that extent.*

"*The Court: Well gentlemen, if Mr. Roddy only appears as assistant that way, I think it is proper that I appoint members of this bar to represent them, I expect that is right. If Mr. Roddy will appear, I wouldn't of course, I would not appoint anybody. I don't see, Mr. Roddy, how I can make a qualified appointment or a limited appointment. Of course, I don't mean to cut off your assistance in any way—Well gentlemen, I think you understand it.*

"*Mr. Moody: I am willing to go ahead and help Mr. Roddy in anything I can do about it, under the circumstances.*

"*The Court: All right, all the lawyers that will; of course I would not require a lawyer to appear if—*

"*Mr. Moody: I am willing to do that for him as a member of the bar; I will go ahead and help do anything I can do.*

"*The Court: All right.*"

And in this casual fashion the matter of counsel in a capital case was disposed of.

.   .   .   .   .   .

. . . *[T]he trials immediately proceeded. The defendants, young, ignorant, illiterate, surrounded by hostile sentiment, haled back and forth under guard of soldiers, charged with an atrocious crime regarded with especial horror in the community where they were to be tried, were thus put in peril of their lives within a few moments after counsel for the first time charged with any degree of responsibility began to represent them.*

It is not enough to assume that counsel thus precipitated into the case thought there was no defense, and exercised their best judgment in proceeding to trial without preparation. Neither they nor the court could say what a prompt and thoroughgoing investigation might disclose as to the facts. No attempt was made to investigate. No opportunity to do so was given. Defendants were immediately hurried to trial. . . . Under the circumstances disclosed, we hold that defendants were not accorded the right of counsel in any substantial sense. To decide otherwise, would simply be to ignore actualities. . . .

.   .   .   .   .   .

Second. *The Constitution of Alabama provides that in all criminal prosecutions the accused shall enjoy the right to have the assistance of counsel; and a state statute requires the court in a capital case, where the defendant is unable to employ counsel, to appoint counsel for him. The state supreme court held that these provisions had not been infringed, and with that holding we are powerless to interfere. The question, however, which it is our duty, and within our power, to decide, is whether the denial of the assistance of counsel contravenes the due process clause of the Fourteenth Amendment to the federal Constitution.*

If recognition of the right of a defendant charged with a felony to have the aid of counsel depended upon the existence of a similar right at common law as it existed in England when our Constitution was adopted, there would be great difficulty in maintaining it as necessary to due process. Originally, in England, a person charged with treason or felony was denied the aid of counsel, except in respect of legal questions which the accused himself might suggest. At the same time parties in civil cases and persons accused of misdemeanors were entitled to the full assistance of counsel. After the revolution of 1688, the rule was abolished as to treason, but was otherwise steadily adhered to until 1836, when by act of Parliament the full right was granted in respect of felonies generally. . . .

An affirmation of the right to the aid of counsel in petty offenses, and its denial in the case of crimes of the gravest character, where such aid is most needed, is so outrageous and so obviously a perversion of all sense of proportion that the rule was constantly, vigorously and sometimes passionately assailed by English statesmen and lawyers. As early as 1758, Blackstone, although recognizing that the rule was settled at common law, denounced it as not in keeping with the rest of the humane treatment of prisoners by the English law. "For upon what face of reason," he says, "can that assistance be denied to save the life of a man, which yet is allowed him in prosecutions for every petty trespass?" . . .

The rule was rejected by the colonies. . . .

.   .   .   .   .   .

. . . [I]n at least twelve of the thirteen colonies the rule of the English common law . . . had been definitely rejected and the right to counsel fully recognized in all criminal prosecutions,

*save that in one or two instances the right was limited to capital
offenses or to the more serious crimes. . . .*

.   .   .   .   .

One test which has been applied to determine whether due
process of law has been accorded in given instances is to ascertain what were the settled usages and modes of proceeding
under the common and statute law of England before the
Declaration of Independence, subject, however, to the qualification that they be shown not to have been unsuited to the civil
and political conditions of our ancestors by having been followed
in this country after it became a nation. . . . Plainly . . . this
test, as thus qualified, has not been met in the present case.

We do not overlook the case of Hurtado v. California, 110
U.S. 516, where this court determined that due process of law
does not require an indictment by a grand jury as a prerequisite
to prosecution by a state for murder. In support of that conclusion the court (pp. 534–535) referred to the fact that the Fifth
Amendment, in addition to containing the due process of law
clause, provides in explicit terms that "No person shall be held to
answer for a capital, or otherwise infamous crime, unless on a
presentment or indictment of a grand jury, . . .", and said that
since no part of this important amendment could be regarded
as superfluous, the obvious inference is that in the sense of the
Constitution due process of law was not intended to include,
ex vi termini, the institution and procedure of a grand jury in any
case; and that the same phrase, employed in the Fourteenth
Amendment to restrain the action of the states, was to be interpreted as having been used in the same sense and with no
greater extent; and that if it had been the purpose of that
Amendment to perpetuate the institution of the grand jury in
the states, it would have embodied, as did the Fifth Amendment,
an express declaration to that effect.

The Sixth Amendment, in terms, provides that in all criminal prosecutions the accused shall enjoy the right "to have the
assistance of counsel for his defense." In the face of the reasoning
of the Hurtado case, if it stood alone, it would be difficult to
justify the conclusion that the right to counsel, being thus
specifically granted by the Sixth Amendment, was also within
the intendment of the due process of law clause. But the Hurtado

case does not stand alone. In the later case of Chicago, Burlington & Quincy R. Co. v. Chicago, 166 U.S. *226, 241, this court held that a judgment of a state court, even though authorized by statute, by which private property was taken for public use without just compensation, was in violation of the due process of law required by the Fourteenth Amendment, notwithstanding that the Fifth Amendment explicitly declares that private property shall not be taken for public use without just compensation. . . .*

Likewise, this court has considered that freedom of speech and of the press are rights protected by the due process clause of the Fourteenth Amendment, although in the First Amendment, Congress is prohibited in specific terms from abridging the right. Gitlow v. New York, 268 U.S. 652, 666. . . .

These later cases establish that notwithstanding the sweeping character of the language in the Hurtado *case, the rule laid down is not without exceptions. The rule is an aid to construction, and in some instances may be conclusive; but it must yield to more compelling considerations whenever such considerations exist. The fact that the right involved is of such a character that it cannot be denied without violating those "fundamental principles of liberty and justice which lie at the base of all our civil and political institutions"* (Hebert v. Louisiana, 272 U.S. 312, 316), *is obviously one of those compelling considerations which must prevail in determining whether it is embraced within the due process clause of the Fourteenth Amendment, although it be specifically dealt with in another part of the federal Constitution. Evidently this court, in the later cases enumerated, regarded the rights there under consideration as of this fundamental character. That some such distinction must be observed is foreshadowed in* Twining v. New Jersey, 211 U.S. 78, 99, *where Mr. Justice Moody, speaking for the court, said that ". . . it is possible that some of the personal rights safeguarded by the first eight Amendments against National action may also be safeguarded against state action, because a denial of them would be a denial of due process of law.* Chicago, Burlington & Quincy R. Co. v. Chicago, 166 U.S. 226. *If this is so, it is not because those rights are enumerated in the first eight Amendments, but because they are of such a nature that they are included in the conception of due process of law." While the question has never been categorically determined by this court, a consideration of the nature of the right and a review of the expressions of this and other courts, makes it clear that the right to the aid of counsel is of this fundamental character.*

It never has been doubted by this court, or any other so far as we know, that notice and hearing are preliminary steps essential to the passing of an enforceable judgment, and that they, together with a legally competent tribunal having jurisdiction of the case, constitute basic elements of the constitutional requirement of due process of law. The words of Webster, so often quoted, that by "the law of the land" is intended "a law which hears before it condemns," have been repeated in varying forms of expression in a multitude of decisions. . . .

What, then, does a hearing include? Historically and in practice, in our own country at least, it has always included the right to the aid of counsel when desired and provided by the party asserting the right. The right to be heard would be, in many cases, of little avail if it did not comprehend the right to be heard by counsel. Even the intelligent and educated layman has small and sometimes no skill in the science of law. If charged with crime, he is incapable, generally, of determining for himself whether the indictment is good or bad. He is unfamiliar with the rules of evidence. Left without the aid of counsel he may be put on trial without a proper charge, and convicted upon incompetent evidence, or evidence irrelevant to the issue or otherwise inadmissible. He lacks both the skill and knowledge adequately to prepare his defense, even though he have a perfect one. He requires the guiding hand of counsel at every step in the proceedings against him. Without it, though he be not guilty, he faces the danger of conviction because he does not know how to establish his innocence. If that be true of men of intelligence, how much more true is it of the ignorant and illiterate, or those of feeble intellect. If in any case, civil or criminal, a state or federal court were arbitrarily to refuse to hear a party by counsel, employed by and appearing for him, it reasonably may not be doubted that such a refusal would be a denial of a hearing, and, therefore, of due process in the constitutional sense.

In the light of the facts outlined in the forepart of this opinion—the ignorance and illiteracy of the defendants, their youth, the circumstances of public hostility, the imprisonment and the close surveillance of the defendants by the military forces, the fact that their friends and families were all in other states and communication with them necessarily difficult, and above all that they stood in deadly peril of their lives—we think the failure of the trial court to give them reasonable time and opportunity to secure counsel was a clear denial of due process.

But passing that, and assuming their inability, even if opportunity had been given, to employ counsel, as the trial court evidently did assume, we are of opinion that, under the circumstances just stated, the necessity of counsel was so vital and imperative that the failure of the trial court to make an effective appointment of counsel was likewise a denial of due process within the meaning of the Fourteenth Amendment. Whether this would be so in other criminal prosecutions, or under other circumstances, we need not determine. . . .

.   .   .   .   .   .

Mr. Justice [Pierce] Butler, *dissenting.*

The Court, putting aside—they are utterly without merit—all other claims that the constitutional rights of petitioners were infringed, grounds its opinion and judgment upon a single assertion of fact. It is that petitioners "were denied the right of counsel, with the accustomed incidents of consultation and opportunity of preparation for trial." If that is true, they were denied due process of law and are entitled to have the judgments against them reversed.

But no such denial is shown by the record.

.   .   .   .   .

The informality disclosed by the colloquy between court and counsel, which is quoted in the opinion of this Court and so heavily leaned on, is not entitled to any weight. It must be inferred from the record that Mr. Roddy at all times was in touch with the defendants and the people who procured him to act for them. Mr. Moody and others of the local bar also acted for defendants at the time of the first arraignment and, as appears from the part of the record that is quoted in the opinion, there-

*after proceeded in the discharge of their duty, including confer-
ences with the defendants. There is not the slightest ground to
suppose that Roddy or Moody were by fear or in any manner
restrained from full performance of their duties. Indeed, it
clearly appears that the State, by proper and adequate show of
its purpose and power to preserve order, furnished adequate
protection to them and the defendants.*

. . . . .

*If correct, the ruling that the failure of the trial court to give
petitioners time and opportunity to secure counsel was denial of
due process is enough, and with this the opinion should end.
But the Court goes on to declare that "the failure of the trial
court to make an effective appointment of counsel was likewise
a denial of due process within the meaning of the Fourteenth
Amendment." This is an extension of federal authority into a
field hitherto occupied exclusively by the several States. Nothing
before the Court calls for a consideration of the point. It was
not suggested below, and petitioners do not ask for its decision
here. The Court, without being called upon to consider it,
adjudges without a hearing an important constitutional question
concerning criminal procedure in state courts.*

. . . . .

*The record wholly fails to reveal that petitioners have been
deprived of any right guaranteed by the Federal Constitution,
and I am of opinion that the judgment should be affirmed.*

MR. JUSTICE MCREYNOLDS *concurs in this opinion.*[28]

In 1942, ten years after *Powell v. Alabama,* the Supreme
Court, in a divided vote, held, in *Betts v. Brady,*[29] that the Fourteenth Amendment did *not* require states to see to it that defendants in *non*capital cases were represented by counsel, except
where the complexity of a particular prosecution seemed to the
Supreme Court to make it impossible for the accused to do an
adequate job of managing his own defense. But to the dissenting
Justices in *Betts v. Brady,* and to numerous students of criminal
procedure, the notion that a layman could usually be counted on
to represent himself intelligently, when faced with a noncapital
felony prosecution in a state court, seemed highly unpersuasive.
Underscoring the unpersuasiveness of the notion was the fact that
in the *federal* courts it was an accepted part of the routine

that counsel should be appointed to represent indigent defendants in all criminal cases, capital or otherwise.

For two decades after *Betts v. Brady* was decided, the asserted due process distinction between capital and noncapital cases came increasingly under fire.[30] Curiously, however, the logical dimensions of the problem became somewhat obscured by a rising doctrinal debate within the Court, of which the right-to-counsel issue was merely one facet. Justices Black and Douglas, who had dissented in *Betts v. Brady*, became the leading proponents of a theory—advanced with great elaborateness in a dissenting opinion in *Adamson v. California*[31]—that the Fourteenth Amendment was intended to protect against *state* interference every *federal* procedural right itemized in the Bill of Rights. This view of the Fourteenth Amendment of course automatically included the Sixth Amendment's right to counsel. Arrayed against Justices Black and Douglas in the larger doctrinal struggle was a majority, usually led by the late Justice Frankfurter, which insisted that the due process of law protected by the Fourteenth Amendment against state authority was not simply a short-hand notation referring back to the specific rights listed in the Bill of Rights, but rather was a generalized guarantee of fundamental fairness—a guarantee whose particular content might vary from case to case and decade to decade. Adherents of this view of the Fourteenth Amendment felt unable, therefore, to commit themselves to the blanket proposition that appointment of counsel was an essential ingredient of fairness in every state criminal prosecution.

Writing a couple of years after the *Adamson* controversy began, Professor Paul A. Freund, one of the most perceptive students of the Supreme Court, proposed a sensible way out of the right-to-counsel portion of the doctrinal log jam:

> *The pressing issue centers on the right of indigent defendants in criminal cases to have counsel appointed as a matter of course. In the federal courts this has been required since 1938 on the ground that it is commanded by the Sixth Amendment. A majority of the Court has been unwilling to apply this blanket rule to state prosecutions, preferring a case-by-case review looking to the essential fairness or unfairness of the procedure. One may hope that a majority of the Court will turn to the view that*

the appointment of counsel is as indispensable to the just and even-handed administration of the criminal law in the state courts as in the federal courts. They would be helped to reach this conclusion by avowing frankly that the Sixth Amendment does not furnish the real reason for the requirement in the federal courts. It seems more nearly true to regard that Amendment as having simply conferred the right on the accused to employ counsel—a right which of course was by no means assured prior to the adoption of the Constitution. If the right to have counsel appointed in the federal courts is acknowledged to rest on a pervasive sense of justice it should be extended to state prosecutions as an element of due process of law. This would be a happy dénouement of the dramatic, the over-dramatic, clash over the Fourteenth Amendment which has drawn so heavily on the energies of the Court.[32]

Professor Freund's words were written in 1949. Well over a decade elapsed before the Court resolved the matter. The case was this: Clarence Earl Gideon was charged, in 1961, with breaking and entering a poolroom, with intent to commit petty larceny, in Panama City, Florida. When his case came up for trial, Gideon, an indigent in his fifties, apparently felt that the legal lore he had picked up in many prior brushes with the law was insufficient to permit him adequately to defend himself. He asked the Florida state judge to appoint a lawyer to represent him. But the request was turned down because Florida courts, fulfilling what they understood to be the minimal mandate of the Constitution, appointed defense counsel only to represent indigents charged with capital offenses. Gideon, perforce, represented himself. And he was convicted and sentenced to a five-year prison term. In due course, Gideon filed a petition for habeas corpus seeking to have his conviction set aside. When he lost in the Florida Supreme Court, Gideon filed with the United States Supreme Court a handwritten petition for certiorari. That Court decided to hear Gideon's case, and appointed one of the senior members of the Washington bar (Abe Fortas, who, in 1965, was to succeed Justice Arthur Goldberg on the Court) to brief and argue it for him. Meanwhile, in view of the widespread implications for all the states of the issue to be argued, the Florida Attorney General urged the attorneys general of other states to file briefs as *amici curiae* (friends of the Court) supporting Florida's position. Two states responded in the affirmative. But twenty-two others, as *amici curiae,* supported Gideon: arguing that *Betts v. Brady* (the 1942 decision establishing a constitutional distinction between capital and noncapital cases) should be over-ruled, these states urged the Supreme Court to hold that the due process clause requires every state to make sure that the accused has counsel in all criminal cases.

When Gideon's case was argued in the Supreme Court, Justices Black and Douglas were the only sitting Justices who had been on the Court when *Betts v. Brady* and *Adamson v. California* were decided; and they, of course, had dissented in both cases. Justice Frankfurter, their great antagonist, who had been with the majority in *Betts v. Brady* and in *Adamson,* had retired a few months before Gideon's case was argued.

The decision, to no one's great surprise, was favorable to Gideon. More surprising, to some, was the fact that the decision was unanimous—although, to be sure, Justices Clark and Harlan did not join in the Court's opinion.

The opinion of the Court in *Gideon v. Wainwright* was written by Justice Black. He did not pursue the approach he and Justice Douglas had followed in *Adamson.* Instead, he sought to demonstrate that *Betts v. Brady* was a departure from more generous principles announced in *Powell v. Alabama* (the first *Scottsboro Case*). Justice Black's comparison of Betts' and Gideon's cases follows:

> *The facts upon which Betts claimed that he had been un-constitutionally denied the right to have counsel appointed to assist him are strikingly like the facts upon which Gideon here bases his federal constitutional claim. Betts was indicted for robbery in a Maryland state court. On arraignment, he told the trial judge of his lack of funds to hire a lawyer and asked the court to appoint one for him. Betts was advised that it was not the practice in that county to appoint counsel for indigent de-fendants except in murder and rape cases. He then pleaded not guilty, had witnesses summoned, cross-examined the State's witnesses, examined his own, and chose not to testify himself. He was found guilty by the judge, sitting without a jury, and sentenced to eight years in prison. Like Gideon, Betts sought*

release by habeas corpus, alleging that he had been denied the right to assistance of counsel in violation of the Fourteenth Amendment. Betts was denied any relief, and on review this Court affirmed. It was held that a refusal to appoint counsel for an indigent defendant charged with a felony did not necessarily violate the Due Process Clause of the Fourteenth Amendment, which for reasons given the Court deemed to be the only applicable federal constitutional provision. The Court said:

> *Asserted denial [of due process] is to be tested by an appraisal of the totality of facts in a given case. That which may, in one setting, constitute a denial of fundamental fairness, shocking to the universal sense of justice, may, in other circumstances, and in the light of other considerations, fall short of such denial. 316 U.S. at 462.*

Treating due process as "a concept less rigid and more fluid than those envisaged in other specific and particular provisions of the Bill of Rights," the Court held that refusal to appoint counsel under the particular facts and circumstances in the Betts case was not so "offensive to the common and fundamental ideas of fairness" as to amount to a denial of due process. Since the facts and circumstances of the two cases are so nearly indistinguishable, we think the Betts v. Brady holding if left standing would require us to reject Gideon's claim that the Constitution guarantees him the assistance of counsel. Upon full reconsideration we conclude that Betts v. Brady should be overruled.

.   .   .   .   .

We accept Betts v. Brady's assumption, based as it was on our prior cases, that a provision of the Bill of Rights which is "fundamental and essential to a fair trial" is made obligatory upon the States by the Fourteenth Amendment. We think the Court in Betts was wrong, however, in concluding that the Sixth Amendment's guarantee of counsel is not one of these fundamental rights. Ten years before Betts v. Brady, this Court, after full consideration of all the historical data examined in Betts, had unequivocally declared that "the right to the aid of counsel is of this fundamental character." Powell v. Alabama, 287 U.S. 45, 68 (1932). While the Court at the close of its Powell opinion did by its language, as this Court frequently does, limit its holding to the particular facts and circumstances of that case, its con-

clusions about the fundamental nature of the right to counsel are unmistakable. . . .

. . . . .

. . . The fact is that in deciding as it did—that "appointment of counsel is not a fundamental right, essential to a fair trial"— the Court in Betts v. Brady *made an abrupt break with its own well-considered precedents. In returning to these old precedents, sounder we believe than the new, we but restore constitutional principles established to achieve a fair system of justice. Not only these precedents but also reason and reflection require us to recognize that in our adversary system of criminal justice, any person haled into court, who is too poor to hire a lawyer, cannot be assured a fair trial unless counsel is provided for him. This seems to us to be an obvious truth. Governments, both state and federal, quite properly spend vast sums of money to establish machinery to try defendants accused of crime. Lawyers to prosecute are everywhere deemed essential to protect the public's interest in an orderly society. Similarly, there are few defendants charged with crime, few indeed, who fail to hire the best lawyers they can get to prepare and present their defenses. That government hires lawyers to prosecute and defendants who have the money hire lawyers to defend are the strongest indications of the widespread belief that lawyers in criminal courts are necessities, not luxuries. The right of one charged with crime to counsel may not be deemed fundamental and essential to fair trials in some countries, but it is in ours. From the very beginning, our state and national constitutions and laws have laid great emphasis on procedural and substantive safeguards designed to assure fair trials before impartial tribunals in which every defendant stands equal before the law. This noble ideal cannot be realized if the poor man charged with crime has to face his accusers without a lawyer to assist him. A defendant's need for a lawyer is nowhere better stated than in the moving words of Mr. Justice Sutherland in* Powell v. Alabama:

> *The right to be heard would be, in many cases, of little avail if it did not comprehend the right to be heard by counsel. Even the intelligent and educated layman has small and sometimes no skill in the science of law. If*

charged with crime, he is incapable, generally, of determining for himself whether the indictment is good or bad. He is unfamiliar with the rules of evidence. Left without the aid of counsel he may be put on trial without a proper charge, and convicted upon incompetent evidence, or evidence irrelevant to the issue or otherwise inadmissible. He lacks both the skill and knowledge adequately to prepare his defense, even though he have a perfect one. He requires the guiding hand of counsel at every step in the proceedings against him. Without it, though he be not guilty, he faces the danger of conviction because he does not know how to establish his innocence. 287 U.S. at 68, 69.

The Court in Betts v. Brady *departed from the sound wisdom upon which the Court's holding in* Powell v. Alabama *rested. Florida, supported by two other States, has asked that* Betts v. Brady *be left intact. Twenty-two States, as friends of the Court, argue that* Betts *was "an anachronism when handed down" and that it should now be overruled. We agree.*[33]

Justice Douglas filed a separate concurring opinion in which, by reciting the pedigree of the doctrine advanced in the *Adamson* dissent, he tried to suggest that the doctrine might one day produce living issue. But the tone of the concurrence, belying the words, sounded more like the doctrine's epitaph:

While I join the opinion of the Court, a brief historical résumé of the relation between the Bill of Rights and the first section of the Fourteenth Amendment seems pertinent. Since the adoption of that Amendment, ten Justices have felt that it protects from infringement by the States the privileges, protections, and safeguards granted by the Bill of Rights.

Justice Field, the first Justice Harlan, and probably Justice Brewer, took that position in O'Neil v. Vermont, *144 U.S. 323, 362–363, 370–371, as did Justices Black, Douglas, Murphy and Rutledge in* Adamson v. California, *332 U.S. 46, 71–72, 124. And see* Poe v. Ullman, *367 U.S. 497, 515–522 (dissenting opinion). That view was also expressed by Justices Bradley and Swayne in the* Slaughter-House Cases, *16 Wall. 36, 118–119, 122, and seemingly was accepted by Justice Clifford when he dissented with Justice Field in* Walker v. Sauvinet, *92 U.S. 90, 92. Unfortunately it has never commanded a Court. Yet, happily, all constitutional questions are always open.* Erie R. Co. v. Tompkins, 304 U.S. 64. *And what we do today does not foreclose the matter.*[34]

Justice Clark's concurrence centered on the irrationality of a constitutional distinction between capital and noncapital cases:

. . . *The Fourteenth Amendment requires due process of law for the deprival of "liberty" just as for deprival of "life," and there cannot constitutionally be a difference in the quality of the process based merely upon a supposed difference in the sanction involved. How can the Fourteenth Amendment tolerate a procedure which it condemns in capital cases on the ground that deprival of liberty may be less onerous than deprival of life—a value judgment not universally accepted—or that only the latter deprival is irrevocable? I can find no acceptable rationalization for such a result, and I therefore concur in the judgment of the Court.*[35]

Justice John M. Harlan's concurrence took sharp issue with the majority view that *Betts v. Brady* was, when announced, a narrowing of prior doctrine. But Justice Harlan agreed that *Betts v. Brady* had, by 1963, outlived its constitutional usefulness:

I agree that Betts v. Brady *should be overruled, but consider it entitled to a more respectful burial than has been accorded, at least on the part of those of us who were not on the Court when that case was decided.*

I cannot subscribe to the view that Betts v. Brady *represented "an abrupt break with its own well-considered precedents." Ante, p. 344. In 1932, in* Powell v. Alabama, *287 U.S. 45, a capital case, this Court declared that under the particular facts there presented—"the ignorance and illiteracy of the defendants, their youth, the circumstances of public hostility . . . and above all that they stood in deadly peril of their lives" (287 U.S., at 71)—the state court had a duty to assign counsel for the trial as a necessary requisite of due process of law. It is evident that these limiting facts were not added to the opinion as an afterthought; they were repeatedly emphasized, see 287 U.S., at 52, 57–58, 71, and were clearly regarded as important to the result.*

Thus when this Court, a decade later, decided Betts v.

Brady, *it did no more than to admit of the possible existence of special circumstances in noncapital as well as capital trials, while at the same time insisting that such circumstances be shown in order to establish a denial of due process. The right to appointed counsel had been recognized as being considerably broader in federal prosecutions, see* Johnson v. Zerbst, *304 U.S. 458, but to have imposed these requirements on the States would indeed have been "an abrupt break" with the almost immediate past. The declaration that the right to appointed counsel in state prosecutions, as established in* Powell v. Alabama, *was not limited to capital cases was in truth not a departure from, but an extension of, existing precedent.*

The principles declared in Powell *and in* Betts, *however, have had a troubled journey throughout the years that have followed first the one case and then the other. Even by the time of the* Betts *decision, dictum in at least one of the Court's opinions had indicated that there was an absolute right to the services of counsel in the trial of state capital cases. Such dicta continued to appear in subsequent decisions, and any lingering doubts were finally eliminated by the holding of* Hamilton v. Alabama, *368 U.S. 52.*

In noncapital cases, the "special circumstances" rule had continued to exist in form while its substance has been substantially and steadily eroded. In the first decade after Betts, *there were cases in which the Court found special circumstances to be lacking, but usually by a sharply divided vote. However, no such decision has been cited to us, and I have found none, after* Quicksall v. Michigan, *339 U.S. 660, decided in 1950. At the same time, there have been not a few cases in which special circumstances were found in little or nothing more than the "complexity" of the legal questions presented, although those questions were often of only routine difficulty. The Court has come to recognize, in other words, that the mere existence of a serious criminal charge constituted in itself special circumstances requiring the services of counsel at trial. In truth the* Betts v. Brady *rule is no longer a reality.*

This evolution, however, appears not to have been fully recognized by many state courts, in this instance charged with the front-line responsibility for the enforcement of constitutional rights. To continue a rule which is honored by this Court only with lip service is not a healthy thing and in the long run will do disservice to the federal system.

The special circumstances rule has been formally abandoned in capital cases, and the time has now come when it should be similarly abandoned in noncapital cases, at least as to offenses which, as the one involved here, carry the possibility of a substantial prison sentence. (Whether the rule should extend to all criminal cases need not now be decided.) This indeed does no more than to make explicit something that has long since been foreshadowed in our decisions.[36]

Justice Harlan's approach to *Gideon v. Wainwright* echoes the evolutionary view of the due process clause long associated with Justice Frankfurter. And this fact gives jurisprudential dimension to the poignant anecdote related by Anthony Lewis in his volume dissecting the *Gideon* case:

Shortly after the Gideon case was decided, Justice Black visited Justice Frankfurter at home and told his ailing colleague about the conference at which the case had been discussed. He had told the other members of the Court, Justice Black said, that if Felix had been there he would have voted—faithful to his own view of due process—to reverse the conviction of Clarence Earl Gideon and overrule Betts v. Brady.

Justice Frankfurter said: "Of course I would."[37]

Doubtless the anecdote is true. In appraising the anecdote, however, one caveat is in order: In telling Justice Black that he would have joined in the Court's judgment in *Gideon* if he had participated in the case, Justice Frankfurter did not and could not employ the language of decision. Justice Frankfurter was estimating, subjunctively, a condition contrary to fact. For he did *not* participate in *Gideon*. And the genius of American constitutional adjudication—*especially* as practiced by Justice Frankfurter—is that the law is shaped from the stubborn clay of particular controversies. Justice Frankfurter once said that "in the end, judgment cannot be escaped—the judgment of this Court."[38] By the same token, there is no substitute for the discipline imposed by sharing in the responsibility of judgment.

The filing of this caveat is not, however, meant to cast doubt on the probability that Justice Frankfurter, had he participated in

Gideon, would have agreed with the result reached by the Court, even if not with Justice Black's opinion. In philosophic as well as in personal terms, the reported quasi-coalescence of the views of the two great Justices has the ring of validity. It implies no surrender of his doctrinal premises by either Justice. Yet it illustrates the capacity of the law—and particularly the law of the Constitution—to draw strength from conflicting doctrines, and thereby to build upon and beyond them.

For Clarence Gideon, victory of the Supreme Court had more immediate implications. He had won the right to a new trial. But this time he was represented by a lawyer. And this time the jury acquitted him. "Do you feel like you accomplished something?", a newspaperman asked Gideon after the verdict. "Well," said Gideon, "I did."[39]

One of the practical problems posed by the decision in *Gideon v. Wainwright,* and not resolved by the opinion, was how far the principle there announced was to extend. The charge against Gideon was a felony—a serious charge. What was not clear was whether the requirement that the state ensure the provision of counsel to criminal defendants would cover misdemeanors as well. In 1965 the Court of Appeals for the Fifth Circuit either held, or came to the verge of holding, that counsel must be provided for persons charged with misdemeanors.[40]

c. Due process as fair process: but what does fairness mean?

Starting with the *Scottsboro Cases,* the Supreme Court managed in a generation to reach a conclusion most laymen would be able to arrive at more quickly than they could say "due process"—that a defendant unrepresented by counsel cannot effectively plead his case. But simply having a lawyer is only the first element of a fair trial. The materials that follow illustrate the Court's efforts to determine what some of the other minimal ingredients of fairness are which inhere in the concept of due process of law.

In *Palko v. Connecticut,* the Supreme Court reviewed a Connecticut murder case which was as obscure as *Scottsboro* was celebrated. What marked out *Palko* as unusual was not the crime, nor the character of the trial, but the fact that the defendant was tried twice.

A second trial for the same offense is not in itself unusual.

Indeed, in the United States it is customary for the state to try a defendant a second time when his first conviction is set aside, on appeal, because of some trial error which may have prejudiced the defendant's case. But *Palko* was different. For there, after securing a conviction for *second degree* murder—and a life sentence—the *state* appealed, and got a reversal in Connecticut's highest court, on the ground that trial court errors *prejudicial to the state* prevented Connecticut from getting a conviction for murder in the *first degree*. Then Palko was retried, found guilty of first degree murder, and sentenced to death.

It was this unusual procedure which Palko challenged in the Supreme Court. He argued that, under these circumstances, his second trial meant that he was "twice put in jeopardy" within the meaning of the Fifth Amendment; and that the Fourteenth Amendment's due process clause by implication adopted the double jeopardy prohibition and imposed that prohibition on the states.

Justice Benjamin N. Cardozo, on behalf of an all-but-unanimous Court, rejected Palko's claim: the right to protection against double jeopardy was not "fundamental," and thus not an element of due process. In reaching his conclusion, Cardozo explained why some kinds of rights—procedural and substantive—were of a higher order than others and therefore became, through case-by-case and liberty-by-liberty evaluation, binding on the states. His characterization of the way in which the nonspecific language of the Fourteenth Amendment progressively acquires concrete meaning remains today the fundamental exposition of that process. It is an exposition which transposes to constitutional adjudication the traditional evolutionary method of the common law. Cardozo—like Holmes, whom he succeeded on the Supreme Court—had been for many years, as a state court judge, a pre-eminent master of the common law. The opinion in *Palko* follows:

MR. JUSTICE CARDOZO *delivered the opinion of the Court.*
A statute of Connecticut permitting appeals in criminal cases to be taken by the state is challenged by appellant as an infringement of the Fourteenth Amendment of the Constitution of the United States. Whether the challenge should be upheld is now to be determined.
Appellant was indicted for the crime of murder in the first

*degree. A jury found him guilty of murder in the second degree,
and he was sentenced to confinement in the state prison for life.
Thereafter the State of Connecticut [appealed, alleging certain
trial errors prejudicial to the prosecution's case]. . . . Upon such
appeal, the Supreme Court of Errors reversed the judgment and
ordered a new trial. . . .*

*Pursuant to the mandate of the Supreme Court of Errors,
defendant was brought to trial again. Before a jury was im-
paneled and also at later stages of the case he made the objection
that the effect of the new trial was to place him twice in jeopardy
for the same offense, and in so doing to violate the Fourteenth
Amendment of the Constitution of the United States. Upon the
overruling of the objection the trial proceeded. The jury returned a verdict of murder in the first degree, and the court
sentenced the defendant to the punishment of death. The Supreme Court of Errors affirmed the judgment of conviction. . . .*

.   .   .   .   .

*. . . The Fifth Amendment, which is not directed to the
states, but solely to the federal government, creates immunity
from double jeopardy. No person shall be "subject for the same
offense to be twice put in jeopardy of life or limb". The Fourteenth Amendment ordains, "nor shall any State deprive any
person of life, liberty, or property, without due process of
law." . . .*

.   .   .   .   .

*We have said that in appellant's view the Fourteenth
Amendment is to be taken as embodying the prohibitions of the
Fifth. His thesis is even broader. Whatever would be a violation
of the original bill of rights (Amendments I to VIII) if done by
the federal government is now equally unlawful by force of the
Fourteenth Amendment if done by a state. There is no such
general rule.*

*The Fifth Amendment provides, among other things, that
no person shall be held to answer for a capital or otherwise infamous crime unless on presentment or indictment of a grand
jury. This court has held that, in prosecutions by a state, presentment or indictment by a grand jury may give way to informa-
tions at the instance of a public officer. Hurtado v. California,
110 U.S. 516; Gaines v. Washington, 277 U.S. 81, 86. The Fifth*

Amendment provides also that no person shall be compelled in any criminal case to be a witness against himself. This court has said that, in prosecutions by a state, the exemption will fail if the state elects to end it. Twining v. New Jersey, 211 U.S. 78, 106, 111, 112. Cf. Snyder v. Massachusetts, supra, p. 105; Brown v. Mississippi, 297 U.S. 278, 285. *The Sixth Amendment calls for a jury trial in criminal cases and the Seventh for a jury trial in civil cases at common law where the value in controversy shall exceed twenty dollars. This court has ruled that consistently with those amendments trial by jury may be modified by a state or abolished altogether.* Walker v. Sauvinet, 92 U.S. 90; Maxwell v. Dow, 176 U.S. 581; New York Central R. Co. v. White, 243 U.S. 188, 208; Wagner Electric Mfg. Co. v. Lyndon, 262 U.S. 226, 232. *As to the Fourth Amendment, one should refer to* Weeks v. United States, 232 U.S. 383, 398, *and as to other provisions of the Sixth, to* West v. Louisiana, 194 U.S. 258.

On the other hand, the due process clause of the Fourteenth Amendment may make it unlawful for a state to abridge by its statutes the freedom of speech which the First Amendment safeguards against encroachment by the Congress, De Jonge v. Oregon, 299 U.S. 353, 364; Herndon v. Lowry, 301 U.S. 242, 259; *or the like freedom of the press,* Grosjean v. American Press Co., 297 U.S. 233; Near v. Minnesota ex rel. Olson, 283 U.S. 697, 707; *or the free exercise of religion,* Hamilton v. Regents, 293 U.S. 245, 262; cf. Grosjean v. American Press Co., supra; Pierce v. Society of Sisters, 268 U.S. 510; *or the right of peaceable assembly, without which speech would be unduly trammeled,* De Jonge v. Oregon, supra; Herndon v. Lowry, supra; *or the right of one accused of crime to the benefit of counsel,* Powell v. Alabama, 287 U.S. 45. *In these and other situations immunities that are valid as against the federal government by force of the specific pledges of particular amendments have been found to be implicit in the concept of ordered liberty, and thus, through the Fourteenth Amendment, become valid as against the states.*

The line of division may seem to be wavering and broken if there is a hasty catalogue of the cases on the one side and the other. Reflection and analysis will induce a different view. There emerges the perception of a rationalizing principle which gives to discrete instances a proper order and coherence. The right to trial by jury and the immunity from prosecution except as the result of an indictment may have value and importance. Even so, they are not of the very essence of a scheme of ordered liberty. To abolish them is not to violate a "principle of justice so rooted in the traditions and conscience of our people as to be ranked as fundamental." Snyder v. Massachusetts, supra, p. 105; Brown v. Mississippi, supra, p. 285; Hebert v. Louisiana, 272 U.S. 312, 316. Few would be so narrow or provincial as to maintain that a fair and enlightened system of justice would be impossible without them. What is true of jury trials and indictments is true also, as the cases show, of the immunity from compulsory self-incrimination. Twining v. New Jersey, supra. This too might be lost, and justice still be done. Indeed, today as in the past there are students of our penal system who look upon the immunity as a mischief rather than a benefit, and who would limit its scope, or destroy it altogether. No doubt there would remain the need to give protection against torture, physical or mental. Brown v. Mississippi, supra. Justice, however, would not perish if the accused were subject to a duty to respond to orderly inquiry. The exclusion of these immunities and privileges from the privileges and immunities protected against the action of the states has not been arbitrary or casual. It has been dictated by a study and appreciation of the meaning, the essential implications, of liberty itself.

We reach a different plane of social and moral values when we pass to the privileges and immunities that have been taken over from the earlier articles of the federal bill of rights and brought within the Fourteenth Amendment by a process of absorption. These in their origin were effective against the federal government alone. If the Fourteenth Amendment has absorbed them, the process of absorption has had its source in the belief that neither liberty nor justice would exist if they were sacrificed. Twining v. New Jersey, supra, p. 99. This is true, for illustration, of freedom of thought, and speech. Of that freedom one may say that it is the matrix, the indispensable condition, of nearly every other form of freedom. With rare aberrations a pervasive recognition of that truth can be traced in our history, political and legal. So it has come about that the domain of liberty, withdrawn by the Fourteenth Amendment from encroachment by the states, has been enlarged by latter-day judgments to include liberty of the mind as well as liberty of action.

The extension became, indeed, a logical imperative when once it was recognized, as long ago it was, that liberty is something more than exemption from physical restraint, and that even in the field of substantive rights and duties the legislative judgment, if oppressive and arbitrary, may be overridden by the courts. Cf. Near v. Minnesota ex rel. Olson, supra; De Jonge v. Oregon, supra. *Fundamental too in the concept of due process, and so in that of liberty, is the thought that condemnation shall be rendered only after trial.* Scott v. McNeal, *154 U.S. 34;* Blackmer v. United States, *284 U.S. 421. The hearing, moreover, must be a real one, not a sham or a pretense.* Moore v. Dempsey, *261 U.S. 86;* Mooney v. Holohan, *294 U.S. 103. For that reason, ignorant defendants in a capital case were held to have been condemned unlawfully when in truth, though not in form, they were refused the aid of counsel.* Powell v. Alabama, supra, *pp. 67, 68. The decision did not turn upon the fact that the benefit of counsel would have been guaranteed to the defendants by the provisions of the Sixth Amendment if they had been prosecuted in a federal court. The decision turned upon the fact that in the particular situation laid before us in the evidence the benefit of counsel was essential to the substance of a hearing.*

Our survey of the cases serves, we think, to justify the statement that the dividing line between them, if not unfaltering throughout its course, has been true for the most part to a unifying principle. On which side of the line the case made out by the appellant has appropriate location must be the next inquiry and the final one. Is that kind of double jeopardy to which the statute has subjected him a hardship so acute and shocking that our polity will not endure it? Does it violate those "fundamental principles of liberty and justice which lie at the base of all our civil and political institutions"? Hebert v. Louisiana, supra. *The answer surely must be "no". What the answer would have to be if the state were permitted after a trial free from error to try the accused over again or to bring another case against him, we have no occasion to consider. We deal with the statute before us and no other. The state is not attempting to wear the accused out by a multitude of cases with accumulated trials. It asks no more than this, that the case against him shall go on until there shall be a trial free from the corrosion of substantial legal error.* State v. Felch, *92 Vt. 477; 105 Atl. 23;* State v. Lee, supra. *This is not cruelty at all, nor even vexation in any immoderate degree. If the trial had been infected with error adverse to the accused, there might have been review at his instance, and as often as necessary to purge the vicious taint. A reciprocal privilege, subject all times to the discretion of the presiding judge, State v. Carabetta, 106 Conn. 114; 127 Atl. 394, has now been granted to the state. There is here no seismic innovation. The edifice of justice stands, its symmetry, to many, greater than before.*

The judgment is

Affirmed.

MR. JUSTICE BUTLER *dissents.*[41]

Palko, which was decided in 1937, is still what lawyers call "good law." And this is so, notwithstanding the fact that a decade later four members of the Court sought to unseat the doctrine and replace it with a rule that the Fourteenth Amendment imposes on the states *all* the restraints the Bill of Rights imposes on the federal government. The leader of this vigorous but unsuccessful attack on *Palko* (and on *Twining v. New Jersey*,[42] upon which *Palko* relied) was Justice Black, the only present member of the Supreme Court who was on the Court when *Palko* was decided.

The occasion for the proposed new departure was the case of *Adamson v. California*. The case, discussed above[43] in connection with the development of the law of right to counsel, arose out of the California murder conviction of Admiral Dewey Adamson.

Under the law prevailing in California—and, generally, throughout the United States—an accused may not be called to testify by the prosecution, and he need not take the witness stand in his own behalf unless he elects to do so. This general rule is the practical expression of the privilege against self-incrimination which binds the federal government and which is also to be found in most state constitutions. In California, however, the failure of a defendant to take the stand in his own behalf and rebut the evidence against him may be commented upon to the jury by the prosecuting attorney and even by the trial judge. Probably—or so at least the Supreme Court assumed—such comment in the federal courts would be regarded as an infringement of the privilege against self-incrimination.

But if Admiral Dewey Adamson were to have taken the witness stand in order to avoid the inference of guilt drawn from his silence, he would have been in greater difficulty. For then the prosecution would have been free to cross-examine him. Moreover, and more important, the prosecution also would have been free to inquire about Adamson's prior convictions for other crimes. Ostensibly, the relevance of such prior convictions is to show that the defendant is untrustworthy, and that, therefore, his testimony is not to be believed. Actually, of course, revelation of other crimes serves the prosecution's purpose of prejudicing the jury against the defendant. Even though the prior crimes are unrelated to the offense charged, their mere existence, if known to the jury, makes it much easier to persuade a jury that the defendant is guilty "beyond a reasonable doubt" of the crime presently laid at his door.

Caught in this squeeze, Adamson argued that California had effectively compelled him to testify against himself—by his silence, or by taking the stand—and thereby denied him the privilege against self-incrimination.

For the majority of the Court, speaking through Justice Reed, the answer was clear. The Fourteenth Amendment does not in terms require states to preserve the privilege against self-incrimination. In *Twining v. New Jersey*, decided in 1908, the Court had decided that the privilege against self-incrimination was not protected by either the "privileges or immunities" clause or the "due process" clause of the amendment. In *Palko*, Cardozo had reaffirmed the general principles of *Twining*; moreover, even though the *Palko* issue was double jeopardy, Cardozo had discussed the privilege against self-incrimination too, finding it not so "fundamental" as to be ranked with the right to counsel, or free speech, and therefore not to be judicially incorporated into the Fourteenth Amendment. Accordingly, in reliance on *Twining* and *Palko*, the Court affirmed Adamson's conviction.[44]

Justices Black and Douglas (with whom Justices Murphy and Rutledge substantially agreed) advanced a different view of the Fourteenth Amendment. According to Black, his study of the relevant "history" conclusively demonstrated that the language of the first section of the Fourteenth Amendment, taken as a whole, was thought by those responsible for its submission to the people, and by those who opposed its submission, sufficiently explicit to guarantee that thereafter no state could deprive its citizens of the privileges and protections of the Bill of Rights.[45] Accordingly, the federal privilege against self-incrimination was, by the Fourteenth Amendment, made a restraint upon the states as well. Therefore, Adamson's conviction should have been reversed.

This Black-Douglas view of the Fourteenth Amendment has been noted earlier,[46] in connection with the discussion of the attempts of the two Justices to justify, textually, the use of the amendment—and especially its privileges or immunities clause —to protect personal, as distinct from economic, liberties. It was there indicated that the full history of the amendment probably does not support their historical conclusions. This historical controversy is too complex to be explored fully here. It is, however, important to note the philosophic objection that Justices Black and Douglas have to the judicial method, exemplified by *Palko,* of identifying certain rights as "fundamental" and incorporating those and only those into the due process clause. To the two Justices, the assumption by judges of competence to decide what is "fundamental" perpetuates the free-handed judicial usurpation of the "liberty of contract" era. They prefer to anchor precious rights in particular words of the Constitution which judges cannot, from generation to generation, choose to ignore or revere at their unbridled discretion. A convenient and (relatively) explicit itemization of such rights—all *personal* rights, except perhaps, the requirement that "just compensation" be paid for private property that the government condemns—is the Bill of Rights. Failure to root the judicial construction of the Fourteenth Amendment in the specifics of the Bill of Rights leaves judges, in the Black-Douglas view, free to flounder in a higher "natural law" of their own devising. As Justice Black put it in *Adamson:*

. . . I further contend that the "natural law" formula which the Court uses to reach its conclusion in this case should be abandoned as an incongruous excrescence on our Constitution. I believe that formula to be itself a violation of our Constitution, in that it subtly conveys to courts, at the expense of legislatures,

ultimate power over public policies in fields where no specific provision of the Constitution limits legislative power. . . .[47]

The late Justice Frankfurter, concurring in *Adamson*, expressed a very different estimate of the judicial process called for by the Fourteenth Amendment:

. . . [W]hen, as in a case like the present, a conviction in a State court is here for review under a claim that a right protected by the Due Process Clause of the Fourteenth Amendment has been denied, the issue is not whether an infraction of one of the specific provisions of the first eight Amendments is disclosed by the record. The relevant question is whether the criminal proceedings which resulted in conviction deprived the accused of the due process of law to which the United States Constitution entitled him. Judicial review of that guaranty of the Fourteenth Amendment inescapably imposes upon this Court an exercise of judgment upon the whole course of the proceedings in order to ascertain whether they offend those canons of decency and fairness which express the notions of justice of English-speaking peoples even toward those charged with the most heinous offenses. These standards of justice are not authoritatively formulated anywhere as though they were prescriptions in a pharmacopoeia. But neither does the application of the Due Process Clause imply that judges are wholly at large. The judicial judgment in applying the Due Process Clause must move within the limits of accepted notions of justice and is not to be based upon the idiosyncrasies of a merely personal judgment. The fact that judges among themselves may differ whether in a particular case a trial offends accepted notions of justice is not disproof that general rather than idiosyncratic standards are applied. . . .[48]

The retention of the *Palko* doctrine does not answer all questions. Indeed (as both its proponents and its detractors recognize) the doctrine dictates an extremely taxing judicial inquiry into the nature of our fundamental institutions. Yet the doctrine does afford some guidelines. Occasionally, however, cases come to the Court that demonstrate the limitations of any legal doctrine that may be espoused. Such was the case of Willie Francis, which the majority and the dissenting Justices alike described as "unique."[49]

Willie Francis was tried in a Louisiana court, convicted, and sentenced to death for the crime of murder. On the appointed day, Willie Francis was taken to the electric chair. Then, according to the affidavit of the attending chaplain:

After he was strapped to the chair the Sheriff of St. Martin Parish asked him if he had anything to say about anything and he said nothing. Then the hood was placed before his eyes. Then the officials in charge of the electrocution were adjusting the mechanisms and when the needle of the meter registered to a certain point on the dial, the electrocutioner pulled down on the switch and at the same time said, "Goodby Willie." At that very moment, Willie Francis' lips puffed out and his body squirmed and tensed and he jumped so that the chair rocked on the floor. Then the condemned man said: "Take it off. Let me breath [sic]." Then the switch was turned off. Then some of the men left and a few minutes after the Sheriff of St. Martin Parish, Mr. E. L. Resweber, came in and announced that the governor had granted the condemned man a reprieve.[50]

A reporter for the *New York Herald-Tribune* talked to Willie Francis later on, and wrote up his story:

Whatever did happen, Willie Francis did not die. . . . Willie Francis, telling it better than any other human being of our time, has described the sensation of dying but not quite achieving death.

"You feel like you got a mouthful of cold peanut butter and you see little blue and pink and green speckles in front of your eyes, the kind that shines in a rooster's tail. All I could think was Willie, you're going out'n this world, . . .

"They begun to strap me against the chair and everything begun to look dazey in the room. It was like the white folks watching was on a big swing and they swung away-y-y back and then right up close to me where I could hear their breathing. I didn't think of my whole life like at the picture show, just Willie, you're going out'n this world in this bad chair. Sometimes I thought it so loud it hurt my head, and when they put the black bag over my head I was all locked up inside the bag with the loud thinking."

And then Willie Francis told the color of death: "Some

folks say it's gold; some say it's white as hominy grits. I reckon it's black. I ought to know, I been mighty close."

The steel cap by now had been applied and the electrodes fastened as tight as Willie's skinny, undernourished legs would allow. The "electric man" said, "Goodbye, Willie," but Willie was too frightened to answer.

"He could have been putting me on a bus for New Orleans the way he said it, and I tried to say goodbye but my tongue got stuck in the peanut butter, and I felt a burning in my head and my left leg and I jumped against the straps. When the straps kept cutting me I hoped I was alive and I asked the electric man to let me breathe."[51]

When Louisiana undertook to execute Willie Francis for the second time, he took his case to the Supreme Court, arguing that the Fourteenth Amendment should protect him against what he felt to be both "double jeopardy" and "cruel and unusual punishment." *Francis v. Resweber,* sustaining the constitutionality of the proposed second execution, was decided on January 13, 1947, two days before the arguments in *Adamson* got under way. Justice Reed, who was to write the *Adamson* majority opinion, wrote for the Court in *Francis v. Resweber.* His opinion, which Justice Black joined, relied on *Palko* (on the double jeopardy issue) with a serenity that seems to belie the possibility that either Justice Reed or Justice Black foresaw the issues which were shortly to divide them. Justice Frankfurter's concurrence, on the other hand, seems instinct with anticipation of the issues to be fought out in *Adamson.* However this may be, the unprecedented (in the lay and legal sense alike) horror of Willie Francis' actual case seemed to overwhelm available doctrines. One feels, in reading the opinions, that those Justices who were armed with *Palko,* and those who were shortly to espouse the thesis contained in the *Adamson* dissent, were equally bereft of constitutional moorings. Yet it is the essence of judicial responsibility that cases, however perplexing, must be decided. ". . . [I]n the end, judgment cannot be escaped—the judgment of this Court."[52] This, then, is how the Court dealt with the case of Willie Francis:

Mr. Justice Reed *announced the judgment of the Court in an opinion in which* The Chief Justice, Mr. Justice Black *and* Mr. Justice Jackson *join.*

This writ of certiorari brings before this Court a unique situation. The petitioner, Willie Francis, is a colored citizen of Louisiana. He was duly convicted of murder and in September, 1945, sentenced to be electrocuted for the crime. Upon a proper death warrant, Francis was prepared for execution and on May 3, 1946, pursuant to the warrant, was placed in the official electric chair of the State of Louisiana in the presence of the authorized witnesses. The executioner threw the switch but, presumably because of some mechanical difficulty, death did not result. He was thereupon removed from the chair and returned to prison where he now is. A new death warrant was issued by the Governor of Louisiana, fixing the execution for May 9, 1946.

Applications to the Supreme Court of the state were filed for writs of certiorari, mandamus, prohibition and habeas corpus, directed to the appropriate officials in the state. Execution of the sentence was stayed. By the applications petitioner claimed the protection of the due process clause of the Fourteenth Amendment on the ground that an execution under the circumstances detailed would deny due process to him because of the double jeopardy provision of the Fifth Amendment and the cruel and unusual punishment provision of the Eighth Amendment. These federal constitutional protections, petitioner claimed, would be denied because he had once gone through the difficult preparation for execution and had once received through his body a current of electricity intended to cause death. The Supreme Court of Louisiana denied the applications on the ground of a lack of any basis for judicial relief. That is, the state court concluded there was no violation of state or national law alleged in the various applications. It spoke of the fact that no "current of sufficient intensity to cause death" passed through petitioner's body. It referred specifically to the fact that the applications of petitioner invoked the provisions of the Louisiana Constitution against cruel and inhuman punishments and putting one in jeopardy of life or liberty twice for the same offense. We granted certiorari on a petition setting forth the aforementioned contentions, to consider the alleged violations of rights under the Federal Constitution in the unusual circumstances of this case. 328 U.S. 833. For matters of state law, the opinion and order of the Supreme Court of Louisiana are binding on this Court, Hebert

v. Louisiana, 272 *U.S.* 312, 317. *So far as we are aware, this case
is without precedent in any court.*

To determine whether or not the execution of the petitioner
may fairly take place after the experience through which he
passed, we shall examine the circumstances under the assumption,
but without so deciding, that violation of the principles of the
Fifth and Eighth Amendments, as to double jeopardy and cruel
and unusual punishment, would be violative of the due process
clause of the Fourteenth Amendment. As nothing has been
brought to our attention to suggest the contrary, we must and do
assume that the state officials carried out their duties under the
death warrant in a careful and humane manner. Accidents
happen for which no man is to blame. We turn to the question
as to whether the proposed enforcement of the criminal law
of the state is offensive to any constitutional requirements to
which reference has been made.

FIRST. *Our minds rebel against permitting the same sovereignty to punish an accused twice for the same offense.* Ex parte
Lange, *18 Wall. 163, 168, 175;* In re Bradley, *318 U.S. 50. Compare* United States *v.* Lanza, *260 U.S. 377, 382. But where the
accused successfully seeks review of a conviction, there is no
double jeopardy upon a new trial.* United States *v.* Ball, *163 U.S.
662, 672.* See People *v.* Trezza, *128 N.Y. 529, 535, 28 N.E.
533. Even where a state obtains a new trial after conviction
because of errors, while an accused may be placed on trial a
second time, it is not the sort of hardship to the accused that is
forbidden by the Fourteenth Amendment.* Palko *v.* Connecticut,
*302 U.S. 319, 328. As this is a prosecution under state law, so far
as double jeopardy is concerned, the* Palko *case is decisive. For
we see no difference from a constitutional point of view between
a new trial for error of law at the instance of the state that results
in a death sentence instead of imprisonment for life and an execution that follows a failure of equipment. When an accident,
with no suggestion of malevolence, prevents the consummation
of a sentence, the state's subsequent course in the administration
of its criminal law is not affected on that account by any requirement of due process under the Fourteenth Amendment. We
find no double jeopardy here which can be said to amount to
a denial of federal due process in the proposed execution.*

SECOND. *We find nothing in what took place here which*

amounts to cruel and unusual punishment in the constitutional sense. The case before us does not call for an examination into any punishments except that of death. See Weems v. United States, 217 U.S. 349. The traditional humanity of modern Anglo-American law forbids the infliction of unnecessary pain in the execution of the death sentence. Prohibition against the wanton infliction of pain has come into our law from the Bill of Rights of 1688. The identical words appear in our Eighth Amendment. The Fourteenth would prohibit by its due process clause execution by a state in a cruel manner.

Petitioner's suggestion is that because he once underwent the psychological strain of preparation for electrocution, now to require him to undergo this preparation again subjects him to a lingering or cruel and unusual punishment. Even the fact that petitioner has already been subjected to a current of electricity does not make his subsequent execution any more cruel in the constitutional sense than any other execution. The cruelty against which the Constitution protects a convicted man is cruelty inherent in the method of punishment, not the necessary suffering involved in any method employed to extinguish life humanely. The fact that an unforeseeable accident prevented the prompt consummation of the sentence cannot, it seems to us, add an element of cruelty to a subsequent execution. There is no purpose to inflict unnecessary pain nor any unnecessary pain involved in the proposed execution. The situation of the unfortunate victim of this accident is just as though he had suffered the identical amount of mental anguish and physical pain in any other occurrence, such as, for example, a fire in the cell block. We cannot agree that the hardship imposed upon the petitioner rises to that level of hardship denounced as denial of due process because of cruelty.

THIRD. *The Supreme Court of Louisiana also rejected petitioner's contention that death inflicted after his prior sufferings would deny him the equal protection of the laws, guaranteed by the Fourteenth Amendment. This suggestion in so far as it differs from the due process argument is based on the idea that execution, after an attempt at execution has failed, would be a more severe punishment than is imposed upon others guilty of a like offense. That is, since others do not go through the strain of preparation for execution a second time or have not experienced a nonlethal current in a prior attempt at execution, as petitioner did, to compel petitioner to submit to execution after these prior experiences denies to him equal protection. Equal protection does not protect a prisoner against even illegal acts of officers in charge of him, much less against accidents during his detention for execution. See Lisenba v. California, 314 U.S. 219, 226. Laws cannot prevent accidents nor can a law equally protect all against them. So long as the law applies to all alike, the requirements of equal protection are met. We have no right to assume that Louisiana singled out Francis for a treatment other than that which has been or would generally be applied.*

.   ·   .   .   .   .

Affirmed.

MR. JUSTICE FRANKFURTER, *concurring.*

When four members of the Court find that a State has denied to a person the due process which the Fourteenth Amendment safeguards, it seems to me important to be explicit regarding the criteria by which the State's duty of obedience to the Constitution must be judged. Particularly is this so when life is at stake.

Until July 28, 1868, when the Fourteenth Amendment was ratified, the Constitution of the United States left the States free to carry out their own notions of criminal justice, except insofar as they were limited by Article I, § 10 of the Constitution which declares: "No State shall . . . pass any Bill of Attainder, [or] ex post facto Law. . . ." The Fourteenth Amendment placed no specific restraints upon the States in the formulation or the administration of their criminal law. It restricted the freedom of the States generally, so that States thereafter could not "abridge the privileges or immunities of citizens of the United States," or "deprive any person of life, liberty, or property, without due process of law," or "deny to any person within its jurisdiction the equal protection of the laws."

These are broad, inexplicit clauses of the Constitution, unlike specific provisions of the first eight amendments formulated by the Founders to guard against recurrence of well-defined historic grievances. But broad as these clauses are, they are not generalities of empty vagueness. They are circumscribed partly by history and partly by the problems of government, large and dynamic though they be, with which they are concerned. The "privileges or immunities of citizens of the United States" concern the dual citizenship under our federal system. The safeguards of "due process of law" and "the equal protection of the laws" summarize the meaning of the struggle for freedom of English-speaking peoples. They run back to Magna Carta but contemplate no less advances in the conceptions of justice and freedom by a progressive society. See the classic language of Mr. Justice Matthews in Hurtado v. California, *110 U.S. 516, 530–31.*

When, shortly after its adoption, the Fourteenth Amendment came before this Court for construction, it was urged that the "privileges or immunities of citizens of the United States" which were not to be abridged by any State were the privileges and immunities which citizens theretofore enjoyed under the Constitution. If that view had prevailed, the Privileges or Immunities Clause of the Fourteenth Amendment would have placed upon the States the limitations which the specific articles of the first eight amendments had theretofore placed upon the agencies of the national government. After the fullest consideration that view was rejected. The rejection has the authority that comes from contemporaneous knowledge of the purposes of the Fourteenth Amendment. See Slaughter-House Cases, *16 Wall. 36, 67–68;* Davidson v. New Orleans, *96 U.S. 97. The notion that the Privileges or Immunities Clause of the Fourteenth Amendment absorbed, as it is called, the provisions of the Bill of Rights that limit the Federal Government has never been given countenance by this Court.*

Not until recently was it suggested that the Due Process Clause of the Fourteenth Amendment was merely a compendious reference to the Bill of Rights whereby the States were now restricted in devising and enforcing their penal code precisely as is the Federal Government by the first eight amendments. On this view, the States would be confined in the enforcement of their criminal codes by those views for safeguarding the rights of the individual which were deemed necessary in the eighteenth century. Some of these safeguards have perduring validity. Some grew out of transient experience or formulated remedies which time might well improve. The

Fourteenth Amendment did not mean to imprison the States into the limited experience of the eighteenth century. It did mean to withdraw from the States the right to act in ways that are offensive to a decent respect for the dignity of man, and heedless of his freedom.

These are very broad terms by which to accommodate freedom and authority. As has been suggested from time to time, they may be too large to serve as the basis for adjudication, in that they allow much room for individual notions of policy. That is not our concern. The fact is that the duty of such adjudication on a basis no less narrow has been committed to this Court.

In an impressive body of decision this Court has decided that the Due Process Clause of the Fourteenth Amendment expresses a demand for civilized standards which are not defined by the specifically enumerated guarantees of the Bill of Rights. They neither contain the particularities of the first eight amendments nor are they confined to them. . . .

. . . .

Once we are explicit in stating the problem before us in terms defined by an unbroken series of decisions, we cannot escape acknowledging that it involves the application of standards of fairness and justice very broadly conceived. They are not the application of merely personal standards but the impersonal standards of society which alone judges, as the organs of Law, are empowered to enforce. When the standards for judicial judgment are not narrower than "immutable principles of justice which inhere in the very idea of free government," Holden v. Hardy, 169 U.S. 366, 389, *"fundamental principles of liberty and justice which lie at the base of all our civil and political institutions,"* Hebert v. Louisiana, 272 U.S. 312, 316, *"immunities . . . implicit in the concept of ordered liberty,"* Palko v. Connecticut, supra, at 324–25, *great tolerance toward a State's conduct is demanded of this Court. . . .*

I cannot bring myself to believe that for Louisiana to leave to executive clemency, rather than to require, mitigation of a sentence of death duly pronounced upon conviction for murder because a first attempt to carry it out was an innocent misadventure, offends a principle of justice "rooted in the traditions and conscience of our people." See Snyder v. Massachusetts

[*291 U.S. 97, 105*]. *Short of the compulsion of such a principle, this Court must abstain from interference with State action no matter how strong one's personal feeling of revulsion against a State's insistence on its pound of flesh. One must be on guard against finding in personal disapproval a reflection of more or less prevailing condemnation. Strongly drawn as I am to some of the sentiments expressed by my brother* BURTON, *I cannot rid myself of the conviction that were I to hold that Louisiana would transgress the Due Process Clause if the State were allowed, in the precise circumstances before us to carry out the death sentence, I would be enforcing my private view rather than that consensus of society's opinion which, for purposes of due process, is the standard enjoined by the Constitution.*

The fact that I reach this conclusion does not mean that a hypothetical situation, which assumes a series of abortive attempts at electrocution or even a single, cruelly willful attempt, would not raise different questions. When the Fourteenth Amendment first came here for application the Court abstained from venturing even a tentative definition of due process. With wise forethought it indicated that what may be found within or without the Due Process Clause must inevitably be left to "the gradual process of judicial inclusion and exclusion, as the cases presented for decision shall require, with the reasoning on which such decisions may be founded." Davidson v. New Orleans, supra, at 104. This is another way of saying that these are matters which depend on "differences of degree. The whole law does so as soon as it is civilized." Holmes, J., in LeRoy Fibre Co. v. Chicago, M. & St. P. R. Co., 232 U.S. 340, 354. Especially is this so as to questions arising under the Due Process Clause. A finding that in this case the State of Louisiana has not gone beyond its powers is for me not the starting point for abstractly logical extension. Since I cannot say that it would be "repugnant to the conscience of mankind," Palko v. Connecticut, supra, at 323, for Louisiana to exercise the power on which she here stands, I cannot say that the Constitution withholds it.

MR. JUSTICE BURTON, *with whom* MR. JUSTICE DOUGLAS, MR. JUSTICE MURPHY *and* MR. JUSTICE RUTLEDGE *concur, dissenting.*

Under circumstances unique in judicial history, the relator asks this Court to stay his execution on the ground that it will violate the due process of law guaranteed to him by the Constitution of the United States. . . .

.   .   .   .   .

The capital case before us presents an instance of the violation of constitutional due process that is more clear than would be presented by many lesser punishments prohibited by the Eighth Amendment or its state counterparts. Taking human life by unnecessarily cruel means shocks the most fundamental instincts of civilized man. It should not be possible under the constitutional procedure of a self-governing people. Abhorrence of the cruelty of ancient forms of capital punishment has increased steadily until, today, some states have prohibited capital punishment altogether. It is unthinkable that any state legislature in modern times would enact a statute expressly authorizing capital punishment by repeated applications of an electric current separated by intervals of days or hours until finally death shall result. The Legislature of Louisiana did not do so. The Supreme Court of Louisiana did not say that it did. The Supreme Court of Louisiana said merely that the pending petitions for relief in this case presented an executive rather than a judicial question. . . .

.   .   .   .   .

Executive clemency provides a common means of avoiding unconstitutional or otherwise questionable executions. When, however, the unconstitutionality of proposed executive procedure is brought before this Court, as in this case, we should apply the constitutional protection. In this case, final recourse is had to the high trusteeship vested in this Court by the people of the United States over the constitutional process by which their own lives may be taken.[53]

Justice Rutledge, together with Justices Douglas and Murphy, joined Justice Burton in dissent. But Justice Rutledge's papers disclose that he also drafted a separate dissent which he never filed. That dissent follows:

MR. JUSTICE RUTLEDGE, *dissenting.*

No one would hold, I think, that Louisiana would be free deliberately to place a convicted man in the electric chair, turn on the current, cut it off before death, remove him and later re-

*electrocute him. That would be sheer torture. Due process out-
laws this barbarism in our scheme, whether as contravening the
most elementary standards of decency in dealing with persons
charged with crime,* Malinski v. New York, 324 U.S. *401, or as
incorporating the commands against cruel and unusual punishments and punishing a man twice for the same offense. See* In re
Kemmler, 136 U.S. 436. *Here this trinity comes to the same
thing:*

*I do not think the element of torture is removed because the
state acts carelessly rather than deliberately. This is the crucial
question. The majority say the failure was due to accident. I
find no basis for this view in the record, except that the failure
was not intended or foreseen. Even so, it was not shown to be
due to causes over which the state had no control. Its duty is to
see that such failures do not occur. It has no right to take
chances with faulty or antique equipment, low current or any
other risk likely to produce such horror. Torture, for the victim,
is not a matter of the executioner's state of mind. It may be inflicted as much by carelessness and bungling or taking a chance
as by design. The facts of this electrocution are more consistent
with such a cause than any other, if only by the absence of any
showing that the failure was due to factors beyond the state's
control. That showing at the least should be compelled in such
a case as this, before a second or perchance a third electrocution
is attempted.*

*I do not think the states are free to take chances in any way
with such a consequence as took place here. I am unwilling to
indulge the presumption on this record that it did not do so.
Men's lives should not hang upon a thread so slender. I know of
no way to force the states to forego such risks and the horrors
both of cruel and of multiple punishments they entail, other
than by applying strictly the constitutional prohibitions against
them. Willie Francis cannot be electrocuted again without
undergoing a second time the death pangs he already has
suffered and which now I think the state has no right to re-
inflict. Needless to add, I am in substantial agreement with the
views expressed by my brothers,* MURPHY *[apparently a reference to a draft dissent prepared by Justice Frank Murphy, and
likewise never filed]* and BURTON.

The foregoing draft opinion by Justice Rutledge first came to public view on January 8, 1965. It appeared in a deeply perceptive study of the Justice entitled *Justice Rutledge and the Bright Constellation*, written by the late Fowler V. Harper, an old friend of the Justice's and a distinguished law teacher and legal scholar. Professor Harper's book was published on the very day Professor Harper died. In an addendum to the Justice's draft opinion, Professor Harper commented:

[Although the *Francis* case is referred to as without precedent in Anglo-American law, the statement is not entirely accurate. At least there was a close analogy in the execution of Captain Kidd in 1701 by hanging. It is reported authoritatively that "the rope broke and he had to be raised from the ground and hanged again."][54]

A month after the Supreme Court's decision, Willie Francis was again executed, this time successfully.

In the summer of 1950, three years after the decision in *Francis v. Resweber*, Justice Frankfurter, who was vacationing in England, was invited to appear as a witness at hearings being conducted by the Royal Commission on Capital Punishment. The Royal Commission was, of course, particularly interested in getting Frankfurter to comment on the American experience with capital punishment. There follows an excerpt from his testimony:

Sir Ernest Gowers: Has either the electric chair or the gas chamber shown itself to be open to any marked objections?

Mr. Justice Frankfurter: . . . We had a very interesting case two or three years ago, a case that told on my conscience a good deal. This was the case of poor Willie Francis, a young coloured fellow convicted of murder. There was no question about his guilt. He went to the electric chair and there was some mischance by which the current or something went wrong, something mechanical; there was no negligence. His counsel then tried to prevent execution and said that on various grounds it would be "cruel and unusual punishment," and, as such, violation of due process. Various objections were put forward and questions arose as to whether it would be a denial of due process, that is, contrary to fundamental principles common to the English-speaking world, to try to execute a man after the first attempt had failed. The Court held that if that is what

Louisiana wants to do, that is for Louisiana to do, so far as the United States Constitution goes. I was very much bothered by the problem, it offended my personal sense of decency to do this. Something inside of me was very unhappy, but I did not see that it violated due process of law. This problem has arisen several times in your history. It was raised in the House of Commons by Harcourt, who had been Home Secretary in the '80's or '90's, and he was outraged by it. I believe it is the law of England, is it not, that if there are two mischances you cannot do it the third time, but you can go wrong twice—or is it thrice?

Sir Alexander Maxwell: I do not think there is any law, but I do seem to remember a case in which the Home Secretary ordered a reprieve because something had gone wrong.

Mr. Justice Frankfurter: There was a full dress debate in Harcourt's time. It was a very interesting debate, and there was the same feeling of revulsion. Sir William Harcourt, I think it was, made a powerful speech, he was outraged by it, as also were others, and there was a reprieve because the third time the rope went wrong again. I mention that because that is the only incident that has come to my knowledge, and I spent quite a good deal of time trying to find out whether there was any dissatisfaction about the electric chair. I think that is accepted now. Hanging is still the mode of execution in some States. I do not know how many States still have hanging. I think on the whole American feeling is strongly against hanging.

Sir Ernest Gowers: What about the gas chamber?

Mr. Justice Frankfurter: I do not know about that. How many States have that, do you happen to know?

Sir Ernest Gowers: Electrocution is used by 22. Eleven use hanging, 8 use lethal gas and in Utah the man has the choice between hanging and shooting. Do you know why electrocution was first substituted for hanging?

Mr. Justice Frankfurter: It was deemed to be quicker, more merciful and to give less opportunity for mischance. It was contested as to its validity, as a matter of due process or in relation to the ex post facto clause of our Constitution. Everything seems to come before the Supreme Court, from the validity of a treaty of peace to whether or not electrocution instead of hanging is such a disadvantageous change in the termination of a life that a prisoner had a right to object to it.[55]

To the extent that one can make any prophecies about the constitutional process, it is probably safe to predict that the thesis advanced by Justices Black and Douglas in *Adamson*—that each of the rights embodied in the Bill of Rights is incorporated in the Fourteenth Amendment—will never gain a Court majority. Justices Murphy and Rutledge, who were substantially aligned with Justices Black and Douglas, both died in 1949, a little more than two years after *Adamson*. (Justices Murphy and Rutledge disagreed with Justices Black and Douglas in the limited sense that they were willing to go farther: they felt that the Fourteenth Amendment also protected other rights not specifically enumerated in the Bill of Rights or elsewhere in the Constitution.) Since 1949, all the Justices composing the *Adamson* majority have died or retired—the last was Justice Frankfurter, who retired in 1962 and died in 1965. But Justices Black and Douglas seem to have won no doctrinal converts among the newer members of the Court. Thus, in 1961, Justice William J. Brennan, Jr., a recent appointee whose demonstrated concern with promoting fairness in the criminal process must have led him to give sympathetic attention to the Black-Douglas position, reviewed the debate from *Palko* forward and concluded, "With all respect, I think that Mr. Justice Cardozo's analysis is more accurate."[56]

On the other hand, although their particular formula has failed of adoption, Justices Black and Douglas have in recent years been increasingly influential in bringing Justice Brennan, Chief Justice Earl Warren, and, during his brief tenure, Justice Arthur J. Goldberg (Justice Frankfurter's successor)—and, on occasion, the Court as a whole—to take a more comprehensive view of the personal rights which are so fundamental as to warrant inclusion in the Fourteenth Amendment. And this trend has been especially evident in the Court's meticulous scrutiny of state criminal convictions.

In 1961, for example, a divided Court, departing from its prior rule, held that a state criminal conviction could not be permitted to stand if evidence secured by illegal police measures (such as breaking into the defendant's house without a warrant) had been admitted at the trial (*Mapp v. Ohio*).[57] In 1963, the Court—this time unanimously, but with some disagreement on the rationale—overturned another major precedent in holding that the states are required to provide indigent defendants with counsel not merely in capital cases but in all serious criminal cases (*Gideon v. Wainwright*).[58] And in 1964, the Court—once again divided—overruled the *Adamson* holding by deciding that a criminal defendant in a state court is protected by the privilege against self-incrimination (*Malloy v. Hogan*).[59] The noteworthy fact is that Justice Brennan's opinion for the Court in *Malloy v. Hogan* did not purport to adopt the rationale which Justices Black and Douglas had advanced in their *Adamson* dissent. The following paragraphs form the core of Justice Brennan's opinion in *Malloy v. Hogan*:

The extent to which the Fourteenth Amendment prevents state invasion of rights enumerated in the first eight Amendments has been considered in numerous cases in this Court since the Amendment's adoption in 1868. Although many Justices have deemed the Amendment to incorporate all eight of the Amendments, the view which has thus far prevailed dates from the decision in 1897 in Chicago, B. & Q. R. Co. v. Chicago, 166 U.S. 226, *which held that the Due Process Clause requires the States to pay just compensation for private property taken for public use. It was on the authority of that decision that the Court said in 1908 in* Twining v. New Jersey, supra, *that "it is possible that some of the personal rights safeguarded by the first eight Amendments against National action may also be safeguarded against state action, because a denial of them would be a denial of due process of law." 211 U.S., at 99.*

The Court has not hesitated to re-examine past decisions according the Fourteenth Amendment a less central role in the preservation of basic liberties than that which was contemplated by its Framers when they added the Amendment to our constitutional scheme. Thus, although the Court as late as 1922 said that "neither the Fourteenth Amendment nor any other provision of the Constitution of the United States imposes upon the States any restrictions about 'freedom of speech' . . . ," Prudential Ins. Co. v. Cheek, 259 U.S. 530, 543, *three years later* Gitlow v. New York, 268 U.S. 652, *initiated a series of decisions which today holds immune from state invasion every First Amendment protection for the cherished rights of mind and spirit—the freedoms of speech, press, religion, assembly, association, and petition for redress of grievances.*

Similarly, Palko *v.* Connecticut, 302 *U.S.* 319, *decided in 1938, suggested that the rights secured by the Fourth Amendment, were not protected against state action, citing at 302 U.S. 324, the statement of the Court in 1914 in* Weeks *v.* United States, 232 *U.S.* 383, 398, *that "the Fourth Amendment is not directed to individual misconduct of [state] officials." In 1961, however, the Court held that in the light of later decisions, it was taken as settled that ". . . the Fourth Amendment's right of privacy has been declared enforceable against the States through the Due Process Clause of the Fourteenth. . . ."* Mapp *v.* Ohio, 367 *U.S.* 643, 655. *Again, although the Court held in 1942 that in a state prosecution for a noncapital offense, "appointment of counsel is not a fundamental right,"* Betts *v.* Brady, 316 *U.S.* 455, 471; *cf.* Powell *v.* Alabama, 287 *U.S.* 45, *only last Term this decision was re-examined and it was held that provision of counsel in all criminal cases was "a fundamental right essential to a fair trial," and thus was made obligatory on the States by the Fourteenth Amendment.* Gideon *v.* Wainwright, 372 *U.S.* 335, 344–345.

We hold today that the Fifth Amendment's exception from compulsory self-incrimination is also protected by the Fourteenth Amendment against abridgment by the States. Decisions of the Court since Twining *and* Adamson *have departed from the contrary view expressed in those cases. . . .*

Brown *v.* Mississippi, 297 *U.S.* 278, *was the first case in which the Court held that the Due Process Clause prohibited the States from using the accused's coerced confessions against him. The Court in* Brown *felt impelled, in light of* Twining, *to say that its conclusion did not involve the privilege against self-incrimination. "Compulsion by torture to extort a confession is a different matter."* 297 *U.S.* 285. *But this distinction was soon abandoned, and today the admissibility of a confession in a state criminal prosecution is tested by the same standard applied in federal prosecutions since 1897, when, in* Bram *v.* United States, 168 *U.S.* 532, *the Court held that "In criminal trials, in the courts of the United States, wherever a question arises whether a confession is incompetent because not voluntary, the issue is controlled by that portion of the Fifth Amendment to the Constitution of the United States, commanding that no person 'shall be* compelled in any criminal case to be a witness against himself.'" Id., at 542. . . .

The marked shift to the federal standard in state cases began with Lisenba v. California, 314 U.S. 219, where the Court spoke of accused's "free choice to admit, to deny, or to refuse to answer." Id., at 241. See Ashcraft v. Tennessee, 322 U.S. 143; Malinski v. New York, 324 U.S. 401; Spano v. New York, 360 U.S. 315; Lynumn v. Illinois, 372 U.S. 528; Haynes v. Washington, 373 U.S. 503. The shift reflects recognition that the American system of criminal prosecution is accusatorial, not inquisitorial, and that the Fifth Amendment privilege is its essential mainstay. Rogers v. Richmond, 365 U.S. 534, 541. Governments, state and federal, are thus constitutionally compelled to establish guilt by evidence independently and freely secured, and may not by coercion prove a charge against an accused out of his own mouth. . . . The Fourteenth Amendment secures against state invasion the same privilege that the Fifth Amendment guarantees against federal infringement—the right of a person to remain silent unless he chooses to speak in the unfettered exercise of his own will, and to suffer no penalty, as held in Twining, for such silence.

This conclusion is fortified by our recent decision in Mapp v. Ohio, 367 U.S. 643, overruling Wolf v. Colorado, supra, which had held "that in a prosecution in a state court for a state crime the Fourteenth Amendment does not forbid the admission of evidence obtained by an unreasonable search and seizure," 338 U.S., at 33. Mapp held that the Fifth Amendment privilege against self-incrimination implemented the Fourth Amendment in such cases, and that the two guarantees of personal security conjoined in the Fourteenth Amendment to make the exclusionary rule obligatory upon the States. . . .[60]

Justice Harlan, dissenting with Justice Clark, saw Justice Brennan's opinion in Malloy v. Hogan as a sort of Adamson dissent in disguise:

I can only read the Court's opinion as accepting in fact what it rejects in theory: the application to the States, via the Fourteenth Amendment, of the forms of federal criminal procedure embodied within the first eight Amendments to the Constitution. . . .[61]

Notwithstanding this observation, it is hard to suppose that any present member of the Supreme Court sees any likelihood that the Court would actually accept and implement the logic of the *Adamson* dissent. For it is a logic which would, for example, seem to mean that every state would be constitutionally required to emulate the federal criminal process by preserving in perpetuity the process of indictment by a grand jury and trial by a petit jury as inalienable rights of the accused in a state criminal trial. Indeed, the same logic would seem to run beyond criminal cases: it would apparently require the maintenance in state courts of the right, which the Seventh Amendment preserves in federal courts, to a jury trial in all civil actions involving more than twenty dollars. Of course many lawyers and judges think that the maintenance of these familiar institutions is desirable. But many others think that modification of at least some of these institutions is appropriate, and perhaps vital, to increase the effectiveness of our state judicial systems. This being so, it would require a boldness bordering on arrogance to insist on a federal constitutional rule which withheld from the states the power to make any significant departures from the forms of criminal and civil trials laid down for federal courts in 1791.

Accordingly, the fair presumption is that the focus of the Supreme Court's attention will continue to be on the central question of whether, in any given setting, a particular mode of trial or of punishment is compatible with prevalent standards of basic fairness.[62]

In the context of this form of constitutional inquiry, it is hard to see how any fundamental question of federal constitutional law would be presented if, for example, New York or North Carolina decided, by way of experimental innovation, to dispense with the right to a jury trial in civil suits involving less than five hundred dollars.

On the other hand, this form of constitutional inquiry leaves open for consideration the question whether practices which have been customary for decades and centuries must, merely by virtue of their familiarity, be regarded as compatible with today's standards of fairness. Thus, to put a concrete issue, it may be anticipated that capital punishment—an historic and widespread incident of the criminal process—will in ensuing years come under more and more searching constitutional inquiry. A sign of more probing judicial concern appeared in 1963, in two capital cases which the Court declined to review. Former Justice Goldberg, joined by Justices Douglas and Brennan, filed an opinion protesting the denials of certiorari:

> *I would grant certiorari in this case and in Snider v. Cunningham, 84 S. Ct. 154, to consider whether the Eighth and Fourteenth Amendments to the United States Constitution permit the imposition of the death penalty on a convicted rapist who has neither taken nor endangered human life.*
>
> *The following questions,* inter alia, *seem relevant and worthy of argument and consideration:*
>
> *(1) In light of the trend both in this country and throughout the world against punishing rape by death, does the imposition of the death penalty by those States which retain it for rape violate "evolving standards of decency that mark the progress of [our] maturing society," or "standards of decency more or less universally accepted"?*
>
> *(2) Is the taking of human life to protect a value other than human life consistent with the constitutional proscription against "punishments which by their excessive . . . severity are greatly disproportioned to the offenses charged"?*
>
> *(3) Can the permissible aims of punishment (e.g., deterrence, isolation, rehabilitation) be achieved as effectively by punishing rape less severely than by death (e.g., by life imprisonment); if so, does the imposition of the death penalty for rape constitute "unnecessary cruelty"?*[63]

Justice Goldberg was proposing to explore the constitutionality of "the taking of human life to protect a value other than human life. . . ." But beyond his proposed inquiry looms a larger question: How long can a civilized community justify the imposition of capital punishment even to protect human life? The imminence and urgency of that question have been heightened as more and more Western nations have abandoned the death sentence even for the crime of murder. Most recently Great Britain has decided to follow suit, leaving France and Spain as the only European nations which retain capital punishment for murder.[64] In this respect the European concept of due process of law would seem to be far in advance of that prevailing in the United States, where only nine of the fifty states have disavowed the death sentence.[65]

There can be no doubt that the questions posed by Justice Goldberg, and cognate questions testing whether "the punishment fits the crime," will come before the Court with greater frequency and greater urgency in future cases. Those future cases will, one by one, give further dimension to the unfolding concept of due process of law. In that process of case-by-case development the process which is the very heart of constitutional adjudication—the arid controversy stirred by the *Adamson* dissent will seem less and less consequential. Recapitulating the doctrinal positions so heatedly espoused by the various Justices back in the late 1940s will become a largely academic exercise. The fit analogy will then become, as Professor Paul A. Freund once prophesied, the anecdote "of the Irish cleric who was asked by a parishioner what the difference was between the cherubim and seraphim, and who answered, 'I think that there was once a difference between them, but they have made it up.' "[66]

d. Insistence that the state prove its case

Occasionally, as in *Gideon v. Wainwright*, the Court is unanimous in its condemnation of state criminal procedure. Another recent example of this is *Thompson v. Louisville*, set forth below. *Thompson v. Louisville* is also remarkable for reasons other than its unanimity. It is believed to be the first case, in the ninety-odd years since the adoption of the Fourteenth Amendment, in which the Supreme Court set aside a state court conviction for the very simple reason that the state had adduced no evidence of the offense charged. Beyond this, the case is remarkable because of its very humdrum nature. It is not a murder or rape case, in which a life sentence, or even execution, hangs in the balance. It is a case in which the accused was convicted of loitering and of disorderly conduct, and in which the punishment was a twenty-dollar fine. It was a police court case of such surpassing ordinariness that no higher court had power to review the conviction. No court, that is, except the Supreme Court of the United States, which thereby evinced its purpose to make the due process of law meaningful throughout the United States at all levels of criminal justice. The opinion in *Thompson v. Louisville* follows:

MR. JUSTICE BLACK *delivered the opinion of the Court.*

Petitioner was found guilty in the Police Court of Louisville, Kentucky, of two offenses—loitering and disorderly conduct. The ultimate question presented to us is whether the charges against petitioner were so totally devoid of evidentiary support as to render his conviction unconstitutional under the Due Process Clause of the Fourteenth Amendment. Decision of this question turns not on the sufficiency of the evidence, but on whether this conviction rests upon any evidence at all.

The facts as shown by the record are short and simple. Petitioner, a long-time resident of the Louisville area, went into the Liberty End Cafe about 6:20 on a Saturday evening, January 24, 1959. In addition to selling food, the cafe was licensed to sell beer to the public and some 12 to 30 patrons were present during the time petitioner was there. When petitioner had been in the cafe about half an hour, two Louisville police officers came in on a "routine check." Upon seeing petitioner "out there on the floor dancing by himself," one of the officers, according to his testimony, went up to the manager who was sitting on a stool nearby and asked him how long petitioner had been in there and if he had bought anything. The officer testified that upon being told by the manager that petitioner had been there "a little over a half-hour and that he had not bought anything," he accosted Thompson and "asked him what was his reason for being in there and he said he was waiting on a bus." The officer then informed petitioner that he was under arrest and took him outside. This was the arrest for loitering. After going outside, the officer testified, petitioner "was very argumentative—he argued with us back and forth and so then we placed a disorderly conduct charge on him." Admittedly the disorderly conduct conviction rests solely on this one sentence description of petitioner's conduct after he left the cafe.

The foregoing evidence includes all that the city offered against him, except a record purportedly showing a total of 54 previous arrests of petitioner. Before putting on his defense, petitioner moved for a dismissal of the charges against him on the ground that a judgment of conviction on this record would deprive him of property and liberty without due process of law under the Fourteenth Amendment in that (1) there was no evidence to support findings of guilt and (2) the two arrests and prosecutions were reprisals against him because petitioner had employed counsel and demanded a judicial hearing to defend himself against prior and allegedly baseless charges by the police. This motion was denied.

Petitioner then put in evidence on his own behalf, none of which in any way strengthened the city's case. . . . At the close of his evidence, petitioner repeated his motion for dismissal of the charges on the ground that a conviction on the foregoing evidence would deprive him of liberty and property without due process under the Fourteenth Amendment. The court denied the motion, convicted him of both offenses, and fined him $10 on each charge. . . .

. . . .

Our examination of the record presented in the petition for certiorari convinced us that although the fines here are small, the due process questions presented are substantial and we therefore granted certiorari to review the police court's judgments. 360 U.S. 916. Compare Yick Wo v. Hopkins, *118 U.S. 356 (San Francisco Police Judges Court judgment imposing a $10 fine, upheld by state appellate court, reversed as in contravention of the Fourteenth Amendment).*

The city correctly assumes here that if there is no support for these convictions in the record they are void as denials of due process. The pertinent portion of the city ordinance under which petitioner was convicted of loitering reads as follows:

> *It shall be unlawful for any person . . . , without visible means of support, or who cannot give a satisfactory account of himself, . . . to sleep, lie, loaf, or trespass in or about any premises, building, or other structure in the City of Louisville, without first having obtained the consent of the owner or controller of said premises, structure, or building; . . . § 85–12, Ordinances of the City of Louisville.*

In addition to the fact that petitioner proved he had "visible means of support," the prosecutor at trial said "This is a loitering charge here. There is no charge of no visible means of support." Moreover, there is no suggestion that petitioner was sleeping, lying or trespassing in or about this cafe. Accordingly he could only have been convicted for being unable to give a satisfactory account of himself while loitering in the cafe, without the con-

*sent of the manager. Under the words of the ordinance itself, if
the evidence fails to prove all three elements of this loitering
charge, the conviction is not supported by evidence, in which
event it does not comport with due process of law. The record is
entirely lacking in evidence to support any of the charges.*

*Here, petitioner spent about half an hour on a Saturday
evening in January in a public cafe which sold food and beer to
the public. When asked to account for his presence there, he said
he was waiting for a bus. The city concedes that there is no
law making it an offense for a person in such a cafe to "dance,"
"shuffle" or "pat" his feet in time to music. The undisputed testimony of the manager, who did not know whether petitioner had
bought macaroni and beer or not but who did see the patting,
shuffling or dancing, was that petitioner was welcome there. The
manager testified that he did not at any time during petitioner's
stay in the cafe object to anything petitioner was doing and that
he never saw petitioner do anything that would cause any objection. Surely this is implied consent, which the city admitted
in oral argument satisfies the ordinance. The arresting officer
admitted that there was nothing in any way "vulgar" about
what he called petitioner's "ordinary dance," whatever relevance, if any, vulgarity might have to a charge of loitering.
There simply is no semblance of evidence from which any person could reasonably infer that petitioner could not give a satisfactory account of himself or that he was loitering or loafing
there (in the ordinary sense of the words) without "the consent
of the owner or controller" of the cafe.*

*Petitioner's conviction for disorderly conduct was under
§ 85–8 of the city ordinance which, without definition, provides
that "[w]hoever shall be found guilty of disorderly conduct in
the City of Louisville shall be fined. . . ." etc. The only evidence of "disorderly conduct" was the single statement of the
policeman that after petitioner was arrested and taken out of
the cafe he was very argumentative. There is no testimony that
petitioner raised his voice, used offensive language, resisted the
officers or engaged in any conduct of any kind likely in any way
to adversely affect the good order and tranquillity of the City of
Louisville. The only information the record contains on what
the petitioner was "argumentative" about is his statement that
he asked the officers "what they arrested me for." We assume,*

for we are justified in assuming, that merely "arguing" with a policeman is not, because it could not be "disorderly conduct" as a matter of the substantive law of Kentucky. See Lanzetta v. New Jersey, *306 U.S. 451. Moreover, Kentucky law itself seems to provide that if a man wrongfully arrested fails to object to the arresting officer, he waives any right to complain later that the arrest was unlawful.* Nickell v. Commonwealth, *285 S.W.2d 495, 496.*

Thus we find no evidence whatever in the record to support these convictions. Just as "Conviction upon a charge not made would be sheer denial of due process," [De Jonge v. Oregon, *299 U.S. 353, 362] so is it a violation of due process to convict and punish a man without evidence of his guilt.*

The judgments are reversed and the cause is remanded to the Police Court of the City of Louisville for proceedings not inconsistent with this opinion.

Reversed and remanded.[67]

e. Insistence that the state's proof of guilt be lawfully obtained

One of the enduring contributions to the quality of American criminal justice was initiated by President Herbert Hoover. He instructed his Attorney General, George Wickersham, to conduct an investigation of major issues affecting law observance and law enforcement. High on the Wickersham Commission's agenda of matters to be investigated was a grave malady infecting the American legal process—the readiness of many prosecutors and many police officers to overstep the bounds of legal behavior in their desire to obtain criminal convictions.

The Wickersham Commission turned the problem over to a law professor, Zechariah Chafee, Jr., and two practicing lawyers, Walter H. Pollak and Carl S. Stern, who prepared a report on *Lawlessness in Law Enforcement* which has become a classic in legal literature.

The malady that troubled President Hoover and the Wickersham Commission still persists. But it is a malady that is on the defensive. And this is so, in large measure, because for the last thirty years the Supreme Court has assumed a major role in the fight to keep law enforcement within legal bounds. The materials that follow (1) identify some of the prevalent types of official lawlessness, and (2) illustrate the Court's method in dealing with these issues. It will be seen that the approach taken by the Court conforms closely to the approach that the Wickersham Commission made explicit in its preface to *Lawlessness in Law Enforcement* more than three decades ago:

> *The widest inquiry into the shortcomings of the administration of justice, which the President enjoined upon this commission, necessarily involves the duty of investigating the justice of complaints, often made, that in their zeal to accomplish results Government officials themselves frequently lose sight of the fact that they are servants of the law, subject to its mandates and peculiarly charged with the duty to observe its spirit and its letter. They should always remember that there is no more sinister sophism than that the end justifies the employment of illegal means to bring offenders to justice. . . .*
>
> *. . . Respect for law, which is the fundamental prerequisite of law observance, hardly can be expected of people in general if the officers charged with enforcement of the law do not set the example of obedience to its precepts.*[68]

(1). *Illegal law enforcement*

(a) *Wiretapping.* Wiretapping, the tapping of telephone conversations in order to get evidence of crime, is not an *unconstitutional* mode of snooping.[69] But wiretapping is very likely to involve a trespass, a physical invasion of somebody's private home or office, and therefore becomes a crime under local law. In addition, the tapping of telephone conversations has been made a federal crime by Congress.[70]

Nevertheless, wiretapping is very commonly engaged in by law-enforcement officers.[71]

(b) *Unlawful searches and seizures.* Searching homes and offices without a warrant, in the hope of finding incriminating evidence, is an occasional practice of federal officials,[72] and a frequent practice of state officials.[73] This is so notwithstanding the facts that (1) the Fourth Amendment bars "unreasonable searches" by *federal* officials, and provides that "no Warrants shall issue, but upon probable cause, supported by Oath or affirmation, and particularly describing the place to be searched, and the person or things to be seized"; and (2) the Supreme

Court has held that the Fourteenth Amendment imposes these Fourth Amendment limitations on *state* officials as well.[74]

(c) *The "third degree."* The most obnoxious form of overzealous law enforcement is the "third degree." This is the practice, still widely employed by local police and prosecutors, of interrogating a suspect who is in police custody for hours on end until he confesses. In point of law, a suspect is not obliged to answer questions unless he wishes to do so. (The Fifth Amendment's self-incrimination clause provides that no federal prisoner "shall be compelled in any criminal case to be a witness against himself"; and the Supreme Court has held that this clause is, via the Fourteenth Amendment, binding on the states as well [*Malloy v. Hogan*]. Moreover, state constitutions have similar provisions.) But most people who have been arrested do not know this until a lawyer so informs them. And, typically, police and prosecutors are not anxious to tell a suspect of his right to stay silent, or even of his right to a lawyer, until he has told them what they want to know about the crime they are investigating.

Sometimes, of course, police questioning can be brief, courteous, and noncoercive. But this is only likely to be the case when the person under arrest is somebody of considerable status in the community—or when he has counsel with him while he is being questioned. Most people arrested for serious crimes are friendless and lawyerless and poorly educated people functioning in a marginal way at the edges of the community. They are ignorant of their legal rights (if they have been arrested before, they may have a false sense of legal sophistication) and tend to be easily intimidated by those wielding the law's authority.

Typically, therefore, police interrogation is an unequal battle. The suspect may, after long hours, confess out of sheer exhaustion.[75] Or, if he is abnormally impressionable, he may be induced to confess through subtle psychological manipulation.[76] Or he may even be subjected to outright physical torture.[77]

But it must be stressed that "third degree" tactics are not merely reprehensible in the sense that, like wiretapping or searches without a warrant, they are *unlawful.* "Third degree" tactics have the further characteristic of producing *untrustworthy* evidence. A police officer breaking into a home without a warrant may find heroin, or gambling slips—or he may find nothing. But if he finds heroin, or gambling slips, even though he had no real reason for suspecting they were there, he has actually come upon objects which may be evidence of criminal behavior. By contrast, a police officer who extracts a confession by beating up a suspect simply has a statement that was made just to avoid further pain. There is no intrinsic reason to assume it is a *true* statement.

(2). *The Supreme Court's response*

Faced with the lawless law-enforcement practices, what does the Supreme Court do? The Court is not itself a prosecuting agency, and therefore has no power to discipline the prosecutors and police who break the law. The Court can only work with a particular criminal conviction that comes before it, in which the defendant claims that his conviction is traceable to so gross an invasion of his rights as to justify setting aside his conviction. To revoke a criminal conviction is serious business, but it does not necessarily mean, as is frequently charged, that the accused goes scot free. What it means is that the state has a further opportunity to try the accused if it has sufficient evidence of guilt which has been obtained by lawful means.

(a) *The "third degree."* When the lawless acquisition of evidence is of the "third degree" variety, the Supreme Court unhesitatingly sets aside the challenged conviction as a denial of due process of law. And this, of course, is so whether the case arose in a federal or a state court.[78] In addition, in order to guard against incipient "third degree" tactics, even where the confession is not shown to be involuntary, the Court has for many years set aside *federal* criminal convictions (over which it feels it has a wider degree of supervisory control) whenever the accused is not brought before a federal committing magistrate, who will advise the accused of his rights, including his right to be silent and his right to counsel, as soon as he is arrested.[79] More recently, the Court has begun to insist that *state and city* police likewise desist from holding prisoners incommunicado, for extended periods of interrogation, before presenting them for arraignment and giving them access to counsel. This newly rigorous surveillance of the procedures commonly employed by state and city police (and commonly tolerated by state courts) has precipitated substantial complaint by local law-enforcement officials that the Supreme Court is hamstringing their efforts to detect and punish those guilty of major crimes. Some sense of this current controversy, and of what issues are at stake, is supplied by the following narrative of the ordeal of George Whitmore, Jr., "a slow-witted 19-year-old Negro drifter," reported by Sidney Zion in *The New York Times* in the spring of 1965:

At 7:30 A.M. on April 24, 1964, George Whitmore, Jr., a slow-witted 19-year-old Negro drifter with no previous arrest record, was ushered into the back room of a Brooklyn police station. Within 22 hours, he had confessed to one attempted rape and three murders—that of Mrs. Minnie Edmonds, a Brooklyn charwoman, and the double killing of career girls Janice Wylie and Emily Hoffert, New York's most sensational crime in recent years.

Now, after two trials, a reversed conviction (in the attempted-rape case), a hung jury (in the Edmonds murder) and, most recently, a dismissed indictment (in the Wylie-Hoffert case), the Whitmore affair has become a cause célèbre.

Already it has seriously undermined the credibility of the New York Police Department and stained the reputations of the Manhattan and Brooklyn District Attorneys' offices. And for the future it promises to have an important impact on the revolution in criminal law now being forged by the Supreme Court of the United States.

That revolution reached its present high point last June—two months after Whitmore's arrest—when the Court issued a devastating, if limited, attack on the use of the confession, which has been the backbone of law enforcement in the United States. The Justices were concerned with a Chicagoan named Danny Escobedo, who had been convicted in 1960 of murdering his brother-in-law. They reversed the conviction on the grounds that his confession, while voluntary, had been made after he had been denied permission to see his lawyer.

The ruling sent shock waves through the nation's prosecutors. From public platforms and in private interviews, they charged that the Court was "coddling the criminal element" and "swinging the pendulum too far" in favor of defendants' rights as against the public's safety. And then George Whitmore Jr. came along and rained on their parade.

In a long harangue directed at a reporter, one of the top assistants of Manhattan District Attorney Frank S. Hogan explained the connection between the Escobedo and Whitmore cases. "Let me give you the perfect example of the importance of confessions in law enforcement," he said, leaning across his desk. "This, more than anything else, will prove how unrealistic and naive the Court is."

His finger punched the air. "Whitmore! The Whitmore case. Do you know that we had every top detective on the Wylie-Hoffert murders and they couldn't find a clue. Not a clue!

"I tell you, if that kid hadn't confessed, we never would have caught the killer!"

Yet, last January, six months after this passionate statement, District Attorney Hogan dropped the charges against Whitmore for the Wylie-Hoffert murders (though the indictment was not quashed until May). In an affidavit filed in State Supreme Court he declared that Whitmore's confession had, upon investigation, been discredited. Shortly thereafter, another man, a drug addict, named Richard Robles, was indicted for the murders. It will be a long time before the public can accept a confession without thinking of George Whitmore, Jr.[79a]

(b) *Wiretapping.* With respect to wiretapping, which is not *unconstitutional* but which is today *illegal,* the Court has taken a far more modest position. *Federal* criminal convictions are set aside in those few cases—and they are very few—where the defendant can *prove* that the evidence against him was obtained by wiretapping.[80] State criminal convictions based on wiretapping are left undisturbed.[81]

(c) *Unlawful searches and seizures.* In 1914, the Supreme Court held, in *Weeks v. United States,*[82] that *federal* criminal convictions based on evidence secured by "unreasonable searches and seizures" (searches without a warrant, or where a warrant had been issued without "probable cause") had to be set aside.

In June of 1949, on the last day of the judicial year, the Supreme Court handed down its decision in the case of Dr. Julius A. Wolf, convicted by a Colorado court of conspiracy to commit abortion. Evidence heavily relied on by the prosecution in *Wolf v. Colorado* included Dr. Wolf's office diaries, taken from his office without a warrant. The court, speaking through Justice Frankfurter, started out as if to reverse Wolf's conviction:

The security of one's privacy against arbitrary intrusion by the police—which is at the core of the Fourth Amendment—is basic to a free society. It is therefore implicit in "the concept of ordered liberty" and as such enforceable against the States through the Due Process Clause.[83]

Nevertheless, Justice Frankfurter held, state courts were not required to follow the *Weeks* rule of excluding evidence acquired by "unreasonable searches and seizures." Justice Frankfurter noted that about a third of the states had adopted the *Weeks* rule on their own initiative. But he indicated doubt whether, even in federal cases, *Weeks* was a *constitutionally required* correlative of the Fourth Amendment rather than simply a judge-made rule of evidence. There are, Justice Frankfurter pointed out, other sanctions available, such as civil and criminal proceedings against the offending officers, to enforce the ban on "unreasonable searches and seizures." So:

Granting that in practice the exclusion of evidence may be an effective way of deterring unreasonable searches, it is not for this Court to condemn as falling below the minimal standards assured by the Due Process Clause a State's reliance upon other methods which, if consistently enforced, would be equally effective. . . .[84]

The senior Justice in point of service, Justice Black, who was on that day completing his twelfth Court term, filed a brief concurring opinion, building on what he had said two years before in the *Adamson* dissent.[85] His opinion was a reminder that he believed the touchstones of Fourteenth Amendment interpretation to be the specific provisions of the Bill of Rights, and not vague notions about "the concept of ordered liberty":

In this case petitioner was convicted of a crime in a state court on evidence obtained by a search and seizure conducted in a manner that this Court has held "unreasonable" and therefore in violation of the Fourth Amendment. And under a rule of evidence adopted by this Court evidence so obtained by federal officers cannot be used against defendants in federal courts. For reasons stated in my dissenting opinion in Adamson v. California, 332 U.S. 46, 68, I agree with the conclusion of the Court that the Fourth Amendment's prohibition of "unreasonable searches and seizures" is enforceable against the states. Consequently, I should be for reversal of this case if I thought the Fourth

Amendment not only prohibited "unreasonable searches and seizures," but also, of itself, barred the use of evidence so unlawfully obtained. But I agree with what appears to be a plain implication of the Court's opinion that the federal exclusionary rule is not a command of the Fourth Amendment but is a judicially created rule of evidence which Congress might negate.[86]

Justice Douglas, and the late Justices Murphy and Rutledge—the three Justices with whom Justice Black generally agreed on issues of criminal due process—dissented. Justice Murphy showed that in fact the victim of an unlawful search can almost never get redress: the only effective sanction, he argued, was to exclude the lawless evidence, thus removing the motivation for the lawless search. Justice Rutledge, in a separate dissenting opinion, put the matter this way:

"Wisdom too often never comes, and so one ought not to reject it merely because it comes late." Similarly, one should not reject a piecemeal wisdom, merely because it hobbles toward the truth with backward glances. Accordingly, although I think that all "the specific guarantees of the Bill of Rights should be carried over intact into the first section of the Fourteenth Amendment," Adamson v. California, 332 U.S. 46, *dissenting opinion at 124, I welcome the fact that the Court, in its slower progress toward this goal, today finds the substance of the Fourth Amendment "to be implicit in the concept of ordered liberty, and thus, through the Fourteenth Amendment, . . . valid as against the states."* Palko v. Connecticut, 302 U.S. 319, 325.

But I reject the Court's simultaneous conclusion that the mandate embodied in the Fourth Amendment, although binding on the states, does not carry with it the one sanction—exclusion of evidence taken in violation of the Amendment's terms—failure to observe which means that "the protection of the Fourth Amendment . . . might as well be stricken from the Constitution." Weeks v. United States, 232 U.S. 383, 393. *For I agree with my brother* MURPHY's *demonstration that the Amendment without the sanction is a dead letter. Twenty-nine years ago this Court, speaking through Justice Holmes, refused to permit the Government to subpoena documentary evidence which it had stolen, copied and then returned, for the reason that such a procedure "reduces the Fourth Amendment to a form of words."*

Silverthorne Lumber Co. v. United States, 251 *U.S.* 385, 392. *But the version of the Fourth Amendment today held applicable to the states hardly rises to the dignity of a form of words; at best it is a pale and frayed carbon copy of the original, bearing little resemblance to the Amendment the fulfillment of whose command I had heretofore thought to be "an indispensable need for a democratic society."* Harris v. United States, 331 *U.S.* 145, *dissenting opinion at 161.*

I also reject any intimation that Congress could validly enact legislation permitting the introduction in federal courts of evidence seized in violation of the Fourth Amendment. I had thought that issue settled by this Court's invalidation on dual grounds, in Boyd v. United States, 116 *U.S.* 616, *of a federal statute which in effect required the production of evidence thought probative by Government counsel—the Court there holding the statute to be "obnoxious to the prohibition of the Fourth Amendment of the Constitution, as well as of the Fifth."* Id. *at 632. See* Adams v. New York, 192 *U.S.* 585, 597, 598. *The view that the Fourth Amendment itself forbids the introduction of evidence illegally obtained in federal prosecutions is one of long standing and firmly established. See* Olmstead v. United States, 277 *U.S.* 438, 462. *It is too late in my judgment to question it now. . . .*

As Congress and this Court are, in my judgment, powerless to permit the admission in federal courts of evidence seized in defiance of the Fourth Amendment, so I think state legislators and judges—if subject to the Amendment, as I believe them to be—may not lend their offices to the admission in state courts of evidence thus seized. Compliance with the Bill of Rights betokens more than lip service.[87]

For a dozen years the Court operated under the *Wolf* rule. But the rule did not yield easy answers in all situations. In *Rochin v. California*, the Court reviewed a California state court conviction for possession of narcotics. Three deputy sheriffs, having no warrant, entered Antonio Rochin's home and forced their way into his bedroom. Rochin put two capsules in his mouth. The deputies grabbed Rochin and tried unsuccessfully to prevent him from swallowing. Then they rushed him to a hospital, where a doctor, administering a "stomach pump," forced Rochin to vomit up the crucial (and highly trustworthy) evidence.

Justice Frankfurter wrote for the Court in setting aside Rochin's conviction. Justice Frankfurter struggled mightily to analogize the case to that of a coerced confession:

. . . *[W]e are compelled to conclude that the proceedings by which this conviction was obtained do more than offend some fastidious squeamishness or private sentimentalism about combatting crime too energetically. This is conduct that shocks the conscience. Illegally breaking into the privacy of the petitioner, the struggle to open his mouth and remove what was there, the forcible extraction of his stomach's contents—this course of proceeding by agents of government to obtain evidence is bound to offend even hardened sensibilities. They are methods too close to the rack and the screw to permit of constitutional differentiation.*

. . . It would be a stultification of the responsibility which the course of constitutional history has cast upon this Court to hold that in order to convict a man the police cannot extract by force what is in his mind but can extract what is in his stomach.

To attempt in this case to distinguish what lawyers call "real evidence" from verbal evidence is to ignore the reasons for excluding coerced confessions. Use of involuntary verbal confessions in State criminal trials is constitutionally obnoxious not only because of their unreliability. They are inadmissible under the Due Process Clause even though statements contained in them may be independently established as true. Coerced confessions offend the community's sense of fair play and decency. So here, to sanction the brutal conduct which naturally enough was condemned by the court whose judgment is before us, would be to afford brutality the cloak of law. Nothing would be more calculated to discredit law and thereby to brutalize the temper of a society.[88]

Justice Black concurred in the Court's judgment.[89] But he felt that Justice Frankfurter's majority opinion, although reaching the right result, proceeded from a dangerous premise. He thought the Constitution did not confer on the Court the power to construe the Fourteenth Amendment in terms so "evanescent" and "accordion-like" as whether a particular practice "shocks the conscience." Justice Black found the California conviction bad because it violated the Fifth Amendment's self-incrimination clause, which he felt to be binding on the states for the reasons expressed in his *Adamson* dissent.

Two years later the Court considered another California case, *Irvine v. California.* Police, sneaking into Patrick Irvine's home in his absence, secreted microphones in his bedroom and elsewhere. With this they overheard conversations which were later introduced into evidence at Irvine's state trial for "making book" and related gambling offenses.

Four members of the Court—Justice Jackson wrote the opinion, and was joined by Chief Justice Warren, Justice Reed, and Justice Sherman Minton—felt that the case was controlled by *Wolf,* which meant that Irvine's conviction should be affirmed.[90] Four other members of the Court felt that *Rochin* controlled the case (Justice Frankfurter and Justice Burton relying on the Frankfurter view of *Rochin,* Justice Black and Justice Douglas relying on the Black view of *Rochin.*)

The casting vote was that of Justice Clark:

Had I been here in 1949 when Wolf *was decided I would have applied the doctrine of* Weeks v. United States, *232 U.S. 383 (1914), to the states. But the Court refused to do so then, and it still refuses today. Thus* Wolf *remains the law and, as such, is entitled to the respect of this Court's membership. . . .*

In light of the "incredible" activity of the police here it is with great reluctance that I follow Wolf. *Perhaps strict adherence to the tenor of that decision may produce needed converts for its extinction. . . .*[91]

In June of 1961, on the last day of the judicial year, the Court decided the case of Doll Ree Mapp.[92] The Ohio courts had found Miss Mapp guilty of possessing pornographic materials— "four little pamphlets, a couple of photographs and a little pencil doodle"[93]—which had belonged to a former boarder and which Miss Mapp had stowed away in a suitcase and a bureau. It had been generally supposed that the Supreme Court had heard Miss Mapp's appeal to consider whether a statute "making criminal the *mere* knowing possession or control of obscene material . . . is consistent with the rights of free thought and expression assured against state action by the Fourteenth Amendment."[94] Justice Stewart, indeed, voted to reverse Miss Mapp's conviction on this ground.[95] But the case also presented a claim, which Miss Mapp's lawyer did not really press with any enthusiasm in the Supreme Court, that Miss Mapp had been the victim of an unlawful search. And several members of the Court, finding this issue in *Mapp v. Ohio*, used it as a basis for re-examining *Wolf*.

Justice Clark (writing for himself, Chief Justice Warren, Justice Douglas, and Justice Brennan) summarized what happened to Miss Mapp as follows:

> On May 23, 1957, three Cleveland police officers arrived at appellant's residence in that city pursuant to information that "a person [was] hiding out in the home, who was wanted for questioning in connection with a recent bombing, and that there was a large amount of policy paraphernalia being hidden in the home." Miss Mapp and her daughter by a former marriage lived on the top floor of the two-family dwelling. Upon their arrival at that house, the officers knocked on the door and demanded entrance but appellant, after telephoning her attorney, refused to admit them without a search warrant. They advised their headquarters of the situation and undertook a surveillance of the house.
>
> The officers again sought entrance some three hours later when four or more additional officers arrived on the scene. When Miss Mapp did not come to the door immediately, at least one of the several doors to the house was forcibly opened and the policemen gained admittance. Meanwhile Miss Mapp's attorney arrived, but the officers, having secured their own entry, and continuing in their defiance of the law, would permit him neither to see Miss Mapp nor to enter the house. It appears that Miss Mapp was halfway down the stairs from the upper floor to the front door when the officers, in this highhanded manner, broke into the hall. She demanded to see the search warrant. A paper, claimed to be a warrant, was held up by one of the officers. She grabbed the "warrant" and placed it in her bosom. A struggle ensued in which the officers recovered the piece of paper and as a result of which they handcuffed appellant because she had been "belligerent" in resisting their official rescue of the "warrant" from her person. Running roughshod over appellant, a policeman "grabbed" her, "twisted [her] hand," and she "yelled [and] pleaded with him" because "it was hurting." Appellant, in handcuffs, was then forcibly taken upstairs to her bedroom

*where the officers searched a dresser, a chest of drawers, a closet
and some suitcases. They also looked into a photo album and
through personal papers belonging to the appellant. The search
spread to the rest of the second floor including the child's bedroom, the living room, the kitchen and a dinette. The basement
of the building and a trunk found therein were also searched.
The obscene materials for possession of which she was ultimately
convicted were discovered in the course of that widespread
search.*

*At the trial no search warrant was produced by the prosecu-
tion, nor was the failure to produce one explained or accounted
for. . . .[96]*

Starting from this, Justice Clark moved forward along lines
which were implicit in his concurrence in *Irvine.* He felt that
Wolf's refusal to impose the exclusionary rule on the states was
illogical, unworkable, and should be overruled. He pointed out
that since *Wolf* a number of state courts had adopted the exclusionary rule of their own accord. He argued that the Supreme
Court should complete the job, imposing the exclusionary rule on
all American courts.

Justices Harlan, Frankfurter, and Whittaker felt (as did
Justice Stewart) that Miss Mapp's lawyer had not really asked
the Court to reconsider *Wolf* and that, therefore, the Court
should not do so. But the three Justices then went on to argue
that, if open to reconsideration, the *Wolf* doctrine should be
retained.

Since Justice Stewart wished to reverse on First Amendment
grounds, his vote, added to that of Justice Clark and the three
Justices who joined Justice Clark's opinion, meant victory for
Miss Mapp. But the larger question, the fate of the *Wolf* doctrine,
seemed to rest with the senior member of the Court, Justice
Black. Aside from Justice Black, the seven Justices who recon-
sidered *Wolf* were split four-to-three against. If Justice Black
adhered to the concurrence he had filed in *Wolf* in 1949, the score
would be four-to-four. In that event, *Wolf* would retain an
uneasy dominion—unless and until, in a subsequent case, Justice
Stewart were to side with Justice Clark and thereby consign
Wolf to past history.

But Justice Black, on the last day of his twenty-fourth Court term, decided he had been wrong twelve years before. And, in a concurring opinion, he explained why:

> *I am still not persuaded that the Fourth Amendment, standing alone, would be enough to bar the introduction into evidence against an accused of papers and effects seized from him in violation of its commands. For the Fourth Amendment does not itself contain any provision expressly precluding the use of such evidence, and I am extremely doubtful that such a provision could properly be inferred from nothing more than the basic command against unreasonable searches and seizures. Reflection on the problem, however, in the light of cases coming before the Court since Wolf, has led me to conclude that when the Fourth Amendment's ban against unreasonable searches and seizures is considered together with the Fifth Amendment's ban against compelled self-incrimination, a constitutional basis emerges which not only justifies but actually requires the exclusionary rule.*
>
> *The close interrelationship between the Fourth and Fifth Amendments, as they apply to this problem, has long been recognized and, indeed, was expressly made the ground for this Court's holding in Boyd v. United States [116 U.S. 616]. There the Court fully discussed this relationship and declared itself "unable to perceive that the seizure of a man's private books and papers to be used in evidence against him is substantially different from compelling him to be a witness against himself." It was upon this ground that Mr. Justice Rutledge largely relied in his dissenting opinion in the Wolf case. And, although I rejected the argument at that time, its force has, for me at least, become compelling with the more thorough understanding of the problem brought on by recent cases. In the final analysis, it seems to me that the Boyd doctrine, though perhaps not required by the express language of the Constitution strictly construed, is amply justified from an historical standpoint, soundly based in reason, and entirely consistent with what I regard to be the proper approach to interpretation of our Bill of Rights—an approach well set out by Mr. Justice Bradley in the Boyd case:*
>
> > *[C]onstitutional provisions for the security of person and property should be liberally construed. A close and literal construction deprives them of half their efficacy, and leads*

to gradual depreciation of the right, as if it consisted more in sound than in substance. It is the duty of the courts to be watchful for the constitutional rights of the citizen, and against any stealthy encroachments thereon.

.   .   .   .   .

. . . As I understand the Court's opinion in this case, we . . . reject the confusing "shock-the-conscience" standard of the Wolf *and* Rochin *cases and, instead, set aside this state conviction in reliance upon the precise, intelligible and more predictable constitutional doctrine enunciated in the* Boyd *case. I fully agree with Mr. Justice Bradley's opinion that the two Amendments upon which the* Boyd *doctrine rests are of vital importance in our constitutional scheme of liberty and that both are entitled to a liberal rather than a niggardly interpretation. The courts of the country are entitled to know with as much certainty as possible what scope they cover. The Court's opinion, in my judgment, dissipates the doubt and uncertainty in this field of constitutional law and I am persuaded, for this and other reasons stated, to depart from my prior views, to accept the* Boyd *doctrine as controlling in this state case and to join the Court's judgment and opinion which are in accordance with that constitutional doctrine.*[97]

(3). *"Our Government is the potent, the omnipresent teacher"*

In a number of the preceding cases, the Supreme Court was simply fulfilling in constitutional terms the most fundamental of judicial responsibilities, trying to make certain that people are not found guilty of crimes they have not committed. When the Court insists that a defendant have a lawyer at his side, or rules out a confession extracted by threats or blandishments, it seeks to insure that American criminal justice works in the way best calculated to get at the truth. For the Justices remember the deaths of Sacco and Vanzetti, and the years in prison served by Mooney and by the Scottsboro boys; and they also know that in scores of less publicized instances, men and women have, by one fortuity or another, been mistakenly convicted.[98]

Moreover, the Justices know that the powerful engine of criminal justice, when placed in the wrong hands, can be an especially apt instrument to reinforce other forms of societal oppression. From their own cases the Justices can, for example, build a documented record of Southern callousness to the due process rights of Negro defendants: In twenty-five years, from February 1936 (when *Brown v. Mississippi,* the path-breaking coerced-confession case, was decided), to June 1961, the Supreme Court set aside state court convictions on coerced-confession grounds on twenty-two occasions. Of the twenty-seven defendants involved in these cases, nineteen were Negroes and six were whites; the race of the other two is not disclosed by the records. Sixteen of the nineteen identifiable Negroes were tried in Southern courts. Only one of the six identifiable whites, and neither of the two racially unidentified defendants, was tried in a Southern court.[99]

Protecting the innocent is a vital judicial responsibility. But the Court has another, closely related, less obvious, but no less important responsibility. This aspect of the Court's work is illustrated by the cases in which it sets aside criminal convictions that are based on wiretapping, or on an unlawful search, or on a coerced confession that is verified by independent and valid evidence. In these instances the Court may have no reason to doubt the guilt of the defendant whose conviction it sets aside. The challenged evidence (as, for example, the morphine capsules forced out of Rochin's stomach) is likely to be trustworthy enough. (Here a word of caution is appropriate: wiretapping and related techniques for recording conversations lend themselves, in corrupt hands, to gross manipulation and fabrication of evidence.) At all events, on the assumption that the challenged evidence is trustworthy, the Court is saying that the integrity of the legal process is dealt a greater blow when courts approve the lawlessness of law-enforcement officers than when courts, by insisting on an untainted trial, permit a particular criminal to delay—or, sometimes, wholly escape—due punishment.

Holmes, in 1928, vainly protesting against wiretapping, put the matter this way:

. . . We have to choose, and for my part I think it a less evil that some criminals escape than that the government should play an ignoble part.[100]

Brandeis, in the same case (*Olmstead v. United States*), pushed the issue one step beyond:

Decency, security, and liberty alike demand that govern-
ment officials shall be subjected to the same rules of conduct
that are commands to the citizen. In a government of laws,
existence of the government will be imperilled if it fails to ob-
serve the law scrupulously. Our Government is the potent, the
omnipresent teacher. For good or for ill, it teaches the whole
people by its example. Crime is contagious. If the Government
becomes a lawbreaker, it breeds contempt for law; it invites
every man to become a law unto himself; it invites anarchy. To
declare that in the administration of the criminal law the end
justifies the means—to declare that the Government may com-
mit crimes in order to secure the conviction of a private crim-
inal—would bring terrible retribution. Against that pernicious
doctrine this Court should resolutely set its face.[101]

In these quoted passages, Holmes and Brandeis were expressing their concern at unfairness practiced by federal investi-
gators. But it should be noted that, by and large, federal investi-
gative agencies and federal prosecutors are far more attuned to,
and respectful of, the procedural rights of the private citizen than
are their state counterparts. (A recent illustration of the enlightened attitudes of responsible officials was the creation, by
then Attorney General Robert F. Kennedy, of a watchdog Office
of Criminal Justice, which would exercise general surveillance
over the processes of federal law enforcement, thereby helping to
"insure that the department over which I preside is more than a
Department of Prosecution and is in fact the Department of
Justice."[102]) This fact—which bears thoughtful consideration by
those who inveigh against the dangers to liberty inherent in
centralized federal law enforcement—is doubtless attributable to
a variety of causes. One may be the difference in character
between most federal crimes and most state crimes. Another,
surely, is that federal law enforcement officers have been exposed
to the Supreme Court's active tutelage for far longer than state
law enforcement officers.

The Court's role, as teacher, has surely been influential.
Slowly, a growing number of police, prosecutors, and lower-court
judges are learning the meaning of due process of law. But there
are still far too many law enforcement officials who are ignorant,
or simply contemptuous, of the Constitution's mandates of fair-

ness. And so the Court—acting simultaneously as teacher, censor, and guardian—continues its necessary task. Justice William J. Brennan, Jr., writing in 1961, put it very succinctly:

> . . . *Far too many cases come from the states to the Supreme Court presenting dismal pictures of official lawlessness, of illegal searches and seizures, illegal detentions attended by prolonged interrogation and coerced admissions of guilt, of the denial of counsel, and downright brutality. Judicial self-restraint which defers too much to the sovereign powers of the states and reserves judicial intervention for only the most revolting cases will not serve to enhance Madison's priceless gift of "the great rights of mankind secured under this Constitution." For these secure the only climate in which the law of freedom can exist.*[103]

The quality of the legal process we require reflects the quality of the civilization we aspire to. The point was made over half a century ago by a gifted young politician who, as Home Secretary, was responsible for British law enforcement. The Home Secretary was Winston Churchill, and in 1910 he spoke to his colleagues in the House of Commons in the following vein:

> *The mood and temper of the public in regard to the treatment of crime and criminals is one of the most unfailing tests of any country. A calm, dispassionate recognition of the rights of the accused, and even of the convicted criminal, against the State— a constant heart-searching by all charged with the duty of punishment—a desire and eagerness to rehabilitate in the world of industry those who have paid their due in the hard coinage of punishment: tireless efforts towards the discovery of curative and regenerative processes: unfailing faith that there is a treasure, if you can only find it, in the heart of every man. These are the symbols, which, in the treatment of crime and criminal, mark and measure the stored up strength of a nation, and are sign and proof of the living virtue within it.*[104]

C. "ALL MEN ARE CREATED EQUAL"

WHEN LINCOLN, at Gettysburg, spoke of the United States as a "nation . . . dedicated to the proposition that all men are created equal," his words took his audience back to Jefferson and the Declaration of Independence. But Lincoln's words were less metaphoric than Jefferson's: six months before the Gettysburg Address, Lincoln had issued his Emancipation Proclamation, freeing the slaves in the states that were in rebellion.

Yet, just as the Emancipation Proclamation was not the triumphant end of the fight for equality, so too it was not the beginning.

1. From the Constitutional Convention to the Civil War

Anti-slavery sentiment had been strong within the Constitutional Convention. But the Georgia and South Carolina delegates agreed to the Constitution only on the basis of the Compromise that preserved the slave trade until 1803. Other provisions of the Constitution also recognized slavery: A slave was to be counted as three-fifths of a free man for purposes of computing "direct" taxes and representation in the House of Representatives. And slaves escaping into free states were to be returned.

The general tenor of the Convention seemed, however, to reflect a confidence that these provisions would be temporary, in the sense that slavery was thought to be a withering weed. Here, of course, the framers' sense of phophecy failed them.

The turn of the century was a time of promise for American democracy. But, whatever Jefferson personally may have wished, and anticipated, his "revolution of 1800" did not usher in equality for the Negro. New ways to gin cotton, new lands to put to cotton—these were the ingredients of a new birth of slavery. And ending the slave trade merely served to protect the infant American service industry of slave breeding.

a. Slavery, foreign commerce, and international relations

The Constitution, as befits a compromise document, cut both ways in its actual impact on slavery. Ultimately, the *Dred Scott Case* was to deny that Congress could exclude slavery from any part of the new western territories. And *Dred Scott* was also, apparently, to say that not even a free Negro in a free state could ever aspire to the citizenship contemplated by the Constitution. But a generation before *Dred Scott*, the beleaguered slaveowners of South Carolina learned that the Constitution could be a very hostile document. They learned that the treaty power and the commerce power vested by the Constitution in the national government were impediments to their own domestic efforts to secure themselves against slave uprisings. And they learned this at the hands of one of South Carolina's most distinguished sons, Justice William Johnson.

In 1823, just a few months before the Supreme Court, in *Gibbons v. Ogden*,[1] held that New York's steamboat monopoly was in conflict with the commerce power, Justice Johnson had encountered a similar conflict, in a very different context, in the federal circuit court in Charleston. Justice Johnson was holding court in Charleston under the then prevailing requirement that Supreme Court Justices spend a good part of their judicial year "riding circuit" to preside in the lower federal courts. As a trial judge, he decided *Elkison v. Deliesseline*.[2] That case, as Justice Johnson's biographer, Professor Donald G. Morgan, makes clear, was to shape Justice Johnson's sweeping concurring opinion in *Gibbons v. Ogden*, asserting the exclusivity of the commerce power, as against state laws, whether or not Congress has undertaken to exercise its commerce power. Professor Morgan's narrative of the *Elkison* case describes with clarity and insight an early chapter in slavery's struggle for survival. Much of that narrative follows:

The law with which Johnson [was] confronted in the lower court—the Negro Seamen Act—had been passed by the South

Carolina legislature in December, 1822. . . . Charleston had been thrown into a state of near-panic when the plans of Denmark Vesey, a free Negro, for a slave revolt had been exposed. While Johnson had publicly and privately regretted the state of the public mind and deplored the severity of the ensuing trials, South Carolina had taken a different view of the affair. The state law, which gave expression to prevailing fears, sought to prevent the spread of subversive ideas among the slaves by prohibiting free Negroes from entering the state. The third section of this measure required that free Negroes or persons of color employed on incoming vessels from ports outside the state be seized and held in jail until the vessels departed. The ships' captains were to pay the costs of detention and in case of default were liable to fine or imprisonment. The Negro seamen in case of such a default were to be sold into slavery.

The enforcement of this provision soon produced complications. Its immediate effect was to disrupt trade in Charleston, and American shipowners and the British minister at Washington loudly protested the restraint on commerce. Secretary of State Adams then conferred with congressmen from South Carolina; from one of them who was also an intimate of Johnson's, Joel Poinsett, Adams received assurances sufficiently strong to impel him in June, 1823, to dispatch a conciliatory reply to the British complaint. For several months the state withheld enforcement of the Seamen Act.

Nevertheless, the statute was not allowed to sleep. Through a private organization, the "South Carolina Association," a group of citizens took up the problem of execution, and at their behest the sheriff of Charleston removed from a British vessel one Henry Elkison, a free Negro and a British subject, who, by the terms of the law, was put in jail. The prisoner then applied to Judge Johnson for a writ of habeas corpus or, failing that, a writ de homine replegiando.

In the courtroom Elkison's counsel attacked the validity of the state law. It was in direct conflict, he argued, with both the commerce power of Congress and a commercial agreement between the United States and Great Britain. No counsel appeared for the state, but two lawyers representing the Association argued at length in support of the state law. One of them, B. F.

Hunt, questioned the court's jurisdiction and went on to defend the act under the state's reserve powers. The law, he said, did not exclude persons of color, but only required their detention in a "very airy and healthy part of the city." The act protected health by preventing bloodshed. As a sovereign state, South Carolina could not surrender rights essential to its self-preservation. The other counsel, Isaac E. Holmes, went even further. According to Johnson, Holmes asserted that rather than see the state surrender this power, he would have preferred a dissolution of the Union. The suggestion shocked the judge. As Johnson himself described the scene: "Everyone saw me lay down my pen, raise my eyes from my notes, and fix them on the speaker's face. He still proceeded, and in a style which bore evidence of preparation and study."

Here was an issue to test the mettle of any judge. The police powers of the state were in conflict with the dormant power of Congress over commerce, and public opinion passionately sided with the state.

William Johnson had foreseen this collision and in fact had sought to prevent it. In January when the state had begun the enforcement of the law, American shipmasters and the British consul had applied to Johnson for protection. Johnson had then instructed the United States District Attorney to bring the question before the state judges, and to do it in the manner "most respectful to them." Johnson's brother-in-law, Governor Thomas Bennett, had with some reluctance approved the initial adoption of the act, and the judge had this to say in explanation of his own conduct:

> *I felt confident that the act had been passed hastily, and without due consideration, and knowing the unfavorable feeling that it was calculated to excite abroad, it was obviously best that relief should come from the quarter from which proceeded the act complained of.*

These negotiations had found the state officials cooperative, and the men had secured their release. Yet the state had made no pledge to withhold enforcement in the future, and this, according to Johnson, had induced the complaining parties to carry their protests to the national capital. That the state had allowed the law to rest, however, won Johnson's praise. The re-

vival of enforcement was to him more a private than a public act.

Now the judge met the issue head on. He held the Seamen Act unconstitutional . . . [H]e might have escaped on the question of jurisdiction. Moreover, he was aware of popular feeling and correctly predicted the public condemnation his opinion would evoke. John Marshall himself had encountered a similar case in his own circuit and had sidestepped the main issue. Taking note of Johnson's predicament, the Chief Justice now confided to Story that for his part he had little taste for "butting against a wall in sport."

In his opinion Johnson examined the object and effect of the state law. Its direct aim was to prohibit from Carolina ports all ships employing Negro seamen regardless of nationality. If "the color of his skin" were sufficient ground for excluding a seaman, why not "the color of his eye or his hair"? The act might as readily apply to Nantucket Indians aboard the ships of Massachusetts. Retaliation might ensue and complete the destruction of Charleston's dwindling commerce.

Such a power in the state collided with the power of Congress to regulate commerce. For the first time since 1789, an American court found in the commerce clause a ground for invalidating state legislation, and this at the hands of a Jeffersonian judge! The scholar under Witherspoon, the son of the blacksmith who had cast a vote for ratification, and the law reader with Pinckney now portrayed the power in bold terms. With that description went a word of tribute for the Constitution itself:

> But the right of the general government to regulate commerce with the sister states and foreign nations is a paramount and exclusive right; and this conclusion we arrive at, whether we examine it with reference to the words of the constitution, or the nature of the grant. That this has been the received and universal construction from the first day of the organization of the general government is unquestionable; and the right admits not of a question any more than the fact. In the Constitution of the United States, the most wonderful instrument ever drawn by the hand of man, there is a comprehension and precision that is unparalleled; and I can truly say, that after spending my life in studying it, I still daily find in it some new excellence.

.   .   .   .   .   .

*Johnson gave his opinion on the seventh of August. When
the Charleston newspapers balked at printing it, he published it
as a pamphlet. He promptly sent a copy to Jefferson with a letter relating the difficulties he was encountering in Charleston.
He was alarmed at the mounting spirit of persecution and at the
activities of the South Carolina Association. His position in the
community was growing increasingly desperate; the idea of
disunion, that "greatest of evils," seemed to be losing its horror.
One may conclude that Johnson had forsaken his customary insistence on clear jurisdiction and pronounced his pronational
opinion in the Elkison case in the hope that his argument would
lop off at the ground these early shoots of state-rights extrem-
ism in South Carolina.*

*That hope was soon to expire. The newspapers of Charles-
ton began to teem with letters attacking the judge and his
opinion. For two full months the attacks kept up. . . .*

*. . . As might have been expected, the judge lost no time
in replying. . . .*

*. . . Several ideas stand out clearly from his columns of
explosive argument. One was antipathy to the notion of disunion
toward which he thought his critics were moving. The words
suggesting that the state might have to violate the Constitution,
he exclaimed, "thrill thro' my frame with an indescribable sensation." The state sovereignty argument he deemed all revolutionary; it converted the Constitution into a mere "letter of
attorney." Here was fresh evidence of Johnson's distress over the
mounting disunion talk.*

*Another idea reappears in these papers. This was Johnson's
concern for the individual. Thus, he detailed the summary procedure by which innocent seamen like Elkison could be sold
into slavery. This strange solitary figure, so inept in many of his
dealings with others, was often moved nonetheless by compas-
sion for the weak and oppressed. He would soon be voicing the
same respect for the individual in the Steamboat case [Gibbons
v. Ogden].*

*Again he gave an expansive interpretation to national pow-
ers. On the matter of the commerce power, he added but little
to the earlier analysis. Commerce he called a "coy damsel,"*

whom laws like the state act under question would drive from Charleston. If states were to exclude seamen, what would become of Congress' power "to regulate, to foster, to encourage commerce"? He here set forth the power in language soon to be elaborated at Washington.

But the treaty-making power he now portrayed with bold strokes. The Constitution gave that power to the President, acting with the "advice and consent of the Senate, . . . provided two thirds of the Senators present concur"; it further constituted treaties made "under the authority of the United States" part of the supreme law of the land. What was the nature and scope of this power? With an explicitness seldom duplicated in the writings of other judges, Johnson examined the power. It had lain, originally, he said, with the thirteen states; and they had relinquished it to the federal government by the Constitution. Because of the unpredictable nature of foreign relations and the need of flexibility in negotiations, it would serve the nation best to leave a wide discretion to treaty-makers. Johnson anticipated by a century the stand of the Supreme Court in asserting that the treaty-making power took in subjects not embraced by the normal congressional powers to legislate.

He made it abundantly clear, however, that there were limits to the power. He found these in the express provisions of the Constitution and gave illustrations. Yet state rights were not among such barriers, for in case of conflict the treaty power was paramount. Turning to history, he said no fewer than thirty-six treaties dating from 1778 on had intruded on reserved powers. Several of these he cited at length. Early expositions, long usage, and acquiescence by the states had established the power on a firm basis. In his effort to assure the nation ample powers to cope with the complexities of foreign affairs for the good of all the people, Johnson had carried broad construction to the delicate matter of treaty-making.

Finally, Johnson sought to calm the fears of his antagonists. Most of those fears he thought groundless. Within its own territory, South Carolina had ample power to control its colored population. Forbearance in the exercise of powers and steady cooperation between national and state governments were the keys to the harmonious working of the federal system.[3]

b. Slavery and the western territories

As things turned out, constitutional controversies like that involved in *Elkison* were not to prove decisive in the later unfolding of the slavery controversy. The dominant issue, from the Missouri Compromise of 1820 onward to the Civil War, was whether slavery was to spread to the new western territories. The Northwest Ordinance of 1787, which antedated the Constitution, had forever barred slavery from the lands north and west of the Ohio River ceded to the United States by the states. As to the status of this region, thereafter organized into free states (Ohio, Indiana, Illinois, Michigan, Wisconsin, and a portion of Minnesota), there was, accordingly, no issue. But the enormous reaches of land beyond the Mississippi—extended by purchase and by war to the Pacific—beckoned the peoples, the statesmen, and the economies of South and North alike. On the status of this empire depended the prosperity of the slave institution, which demanded more and more new land; and on it also depended the national political strength of the slave institution. In the House of Representatives, the established slave states were irretrievably outvoted by the established free states. But approximate parity could be maintained in the Senate if one slave state with two slave senators could be admitted into the Union to counter each newly admitted free state.

The Missouri Compromise eased the tensions of 1820 by drawing a line through the west—36°30′ north latitude—and banning slavery north of the line. But as years passed, as the Mexican war added more southwestern and western lands, and as people moved west to fill the new lands, the tenuous equilibrium disintegrated. The Compromise of 1850 brought in California as a free state; but the Utah and New Mexico territories were to be organized on the basis of "popular sovereignty"—the settlers themselves were to decide for or against slavery. Then came 1854, and the controversy reached fever pitch over the status of the Nebraska territory, which lay north of 36°30′. Under the guidance of a Democrat from Illinois, Senator Stephen A. Douglas, Congress passed the Kansas-Nebraska Act. "Popular sovereignty" was the principle of this act too; and the Missouri Compromise was declared "null and void."

In Kansas, the Kansas-Nebraska Act meant a surging influx

of the supporters of slavery and of those of freedom, racing to organize the territory and vote slavery up or down. And by 1856 it meant bloodshed, on both sides. (With the murders at Ossawatomie, John Brown began the tragic vengeance which was to lead him, three years later, to Harper's Ferry.)

In the nation at large, the Kansas-Nebraska Act meant the beginnings of organized political protest against the repeal of the Missouri Compromise. The "Anti-Nebraska" forces had, by 1856, coalesced into a new national political force, the Republican Party. The party's first presidential candidate, John C. Frémont, lost the hard-fought 1856 election to the Democratic candidate James Buchanan.

In the winter months before Buchanan's inauguration, Washington became aware of the pendency in the Supreme Court of a case touching on the paramount political question of the day, the power of Congress to regulate slavery in the territories.

(1). *The Dred Scott Case* (1857)

The case was a suit started in 1853 in the Missouri federal court by a Missouri Negro, Dred Scott, against a New Yorker, John F. A. Sandford, to whom Scott had been "sold." But Scott's claim—for which he wanted judicial validation—was that he had not been sold, because he was no longer a slave. He said he had stopped being a slave when he was taken by a former master into, first, the free state of Illinois, carved out of the free Northwest Territory, and, second, the northern reaches of the territory then governed by the Missouri Compromise. Having lost in the lower court, he had appealed to the Supreme Court.

The case presented three main questions. *First:* Could a Negro be a "citizen" of a state, within the meaning of Article III of the Constitution, which gives federal courts jurisdiction over suits between "citizens of different states"? If not, the Missouri federal court could not entertain the lawsuit, regardless of whether Scott had lost his slave status. *Second:* Was Scott in any event precluded because he had already lost a similar lawsuit in the Missouri state courts before he began his federal suit? *Third:* If the answer to *neither* of the first two questions barred Scott's suit, could he be emancipated by his stay in the free state or the free territory? This last question, if the Court were compelled to reach it, might raise questions of congressional power to pass an act, like the Missouri Compromise, barring slaves in the territories.

At first (according to the researches of Charles Warren, the author of the standard history of the Supreme Court) it was the consensus of the Justices that the case could be disposed of adversely to Scott on the basis of the second point alone—the previous Missouri state court judgment. But two Justices, John McLean and Benjamin R. Curtis, announced they would dissent and would, in their dissents, sustain the power exercised in the Missouri Compromise. The majority then concluded that they also should reach the merits of the constitutional problem. To secure as strong a majority front as possible, Justice James M. Wayne, on February 19, 1857, took the remarkable step of writing President-elect Buchanan the following letter, urging Buchanan to help bring Justice Robert C. Grier into line:

The Dred Scott case has been before the Judges several times since last Saturday, and I think you may safely say in your Inaugural: "That the question involving the constitutionality of the Missouri Compromise line is presented to the appropriate tribunal to decide: to wit, to the Supreme Court of the United States. It is due to its high and independent character to suppose that it will decide and settle a controversy which has so long and seriously agitated the country, and which must ultimately be decided by the Supreme Court. And until the case now before it (on two arguments) presenting the direct question, is disposed of, I would deem it improper to express any opinion on the subject." A majority of my brethren will be forced up to this point by two dissentients. Will you drop Grier a line, saying how necessary it is, and how good the opportunity is, to settle the agitation by an affirmative decision of the Supreme Court, the one way or the other. He ought not to occupy so doubtful a ground as the outside issue—that admitting the constitutionality of the Missouri Compromise Law of 1820, still, as no domicile was acquired by the negro at Fort Snelling, and he returned to Missouri, he was not free. He has no doubt about the question on the main contest, but has been persuaded to take the smooth handle for the sake of repose.[4]

Evidently Buchanan complied, because four days later Justice Grier wrote Buchanan as follows:

We fully appreciate and concur in your views as to the desirableness at this time of having an expression of the opinion of the Court on this troublesome question. With their concurrence, I will give you in confidence the history of the case before us, with the probable result. Owing to the sickness and absence of a member of the Court, the case was not taken up in conference till lately. The first question which presented itself was the right of a negro to sue in the Courts of the United States. A majority of the Court were of the opinion that the question did not arise on the pleadings and that we were compelled to give an opinion on the merits. After much discussion it was finally agreed that the merits of the case might be satisfactorily decided without giving an opinion on the question of the Missouri Compromise; and the case was committed to Judge Nelson to write the opinion of the Court affirming the judgment of the Court below, but leaving these difficult questions untouched. But it appeared that our brothers who dissented from the majority, especially Justice McLean, were determined to come out with a long and labored dissent, including their opinions and arguments on both the troublesome points, although not necessary to a decision of the case. In our opinion both the points are in the case and may be legitimately considered. Those who hold a different opinion from Messrs. McLean and Curtis on the power of Congress and the validity of the Compromise Act feel compelled to express their opinions on the subject. Nelson and myself refusing to commit ourselves. A majority including all the Judges south of Mason and Dixon's line agreeing in the result, but not in their reasons,—as the question will be thus forced upon us, I am anxious that it should not appear that the line of latitude should mark the line of division in the Court. I feel also that the opinion of the majority will fail of much of its effect if founded on clashing and inconsistent arguments. On conversation with the Chief Justice, I have agreed to concur with him. Brother Wayne and myself will also use our endeavors to get brothers Daniel and Campbell and Catron to do the same. So that if the question must be met, there will be an opinion of the Court upon it, if possible, without the contradictory views which would weaken its force. But I fear some rather extreme views may be thrown out by some of our southern brethren. There will therefore be six, if not seven (perhaps Nelson will remain neutral)

who will decide the Compromise law of 1820 to be of non-effect.
*But the opinions will not be delivered before Friday the 6th of
March. We will not let any others of our brethren know anything about* the cause of our anxiety *to produce this result, and
though contrary to our usual practice, we have thought it due
to you to state to you in candor and confidence the real state of
the matter.*[5]

The Court was as good as Grier's word. On Friday, March 6,
Chief Justice Taney delivered the Court's opinion in *Dred Scott.*
His opinion, contrary to every ordinary canon of judicial limitation, reached all the available issues: the lower court had no
jurisdiction; the prior state decision was conclusive; and the
(defunct) Missouri Compromise was unconstitutional. And that
constitutional holding, it should be noted, rested on the then
fairly novel constitutional proposition that the Fifth Amendment's
due process clause created not merely *procedural* rights to fairness but *substantive* rights in "property"—i.e., slaves—which put
that "property" beyond the scope of congressional regulation.
Thus, Taney can claim some dubious dram of credit for helping
launch the view of "due process" which was to lead the Court into
the "liberty of contract" jungle half a century thereafter.

But the immediate impact of the case was even more mo-
mentous than the ultimate doctrinal aberrations it spawned. By
reaching out for a major constitutional problem, Taney and his
colleagues—with the apparent cooperation of the President-elect
—deliberately injected themselves into the dominant political
issue of the day. Rather than settle the issue, they in effect
exacerbated it to the point where it could be resolved only by
war. It was this supreme act of judicial irresponsibility which was
to lead the late Justice Jackson, in his comment on Taney's inability to enforce the writ of habeas corpus in *Ex parte Merryman,* to see a kind of retribution in the ultimate impotence of the
judicial process.[6] *Dred Scott,* substantially abridged, follows:

MR. CHIEF JUSTICE TANEY *delivered the opinion of the court:*

.   .   .   .   .

[The following factual statement appears mid-way in the
Chief Justice's opinion. To clarify the facts, the statement has
been moved forward.]

The plaintiff was a negro slave, belonging to Dr. Emerson, who was a surgeon in the army of the United States. In the year 1834, he took the plaintiff from the State of Missouri to the military post at Rock Island, in the State of Illinois, and held him there as a slave until the month of April or May, 1836. At the time last mentioned, said Dr. Emerson removed the plaintiff from said military post at Rock Island to the military post at Fort Snelling, situate on the west bank of the Mississippi River, in the Territory known as Upper Louisiana, acquired by the United States of France, and situate north of the latitude of thirty-six degrees thirty minutes north, and north of the State of Missouri. Said Dr. Emerson held the plaintiff in slavery at said Fort Snelling, from said last mentioned date until the year 1838.

In the year 1835, Harriet, who is named in the second count of the plaintiff's declaration, was a negro slave of Major Taliaferro, who belonged to the army of the United States. In that year, 1835, said Major Taliaferro took said Harriet to said Fort Snelling, a military post, situated as hereinbefore stated, and kept her there as a slave until the year 1836, and then sold and delivered her as a slave, at said Fort Snelling, unto the said Dr. Emerson hereinbefore named. Said Dr. Emerson held said Harriet in slavery at said Fort Snelling, until the year 1838.

In the year 1836, the plaintiff and Harriet intermarried, at Fort Snelling, with the consent of Dr. Emerson, who then claimed to be their master and owner. Eliza and Lizzie, named in the third count of the plaintiff's declaration, are the fruit of that marriage. Eliza is about fourteen years old, and was born on board the steamboat Gipsey, north of the north line of the State of Missouri, and upon the river Mississippi. Lizzie is about seven years old, and was born in the State of Missouri, at the military post called Jefferson Barracks.

In the year 1838, said Dr. Emerson removed the plaintiff and said Harriet, and their said daughter Eliza, from said Fort Snelling, to the State of Missouri, where they have ever since resided.

Before the commencement of this suit, said Dr. Emerson sold and conveyed the plaintiff, and Harriet, Eliza, and Lizzie, to the defendant, as slaves, and the defendant has ever since claimed to hold them, and each of them, as slaves. . . .

[The foregoing facts provide the basis for the Chief Justice's legal discussion, which follows.]

. . . *The defendant pleaded in abatement to the jurisdiction of the court, that the plaintiff was not a citizen of the State of Missouri, as alleged in his declaration, being a negro of African descent, whose ancestors were of pure African blood, and who were brought into this country and sold as slaves.*

. ⠀⠀⠀⠀ . ⠀⠀⠀⠀ . ⠀⠀⠀⠀ . ⠀⠀⠀⠀ . ⠀⠀⠀⠀ .

The question is simply this: Can a negro, whose ancestors were imported into this country and sold as slaves, become a member of the political community formed and brought into existence by the Constitution of the United States, and as such become entitled to all the rights, and privileges, and immunities, guaranteed by that instrument to the citizen. One of which rights is the privilege of suing in a court of the United States in the cases specified in the Constitution.

. ⠀⠀⠀⠀ . ⠀⠀⠀⠀ . ⠀⠀⠀⠀ . ⠀⠀⠀⠀ .

In discussing this question, we must not confound the rights of citizenship which a State may confer within its own limits, and the rights of citizenship as a member of the Union. It does not by any means follow, because he has all the rights and privileges of a citizen of a State, that he must be a citizen of the United States. . . . Each State may still confer them upon an alien, or any one it thinks proper, or upon any class or description of persons; yet he would not be a citizen in the sense in which that word is used in the Constitution of the United States, nor entitled to sue as such in one of its courts, nor to the privileges and immunities of a citizen in the other States. . . .

. ⠀⠀⠀⠀ . ⠀⠀⠀⠀ . ⠀⠀⠀⠀ . ⠀⠀⠀⠀ .

It becomes necessary, therefore, to determine who were citizens of the several States when the Constitution was adopted. . . .

In the opinion of the court, the legislation and histories of the times, and the language used in the Declaration of Independence, show, that neither the class of persons who had been imported as slaves, nor their descendants, whether they had become free or not, were then acknowledged as a part of the people, nor intended to be included in the general words used in that memorable instrument.

It is difficult at this day to realize the state of public opinion in relation to that unfortunate race, which prevailed in the civilized and enlightened portions of the world at the time of the Declaration of Independence, and when the Constitution of the United States was framed and adopted. But the public history of every European nation displays it in a manner too plain to be mistaken.

They had for more than a century before been regarded as beings of an inferior order, and altogether unfit to associate with the white race, either in social or political relations; and so far inferior, that they had no rights which the white man was bound to respect; and that the negro might justly and lawfully be reduced to slavery for his benefit. . . .

. . . And, accordingly, a negro of the African race was regarded by them as an article of property, and held, and bought and sold as such, in every one of the thirteen Colonies which united in the Declaration of Independence, and afterwards formed the Constitution of the United States. The slaves were more or less numerous in the different Colonies, as slave labor was found more or less profitable. But no one seems to have doubted the correctness of the prevailing opinion of the time. . . .

. . . .

No one, we presume, supposes that any change in public opinion or feeling in relation to this unfortunate race, in the civilized nations of Europe or in this country, should induce the court to give to the words of the Constitution a more liberal construction in their favor than they were intended to bear when the instrument was framed and adopted. Such an argument would be altogether inadmissible in any tribunal called on to interpret it. If any of its provisions are deemed unjust, there is a mode prescribed in the instrument itself by which it may be amended; but while it remains unaltered, it must be construed now as it was understood at the time of its adoption. . . . Any other rule of construction would abrogate the judicial character of this court, and make it the mere reflex of the popular opinion or passion of the day. This court was not created by the Constitution for such purposes. Higher and graver trusts have been confided to it, and it must not falter in the path of duty.

. . . .

. . . [*The plaintiff*] *admits that he and his wife were born slaves, but endeavors to make out his title to freedom and citizenship by showing that they were taken by their owner to certain places . . . where slavery could not by law exist, and that they thereby became free, and upon their return to Missouri became citizens of that State.*

Now, if the removal of which he speaks did not give them their freedom, then by his own admission he is still a slave; and whatever opinions may be entertained in favor of the citizenship of a free person of the African race, no one supposes that a slave is a citizen of the State or of the United States. If, therefore, the acts done by his owner did not make them free persons, he is still a slave, and certainly incapable of suing in the character of a citizen.

.   .   .   .   .

But, before we proceed to examine this part of the case, it may be proper to notice an objection taken to the judicial authority of this court to decide it; and it has been said, that as this court has decided against the jurisdiction of the Circuit Court . . . anything it may say upon [*this*] *part of the case will be extrajudicial, and mere obiter dicta.*

This is a manifest mistake. . . .

.   .   .   .   .

In considering this part of the controversy, two questions arise: 1. Was he, together with his family, free in Missouri by reason of the stay in the territory of the United States hereinbefore mentioned? And 2. If they were not, is Scott himself free by reason of his removal to Rock Island, in the State of Illinois, as stated in the above admissions?

We proceed to examine the first question.

The act of Congress, upon which the plaintiff relies, declares that slavery and involuntary servitude, except as a punishment for crime, shall be forever prohibited in all that part of the territory ceded by France, under the name of Louisiana, which lies north of thirty-six degrees thirty minutes north latitude, and not included within the limits of Missouri. And the difficulty which meets us at the threshold of this part of the inquiry is, whether Congress was authorized to pass this law under any of the powers granted to it by the Constitution; for if the authority is not given by that instrument, it is the duty of this court to declare it void and inoperative, and incapable of conferring freedom upon one who is held as a slave under the laws of any one of the States.

The counsel for the plaintiff has laid much stress upon that article in the Constitution which confers on Congress the power "to dispose of and make all needful rules and regulations respecting the territory or other property belonging to the United States"; but, in the judgment of the court, that provision has no bearing on the present controversy, and the power there given, whatever it may be, is confined, and was intended to be confined, to the territory which at that time belonged to, or was claimed by, the United States, and was within their boundaries as settled by the treaty with Great Britain, and can have no influence upon a territory afterwards acquired from a foreign Government. . . .

. . . . . .

Now . . . the right of property in a slave is distinctly and expressly affirmed in the Constitution. The right to traffic in it, like an ordinary article of merchandise and property, was guaranteed to the citizens of the United States, in every State that might desire it, for twenty years. And the government in express terms is pledged to protect it in all future time, if the slave escapes from its owner. This is done in plain words—too plain to be misunderstood. And no word can be found in the Constitution which gives Congress a greater power over slave property, or which entitles property of that kind to less protection than property of any other description. The only power conferred is the power coupled with the duty of guarding and protecting the owner in his rights.

Upon these considerations, it is the opinion of the court that the Act of Congress which prohibited a citizen from holding and owning property of this kind in the territory of the United States north of the line therein mentioned, is not warranted by the Constitution, and is therefore void; and that neither Dred Scott himself, nor any of his family, were made free by being carried into this territory; even if they had been carried there by the owner, with the intention of becoming a permanent resident.

We have so far examined the case, as it stands under the

*Constitution of the United States, and the powers thereby
delegated to the Federal Government.*

*But there is another point in the case which depends on
State power and State law. And it is contended, on the part of
the plaintiff, that he is made free by being taken to Rock Island,
in the State of Illinois, independently of his residence in the
territory of the United States; and being so made free he was
not again reduced to a state of slavery by being brought back
to Missouri.*

Our notice of this part of the case will be very brief. . . .

.   .   .   .

*. . . [T]he plaintiff, it appears, brought a similar action
against the defendant in the State court of Missouri, claiming the
freedom of himself and his family upon the same grounds and
the same evidence upon which he relies in the case before the
court. The case was carried before the Supreme Court of the
State; was fully argued there; and that court decided that neither
the plaintiff nor his family were entitled to freedom, and were
still the slaves of the defendant. . . .*

.   .   .   .

*Upon the whole, therefore, it is the judgment of this court,
that it appears by the record before us that the plaintiff in
error is not a citizen of Missouri, in the sense in which that
word is used in the Constitution; and that the Circuit Court of
the United States, for that reason, had no jurisdiction in the
case, and could give no judgment in it. Its judgment for the
defendant must, consequently, be reversed, and a mandate
issued, directing the suit to be dismissed for want of jurisdiction.*
MR. JUSTICE WAYNE:

*Concurring as I do entirely in the opinion of the court, as it
has been written and read by the Chief Justice—without any
qualification of its reasoning or its conclusions—I shall neither
read nor file an opinion of my own in this case, which I prepared when I supposed it might be necessary and proper for me
to do so.*

*The opinion of the court meets fully and decides every point
which was made in the argument of the case by the counsel on
either side of it. Nothing belonging to the case, has been left
undecided, nor has any point been discussed and decided which*

was not called for by the record, or which was not necessary for the judicial disposition of it, in the way that it has been done, by more than a majority of the court.

In doing this, the court neither sought nor made the case. It was brought to us in the course of that administration of the laws which Congress has enacted, for the review of cases from the Circuit Courts by the Supreme Court.

In our action upon it, we have only discharged our duty as a distinct and efficient department of the Government, as the framers of the Constitution meant the judiciary to be, and as the States of the Union and the people of those States intended it should be, when they ratified the Constitution of the United States.

The case involves private rights of value, and constitutional principles of the highest importance, about which there had become such a difference of opinion, that the peace and harmony of the country required the settlement of them by judicial decision.

It would certainly be a subject of regret, that the conclusions of the court have not been assented to by all of its members, if I did not know from its history and my own experience how rarely it has happened that the judges have been unanimous upon constitutional questions of moment, and if our decision in this case had not been made by as large a majority of them as has been usually had on constitutional questions of importance.

Two of the judges, Mr. Justices McLean and Curtis, dissent from the opinion of the court. A third, Mr. Justice Nelson, gives a separate opinion upon a single point in the case, with which I concur, assuming that the Circuit Court had jurisdiction; but he abstains altogether from expressing any opinion upon the eighth section of the act of 1820, known commonly as the Missouri Compromise law, and six of us declare that it was unconstitutional.

.   .   .   .   .

[The other concurring and dissenting opinions are omitted.][7]

> (2). *Senatorial candidate Abraham Lincoln challenges incumbent Senator Stephen Douglas on* Dred Scott *(1858)*

In 1858, Stephen A. Douglas was opposed for re-election, as Senator from Illinois, by a lawyer who had helped organize the rising Republican Party in Illinois, Abraham Lincoln. The opponents stumped the state, debating each other. The Lincoln-Douglas debates centered largely on the *Dred Scott* decision. That decision had apparently stamped as "unconstitutional" Republican demands for a return to congressional restraints on the further spread of slavery in the territories. Douglas taxed Lincoln with undermining the authority of the Supreme Court. At Springfield, on July 17, 1858, Lincoln replied:

Now, as to the Dred Scott decision; for upon that he makes his last point at me. He boldly takes ground in favor of that decision.

This is one-half the onslaught, and one-third of the entire plan of the campaign. I am opposed to that decision in a certain sense, but not in the sense which he puts on it. I say that in so far as it decided in favor of Dred Scott's master and against Dred Scott and his family, I do not propose to disturb or resist the decision.

I never have proposed to do any such thing. I think, that in respect for judicial authority, my humble history would not suffer in a comparison with that of Judge Douglas. He would have the citizen conform his vote to that decision; the member of Congress, his; the President, his use of the veto power. He would make it a rule of political action for the people and all the departments of the government. I would not. By resisting it as a political rule, I disturb no right of property, create no disorder, excite no mobs.

When he spoke at Chicago, on Friday evening of last week, he made this same point upon me. On Saturday evening I replied and reminded him of a Supreme Court decision which he opposed for at least several years. Last night, at Bloomington, he took some notice of that reply; but entirely forgot to remember that part of it.

He renews his onslaught upon me, forgetting to remember that I have turned the tables against himself on that very point. I renew the effort to draw his attention to it. I wish to stand erect before the country as well as Judge Douglas, on this question of judicial authority; and therefore I add something to the authority in favor of my own position. I wish to show that I am sustained by authority, in addition to that heretofore presented. I do not expect to convince the Judge. It is part of the plan of his campaign, and he will cling to it with a desperate gripe. Even, turn it upon him—turn the sharp point against him, and gaff him through—he will still cling to it till he can invent some new dodge to take the place of it.

In public speaking it is tedious reading from documents; but I must beg to indulge the practice to a limited extent. I shall read from a letter written by Mr. Jefferson in 1820, and now to be found in the seventh volume of his correspondence, at page 177. It seems he had been presented by a gentleman by the name of Jarvis with a book, or essay, or periodical, called the "Republican," and he was writing in acknowledgment of the present, and noting some of its contents. After expressing the hope that the work will produce a favorable effect upon the minds of the young, he proceeds to say:

That it will have this tendency may be expected, and for that reason I feel an urgency to note what I deem an error in it, the more requiring notice as your opinion is strengthened by that of many others. You seem in pages 84 and 148, to consider the judges as the ultimate arbiters of all constitutional questions—a very dangerous doctrine indeed and one which would place us under the despotism of an oligarchy. Our judges are as honest as other men, and not more so. They have, with others, the same passions for party, for power, and the privilege of their corps. Their maxim is, "boni judicis est ampliare jurisdictionem"; and their power is the more dangerous as they are in office for life, and not responsible, as the other functionaries are, to the elective control. The constitution has erected no such single tribunal, knowing that to whatever hands confided, with the corruptions of time and party, its members would become despots. It has more wisely made all the departments co-equal and co-sovereign within themselves.

Thus we see the power claimed for the Supreme Court by Judge Douglas, Mr. Jefferson holds, would reduce us to the despotism of an oligarchy.

Now, I have said no more than this—in fact, never quite so much as this—at least I am sustained by Mr. Jefferson.

Let us go a little further. You remember we once had a

national bank. Some one owed the bank a debt; he was sued and sought to avoid payment, on the ground that the bank was unconstitutional. The case went to the Supreme Court, and therein it was decided that the bank was constitutional. The whole Democratic party revolted against that decision. General Jackson himself asserted that he, as President, would not be bound to hold a national bank to be constitutional, even though the Court had decided it to be so. He fell in precisely with the view of Mr. Jefferson, and acted upon it under his official oath, in vetoing a charter for a national bank. The declaration that Congress does not possess this constitutional power to charter a bank, has gone into the Democratic platform, at their national conventions, and was brought forward and reaffirmed in their last convention at Cincinnati. They have contended for that declaration, in the very teeth of the Supreme Court, for more than a quarter of a century. In fact, they have reduced the decision to an absolute nullity. That decision, I repeat, is repudiated in the Cincinnati platform; and still, as if to show that effrontery can go no further, Judge Douglas vaunts in the very speeches in which he denounces me for opposing the Dred Scott decision, that he stands on the Cincinnati platform.

Now, I wish to know what the Judge can charge upon me, with respect to decisions of the Supreme Court which does not lie in all its length, breadth, and proportions at his own door. The plain truth is simply this: Judge Douglas is for Supreme Court decisions when he likes and against them when he does not like them. He is for the Dred Scott decision because it tends to nationalize slavery—because it is part of the original combination for that object. It so happens, singularly enough, that I never stood opposed to a decision of the Supreme Court till this. On the contrary, I have no recollection that he was ever particularly in favor of one till this. He never was in favor of any, nor opposed to any, till the present one, which helps to nationalize slavery.

Free men of Sangamon—free men of Illinois—free men everywhere—judge ye between him and me, upon this issue.[8]

Douglas' own political position was a delicate one. His "popular sovereignty" doctrine had presumed that an antislave majority could organize a territory on a free basis. To avoid totally alienating northern sentiment, he tried to show that this doctrine could be reconciled with *Dred Scott* on the basis that slavery could not, as a practical matter, survive unless the local territorial government enacted and enforced favorable legislation. But Lincoln, speaking at Alton on October 18, 1858, in the last of the joint debates, refused to let Douglas take this middle ground:

I understand I have ten minutes yet. I will employ it in saying something about this argument Judge Douglas uses, while he sustains the Dred Scott decision, that the people of the territories can still somehow exclude slavery. The first thing I ask attention to is the fact that Judge Douglas constantly said, before the decision, that whether they could or not, was a question for the Supreme Court. [Cheers.] But after the Court has made the decision he virtually says it is not a question for the Supreme Court, but for the people. [Renewed applause.] And how is it he tells us they can exclude it? He says it needs "police regulations," and that admits of "unfriendly legislation." Although it is a right established by the Constitution of the United States to take a slave into a territory of the United States and hold him as property, yet unless the territorial legislature will give friendly legislation, and, more especially, if they adopt unfriendly legislation, they can practically exclude him. Now, without meeting this proposition as a matter of fact, I pass to consider the real constitutional obligation. Let me take the gentleman who looks me in the face before me, and let us suppose that he is a member of the territorial legislature. The first thing he will do will be to swear that he will support the Constitution of the United States. His neighbor by his side in the territory has slaves and needs territorial legislation to enable him to enjoy that constitutional right. Can he withhold the legislation which his neighbor needs for the enjoyment of a right which is fixed in his favor in the Constitution of the United States which he has sworn to support? Can he withhold it without violating his oath? And more especially, can he pass unfriendly legislation to violate his oath? Why this is a monstrous sort of talk about the Constitution of the United States! [Great applause.] There has never been as outlandish or lawless a doctrine from the mouth of any respectable man on earth. [Tremendous cheers.] I do not believe it is a constitutional right to hold slaves in a territory

*of the United States. I believe the decision was improperly made
and I go for reversing it. Judge Douglas is furious against those
who go for reversing a decision. But he is for legislating it out
of all force while the law itself stands. I repeat that there has
never been so monstrous a doctrine uttered from the mouth of
a respectable man. [Loud cheers.]*

*. . . I say if that Dred Scott decision is correct then the right
to hold slaves in a territory is equally a constitutional right with
the [conceded explicit constitutional] right of a slaveholder to
have his runaway returned. No one can show the distinction
between them. The one is express, so that we cannot deny it. The
other is construed to be in the Constitution, so that he who
believes the decision to be correct believes in the right. And the
man who argues that by unfriendly legislation, in spite of that
constitutional right, slavery may be driven from the territories,
cannot avoid furnishing an argument by which Abolitionists
may deny the obligation to return fugitives, and claim the power
to pass laws unfriendly to the right of the slaveholder to reclaim
his fugitive. I do not know how such an argument may strike a
popular assembly like this, but I defy anybody to go before a
body of men whose minds are educated to estimating evidence
and reasoning, and show that there is an iota of difference between the constitutional right to reclaim a fugitive, and the constitutional right to hold a slave, in a territory, provided this
Dred Scott decision is correct. [Cheers.] I defy any man to make
an argument that will justify unfriendly legislation to deprive a
slaveholder of his right to hold his slave in a territory, that will
not equally, in all its length, breadth and thickness furnish an
argument for nullifying the fugitive slave law. Why there is not
such an Abolitionist in the nation as Douglas, after all. [Loud
and enthusiastic applause.]*[9]

In the fall of 1858, Douglas was re-elected to the Senate.
Although the Republicans carried Illinois in 1858 by a slight
popular majority, the margin was not great enough to carry
Lincoln's cause in the state legislature (state legislatures selected
United States Senators until the Seventeenth Amendment,
adopted in 1913, decreed that Senators should be directly
elected).

But Lincoln, in losing the Senate race, had been "effectively
destroying Douglas as the leader of a national coalition. . . ."[10]

In 1860, Stephen Douglas found himself the presidential nominee of a divided Democratic Party. And the defection of the southern Democrats threw the election to the Republican, Abraham Lincoln. And so the war came.

c. War and emancipation

On January 1, 1863, Lincoln, *as a war measure*, emancipated the slaves in those parts of the Union which were in rebellion:

Now, therefore, I, ABRAHAM LINCOLN, *President of the United States, by virtue of the power in me vested as commander-in-chief of the army and navy of the United States, in time of actual armed rebellion against the authority and Government of the United States, and as a fit and necessary war measure for suppressing said rebellion, do . . . order and declare that all persons held as slaves within said designated states and parts of states are, and henceforward shall be, free; and that the Executive Government of the United States, including the military and naval authorities thereof, will recognize and maintain the freedom of said persons.*

And I hereby enjoin upon the people so declared to be free to abstain from all violence, unless in necessary self-defence; and I recommend to them that, in all cases when allowed, they labor faithfully for reasonable wages.

And I further declare and make known that such persons, of suitable condition, will be received into the armed service of the United States to garrison forts, positions, stations, and other places, and to man vessels of all sorts in said service.

And upon this act, sincerely believed to be an act of justice, warranted by the Constitution upon military necessity, I invoke the considerate judgment of mankind and the gracious favor of Almighty God.[11]

2. Emancipation and the three post-Civil-War amendments

In 1865, the Thirteenth Amendment wrote into the Constitution, for all time and for all parts of the Union, the freedom that Lincoln had proclaimed by military fiat in the seceding states.

Then, in 1868, came the Fourteenth Amendment. The Fourteenth Amendment overturned *Dred Scott* by making Negroes (and all others born or naturalized in the United States) "citizens" of the United States. The amendment also sought to protect "citizens" from state interference in the enjoyment of national privileges or immunities (vague categories judicially whittled away to almost-nothingness). And it guaranteed "persons" (citizens and noncitizens alike) *federal* protection from *state* denials of due process of law and the equal protection of the laws. Further (as with the Thirteenth Amendment), the Fourteenth Amendment gave Congress power to enforce the new constitutional rights.

The Fourteenth Amendment also sought, by indirection, to guarantee Negro suffrage. Section 2 of the amendment provided that denial of the right of any adult male to vote, either for federal or state office, for any reason other than "participation in rebellion, or other crime," should result in a proportional diminution of that state's representation in the House of Representatives. This potent provision has never been enforced in any way. The assumption has always been that only Congress could effectuate the necessary redistribution of representatives—a course which has been politically unfeasible ever since the end of Reconstruction. (In 1960 there appeared an article proposing that judicial enforcement be undertaken.[12])

Section 2 of the Fourteenth Amendment on its face left a state willing to suffer a concomitant loss in representation free to exclude Negroes, or others, from the franchise (subject, however, to the overlapping limitation of the equal protection clause). But in 1870, in the Fifteenth Amendment, the Constitution dealt with enfranchisement of the Negro more directly. Henceforth, no person was to be excluded from a federal or state election "on account of race, color, or previous condition of servitude." Nevertheless, the generation following the adoption of the Fifteenth Amendment witnessed the systematic disenfranchisement of southern Negroes. And for all practical purposes Negroes continued to have no role in the southern political process throughout the first four decades of the twentieth century. But the past quarter-century has witnessed the beginnings of change: *first,* as a result of the Supreme Court's decisions in the so-called "white-primary" cases;[13] *second,* because of intensive federal efforts to implement the Civil Rights Acts of 1957 and 1960 and the Voting Rights Act of 1965; and, *third,* by virtue of the massive voter registration programs undertaken by civil rights groups after passage of the recent federal legislation.

The background and the purposes of the Thirteenth, Fourteenth, and Fifteenth Amendments were fully explored by Justice Miller in the opinion in the *Slaughter-House Cases,* quoted in volume 1.[14] There is, therefore, no need to recapitulate these matters here—beyond recalling what Justice Miller had to say about the equal protection clause, whose meaning was to become the dominant constitutional issue in subsequent Supreme Court litigation dealing with problems of racial discrimination:

In the light of the history of these amendments, and the pervading purpose of them, which we have already discussed, it is not difficult to give a meaning to this clause. The existence of laws in the states where the newly emancipated negroes resided, which discriminated with gross injustice and hardship against them as a class, was the evil to be remedied by this clause, and by it such laws are forbidden.[15]

This understanding of equal protection seemed to be confirmed, and strengthened, when the Court first considered state laws discriminating against Negroes. In 1880, in *Strauder v. West Virginia,* the Court reversed the murder conviction of a Negro because the defendant was tried by a jury selected under a West Virginia statute which confined jury service to white males:

. . . [I]t [the Fourteenth Amendment] is to be construed liberally, to carry out the purposes of its framers. . . . It ordains that no State shall deprive any person of life, liberty or property, without due process of law, or deny to any person within its jurisdiction the equal protection of the laws. What is this but declaring that the law in the States shall be the same for the black as for the white; that all persons, whether colored or white, shall stand equal before the laws of the States, and, in regard to the colored race, for whose protection the amendment was primarily designed, that no discrimination shall be made against them by law because of their color? . . .[16]

(*Strauder,* and the companion case of *Ex parte Virginia,*[17] began a long line of cases on jury discrimination still coming before the Court. After statutes explicitly barring Negroes from

juries were invalidated, the southern states adopted racially exclusionary practices without writing them into the jury selection laws. The Court soon declared [in a nonjury case, *Yick Wo
v. Hopkins*[18]] that a state law "fair on its face" was bad if
administered in a discriminatory fashion. Ever since, the Court
has pursued the difficult job of testing, on a case-by-case basis,
whether the absence of Negroes from juries reflects such official
but unavowed discrimination.[19])

3. The *Civil Rights Cases* of 1883 and the "sit-ins" of the 1960s

If *Strauder* seemed to imply a sympathetic judicial response
to the post-Civil-War amendments, that implication was dispelled
three years later. In 1883, the Court, in the *Civil Rights Cases*,[20]
invalidated Section 1 of the Civil Rights Act of 1875, which
provided as follows:

*That all persons within the jurisdiction of the United States
shall be entitled to the full and equal enjoyment of the accommodations, advantages, facilities and privileges of inns, public conveyances on land or water, theatres, and other places of public
amusement; subject only to the conditions and limitations established by law, and applicable alike to citizens of every race and
color, regardless of any previous condition of servitude.*

This statute, which was the last significant legislative attack on
racial discrimination launched by the Radical Republicans,
sought to curtail racial discrimination by those engaged in certain
businesses serving the public generally. The legislation was urged
to be a proper mode of enforcing the Thirteenth and Fourteenth
Amendments; and the particular provision relating to "public
conveyances on land and water" was also buttressed by the
commerce power. But the Court, with only the first Justice
Harlan dissenting, struck down the entire statute.

The Court's reasoning on the "public conveyances" part of
the 1875 law is a little obscure. The Court, speaking through
Justice Bradley, simply said that the validity of an exercise of the
commerce power to accomplish purposes of this kind "is not now

before us, as the sections in question are not conceived in any such view"[21]—an assertion that must have come as a surprise to counsel, who had plainly argued that aspect of the case on commerce grounds. Certainly, to question the scope of the commerce power directly would have been extremely hard for the Court, in view of what it had said only five years before in *Hall v. DeCuir*.[22] There the Court struck down a comparable Louisiana statute because it interfered with the unarticulated congressional purpose to keep Mississippi riverboats unencumbered by such legislation. "If the public good requires such legislation," Chief Justice Waite had said, "it must come from Congress and not from the states." The Chief Justice's observation in *Hall v. DeCuir* bespeaks complete unawareness that in fact Congress had passed such legislation as part of the Civil Rights Act of 1875.

But the great importance of the *Civil Rights Cases* lies in its disposition of the issues raised under the Thirteenth and Fourteenth Amendments. The discriminations complained of were, the Court felt, no part of "slavery," and therefore were not reached by congressional power under the Thirteenth Amendment. And the Fourteenth Amendment did not sustain the legislation, since the discrimination was by private persons and the amendment speaks only to deprivations and discriminations flowing from a "state":

. . . [I]s the Constitution violated until the denial of the right has some state sanction or authority? Can the act of a mere individual, the owner of the inn, the public conveyance or place of amusement, refusing the accommodation, be justly regarded as imposing any badge of slavery or servitude upon the applicant, or only as inflicting an ordinary civil injury, properly cognizable by the laws of the State, and presumably subject to redress by those laws until the contrary appears?

After giving to these questions all the consideration which their importance demands, we are forced to the conclusion that such an act of refusal has nothing to do with slavery or involuntary servitude, and that if it is violative of any right of the party, his redress is to be sought under the laws of the State; or if those laws are adverse to his rights and do not protect him, his remedy will be found in the corrective legislation which Congress has adopted, or may adopt, for counteracting the effect of State laws, *or State action, prohibited by the Fourteenth Amendment. It would be running the slavery argument into the ground to make it apply to every act of discrimination which a person may see fit to make as to the guests he will entertain, or as to the people he will take into his coach or cab or car, or admit to his concert or theatre, or deal with in other matters of intercourse or business. Innkeepers and public carriers, by the laws of all the States, so far as we are aware, are bound, to the extent of their facilities, to furnish proper accommodation to all unobjectionable persons who in good faith apply for them. If the laws themselves make any unjust discrimination, amenable to the prohibitions of the Fourteenth Amendment, Congress has full power to afford a remedy under that amendment and in accordance with it.[23]*

Since the decision in the *Civil Rights Cases*, the inapplicability of the Fourteenth Amendment to discrimination of a private, nonstate character has been regarded as a settled constitutional principle. However, life has become more complex than it was in 1883, and, as was noted in the discussion of *Marsh v. Alabama*,[24] the boundary betweeen state action and nonstate action has become progressively harder to determine. For example, in 1949 the New York Court of Appeals considered the question whether Stuyvesant Town, a huge apartment development in New York City, was violating the Fourteenth Amendment by refusing to rent apartments to Negroes. Stuyvesant Town was financed and built, as an investment, by the Metropolitan Life Insurance Company. But New York City, pursuant to a state statute, materially aided Metropolitan by blocking off several city streets, exercising its power of seizure (eminent domain) to buy up the necessary land, and granting Stuyvesant Town a twenty-five year tax exemption. On this basis, three judges decided Stuyvesant Town was in effect a state instrumentality, bound by the Fourteenth Amendment; but a majority of four held it was not.[25]

Stuyvesant Town is an instance where the ties between the private entity and the state are pretty clearly identified. Yet even without special subsidies of this character, every business corporation derives its corporate charter, and hence its "existence," from the state. Moreover, every business enterprise, whether or not incorporated, depends routinely on all the state's supporting services. As has been said of the enterprises involved in the *Civil Rights Cases,* "Without state recognition of their proprietorship, the owners could not have properly commanded the premises."[26]

But to say this is simply to recognize that all human institutions depend at bottom on an enforceable legal structure. One's home is one's castle only if the police are available at a moment's notice to guard the moat. To determine where, on the scale of state-involvement, the Fourteenth Amendment takes hold, is to make a very subtle judgment of the "publicness" of the particular institution involved. And that judgment may change from generation to generation. The inn or theater that was free to discriminate, in the view of the Court that decided the *Civil Rights Cases,* might not be regarded as free to discriminate in the middle of the twentieth century. Or, at all events, it might not be so regarded if Congress were, by positive legislation, to express a renewed conviction that the Fourteenth Amendment should extend to such enterprises.

These conjectures were given present relevance by the "sit-ins," which began in 1960. By simply sitting and waiting to be served, Negro youths (sometimes joined by whites) throughout the South expressed their view that retail lunch counters should sell coffee and hamburgers to Negroes as well as whites. And especially so, where the lunch counter is a subdivision of a store which cheerfully sells lipstick and safety pins to Negroes and whites alike right across the aisle.

Opponents of the sit-ins relied on the *Civil Rights Cases* as authority for a retail merchant's right to pick his customers on any basis he pleases. It has, of course, been clear for many years that states and cities can pass legislation barring businesses from engaging in discrimination—e.g., the many state fair employment laws, and the increasing number of state and municipal laws forbidding discrimination in the rental and sale of residential dwellings.[27] But, in the absence of such laws, free enterprise and the Fourteenth Amendment are said to support freedom to discriminate. Perhaps so, although the *Civil Rights Cases* are not as clear authority for the proposition as is sometimes supposed. To revert to the quotation from Justice Bradley's opinion, it deserves emphasis that he spoke of the kind of exclusion sought to be reached by the 1875 Act "as inflicting an ordinary civil injury, properly cognizable by the laws of the State, and pre-

sumably subject to redress by those laws until the contrary
appears. . . . Innkeepers and public carriers, by the laws of all
the States, so far as we are aware, are bound, to the extent of
their facilities, to furnish proper accommodation to all unobjectionable persons who in good faith apply for them. If the laws
themselves make any unjust discrimination, amenable to the
prohibitions of the Fourteenth Amendment, Congress has full
power to afford a remedy under that amendment and in accordance with it."[28]

Did Justice Bradley mean that proof that the exclusions
reached by the 1875 Act were *not* "subject to redress by those
[state] laws" would justify protective federal legislation? Did he
mean that the Fourteenth Amendment imposes a duty on the
states to protect against exclusions of this kind? Or, did he merely
mean, what is certainly true, that state laws may not—consistently with the Fourteenth Amendment—protect whites but
not Negroes from exclusion? Even if he meant no more than the
latter, he was certainly indulging an assumption that all the states
require "innkeepers and public carriers" to accommodate "all
unobjectionable persons." But it has been a matter of everyday
experience that many hotels in many parts of the country do not
accommodate Negroes, and that some do not receive Jews. And
comparable establishments—restaurants and lunch counters—
have long engaged in comparable discrimination. Are those "innkeepers" who discriminate violating a requirement of equal accommodation which, Justice Bradley seems to have felt, was
embodied in the common law of every state? If so, and if those
discriminations are not "subject to redress" in the state courts, is
there not a denial of equal protection of the laws?

Beyond the matter of pursuing the implications of Justice
Bradley's opinion, there are further problems that demand
thoughtful consideration:

Those who defend the constitutionality of the racial discrimination practiced in retail stores, lunch counters, motels, and
other private businesses rely on the proposition that today such
discrimination is for the most part mere customary behavior, not
coerced compliance with discriminatory state or local laws. In the
absence of legal compulsion, so the conventional argument runs,
there is no "state action," and therefore nothing to which the
provisions of the Fourteenth Amendment can attach. But the

question arises whether this analysis really comes to grips with what "law" is. Justice Douglas, for example, addressing himself to whether there is today such an operative phenomenon as "international law," has observed:

> . . . [*T*]*he true gauge of law is not command but conduct. Those who move to the measured beat of customs, mores or community or world mandates are obeying law in a real and vivid sense of the term.*[29]

Moreover, apart from this somewhat abstract inquiry into the nature of law, there are two other levels on which, so it has been argued, racial discrimination in places of public accommodation involves "state action" and therefore brings into play the constitutional prohibitions of the Fourteenth Amendment's equal protection clause. First, it is said that the very fact that restaurants and hotels are licensed and extensively supervised by state and local governments, in order to protect the health and comfort of the consuming public, gives them a public caste which they cannot constitutionally repudiate. Second, to the extent that a restaurant or a hotel relies on police and prosecutors and courts to enforce racially discriminatory policies of customer selection, the involvement of those state officials is said to be a constitutionally prohibited state enforcement of what otherwise might be regarded as private discrimination. This latter branch of the argument largely rests upon a case decided by the Supreme Court in 1948. The case was *Shelley v. Kraemer.*[30] There the Supreme Court held that a state court could not enforce a so-called restrictive covenant under which neighboring homeowners agreed with one another not to sell to a Negro (or to a Jew, or to a Catholic, or to a member of any other racially or religiously disfavored group). The Court said in effect that (in the absence of any legislation prohibiting racial and religious discrimination in the sale of housing) neighboring homeowners might enter into such restrictive covenants and live up to them on a voluntary basis. However, in the event of breach of such a covenant, for a court to compel observance of the discriminatory provision (e.g., by ousting a Negro purchaser from his new home, or by permitting a damage action against the white seller) was an unconstitutional state enforcement of what would otherwise be private discrimination.[31]

The first group of sit-in cases came before the Supreme Court in 1961, and the second group in 1963. The 1961 cases were prosecutions for breach of the peace; the 1963 cases were trespass prosecutions. In both instances the Supreme Court set aside the convictions; but in both instances only Justice Douglas addressed himself to the central constitutional questions which the cases presented. In the principal 1961 decision, Chief Justice Warren (following the test laid down in *Thompson v. Louisville*,[32]) found that the state had failed to produce any evidence that the entirely passive behavior of the defendants presented any likelihood of provoking a breach of the public peace.[33] And in the principal 1963 decision, Chief Justice Warren found that local officials had played so active a part in fostering a community policy of racial segregation that the case could not be viewed as one in which the proprietor of the restaurant was pursuing a purely private business decision; the case was, in the Court's view, the constitutional equivalent of a situation in which the state or city involved was enforcing a law requiring segregation in restaurants.[34]

A year later, in June of 1964, the Supreme Court addressed itself to the "sit-in" problem for the third time. In *Bell v. Maryland*, once again, a majority of the Court (Justice Brennan, joined by the Chief Justice and by Justices Clark, Stewart, and Goldberg) thought it unnecessay to reach ultimate constitutional questions.[35] The reasoning of the majority, as expressed in Justice Brennan's opinion for the Court, was as follows:

> *Petitioners, 12 Negro students, were convicted in a Maryland state court as a result of their participation in a "sit-in" demonstration at Hooper's restaurant in the City of Baltimore in 1960. The convictions were based on a record showing in summary that a group of 15 to 20 Negro students, including petitioners, went to Hooper's restaurant to engage in what their counsel describes as a "sit-in protest" because the restaurant would not serve Negroes. The "hostess," on orders of Mr. Hooper, the president of the corporation owning the restaurant, told them, "solely on the basis of their color," that they would not be served. Petitioners did not leave when requested to by the hostess and the manager; instead they went to tables, took seats, and refused to leave, insisting that they be served. On orders of the owner the police were called, but they advised that a warrant would be necessary*

*before they could arrest petitioners. The owner then went to the
police station and swore out warrants, and petitioners were accordingly arrested.*

*The statute under which the convictions were obtained was
the Maryland criminal trespass law, § 577 of Art. 27 of the Maryland Code, 1957 edition, under which it is a misdemeanor to
"enter upon or cross over the land, premises or private property
of any person or persons in this State after having been duly
notified by the owner or his agent not to do so." The convictions
were affirmed by the Maryland Court of Appeals, 227 Md. 302,
176 A. 2d 771 (1962), and we granted certiorari. 374 U.S. 805.*

*We do not reach the questions that have been argued under
the Equal Protection and Due Process Clauses of the Fourteenth
Amendment. It appears that a significant change has taken place
in the applicable law of Maryland since these convictions were
affirmed by the Court of Appeals. Under this Court's settled
practice in such circumstances, the judgments must consequently
be vacated and reversed and the case remanded so that the state
court may consider the effect of the supervening change in state
law.*

*Petitioners' convictions were affirmed by the Maryland Court
of Appeals on January 9, 1962. Since that date, Maryland has
enacted laws that abolish the crime of which petitioners were
convicted. These laws accord petitioners a right to be served in
Hooper's restaurant, and make unlawful conduct like that of
Hooper's president and hostess in refusing them service because
of their race. On June 8, 1962, the City of Baltimore enacted its
Ordinance No. 1249, adding § 10A to Art. 14A of the Baltimore
City Code (1950 ed.). The ordinance, which by its terms took
effect from the date of its enactment, prohibits owners and
operators of Baltimore places of public accommodation, including restaurants, from denying their service or facilities to any
person because of his race. A similar "public accommodations
law," applicable to Baltimore City and Baltimore County though
not to some of the State's other counties, was adopted by the
State Legislature on March 29, 1963. 49B Md. Code § 11 (1963
Supp.). This statute went into effect on June 1, 1963, as provided
by § 4 of the Act, Acts 1963, c. 227. The statute provides that:*

> *It is unlawful for an owner or operator of a place of
> public accommodation or an agent or employee of said*

owner or operator, because of the race, creed, color, or national origin of any person, to refuse, withhold from, or deny to such person any of the accommodations, advantages, facilities and privileges of such place of public accommodation. For the purpose of this subtitle, a place of public accommodation means any hotel, restaurant, inn, motel or an establishment commonly known or recognized as regularly engaged in the business of providing sleeping accommodations, or serving food, or both, for a consideration, and which is open to the general public. . . .

It is clear from these enactments that petitioners' conduct in entering or crossing over the premises of Hooper's restaurant after being notified not to do so because of their race would not be a crime today; on the contrary, the law of Baltimore and of Maryland now vindicates their conduct and recognizes it as the exercise of a right, directing the law's prohibition not at them but at the restaurant owner or manager who seeks to deny them service because of their race.

An examination of Maryland decisions indicates that under the common law of Maryland, the supervening enactment of these statutes abolishing the crime for which petitioners were convicted would cause the Maryland Court of Appeals at this time to reverse the convictions and order the indictments dismissed. . . . It is not for us, however, to decide this question of Maryland law, or to reach a conclusion as to how the Maryland Court of Appeals would decide it. Such a course would be inconsistent with our tradition of deference to state courts on questions of state law. Nor is it for us to ignore the supervening change in state law and proceed to decide the federal constitutional questions presented by this case. To do so would be to decide questions which, because of the possibility that the state court would now reverse the convictions, are not necessarily presented for decision. Such a course would be inconsistent with our constitutional inability to render advisory opinions, and with our consequent policy of refusing to decide a federal question in a case that might be controlled by a state ground of decision. See Murdock v. Memphis, 20 Wall. 590, 634–636. To avoid these pitfalls—to let issues of state law be decided by state courts and to preserve our policy of avoiding gratuitous decisions of federal questions—we have long followed a uniform practice where a *supervening event raises a question of state law pertaining to a case pending on review here. That practice is to vacate and reverse the judgment and remand the case to the state court, so that it may reconsider it in the light of the supervening change in state law.*[36]

It may safely be surmised that there was another fact, not mentioned in Justice Brennan's opinion, which bore heavily on the decision of the majority to avoid for a third time any disposition of ultimate constitutional issues. That fact was that Congress was on the verge of completing action on H.R. 7152. One of the key titles of the pending bill—which is now better known as the Civil Rights Act of 1964—declared a federal right to equality of service in all places of public accommodation which (a) have some meaningful relation to interstate commerce, or (b) are in some meaningful sense creatures of state law. Therefore it seems reasonable to suppose that the Supreme Court majority in *Bell v. Maryland* was reluctant to reach constitutional issues whose disposition might well become largely superfluous on the going into force of the new federal legislation. Of course the majority was well aware that the new legislation would itself generate large constitutional questions. But the majority may well have felt that judicial prudence indicated the desirability of awaiting those questions, which would be sure to arise in due course, rather than anticipating and perhaps confusing the ultimate resolution of those questions by spacious judicial pronouncements about the scope of federal constitutional rights to equal service in the absence of any federal legislation purporting to define those rights and the remedies for their breach.

Whatever force these prudential considerations may have had for a majority of the Court, four of the Justices felt that the ultimate constitutional questions presented in *Bell v. Maryland* demanded an immediate answer. One of the four was Justice Douglas, who had already indicated his constitutional views in the 1961 and 1963 "sit-in" cases. For the Court in 1964 to dispose of *Bell* in nonconstitutional terms was, Justice Douglas felt, an evasion of judicial duty:

We have in this case a question that is basic to our way of life and fundamental in our constitutional scheme. No question preoccupies the country more than this one; it is plainly justiciable; it presses for a decision one way or another; we should resolve it.

The people should know that when filibusters occupy other forums, when oppressions are great, when the clash of authority between the individual and the State is severe, they can still get justice in the courts. When we default, as we do today, the prestige of law in the life of the Nation is weakened.[37]

On this note, Justice Douglas proceeded to the merits: In brief, he felt that a state could not utilize its trespass laws to enforce a corporation's preference for "apartheid."

Justice Black, joined by Justices Harlan and White, also felt that the central constitutional questions had to be faced:

. . . We fully recognize the salutary general judicial practice of not unnecessarily reaching out to decide constitutional questions. But this is neither a constitutional nor a statutory requirement. Nor does the principle properly understood and applied impose a rigid, arbitrary, and inexorable command that courts should never decide a constitutional question in any single case if subtle ingenuity can think up any conceivable technique that might, if utilized, offer a distant possibility of avoiding decision. Here we believe the constitutionality of this trespass statute should be decided.

This case is but one of five involving the same kind of sit-in trespass problems we selected out of a large and growing group of pending cases to decide this very question. We have today granted certiorari in two more of this group of cases. We know that many similar cases are now on the way and that many others are bound to follow. We know, as do all others, that the conditions and feelings that brought on these demonstrations still exist and that rights of private property owners on the one hand and demonstrators on the other largely depend at this time on whether state trespass laws can constitutionally be applied under these circumstances. Since this question is, as we have pointed out, squarely presented in this very case and is involved in other cases pending here and others bound to come, we think it is wholly unfair to demonstrators and property owners alike as well as against the public interest not to decide it now. Since Marbury v. Madison, 1 Cranch 137 (1803), it has been this Court's recognized responsibility and duty to decide constitutional questions properly and necessarily before it. . . . Under these circumstances we think that it would be an unjustified abdication of our duty to leave the question undiscussed. This we are not willing to do. So we proceed to state our views on the merits of the constitutional challenges to the Maryland law.[38]

Thus, Justices Black, Harlan, and White fully agreed with Justice Douglas that the majority's avoidance of ultimate constitutional issues constituted a failure to fulfill plain judicial responsibility. But when it came to the constitutional merits, the three Justices flatly disagreed with Justice Douglas. Their conclusions, as voiced by Justice Black, were as follows:

> Section 1 of the Fourteenth Amendment provides in part:
>
> No State shall . . . deprive any person of life, liberty, or property, without due process of law; nor deny to any person within its jurisdiction the equal protection of the laws.
>
> This section of the Amendment, unlike other sections,[11] [footnote by Justice Black: 11. E.g., § 5: "The Congress shall have power to enforce, by appropriate legislation, the provisions of this article."] is a prohibition against certain conduct only when done by a State—"state action" as it has come to be known—and "erects no shield against merely private conduct, however discriminatory or wrongful." Shelley v. Kraemer, 334 U.S. 1, 13 (1948). . . .
>
> .   .   .   .   .
>
> Petitioners, . . . contend that their conviction for trespass under the state statute was by itself the kind of discriminatory state action forbidden by the Fourteenth Amendment. This contention, on its face, has plausibility when considered along with general statements to the effect that under the Amendment forbidden "state action" may be that of the Judicial as well as of the Legislative or Executive Branches of Government. But a mechanical application of the Fourteenth Amendment to this case cannot survive analysis. The Amendment does not forbid a State to prosecute for crimes committed against a person or his property, however prejudiced or narrow the victim's views may be. Nor can whatever prejudice and bigotry the victim of a crime may have be automatically attributed to the State that prosecutes. Such a doctrine would not only be based on a fiction; it would also severely handicap a State's efforts to maintain a peaceful and orderly society. Our society has put its trust in a system of criminal laws to punish lawless conduct. To avert per-

*sonal feuds and violent brawls it has led its people to believe and
expect that wrongs against them will be vindicated in the courts.
Instead of attempting to take the law into their own hands,
people have been taught to call for police protection to protect
their rights wherever possible. It would betray our whole plan
for a tranquil and orderly society to say that a citizen, because of
his personal prejudices, habits, attitudes, or beliefs, is cast outside
the law's protection and cannot call for the aid of officers sworn
to uphold the law and preserve the peace. The worst citizen no
less than the best is entitled to equal protection of the laws of his
State and of his Nation. None of our past cases justifies reading
the Fourteenth Amendment in a way that might well penalize
citizens who are law-abiding enough to call upon the law and its
officers for protection instead of using their own physical strength
or dangerous weapons to preserve their rights.*

In contending that the State's prosecution of petitioners for
trespass is state action forbidden by the Fourteenth Amendment,
petitioners rely chiefly on Shelley v. Kraemer, supra. That reliance is misplaced. Shelley *held that the Fourteenth Amendment
was violated by a State's enforcement of restrictive covenants
providing that certain pieces of real estate should not be used
or occupied by Negroes, orientals, or any other noncaucasians,
either as owners or tenants, and that in case of use or occupancy
by such proscribed classes, the title of any person so using or
occupying it should be divested. Many briefs were filed in that
case by the parties and by* amici curiae. *To support the holding
that state enforcement of the agreements constituted prohibited
state action even though the agreements were made by private
persons to whom, if they act alone, the Amendment does not
apply, two chief grounds were urged: (1) This type of agreement
constituted a restraint on alienation of property, sometimes in
perpetuity, which, if valid, was in reality the equivalent of and
had the effect of state and municipal zoning laws, accomplishing
the same kind of racial discrimination as if the State had passed
a statute instead of leaving this objective to be accomplished by
a system of private contracts, enforced by the State. See* Marsh v.
Alabama, 326 U.S. 501 (1946); Terry v. Adams, 345 U.S. 461
(1953); cf. Yick Wo v. Hopkins, 118 U.S. 356 (1886); Nashville,
C. & St. L. R. Co. v. Browning, 310 U.S. 362 (1940). (2) *Nearly all
the briefs in* Shelley *which asked invalidation of the restrictive*

covenants iterated and reiterated that judicial enforcement of this system of covenants was forbidden state action because the right of a citizen to own, use, enjoy, occupy, and dispose of property is a federal right protected by the Civil Rights Acts of 1866 and 1870, validly passed pursuant to congressional power authorized by section 5 of the Fourteenth Amendment. This argument was buttressed by citation of many cases, some of which are referred to in this Court's opinion in Buchanan v. Warley, *245 U.S. 60 (1917). In that case this Court, acting under the Fourteenth Amendment and the Civil Rights Acts of 1866 and 1870, struck down a city ordinance which zoned property on the basis of race, stating, 245 U.S., at 81, "The right which the ordinance annulled was the civil right of a white man to dispose of his property if he saw fit to do so to a person of color, and of a colored person to make such disposition to a white person."* Buchanan v. Warley *was heavily relied on by this Court in* Shelley v. Kraemer, *supra, where this statement from* Buchanan *was quoted: "The Fourteenth Amendment and these statutes [of 1866 and 1870] enacted in furtherance of its purpose operate to qualify and entitle a colored man to acquire property without state legislation discriminating against him solely because of color." 334 U.S., at 11–12. And the Court in* Shelley *went on to cite with approval two later decisions of this Court which, relying on* Buchanan v. Warley, *had invalidated other city ordinances.*

It seems pretty clear that the reason judicial enforcement of the restrictive covenants in Shelley *was deemed state action was, not merely the fact that a state court had acted, but rather that it had acted "to deny to petitioners, on the grounds of race or color, the enjoyment of property rights in premises which petitioners are willing and financially able to acquire and which the grantors are willing to sell." 334 U.S., at 19. In other words, this Court held that state enforcement of the covenants had the effect of denying to the parties their federally guaranteed right to own, occupy, enjoy, and use their property without regard to race or color. Thus, the line of cases from* Buchanan *through* Shelley *establishes these propositions: (1) When an owner of property is willing to sell and a would-be purchaser is willing to buy, then the Civil Rights Act of 1866, which gives all persons the same right to "inherit, lease, sell, hold, and convey" property, prohibits a State, whether through its legislature, executive, or judiciary, from preventing the sale on the grounds of the race or color of one of the parties.* Shelley v. Kraemer, supra, 334 U.S., at 19. *(2) Once a person has become a property owner, then he acquires all the rights that go with ownership: "the free use, enjoyment, and disposal of a person's acquisitions without control or diminution save by the law of the land."* Buchanan v. Warley, supra, 245 U.S., at 74. *This means that the property owner may, in the absence of a valid statute forbidding it, sell his property to whom he pleases and admit to that property whom he will; so long as both parties are willing parties, then the principles stated in* Buchanan *and* Shelley *protect this right. But equally, when one party is unwilling, as when the property owner chooses not to sell to a particular person or not to admit that person, then, as this Court emphasized in* Buchanan, *he is entitled to rely on the guarantee of due process of law, that is, "law of the land," to protect his free use and enjoyment of property and to know that only by valid legislation, passed pursuant to some constitutional grant of power, can anyone disturb this free use. But petitioners here would have us hold that, despite the absence of any valid statute restricting the use of his property, the owner of Hooper's restaurant in Baltimore must not be accorded the same federally guaranteed right to occupy, enjoy, and use property given to the parties in* Buchanan *and* Shelley; *instead, petitioners would have us say that Hooper's federal right must be cut down and he be compelled—though no statute said he must—to allow people to force their way into his restaurant and remain there over his protest. We cannot subscribe to such a mutilating, one-sided interpretation of federal guarantees the very heart of which is equal treatment under law to all. We must never forget that the Fourteenth Amendment protects "life, liberty, or property" of all people generally, not just some people's "life," some people's "liberty," and some kinds of "property."*

This Court has done much in carrying out its solemn duty to protect people from unlawful discrimination. And it will, of course, continue to carry out this duty in the future as it has in the past. But the Fourteenth Amendment of itself does not compel either a black man or a white man running his own private business to trade with anyone else against his will. We do not believe that section 1 of the Fourteenth Amendment was written or designed to interfere with a storekeeper's right to choose his customers or with a property owner's right to choose his social or business associates, so long as he does not run counter to valid state or federal regulation. The case before us does not involve the power of the Congress to pass a law compelling privately owned businesses to refrain from discrimination on the basis of race and to trade with all if they trade with any. We express no views as to the power of Congress, acting under one or another provision of the Constitution, to prevent racial discrimination in the operation of privately owned businesses, nor upon any particular form of legislation to that end. Our sole conclusion is that section 1 of the Fourteenth Amendment, standing alone, does not prohibit privately owned restaurants from choosing their own customers. It does not destroy what has until very recently been universally recognized in this country as the unchallenged right of a man who owns a business to run the business in his own way so long as some valid regulatory statute does not tell him to do otherwise.

.39

Chief Justice Warren and former Justice Goldberg were two of the five Justices who joined Justice Brennan's majority opinion in *Bell v. Maryland*, thereby expressing their preference for disposition of the case on a nonconstitutional level. However, because Justices Black, Harlan, and White had found it necessary to reach the constitutional merits and had, in their dissent, expressed conclusions "with which [the Chief Justice and Justice Goldberg] profoundly disagree[d]," the two latter Justices felt "impelled to state the reasons for [their] conviction that the Constitution guarantees to all Americans the right to be treated as equal members of the community with respect to public accommodations."[40] With this preface, the two Justices, in an opinion by Justice Goldberg, formulated at length their view that the right to "sit-in" was protected against state interference by the Fourteenth Amendment. Their views (which Justice Douglas joined) were as follows:

The historical evidence amply supports the conclusion of the Government, stated by the Solicitor General [Archibald Cox] in this Court, that:

it is an inescapable inference that Congress, in recommend-
ing the Fourteenth Amendment, expected to remove the dis-
abilities barring Negroes from the public conveyances and
places of public accommodation with which they were fa-
miliar, and thus to assure Negroes an equal right to enjoy
these aspects of the public life of the community.

.   .   .   .   .

The first sentence of § 1 of the Fourteenth Amendment, the
spirit of which pervades all the Civil War Amendments, was ob-
viously designed to overrule Dred Scott v. Sanford, 19 How. 393,
and to ensure that the constitutional concept of citizenship with
all attendant rights and privileges would henceforth embrace
Negroes. It follows that Negroes as citizens necessarily became
entitled to share the right, customarily possessed by other citi-
zens, of access to public accommodations. The history of the
affirmative obligations existing at common law serves partly to
explain the negative—"deny to any person"—language of the
Fourteenth Amendment.

.   .   .   .   .

Thus a fundamental assumption of the Fourteenth Amend-
ment was that the States would continue, as they had for ages, to
enforce the right of citizens freely to enter public places. This
assumption concerning the affirmative duty attaching to places
of public accommodation was so rooted in the experience of the
white citizenry that law and custom blended together indistin-
guishably. . . .
The Civil Rights Act of 1875, enacted seven years after the
Fourteenth Amendment, specifically provided that all citizens
must have "the full and equal enjoyment of the accommodations,
advantages, facilities, and privileges of inns, public conveyances
on land or water, theatres, and other places of public amuse-
ment. . . ." 18 Stat. 335. The constitutionality of this federal leg-
islation was reviewed by this Court in 1883 in the Civil Rights
Cases, 109 U.S. 1. The dissent in the present case purports to
follow the "state action" concept articulated in that early deci-
sion. There the Court had declared that under the Fourteenth
Amendment:

> *It is State action of a particular character that is pro-*
> *hibited. Individual invasion of individual rights is not the*

subject-matter of the amendment. It has a deeper and broader scope. It nullifies and makes void all State legislation, and State action, of every kind, which impairs the privileges and immunities of the citizens of the United States, or which injures them in life, liberty or property without due process of law, or which denies to any of them the equal protection of the laws. 109 U.S., at 11. (Emphasis added.)

Mr. Justice Bradley, writing for the Court over the strong dissent of Mr. Justice Harlan, held that a proprietor's racially motivated denial of equal access to a public accommodation did not, without more, involve state action. It is of central importance to the case at bar that the Court's decision was expressly predicated:

on the assumption that a right to enjoy equal accommodation and privileges in all inns, public conveyances, and places of public amusement, is one of the essential rights of the citizen which no State can abridge or interfere with. Id., at 19.

The Court added that:

Innkeepers and public carriers, by the laws of all the States, so far as we are aware, are bound, to the extent of their facilities, to furnish proper accommodation to all unobjectionable persons who in good faith apply for them. Id., at 25.

This assumption, whatever its validity at the time of the 1883 decision, has proved to be unfounded. . . .

A State applying its statutory or common law to deny rather than protect the right of access to public accommodations has clearly made the assumption of the opinion in the Civil Rights Cases inapplicable and has, as the author of that opinion would himself have recognized, denied the constitutionally intended equal protection.

.   .   .   .   .   .

In the present case the responsibility of the judiciary in applying the principles of the Fourteenth Amendment is clear. The State of Maryland has failed to protect petitioners' constitutional right to public accommodations and is now prosecuting them for attempting to exercise that right. The decision of Maryland's highest court in sustaining these trespass convictions cannot be described as "neutral," for the decision is as affirmative in effect as if the State had enacted an unconstitutional law ex-

plicitly authorizing racial discrimination in places of public accommodation. A State, obligated under the Fourteenth Amendment to maintain a system of law in which Negroes are not denied protection of their claim to be treated as equal members of the community, may not use its criminal trespass laws to frustrate the constitutionally granted right. . . .[41]

The *Bell* case was decided on June 22, 1964. Ten days later, on July 2, Congress completed action on H.R. 7152; and that evening President Lyndon B. Johnson signed the bill into law as the Civil Rights Act of 1964. The background of the new law, and the initial litigation arising under that law, are considered below.[42]

4. "Separate but equal": its rise and fall

In 1878, in *Hall v. DeCuir,*[43] the Supreme Court *invalidated* a Louisiana statute requiring "equal rights and privileges upon any conveyance of a public character." In 1883, in the *Civil Rights Cases,*[44] the Court *invalidated* the federal act of 1875 requiring for all races "the full and equal enjoyment of the accommodations of . . . public conveyances on land and water." And, in 1896, in *Plessy v. Ferguson,* the Court *sustained* a Louisiana law requiring "all railway companies to provide . . . equal but separate accommodations for the white and colored races."[44a]

Mrs. DeCuir, the Negro plaintiff in *Hall v. DeCuir,* was voyaging from New Orleans to Hermitage, Louisiana; but because "The Governor Allen" was voyaging in interstate commerce—i.e., going to Vicksburg, Mississippi—*the local equal accommodations statute* was unavailing to protect her from being put in a separate cabin for Negroes. Mrs. Robinson, the Negro complainant in one of the *Civil Rights Cases,* wanted to sit in the "ladies car" on a train described by her lawyer as proceeding from one state "through another State, for the purpose of reaching a place in a third State."[45] But the *federal equal accommodations statute* did not help her because, according to the Supreme Court, it was not "conceived" in terms of the commerce power.

Mr. Homer Plessy, the Negro appellant in *Plessy v. Ferguson,* did not want to be seated in a separate car for Negroes on his sixty-mile train trip from New Orleans to Covington, Louisiana; but the *local segregation statute* bound him because "the East Louisiana Railway appears to have been purely a local line, with both its termini within the state of Louisiana."[46] (This characterization of the East Louisiana Railway was accurate so far as it went; but thirty-six of the East Louisiana's sixty miles, from New Orleans to Pearl River, ran on the tracks of the New Orleans and North Eastern Railroad, the southernmost segment of the "Queen and Crescent Route" linking New Orleans to Cincinnati and New York. Pearl River, where the East Louisiana's own track branched off to Covington, appears to have been a transfer point between the East Louisiana and the N.O.&N.E.R.R.[47] The East Louisiana Railway was very likely within the scope of potential congressional power over commerce. Compare *Southern Railway Co. v. United States.*[48])

a. The Court upholds "Jim Crow"

But the great point in *Plessy v. Ferguson* was not, of course, the commerce question. Indeed, in 1892, several months before Homer Plessy's case was considered by the Louisiana Supreme Court, that court had decided that the Louisiana statute requiring "equal but separate" railway cars for the two races could not constitutionally be applied to interstate passengers.[49] The great point in *Plessy* was the validity of the Louisiana statute as against the equal protection clause of the Fourteenth Amendment. By sustaining the statute, the United States Supreme Court gave constitutional underpinning to a vast proliferation of segregation laws which started to crisscross the South in the late 1880s, a decade after the end of Reconstruction. These so-called "Jim Crow" statutes soon blanketed every aspect of southern life; everything from drinking fountains to marriage was divided by law along racial lines. (A typical batch of "Jim Crow" statutes is the catalogue of Louisiana segregation laws listed by Justice Douglas in his concurring opinion in *Garner v. Louisiana,* 368 U.S. 157, 176 [1961].)

The statute challenged by Homer Plessy was enacted by the Louisiana legislature in 1890. Recent researches by Professor C.

Vann Woodward indicate that the statute very nearly failed of adoption:

> When the Jim Crow car bill was introduced in the Louisiana Legislature, New Orleans Negroes organized to fight it. Negroes were still voting in large numbers, and there were sixteen colored senators and representatives in the Louisiana General Assembly at that time. On May 24, 1890, that body received "A Protest of the American Citizens' Equal Rights Association of Louisiana Against Class Legislation," an organization of colored people. The Association protested that the pending separate-car bill was "unconstitutional, unamerican, unjust, dangerous and against sound public policy." It would, declared the protest, "be a free license to the evilly-disposed that they might with impunity insult, humiliate, and otherwise maltreat inoffensive persons, and especially women and children who should happen to have a dark skin."
>
> Nevertheless, on July 10, 1890, the Assembly passed the bill, the Governor signed it, and it became law. Entitled "An Act to promote the comfort of passengers," the new law required railroads "to provide equal but separate accommodations for the white and colored races." Two members of the Equal Rights Association, L. A. Martinet, editor of the New Orleans Crusader, and R. I. Desdunes, placed heavy blame on the sixteen colored members of the Assembly for the passage of the bill. According to Martinet, "they were completely the masters of the situation." They had but to withhold their support for a bill desired by the powerful Louisiana Lottery Company until the Jim Crow bill was killed. "But in an evil moment," he added, "our Representatives turned their ears to listen to the golden siren," and voted for the lottery bill "for a 'consideration.'" [50]

After the failure in the legislature, editor Martinet and other Negro leaders decided to mount a challenge to the statute in the courts. They secured as counsel an upstate New York lawyer, Albion W. Tourgée. Tourgée had, after the Civil War, spent several years in North Carolina as a carpetbagging Republican leader, and he even had for a time been a North Carolina judge; in addition, this versatile man had in the post-Reconstruction years published half a dozen novels.

In addition to securing Tourgée's services, Martinet and his associates gained the tacit cooperation of the railroads: separate cars were an unduly expensive form of service. Professor Woodward has surmised that the railway conductor's advance knowledge of the proposed test case was essential to accomplish the arrest of Homer Plessy for refusing to sit in the Jim Crow car; for Plessy, by his own statement, was a person of "seven-eights Caucasian and one-eighth African blood" in whom "the admixture of colored blood is not discernible."

Following Plessy's arrest, Tourgée asked the Louisiana Supreme Court for a writ of prohibition—i.e., a writ commanding the trial judge to proceed no farther with the case—on the ground that the 1890 statute contravened the Fourteenth Amendment. In 1893 the Louisiana Supreme Court unanimously sustained the statute, writing an opinion of some length "because the dissatisfaction felt with it [the statute] by a portion of the people seems to us so unreasonable that we can account for it only the ground of some misconception. Even were it true that the statute is prompted by prejudice on the part of one race to be thrown in such contact with the other, one would suppose that to be a sufficient reason why the pride and self-respect of the other race should equally prompt it to avoid such contact, if it could be done without the sacrifice of equal accommodations."[51]

Tourgée then appealed Plessy's case to the United States Supreme Court. The following excerpt from Professor Woodward's recent monograph conveys the sense of the unavailing argument which Tourgée advanced in his brief in the Supreme Court:

At the very outset . . . Tourgée advanced an argument in behalf of his client that unconsciously illustrated the paradox that had from the start haunted the American attempt to reconcile strong color prejudice with equalitarian commitments. Plessy, he contended, had been deprived of property without due process of law. The "property" in question was the "reputation of being white." It was "the most valuable sort of property, being the master-key that unlocks the golden door of opportunity." Intense race prejudice excluded any man suspected of having Negro blood "from the friendship and companionship of the white man," and therefore from the avenues to wealth, prestige, and

*opportunity. "Probably most white persons if given the choice,"
he held, "would prefer death to life in the United States as colored persons."*

*Since Tourgée had proposed that a person who was "nearly
white" be selected for the test case, it may be presumed that he
did so with this argument in mind. Of course, this was not a
defense of the colored man against discrimination by whites, but
a defense of the "nearly" white man against the penalties of color.
From such penalties the colored man himself admittedly had no
defenses. The argument, whatever its merits, apparently did not
impress the Court.*

*Tourgée went on to develop more relevant points. He em-
phasized especially the incompatibility of the segregation law
with the spirit and intent of the Thirteenth and Fourteenth
Amendments, particularly the latter. Segregation perpetuated
distinctions "of a servile character, coincident with the institution of slavery." He held that "slavery was a caste, a legal condition of subjection to the dominant class, a bondage quite sepa-
rable from the incident of ownership." He scorned the pretense
of impartiality and equal protection advanced in defense of the
"separate but equal" doctrine. "The object of such a law," he
declared, "is simply to debase and distinguish against the inferior race. Its purpose has been properly interpreted by the general designation of 'Jim Crow Car' law. Its object is to separate
the Negroes from the whites in public conveyances for the
gratification and recognition of the sentiment of white superiority and white supremacy of right and power." He asked the
members of the Court to imagine the tables turned and themselves ordered into a Jim Crow car. "What humiliation, what
rage would then fill the judicial mind!" he exclaimed.*

*The clue to the true intent of the Louisiana statute was that
it did not apply "to nurses attending the children of the other
race." On this clause he observed:*

> *The exemption of nurses shows that the real evil lies not
> in the color of the skin but in the relation the colored person
> sustains to the white. If he is a dependent, it may be en-
> dured: if he is not, his presence is insufferable. Instead of
> being intended to promote the general comfort and moral
> well-being, this act is plainly and evidently intended to
> promote the happiness of one class by asserting its suprem-*

acy and the inferiority of another class. Justice is pictured blind and her daughter, the Law, ought at least to be color-blind.[52]

As will be seen below, much of the spirit of Tourgée's argument—including the exhortation that the law "be color-blind"—found its echo in a dissenting opinion. But the seven members of the majority (one member of the Court, Justice David Brewer, did not participate) were quite unmoved: permeating the *Plessy* decision is a scarcely veiled assertion of the desirability of racial segregation by law: "In determining reasonableness [the legislature] is at liberty to act with reference to the established usages, customs, and traditions of the people. . . . Legislation is powerless to eradicate racial instincts or to abolish distinctions based upon physical differences, and the attempt to do so can only result in accentuating the difficulties of the present situation."[53] The Court's language was a far cry from its language in *Strauder v. West Virginia*, sixteen years before: "What is this but declaring that the law in the States shall be the same for the black as for the white . . . ?"[54]

The lone dissenter in *Plessy* was the first Justice Harlan, who had also dissented alone in the *Civil Rights Cases*. Harlan had courage and frequently he had an instinct for the right decision.[55] But he could also be very wrong, indeed.[56] Probably Holmes' unkind remark about Harlan was justified. "[H]e had a powerful vise the jaws of which couldn't be got nearer than two inches to each other."[57] At all events, Harlan was terribly right in *Plessy v. Ferguson*: "In my opinion, the judgment this day rendered will, in time, prove to be quite as pernicious as the decision made by this tribunal in the *Dred Scott* case."[58] *Plessy v. Ferguson* follows:

Mr. Justice BROWN *delivered the opinion of the court:*
This case turns upon the constitutionality of an act of the general assembly of the state of Louisiana, passed in 1890, providing for separate railway carriages for the white and colored races. Acts 1890, No. 111, p. 152.

The petition for the writ of prohibition [against being prosecuted criminally] averred that petitioner was seven eighths Cau-

casian and one eighth African blood; that the mixture of colored blood was not discernible in him, and that he was entitled to every right, privilege, and immunity secured to citizens of the United States of the white race; and that, upon such theory, he took possession of a vacant seat in a coach where passengers of the white race were accommodated, and was ordered by the conductor to vacate said coach and take a seat in another assigned to persons of the colored race, and having refused to comply with such demand he was forcibly ejected with the aid of a police officer, and imprisoned in the parish jail to answer a charge of having violated the above act.

The constitutionality of this act is . . . attacked upon the ground that it conflicts both with the Thirteenth Amendment of the Constitution, abolishing slavery, and the Fourteenth Amendment, which prohibits certain restrictive legislation on the part of the states.

.   .   .   .   .

A statute which implies merely a legal distinction between the white and colored races—a distinction which is founded in the color of the two races, and which must always exist so long as white men are distinguished from the other race by color—has no tendency to destroy the legal equality of the two races, or re-establish a state of involuntary servitude. Indeed, we do not understand that the Thirteenth Amendment is strenuously relied upon. . . .

.   .   .   .   .

The object of the [Fourteenth] amendment was undoubtedly to enforce the absolute equality of the two races before the law, but in the nature of things it could not have been intended to abolish distinctions based upon color, or to enforce social, as distinguished from political equality, or a commingling of the two races upon terms unsatisfactory to either. Laws permitting, and even requiring, their separation in places where they are liable to be brought into contact do not necessarily imply the inferiority of either race to the other, and have been generally, if not universally, recognized as within the competency of the state legislatures in the exercise of their police power. The most common instance of this is connected with the establishment of separate schools for white and colored children, which has been *held to be a valid exercise of the legislative power even by courts of States where the political rights of the colored race have been longest and most earnestly enforced.*

. . . . . .

Upon the other hand, where a statute of Louisiana required those engaged in the transportation of passengers among the States to give to all persons travelling within that State, upon vessels employed in that business, equal rights and privileges in all parts of the vessel, without distinction on account of race or color, and subjected to an action for damages the owner of such a vessel, who excluded colored passengers on account of their color from the cabin set aside by him for the use of whites, it was held to be so far as it applied to interstate commerce, unconstitutional and void. Hall v. De Cuir, 95 U.S. 485. *The court in this case, however, expressly disclaimed that it had anything whatever to do with the statute as a regulation of internal commerce, or affecting anything else than commerce among the States.*

. . . . . .

. . . In the present case no question of interference with interstate commerce can possibly arise, since the East Louisiana Railway appears to have been purely a local line, with both its termini within the State of Louisiana. . . .

. . . . . .

So far . . . as a conflict with the Fourteenth Amendment is concerned, the case reduces itself to the question whether the statute of Louisiana is a reasonable regulation, and with respect to this there must necessarily be a large discretion on the part of the legislature. In determining the question of reasonableness it is at liberty to act with reference to the established usages, customs, and traditions of the people, and with a view to the promotion of their comfort, and the preservation of the public peace and good order. Gauged by this standard, we cannot say that a law which authorizes or even requires the separation of the two races in public conveyances is unreasonable or more obnoxious to the Fourteenth Amendment than the acts of Congress requiring separate schools for colored children in the District of Columbia, the constitutionality of which does not seem to have been questioned, or the corresponding acts of state legislatures.

We consider the underlying fallacy of the plaintiff's argument to consist in the assumption that the enforced separation of the two races stamps the colored race with a badge of inferiority. If this be so, it is not by reason of anything found in the act, but solely because the colored race chooses to put that construction upon it. The argument necessarily assumes that if, as has been more than once the case, and is not unlikely to be so again, the colored race should become the dominant power in the state legislature, and should enact a law in precisely similar terms, it would thereby relegate the white race to an inferior position. We imagine that the white race, at least, would not acquiesce in this assumption. The argument also assumes that social prejudices may be overcome by legislation, and that equal rights cannot be secured to the negro except by an enforced commingling of the two races. We cannot accept this proposition. If the two races are to meet on terms of social equality, it must be the result of natural affinities, a mutual appreciation of each other's merits and a voluntary consent of individuals. As was said by the Court of Appeals of New York in People v. Gallagher, 93 N.Y. 438, 448, *"this end can neither be accomplished nor promoted by laws which conflict with the general sentiment of the community upon whom they are designed to operate. When the government, therefore, has secured to each of its citizens equal rights before the law and equal opportunities for improvement and progress, it has accomplished the end for which it is organized and performed all of the functions respecting social advantages with which it is endowed." Legislation is powerless to eradicate racial instincts or to abolish distinctions based upon physical differences, and the attempt to do so can only result in accentuating the difficulties of the present situation. If the civil and political rights of both races be equal one cannot be inferior to the other civilly or politically. If one race be inferior to the other socially, the Constitution of the United States cannot put them upon the same plane.*

.   .   .   .   .

The judgment of the court below is, therefore, Affirmed

Mr. Justice BREWER *did not hear the argument or participate in the decision of this case.*

Mr. Justice HARLAN *dissenting.*

.   .   .   .   .

The white race deems itself to be the dominant race in this country. And so it is, in prestige, in achievements, in education, in wealth and in power. So, I doubt not, it will continue to be for all time, if it remains true to its great heritage and holds fast to the principles of constitutional liberty. But in view of the Constitution, in the eye of the law, there is in this country no superior, dominant, ruling class of citizens. There is no caste here. Our Constitution is color-blind, and neither knows nor tolerates classes among citizens. In respect of civil rights, all citizens are equal before the law. The humblest is the peer of the most powerful. The laws regards man as man, and takes no account of his surroundings or of his color when his civil rights as guaranteed by the supreme law of the land are involved. It is therefore to be regretted that this high tribunal, the final expositor of the fundamental law of the land, has reached the conclusion that it is competent for a State to regulate the enjoyment by citizens of their civil rights solely upon the basis of race.

In my opinion, the judgment this day rendered will, in time, prove to be quite as pernicious as the decision made by this tribunal in the Dred Scott case. It was adjudged in that case that the descendants of Africans who were imported into this country and sold as slaves were not included nor intended to be included under the word "citizens" in the Constitution, and could not claim any of the rights and privileges which that instrument provided for and secured to citizens of the United States; that at the time of the adoption of the Constitution they were "considered as a subordinate and inferior class of beings, who had been subjugated by the dominant race, and, whether emancipated or not, yet remained subject to their authority, and had no rights or privileges but such as those who held the power and the government might choose to grant them." 19 How. 393, 404. The recent amendments of the Constitution, it was supposed, had eradicated these principles from our institutions. But it seems that we have yet, in some of the States a dominant race—a superior class of citizens, which assumes to regulate the enjoyment of civil rights, common to all citizens, upon the basis of race. The present decision, it may well be apprehended, will not stimulate aggressions, more or less brutal and irritating, upon the admitted rights of colored citizens, but will encourage the belief that it is possible, by means of state enactments, to defeat the beneficent purposes which the people of the United States had in view when they *adopted the recent amendments of the Constitution, by one of which the blacks of this country were made citizens of the United States and of the States in which they respectively reside and whose privileges and immunities, as citizens, the States are forbidden to abridge. Sixty millions of whites are in no danger from the presence here of eight millions of blacks. The destinies of the two races, in this country, are indissolubly linked together, and the interests of both require that the common government of all shall not permit the seeds of race hate to be planted under the sanction of law.*

.   .   .   .   .   .

I am of opinion that the statute of Louisiana is inconsistent with the personal liberty of citizens, white and black, in that State, and hostile to both the spirit and letter of the Constitution of the United States. If laws of like character should be enacted in the several States of the Union, the effect would be in the highest degree mischievous. Slavery, as an institution tolerated by law would, it is true, have disappeared from our country, but there would remain a power in the States, by sinister legislation, to interfere with the full enjoyment of the blessings of freedom; to regulate civil rights, common to all citizens, upon the basis of race; and to place in a condition of legal inferiority a large body of American citizens, now constituting a part of the political community, called the People of the United States, for whom, and by whom through representatives, our government is administered. Such a system is inconsistent with the guarantee given by the Constitution to each State of a republican form of government, and may be stricken down by Congressional action, or by the courts in the discharge of their solemn duty to maintain the supreme law of the land, anything in the constitution or laws of any State to the contrary notwithstanding.

For the reasons stated, I am constrained to withhold my assent from the opinion and judgment of the majority.[59]

The Court, in *Plessy*, did more than endorse separate railway cars and separate schools. It gave constitutional momentum to the growth of an entire way of life: the racially divided pattern that is known as Jim Crow. As Professor C. Vann Woodward has put it:

. . . [T]*he Jim Crow laws applied to all Negroes—not merely the rowdy, or drunken, or surly, or ignorant ones. The new laws did not countenance the old conservative tendency to distinguish between classes of the race, to encourage the "better" element, and to draw it into a white alliance. Those laws backed up the Alabamian who told the disfranchising convention of his state that no Negro in the world was the equal of "the least, poorest, lowest-down white man I ever knew";* . . . *The Jim Crow laws put the authority of the state or city in the voice of the streetcar conductor, the railway brakeman, the bus driver, the theater usher, and also into the voice of the hoodlum of the public parks and playgrounds. They gave free rein and the majesty of the law to mass aggressions that might otherwise have been curbed, blunted, or deflected. . . .*

The Jim Crow laws, unlike feudal laws, did not assign the subordinate group a fixed status in society. They were constantly pushing the Negro farther down.[60]

The *Plessy* rule endured for nearly sixty years. The southern states seldom undertook, especially in the field of education, to provide genuinely equal facilities for Negroes. Even so, the burden of maintaining dual facilities threatened the South with financial, as well as moral, insolvency. And the financial burden on the poorest section of the Union grew heavier as Negroes, under the resolute leadership of the National Association for the Advancement of Colored People, turned to the courts again and again to "equalize" the public schools. Schools were the crucial area of litigation. There, each morning, Negro children were required to repeat the indignity of being marked as inferior by the law.

b. The Court outlaws "Jim Crow"

Finally, in the 1950s, the NAACP brought five new cases to the Supreme Court—four from southern and border states, and one from the District of Columbia. In these cases quantitative equality of school buildings, equipment, and curricula was acknowledged. The only question was the *Plessy* question once again. Was not racial segregation itself inherently unequal? Had not Americans come to believe that any legal distinctions based on race alone were incompatible with American ideals? Did not new insights into emotional development, and a deeper national commitment to human dignity and equality, dictate an answer different from that handed down in 1896? Or was *Plessy* still good law? Indeed, could not a plausible argument be made that the Supreme Court had reinvigorated *Plessy* when, in the midst of World War II, in *Korematsu v. United States,* the Court had sustained the power of the national government to require American citizens of Japanese ancestry, *solely because of that allegedly suspect ancestry,* to move from their West Coast homes to relocation camps in the interior?[61]

The Court heard the appeals in the five consolidated school cases and then ordered further argument, directing counsel particularly to give the Court guidance in the form of fresh research into the history of the Fourteenth Amendment. Did the framers want to end segregated education? If so, was the judiciary the branch of government to order the change?

The proper answers to these questions were (it was an almost foregone conclusion) both "no" and "yes." The one thing that seemed to have been tolerably clear in the thinking of the framers of the Fourteenth Amendment was that extensions of racial equality, pursuant to the amendment, were expected to be undertaken by Congress rather than by the courts. But this expectation was merely the mistaken anticipation of the Radical Republicans that effective leadership on civil rights matters would continue to be found in Congress. According to Professor Alexander M. Bickel, "It indicates no judgment about the powers and functions properly to be exercised by the other branches."[62] There was no plain consensus among the framers as to what steps might in the future be taken to give content to the Fourteenth Amendment. "Some no doubt felt more certain than others that the new amendment would make possible further strides toward the ideal of equality. That remained to be decided, and there is no indication of the way in which anyone thought the decision would go on any specific issue. It depended a good deal on the trend in public opinion." Thus, for a Court faced in 1954 with the responsibility of re-examining *Plessy,* "the record of history, properly understood, left the way open to, in fact invited, a decision based on the moral and material state of the nation in 1954, not 1866."[63]

On May 17, 1954, the Court, through its newly appointed Chief Justice, Earl Warren, handed down the two *unanimous* opinions which together constitute the *School Segregation Cases*. The first, *Brown v. Board of Education*, dealt with segregated schools in the states. The second, *Bolling v. Sharpe*, dealt with segregated schools in the District of Columbia. The District of Columbia problem was a separate one doctrinally because there is no equal protection clause limiting federal action. Therefore, the District of Columbia case had to be disposed of under the Fifth Amendment's "due process" clause.

The basic opinion was *Brown v. Board of Education*. The text of the opinion follows:

MR. CHIEF JUSTICE WARREN *delivered the opinion of the Court.*

These cases come to us from the States of Kansas, South Carolina, Virginia, and Delaware. They are premised on different facts and different local conditions, but a common legal question justifies their consideration together in this consolidated opinion.

In each of the cases, minors of the Negro race, through their legal representatives, seek the aid of the courts in obtaining admission to the public schools of their community on a nonsegregated basis. In each instance, they had been denied admission to schools attended by white children under laws requiring or permitting segregation according to race. This segregation was alleged to deprive the plaintiffs of the equal protection of the laws under the Fourteenth Amendment. In each of the cases other than the Delaware case, a three-judge federal district court denied relief to the plaintiffs on the so-called "separate but equal" doctrine announced by this Court in Plessy v. Ferguson, *163 U.S. 537. Under that doctrine, equality of treatment is accorded when the races are provided substantially equal facilities, even though these facilities be separate. In the Delaware case, the Supreme Court of Delaware adhered to that doctrine, but ordered that the plaintiffs be admitted to the white schools because of their superiority to the Negro schools.*

The plaintiffs contend that segregated public schools are not "equal" and cannot be made "equal," and that hence they are deprived of the equal protection of the laws. Because of the obvious importance of the question presented, the Court took jurisdiction. Argument was heard in the 1952 Term, and re-

*argument was heard this Term on certain questions propounded
by the Court.*

*Reargument was largely devoted to the circumstances sur-
rounding the adoption of the Fourteenth Amendment in 1868. It
covered exhaustively consideration of the Amendment in Congress, ratification by the states, then existing practices in racial
segregation, and the views of proponents and opponents of the
Amendment. This discussion and our own investigation convince
us that, although these sources cast some light, it is not enough
to resolve the problem with which we are faced. At best, they
are inconclusive. The most avid proponents of the post-War
Amendments undoubtedly intended them to remove all legal distinctions among "all persons born or naturalized in the United
States." Their opponents, just as certainly, were antagonistic to
both the letter and the spirit of the Amendments and wished
them to have the most limited effect. What others in Congress
and the state legislatures had in mind cannot be determined with
any degree of certainty.*

*An additional reason for the inconclusive nature of the
Amendment's history, with respect to segregated schools, is the
status of public education at that time. In the South, the movement toward free common schools, supported by general taxation, had not yet taken hold. Education of white children was
largely in the hands of private groups. Education of Negroes was
almost non-existent, and practically all of the race were illiterate.
In fact, any education of Negroes was forbidden by law in some
states. Today, in contrast, many Negroes have achieved outstanding success in the arts and sciences as well as in the business and
professional world. It is true that public school education at the
time of the Amendment had advanced further in the North, but
the effect of the Amendment on Northern States was generally
ignored in the congressional debates. Even in the North, the conditions of public education did not approximate those existing
today. The curriculum was usually rudimentary; ungraded
schools were common in rural areas; the school term was but
three months a year in many states; and compulsory school attendance was virtually unknown. As a consequence, it is not
surprising that there should be so little in the history of the Fourteenth Amendment relating to its intended effect on public education.*

In the first cases in this Court construing the Fourteenth Amendment, decided shortly after its adoption, the Court interpreted it as proscribing all state-imposed discriminations against the Negro race. The doctrine of "separate but equal" did not make its appearance in this Court until 1896 in the case of Plessy v. Ferguson, supra, involving not education but transportation. American courts have since labored with the doctrine for over half a century. In this Court, there have been six cases involving the "separate but equal" doctrine in the field of public education. In Cumming v. County Board of Education, 175 U.S. 528, and Gong Lum v. Rice, 275 U.S. 78, the validity of the doctrine itself was not challenged. In more recent cases, all on the graduate school level, inequality was found in that specific benefits enjoyed by white students were denied to Negro students of the same educational qualifications. Missouri ex rel. Gaines v. Canada, 305 U.S. 337; Sipuel v. Oklahoma, 332 U.S. 631; Sweatt v. Painter, 339 U.S. 629; McLaurin v. Oklahoma State Regents, 339 U.S. 637. In none of these cases was it necessary to re-examine the doctrine to grant relief to the Negro plaintiff. And in Sweatt v. Painter, supra, the Court expressly reserved decision on the question whether Plessy v. Ferguson should be held inapplicable to public education.

In the instant cases, that question is directly presented. Here, unlike Sweatt v. Painter, there are findings below that the Negro and white schools involved have been equalized, or are being equalized, with respect to buildings, curricula, qualifications and salaries of teachers, and other "tangible" factors. Our decision, therefore, cannot turn on merely a comparison of these tangible factors in the Negro and white schools involved in each of the cases. We must look instead to the effect of segregation itself on public education.

In approaching this problem, we cannot turn the clock back to 1868 when the Amendment was adopted, or even to 1896 when Plessy v. Ferguson was written. We must consider public education in the light of its full development and its present place in American life throughout the Nation. Only in this way can it be determined if segregation in public schools deprives these plaintiffs of the equal protection of the laws.

Today, education is perhaps the most important function of state and local governments. Compulsory school attendance laws *and the great expenditures for education both demonstrate our recognition of the importance of education to our democratic society. It is required in the performance of our most basic public responsibilities, even service in the armed forces. It is the very foundation of good citizenship. Today it is a principal instrument in awakening the child to cultural values, in preparing him for later professional training, and in helping him to adjust normally to his environment. In these days, it is doubtful that any child may reasonably be expected to succeed in life if he is denied the opportunity of an education. Such an opportunity, where the state has undertaken to provide it, is a right which must be made available to all on equal terms.*

We come then to the question presented: Does segregation of children in public schools solely on the basis of race, even though the physical facilities and other "tangible" factors may be equal, deprive the children of the minority group of equal educational opportunities? We believe that it does.

In Sweatt v. Painter, supra, in finding that a segregated law school for Negroes could not provide them equal educational opportunities, this Court relied in large part on "those qualities which are incapable of objective measurement but which make for greatness in a law school." In McLaurin v. Oklahoma State Regents, supra, the Court, in requiring that a Negro admitted to a white graduate school be treated like all other students, again resorted to intangible considerations: ". . . his ability to study, to engage in discussions and exchange views with other students, and, in general, to learn his profession." Such considerations apply with added force to children in grade and high schools. To separate them from others of similar age and qualifications solely because of their race generates a feeling of inferiority as to their status in the community that may affect their hearts and minds in a way unlikely ever to be undone. The effect of this separation on their educational opportunities was well stated by a finding in the Kansas case by a court which nevertheless felt compelled to rule against the Negro plaintiffs:

> *Segregation of white and colored children in public schools has a detrimental effect upon the colored children. The impact is greater when it has the sanction of the law; for the policy of separating the races is usually interpreted as denoting the inferiority of the negro group. A sense of in-*

feriority affects the motivation of a child to learn. Segregation with the sanction of law, therefore, has a tendency to
[retard] the educational and mental development of negro
children and to deprive them of some of the benefits they
would receive in a racial[ly] integrated school system.

Whatever may have been the extent of psychological knowledge
at the time of Plessy v. Ferguson, this finding is amply supported
by modern authority. [Here the Court, in a footnote 11, cited the
following materials: "K. B. Clark, Effect of Prejudice and Dis-
crimination on Personality Development (Midcentury White
House Conference on Children and Youth, 1950); Witmer and
Kotinsky, Personality in the Making (1952), c. VI; Deutscher and
Chein, The Psychological Effects of Enforced Segregation: A
Survey of Social Science Opinion, 26 J. Psychol. 259 (1948);
Chein, What Are the Psychological Effects of Segregation Under
Conditions of Equal Facilities?, 3 Int. J. Opinion and Attitude
Res. 229 (1949); Brameld, Educational Costs, in Discrimination
and National Welfare (MacIver, ed., 1949), 44–48; Frazier, The
Negro in the United States (1949), 678–681. And see generally
Myrdal, An American Dilemma (1944)."] Any language in Plessy
v. Ferguson contrary to this finding is rejected.

We conclude that in the field of public education the doctrine of "separate but equal" has no place. Separate educational
facilities are inherently unequal. Therefore, we hold that the
plaintiffs and others similarly situated for whom the actions have
been brought are, by reason of the segregation complained of,
deprived of the equal protection of the laws guaranteed by the
Fourteenth Amendment. This disposition makes unnecessary any
discussion whether such segregation also violates the Due Process
Clause of the Fourteenth Amendment.

Because these are class actions, because of the wide applicability of this decision, and because of the great variety of local
conditions, the formulation of decrees in these cases presents
problems of considerable complexity. On reargument, the consideration of appropriate relief was necessarily subordinated to
the primary question—the constitutionality of segregation in
public education. We have now announced that such segregation is a denial of the equal protection of the laws. In order that
we may have the full assistance of the parties in formulating
decrees, the cases will be restored to the docket, and the parties

are requested to present further argument on Questions 4 and 5 [relating to the timing of desegregation decrees and to what courts should police such decrees] previously propounded by the Court for the reargument this Term. The Attorney General of the United States is again invited to participate. The Attorneys General of the states requiring or permitting segregation in public education will also be permitted to appear as amici curiae *upon request to do so by September 15, 1954, and submission of briefs by October 1, 1954.*

It is so ordered.[64]

Having dealt with public school segregation in the states, the Supreme Court, in *Bolling v. Sharpe*, which follows, turned to public school segregation in the Nation's capital:

MR. CHIEF JUSTICE WARREN *delivered the opinion of the Court.*

This case challenges the validity of segregation in the public schools of the District of Columbia. The petitioners, minors of the Negro race, allege that such segregation deprives them of due process of law under the Fifth Amendment. They were refused admission to a public school attended by white children solely because of their race. They sought the aid of the District Court for the District of Columbia in obtaining admission. That court dismissed their complaint. The Court granted a writ of certiorari before judgment in the Court of Appeals because of the importance of the constitutional question presented. 344 U.S. 873.

We have this day held that the Equal Protection Clause of the Fourteenth Amendment prohibits the states from maintaining racially segregated public schools. The legal problem in the District of Columbia is somewhat different, however. The Fifth Amendment, which is applicable in the District of Columbia, does not contain an equal protection clause as does the Fourteenth Amendment which applies only to the states. But the concepts of equal protection and due process, both stemming from our American ideal of fairness, are not mutually exclusive. The "equal protection of the laws" is a more explicit safeguard of prohibited unfairness than "due process of law," and, therefore, we do not imply that the two are always interchangeable phrases.

But, as this Court has recognized, discrimination may be so un-justifiable as to be violative of due process.

Classifications based solely upon race must be scrutinized with particular care, since they are contrary to our traditions and hence constitutionally suspect. As long ago as 1896, this Court declared the principle "that the Constitution of the United States, in its present form, forbids, so far as civil and political rights are concerned, discrimination by the General Government, or by the States, against any citizen because of his race." [Gibson v. Mississippi, 162 U.S. 565, 591.] And in Buchanan v. Warley, 245 U.S. 60, the Court held that a statute which limited the right of a property owner to convey his property to a person of another race was, as an unreasonable discrimination, a denial of due process of law.

Although the Court has not assumed to define "liberty" with any great precision, that term is not confined to mere freedom from bodily restraint. Liberty under law extends to the full range of conduct which the individual is free to pursue, and it cannot be restricted except for a proper governmental objective. Segregation in public education is not reasonably related to any proper governmental objective, and thus it imposes on Negro children of the District of Columbia a burden that constitutes an arbitrary deprivation of their liberty in violation of the Due Process Clause.

In view of our decision that the Constitution prohibits the states from maintaining racially segregated public schools, it would be unthinkable that the same Constitution would impose a lesser duty on the Federal Government. We hold that racial segregation in the public schools of the District of Columbia is a denial of the due process of law guaranteed by the Fifth Amendment to the Constitution.

For the reasons set out in Brown v. Board of Education, *this case will be restored to the docket for reargument on Questions 4 and 5 previously propounded by the Court. 345 U.S. 972.*

It is so ordered.[65]

A year later the Court, after reargument, decreed that the new rule should be implemented by the federal district courts (from which most of the cases had arisen) and that implementation should go forward "with all deliberate speed."[66]

c. The impact of the *School Segregation Cases*

Except for waging and winning the Civil War and World Wars I and II, the decision in the *School Segregation Cases* was probably the most important American governmental act of any kind since the Emancipation Proclamation. Necessarily, it met with warm support and warm antagonism. The latter was perhaps less widespread, but surely more vocal, than the former.

Ninety-six southern Congressmen joined in attacking the decisions:

. . . The decision of the Supreme Court in the school cases . . . [is] clear abuse of judicial power. . . . The original Constitution does not mention education. Neither does the Fourteenth Amendment or any other amendment. . . .[67]

But, of course, as Justice Jackson had said for the Court—eleven years before the *School Segregation Cases*—in striking down a state requirement that school children salute the flag:

The Fourteenth Amendment . . . protects the citizen against the State itself and all of its creatures—Boards of Education not excepted. These have, of course, important, delicate, and highly discretionary functions, but none that they may not perform within the limits of the Bill of Rights. . . .[68]

There has also been a frequent complaint that the *School Segregation Cases* do not rest on "law" but on the Court's personal views in the field of "sociology" or "psychology." These criticisms have tended to center around the Court's apparent reliance on the social science materials listed by the Court in footnote 11 of its opinion (347 U.S. 494). But the criticisms are misdirected. The Court simply used the footnote to show that systematic observation of human behavior confirmed what the Justices knew intuitively—that segregation imposed by law degrades its victims. What the Court really decided was—as the late Justice Sherman Minton put it after he left the bench—that segregation imposed by law is "invidious."[69] The Court was simply making a judgment about the dominant moral values of the American community, values which have altered in substantial measure since *Plessy* was decided in 1896. Weighing such moral values is an accredited, indeed essential, part of constitutional adjudication. It is part of the process of defining "the very essence of a scheme of ordered liberty"—the process of constitutional definition described in *Palko v. Connecticut*. And, as Professor Bickel has demonstrated, "the record of [the Fourteenth Amendment's] history . . . invited, a decision based on the moral and material state of the nation in 1954. . . ."[70]

Indeed, to the extent that it is said to be wrong for a decision to concern itself with nonlegal principles, censure should start with *Plessy*. The opinion, as has been pointed out, is deeply charged with judicial presuppositions about intractable natural differences between Negroes and whites to which the community should and must accommodate itself. The judicial presuppositions, probably owing much to the then influential sociological writings of William Graham Sumner, "ought to interest those who complain today about judges relying on 'sociology' rather than on 'law.' "[71]

In a sense there was a special fitness in utilizing a public school case as a vehicle for jettisoning the apartheid of *Plessy*. "Today," as the Court recognized, "education is perhaps the most important function of state and local governments."[72] But underlying this practical observation was an ethical—one might even say a constitutional—proposition. "The public school," as Justice Frankfurter had remarked a few years earlier, "is at once the symbol of our democracy and the most pervasive means for promoting our common destiny."[73]

But the public school is not yet the symbol of our democracy. A decade after the decision, only 10 per cent of the 3,250,000 Negro public school children in the seventeen southern and border states and the District of Columbia had been enrolled in desegregated schools.[74]

Thus far the "all deliberate speed" decreed by the Court has emphasized deliberation, not speed.[75] (Meanwhile it has been becoming increasingly apparent that many northern communities operate what are, in effect, segregated school systems—most often by virtue of residential patterns, but sometimes through discriminatory design.[76])

Nevertheless, the curve of desegregation is upward, and the rate is bound to accelerate. For the Court's mandate is clear. And the Court's purpose to enforce that mandate is also clear.

(1). *Little Rock in 1957: a governor defies the federal courts*

The strength of the Supreme Court's resolve is best illustrated by the view it took of the tragic events which occurred in Little Rock, Arkansas, in the late summer of 1957. Little Rock was a city which, back in 1954, seemed to have recognized its obligation to initiate compliance with the holding in the *School Segregation Cases*. But three years later, under the leadership of the Governor, Orval Faubus, public officials adopted the ruinous course of forceful defiance of a federal court school-integration decree. The doleful history of Little Rock is best told in the Supreme Court's own words:

> On May 20, 1954, three days after the first Brown opinion, the Little Rock District School Board adopted, and on May 23, 1954, made public, a statement of policy entitled "Supreme Court Decision—Segregation in Public Schools." In this statement the Board recognized that
>
> > It is our responsibility to comply with Federal Constitutional Requirements and we intend to do so when the Supreme Court of the United States outlines the method to be followed.
>
> Thereafter the Board undertook studies of the administrative problems confronting the transition to a desegregated public school system at Little Rock. It instructed the Superintendent of Schools to prepare a plan for desegregation, and approved such a plan on May 24, 1955, seven days before the second Brown opinion. The plan provided for desegregation at the senior high school level (grades 10 through 12) as the first stage. Desegregation at the junior high and elementary levels was to follow. It was contemplated that desegregation at the high school level would commence in the fall of 1957, and the expectation was that complete desegregation of the school system would be accomplished by 1963. Following the adoption of this plan, the Superintendent of Schools discussed it with a large number of citizen groups in the city. As a result of these discussions, the Board reached the conclusion that "a large majority of the residents" of Little Rock were of "the belief . . . that the Plan, although objectionable in principle," from the point of view of

those supporting segregated schools, "was still the best for the interests of all pupils in the District."

Upon challenge by a group of Negro plaintiffs desiring mo;e rapid completion of the desegregation process, the District Court upheld the School Board's plan, Aaron v. Cooper, 143 F. Supp. 855. The Court of Appeals affirmed. 243 F. 2d 361. Review of that judgment was not sought here.

While the School Board was thus going forward with its preparation for desegregating the Little Rock school system, other state authorities, in contrast, were actively pursuing a program designed to perpetuate in Arkansas the system of racial segregation which this Court had held violated the Fourteenth Amendment. First came, in November 1956, an amendment to the State Constitution flatly commanding the Arkansas General Assembly to oppose "in every Constitutional manner the Unconstitutional desegregation decisions of May 17, 1954 and May 31, 1955 of the United States Supreme Court," Ark. Const., Amend. 44, and, through the initiative, a pupil assignment law, Ark. Stat. 80–1519 to 80–1524. Pursuant to this state constitutional command, a law relieving school children from compulsory attendance at racially mixed schools, Ark. Stat. 80–1525, and a law establishing a State Sovereignty Commission, Ark. Stat. 6–801 to 6–824, were enacted by the General Assembly in February 1957.

The School Board and the Superintendent of Schools nevertheless continued with preparations to carry out the first stage of the desegregation program. Nine Negro children were scheduled for admission in September 1957 to Central High School, which has more than two thousand students. Various administrative measures, designed to assure the smooth transition of this first stage of desegregation, were undertaken.

On September 2, 1957, the day before these Negro students were to enter Central High, the school authorities were met with drastic opposing action on the part of the Governor of Arkansas who dispatched units of the Arkansas National Guard to the Central High School grounds and placed the school "off limits" to colored students. As found by the District Court in subsequent proceedings, the Governor's action had not been requested by the school authorities, and was entirely unheralded. The findings were these:

Up to this time [September 2], no crowds had gathered about Central High School and no acts of violence or threats of violence in connection with the carrying out of the plan had occurred. Nevertheless, out of an abundance of caution, the school authorities had frequently conferred with the Mayor and Chief of Police of Little Rock about taking appropriate steps by the Little Rock police to prevent any possible disturbances or acts of violence in connection with the attendance of the 9 colored students at Central High School. The Mayor considered that the Little Rock police force could adequately cope with any incidents which might arise at the opening of school. The Mayor, the Chief of Police, and the school authorities made no request to the Governor or any representative of his for State assistance in maintaining peace and order at Central High School. Neither the Governor nor any other official of the State government consulted with the Little Rock authorities about whether the Little Rock police were prepared to cope with any incidents which might arise at the school, about any need for State assistance in maintaining peace and order, or about stationing the Arkansas National Guard at Central High School. Aaron v. Cooper, 156 F. Supp. 220, 225.

The Board's petition for postponement in this proceeding states: "The effect of that action [of the Governor] was to harden the core of opposition to the Plan and cause many persons who theretofore had reluctantly accepted the Plan to believe there was some power in the State of Arkansas which, when exerted, could nullify the Federal law and permit disobedience of the decree of this [District] Court, and from that date hostility to the Plan was increased and criticism of the officials of the [School] District has become more bitter and unrestrained." The Governor's action caused the School Board to request the Negro students on September 2 not to attend the high school "until the legal dilemma was solved." The next day, September 3, 1957, the Board petitioned the District Court for instructions, and the court, after a hearing, found that the Board's request of the Negro students to stay away from the high school had been made because of the stationing of the military guards by the state authorities. The court determined that this was not a reason for departing from the approved plan, and ordered the School Board and Superintendent to proceed with it.

On the morning of the next day, September 4, 1957, the Negro children attempted to enter the high school but, as the District Court later found, units of the Arkansas National Guard *"acting pursuant to the Governor's order, stood shoulder to shoulder at the school grounds and thereby forcibly prevented the 9 Negro students . . . from entering,"* as they continued to do every school day during the following three weeks. 156 F. Supp., at 225.

That same day, September 4, 1957, the United States Attorney for the Eastern District of Arkansas was requested by the District Court to begin an immediate investigation in order to fix responsibility for the interference with the orderly implementation of the District Court's direction to carry out the desegregation program. Three days later, September 7, the District Court denied a petition of the School Board and the Superintendent of Schools for an order temporarily suspending continuance of the program.

Upon completion of the United States Attorney's investigation, he and the Attorney General of the United States, at the District Court's request, entered the proceedings and filed a petition on behalf of the United States, as amicus curiae, to enjoin the Governor of Arkansas and officers of the Arkansas National Guard from further attempts to prevent obedience to the court's order. After hearings on the petition, the District Court found that the School Board's plan had been obstructed by the Governor through the use of National Guard troops, and granted a preliminary injunction on September 20, 1957, enjoining the Governor and the officers of the Guard from preventing the attendance of Negro children at Central High School, and from otherwise obstructing or interfering with the orders of the court in connection with the plan. 156 F. Supp. 220, affirmed, Faubus v. United States, 254 F. 2d 797. The National Guard was then withdrawn from the school.

The next school day was Monday, September 23, 1957. The Negro children entered the high school that morning under the protection of the Little Rock Police Department and members of the Arkansas State Police. But the officers caused the children to be removed from the school during the morning because they had difficulty controlling a large and demonstrating crowd which had gathered at the high school. 163 F. Supp., at 16. On Septem-

ber 25, however, the President of the United States dispatched federal troops to Central High School and admission of the Negro students to the school was thereby effected. . . .[77]

That morning, just before the Negro students were brought into Central High School, Major General Edwin A. Walker, commanding the federal troops dispatched by President Eisenhower, addressed a special assembly of the white students attending Central High School:

Young ladies and gentlemen of Central High School. Mr. Blossom, your Superintendent of Schools, has asked me to come to your school this morning and discuss with you the situation in Little Rock and what it means to you students. I welcome this opportunity to do so.

As you know, the Fourteenth Amendment to the Constitution of the United States guarantees to all citizens the equal protection of the laws. Since the adoption of this amendment many states have provided separate schools for their children on the basis of color. The laws establishing such schools have, however, been challenged in the courts; and about three years ago, the Supreme Court of the United States determined that such laws are contrary to the provisions of the Fourteenth Amendment and consequently invalid. This decision by the highest court in the land is, of course, an authoritative interpretation of our Constitution, is binding on all citizens and government officers, both state and Federal, and may not, under our law, be changed except by an amendment to the Constitution.

Because of the Supreme Court's decision, it became necessary for those states maintaining separate schools to revise their systems to eliminate distinctions on the basis of color. The nature of these plans was left to the states and local communities, subject to approval by the local Federal District courts. The Little Rock School District prepared such a plan which was approved by both the District Court and Circuit Court of Appeals. This plan provides for a very gradual abandonment of the separate school system starting this year.

Subsequent to the approval of this plan, attempts were made in the courts to prevent the school authorities from putting it into effect.

I need not go into the details of this litigation; sufficient to say, it was unsuccessful, and that the plan as originally approved remains unchanged and in full force and effect.

During the past few weeks, as you are well aware, the situation in Little Rock has been such as to prevent the entrance of a few students into your high school. Therefore, to see that the laws of the land be faithfully executed, the President has found it necessary to call the National Guard of Arkansas into the Federal service and has directed that this force and such other armed force as may be made available be used to enforce the orders of the court. As an officer of the United States Army, I have been chosen to command these forces and to execute the President's orders.

What does all this mean to you students? You have often heard it said, no doubt, that the United States is a nation under law and not under men. This means that we are governed by laws, properly decided upon by duly constituted authority, and not by the decrees of one man or one class of men. Since this is true, it means that we are all subject to all the laws, whether we approve of them personally or not, and as law-abiding citizens, have an obligation in conscience to obey them. There can be no exceptions; if it were otherwise, we would not be a strong nation but a mere unruly mob.

I believe that you are well-intentioned, law-abiding citizens, who understand the necessity of obeying the law, and are determined to do so. You have nothing to fear from my soldiers, and no one will interfere with your coming, going or your peaceful pursuit of your studies. However, I would be less than honest if I failed to tell you that I intend to use all means necessary to prevent any interference with the execution of your school board's plan. This is what I have been ordered to do, and I intend to carry out my orders. Those who interfere or disrupt the proper administration of the school will be removed by the soldiers on duty and turned over to the local police for disposition in accordance with the laws of your community.

One last word about my soldiers. They are here because they have been ordered to be here. They are seasoned, well-trained soldiers, many of them combat veterans. Being soldiers, they are as determined as I to carry out their orders. However, as I stated before, the law-abiding people have nothing to fear from them.

They have been carefully instructed not to molest any law-abiding citizen in his person or property, and they will obey these orders. Since a peaceful atmosphere must be maintained in the school and its vicinity, it may be necessary for them to issue instructions concerning such things as loitering, assembling in large groups, and otherwise making it difficult for them to perform their duties. I earnestly ask that you cooperate, for your own benefit and ours.

I wish you all success in your school year and Mr. Matthews [school principal] I thank you for the opportunity to talk to the student body.[78]

Troops—and eight of the Negro students—remained in Central High throughout the academic year of 1957–58. In the course of the winter the Little Rock school officials initiated the proceeding which brought Little Rock's problems to the Supreme Court the following September, in the case of *Cooper v. Aaron:*

. . . On February 20, 1958, the School Board and the Superintendent of Schools filed a petition in the District Court seeking a postponement of their program for desegregation. Their position in essence was that because of extreme public hostility, which they stated had been engendered largely by the official attitudes and actions of the Governor and the Legislature, the maintenance of a sound educational program at Central High School, with the Negro students in attendance, would be impossible. The Board therefore proposed that the Negro students already admitted to the school be withdrawn and sent to segregated schools, and that all further steps to carry out the Board's desegregation program be postponed for a period later suggested by the Board to be two and one-half years.

After a hearing the District Court granted the relief requested by the Board. Among other things the court found that the past year at Central High School had been attended by conditions of "chaos, bedlam and turmoil"; that there were "repeated incidents of more or less serious violence directed against the Negro students and their property"; that there was "tension and unrest among the school administrators, the classroom teachers, the pupils, and the latters' parents, which inevitably had an adverse effect upon the educational program"; that a school official was threatened with violence; that a "serious financial burden" had been cast on the School District; that the education of the students had suffered "and under existing conditions will continue to suffer"; that the Board would continue to need "military assistance or its equivalent"; that the local police department would not be able "to detail enough men to afford the necessary protection"; and that the situation was "intolerable." 163 F. Supp., at 20–26.

. . . . .

In affirming the judgment of the Court of Appeals which reversed the District Court we have accepted without reservation the position of the School Board, the Superintendent of Schools, and their counsel that they displayed entire good faith in the conduct of these proceedings and in dealing with the unfortunate and distressing sequence of events which has been outlined. We likewise have accepted the findings of the District Court as to the conditions at Central High School during the 1957–1958 school year, and also the findings that the educational progress of all the students, white and colored, of that school has suffered and will continue to suffer if the conditions which prevailed last year are permitted to continue.

The significance of these findings, however, is to be considered in light of the fact, indisputably revealed by the record before us, that the conditions they depict are directly traceable to the actions of legislators and executive officials of the State of Arkansas, taken in their official capacities, which reflect their own determination to resist this Court's decision in the Brown *case and which have brought about violent resistance to that decision in Arkansas. In its petition for certiorari filed in this Court, the School Board itself describes the situation in this language: "The legislative, executive, and judicial departments of the state government opposed the desegregation of Little Rock schools by enacting laws, calling out troops, making statements villifying [sic] federal law and federal courts, and failing to utilize state law enforcement agencies and judicial processes to maintain public peace."*

One may well sympathize with the position of the Board in the face of the frustrating conditions which have confronted it, but, regardless of the Board's good faith, the actions of the other state agencies responsible for those conditions compel us to reject the Board's legal position. Had Central High School been under the direct management of the State itself, it could hardly be suggested that those immediately in charge of the school should be heard to assert their own good faith as a legal excuse for delay in implementing the constitutional rights of these respondents, when vindication of those rights was rendered difficult or impossible by the actions of other state officials. The situation here is in no different posture because the members of the School Board and the Superintendent of Schools are local officials; from the point of view of the Fourteenth Amendment, they stand in this litigation as the agents of the State.

The constitutional rights of respondents are not to be sacrificed or yielded to the violence and disorder which have followed upon the actions of the Governor and Legislature. As this Court said some 41 years ago in a unanimous opinion in a case involving another aspect of racial segregation: "It is urged that this proposed segregation will promote the public peace by preventing race conflicts. Desirable as this is, and important as is the preservation of the public peace, this aim cannot be accomplished by laws or ordinances which deny rights created or protected by the Federal Constitution." Buchanan v. Warley, 245 U.S. 60, 81. Thus law and order are not here to be preserved by depriving the Negro children of their constitutional rights. The record before us clearly establishes that the growth of the Board's difficulties to a magnitude beyond its unaided power to control is the product of state action. Those difficulties, as counsel for the Board forthrightly conceded on the oral argument in this Court, can also be brought under control by state action.

The controlling legal principles are plain. The command of the Fourteenth Amendment is that no "State" shall deny to any person within its jurisdiction the equal protection of the laws. "A State acts by its legislative, its executive, or its judicial authorities. It can act in no other way. The constitutional provision, therefore, must mean that no agency of the State, or of the officers or agents by whom its powers are exerted, shall deny to any person within its jurisdiction the equal protection of the laws. Whoever, by virtue of public position under a State government, . . . denies or takes away the equal protection of the laws, violates the constitutional inhibition; and as he acts in the name and for the State, and is clothed with the State's power, his act is that of the State. This must be so, or the constitutional prohibition has no meaning." Ex parte Virginia, *100 U.S. 339, 347. Thus the prohibitions of the Fourteenth Amendment extend to all action of the State denying equal protection of the laws; whatever the agency of the State taking the action, see* Virginia v. Rives, *100 U.S. 313;* Pennsylvania v. Board of Directors of City Trusts cf Philadelphia, *353 U.S. 230;* Shelley v. Kraemer, *334 U.S. 1; or whatever the guise in which it is taken, see* Derrington v. Plummer, *240 F. 2d 922;* Department of Conservation and Development v. Tate, *231 F. 2d 615. In short, the constitutional rights of children not to be discriminated against in school admission on grounds of race or color declared by this Court in the* Brown *case can neither be nullified openly and directly by state legislators or state executive or judicial officers, nor nullified indirectly by them through evasive schemes for segregation whether attempted "ingeniously or ingenuously."* Smith v. Texas, *311 U.S. 128, 132.*

What has been said, in the light of the facts developed, is enough to dispose of the case. However, we should answer the premise of the actions of the Governor and Legislature that they are not bound by our holding in the Brown *case. It is necessary only to recall some basic constitutional propositions which are settled doctrine.*

Article VI of the Constitution makes the Constitution the "supreme Law of the Land." In 1803, Chief Justice Marshall, speaking for a unanimous Court, referring to the Constitution as "the fundamental and paramount law of the nation," declared in the notable case of Marbury v. Madison, *1 Cranch 137, 177, that "It is emphatically the province and duty of the judicial department to say what the law is." This decision declared the basic principle that the federal judiciary is supreme in the exposition of the law of the Constitution, and that principle has ever since been respected by this Court and the Country as a permanent and indispensable feature of our constitutional system. It follows that the interpretation of the Fourteenth Amendment enunciated by this Court in the* Brown *case is the supreme law of the land, and Art. VI of the Constitution makes it of binding effect on the States "any Thing in the Constitution or Laws of any State to the Contrary notwithstanding." Every state legislator and executive and judicial officer is solemnly committed by oath taken pursuant* to Art. VI, cl. 3, "to support this Constitution." Chief Justice Taney, speaking for a unanimous Court in 1859, said that this requirement reflected the framers' "anxiety to preserve it [the Constitution] in full force, in all its powers, and to guard against resistance to or evasion of its authority, on the part of a State. . . ." Ableman v. Booth, 21 How. 506, 524.

No state legislator or executive or judicial officer can war against the Constitution without violating his undertaking to support it. Chief Justice Marshall spoke for a unanimous Court in saying that: "If the legislatures of the several states may, at will, annul the judgments of the courts of the United States, and destroy the rights acquired under those judgments, the constitution itself becomes a solemn mockery. . . ." United States v. Peters, 5 Cranch 115, 136. A Governor who asserts a power to nullify a federal court order is similarly restrained. If he had such power, said Chief Justice Hughes, in 1932, also for a unanimous Court, "it is manifest that the fiat of a state Governor, and not the Constitution of the United States, would be the supreme law of the land; that the restrictions of the Federal Constitution upon the exercise of state power would be but impotent phrases. . . ." Sterling v. Constantin, 287 U.S. 378, 397–398.

It is, of course, quite true that the responsibility for public education is primarily the concern of the States, but it is equally true that such responsibilities, like all other state activity, must be exercised consistently with federal constitutional requirements as they apply to state action. The Constitution created a government dedicated to equal justice under law. The Fourteenth Amendment embodied and emphasized that ideal. State support of segregated schools through any arrangement, management, funds, or property cannot be squared with the Amendment's command that no State shall deny to any person within its jurisdiction the equal protection of the laws. The right of a student not to be segregated on racial grounds in schools so maintained is indeed so fundamental and pervasive that it is embraced in the concept of due process of law. Bolling v. Sharpe, 347 U.S. 497. The basic decision in Brown was unanimously reached by this Court only after the case had been briefed and twice argued and the issues had been given the most serious consideration. Since the first Brown opinion three new Justices have come to the Court. They are at one with the Justices still on the Court who

*participated in that basic decision as to its correctness, and that
decision is now unanimously reaffirmed. The principles announced in that decision and the obedience of the States to them,
according to the command of the Constitution, are indispensable
for the protection of the freedoms guaranteed by our fundamental
charter for all of us. Our constitutional ideal of equal justice
under law is thus made a living truth.*[79]

(2). New Orleans in 1960: a legislature tries "interposition"

Rioting, together with official opposition to federal court orders,
recurred in the fall of 1960, in New Orleans.[80] This time a
state legislature embraced the doctrine of "interposition"—the
notion, which traces its dubious parentage back to Madison's and
Jefferson's Virginia and Kentucky Resolutions, that a state can
decide for itself the extent of the obligations imposed upon it by
the federal Constitution. In this instance, the Louisiana legislature adopted "a series of enactments . . . designed to prevent
partial desegregation of the races in certain public schools in New
Orleans pursuant to an earlier federal court order."[81] A three-
judge federal court promptly declared the Louisiana laws unconstitutional. The state asked the Supreme Court for a stay of the
lower court's order pending an appeal to the Supreme Court. But
the Supreme Court unanimously refused a stay. In a brief opinion
in *Bush v. Orleans School Board*, the Court made plain that it
would countenance no repetition of the official intransigence
which had precipitated the Little Rock crisis:

> *These are motions for stay of an injunction by a three-judge
> District Court which nullified a series of enactments of the State
> of Louisiana. The scope of these enactments and the basis on
> which they were found in conflict with the Constitution of the
> United States are not matters of doubt. The nub of the decision
> of the three-judge court is this:*
>
> > *The conclusion is clear that interposition is not a con-
> > stitutional doctrine. If taken seriously, it is illegal defiance of
> > constitutional authority. United States v. Louisiana, 188 F.
> > Supp. 916, 926.*
>
> *The main basis for challenging this ruling is that the State of
> Louisiana "has interposed itself in the field of public education*

over which it has exclusive control." This objection is without
substance, as we held, upon full consideration, in Cooper v.
Aaron, 358 U.S. 1. The others are likewise without merit.
Accordingly, the motions for stay are denied.[82]

(3). Oxford in 1962: a second governor defies the federal courts

In 1962 the Constitution entered Mississippi, the heartland of
segregation. The Court of Appeals for the Fifth Circuit directed
the admission to the University of Mississippi of James H. Meredith, a twenty-nine-year-old Negro Air Force veteran.[83] The
trustees of the university prepared to seek Supreme Court review,
via a petition for certiorari. Meanwhile, the late Judge Ben F.
Cameron, a judge of the Fifth Circuit who had not participated
in the decision, stayed enforcement of the orders entered by his
brethren pending Supreme Court action on the certiorari petition.
Since a stay would have further postponed Meredith's long over-
due enrollment at Ole Miss, the Fifth Circuit set aside the order of
their single colleague. But Judge Cameron persisted in entering
new orders purporting to countermand the instructions of the
Fifth Circuit, whereupon Meredith's attorneys sought relief from
Justice Black, the member of the Supreme Court with supervisory
responsibility for the Fifth Circuit. Since the Supreme Court was
still in summer recess, Justice Black had unquestioned authority
to review Judge Cameron's stay orders himself. And since Justice
Black concluded (1) "that the stays . . . can only work further
delay and injury to movant [Meredith] while immediate enforcement of the judgment can do no appreciable harm to the University," and (2) "that there is very little likelihood that this Court
will grant certiorari to review the judgment of the Court of
Appeals, which essentially involves only factual issues,"[84] an
order vacating Judge Cameron's orders should have followed as a
matter of course. But Justice Black, aware of the sensitivity of the
case, took the unusual step of consulting each of his brethren, and
they all agreed that he ought to set aside Judge Cameron's orders.
Therefore, on September 10, 1962, Justice Black directed that
"the judgment and mandate of the Court of Appeals should be
obeyed," and enjoined the trustees "from taking any steps to
prevent enforcement of the Court of Appeals' judgment and
mandate."[85]

On September 24, Mississippi's Governor, Ross R. Barnett, responded with a proclamation:

WHEREAS, *the Constitution of the United States of America provides that each state is sovereign with respect to certain rights and powers; and*

WHEREAS, *pursuant to the Tenth Amendment to the Constitution of the United States, the powers not specifically delegated to the Federal Government are reserved to the several states; and*

WHEREAS, *we are now face to face with the direct usurpation of this power by the Federal Government through the illegal use of judicial decree; and*

WHEREAS, *all public officials of the State of Mississippi have the legal right, obligation and duty not to acquiesce, impair, waive or surrender any of the rights of the Sovereign State of Mississippi; and*

WHEREAS, *any acts upon the part of representatives of the federal government to arrest or fine any state official who endeavors to enforce the law of Mississippi, are illegal according to the law of the State of Mississippi, and federal courts have likewise established ample and perfect precedence in the matter:*

NOW, THEREFORE, *I, Ross R. Barnett, Governor of the State of Mississippi, by the authority vested in me under the Constitution and laws of the State of Mississippi, do hereby proclaim and direct that the arrest or attempts to arrest, or the fining or the attempts to fine, of any state official in the performance of his official duties, by any representative of the federal government, is illegal and such representative or representatives of said federal government are to be summarily arrested and jailed by reason of any such illegal acts in violation of this Executive Order and in violation of the laws of the State of Mississippi. . . .*[86]

Meanwhile, Governor Barnett had the university trustees appoint him "special registrar" and he personally, aided by the lieutenant governor, refused to enroll Meredith for the fall term.

Thus was the stage set for conflict. With the state government operating in outright defiance of federal court orders, and with tens of thousands of white Mississippians rallying to support Governor Barnett, President Kennedy on September 30 issued a proclamation asserting the supremacy of federal law:

Whereas the Governor of the State of Mississippi and certain law enforcement officers and other officials of that State, and other persons, individually and in unlawful assemblies, combinations and conspiracies, have been and are willfully opposing and obstructing the enforcement of orders entered by the United States District Court for the Southern District of Mississippi and the United States Court of Appeals for the Fifth Circuit; and

Whereas such unlawful assemblies, combinations and conspiracies oppose and obstruct the execution of the laws of the United States, impede the course of justice under those laws and make it impracticable to enforce those laws in the State of Mississippi by the ordinary course of judicial proceedings; and

Whereas I have expressly called the attention of the Governor of Mississippi to the perilous situation that exists and to his duties in the premises, and have requested but have not received from him adequate assurances that the orders of the courts of the United States will be obeyed and that law and order will be maintained;

Now, therefore, I, John F. Kennedy, President of the United States, under and by virtue of the authority vested in me by the Constitution and laws of the United States, including Chapter 15 of Title 10 of the United States Code, particularly sections 332, 333 and 334 thereof, do command all persons engaged in such obstructions of justice to cease and desist therefrom and to disperse and retire peacefully forthwith. . . .[87]

To implement this proclamation, the President, on the same day, took over command of the Mississippi national guard and "authorized and directed [the Secretary of Defense] to enforce all orders" of the federal courts "and to remove all obstructions of justice in the State of Mississippi."[88]

On the evening of September 30, with thousands of federal troops mobilized for any necessary supporting action, Meredith was taken to the Ole Miss campus at Oxford, under the protection of federal marshals. That same evening the President, on television, explained to the nation—and especially to the citizens of Mississippi and the students at the university—what had impelled his action:

Good evening, my fellow citizens:
The orders of the court in the case of Meredith v. Fair *are*

beginning to be carried out. Mr. James Meredith is now in residence on the campus of the University of Mississippi. This has been accomplished thus far without the use of National Guard or other troops—and it is to be hoped that the law enforcement officers of the State of Mississippi will continue to be sufficient in the future. All students, members of the faculty and public officials in both Mississippi and the Nation, it is to be hoped, can now return to their normal activities with full confidence in the integrity of American law.

This is as it should be. For our Nation is founded on the principle that observance of the law is the eternal safeguard of liberty—and defiance of the law is the surest path to tyranny. The law which we obey includes the final rulings of our courts as well as the enactments of our legislative bodies. Even among law-abiding men, few laws are universally loved—but they are uniformly respected and not resisted.

Americans are free, in short, to disagree with the law—but not to disobey it. For in a government of laws, and not of men, no man—however prominent or powerful—and no mob—however unruly or boisterous—is entitled to defy a court of law. If this country should ever reach the point where any man or group of men, by force, or threat of force, could long defy the commands of our courts and Constitution, then no law would stand free from doubt, no judge would be sure of his writ and no citizen would be safe from his neighbors.

In this case—in which the United States Government was not until recently involved—Mr. Meredith brought a private suit in federal court against those who were excluding him from the university.

A series of federal courts—all the way up to the Supreme Court—repeatedly ordered Mr. Meredith's admission to the university. When those orders were defied and those who sought to implement them threatened with arrest and violence, the United States Court of Appeals—consisting of Chief Judge Tuttle of Georgia, Judge Hutcheson of Texas, Judge Rives of Alabama, Judge Jones of Florida, Judge Brown of Texas, Judge Wisdom of Louisiana, Judge Gewin of Alabama and Judge Bell of Georgia— made clear the fact that the enforcement of its orders had become the obligation of the United States Government.

Even though this Government had not originally been a party to this case, my responsibility as President was therefore inescapable. I accept. My obligation, under the Constitution and the statutes of the United States, was and is to implement the orders of the court with whatever means were necessary, and with as little force and civil disorder as the circumstances permit.

It was for this reason that I federalized the Mississippi National Guard as the most appropriate instrument should any be needed to preserve law and order while United States marshals carried out the orders of the court and prepared to back them up with whatever other civil or military enforcement might have been required.

I deeply regret the fact that any action by the Executive Branch was necessary in this case, but all other avenues and alternatives, including persuasion and conciliation, had been tried and exhausted. Had the police powers of Mississippi been used to support the orders of the court, instead of deliberately and unlawfully blocking them, had the University of Mississippi fulfilled its standard of excellence by quietly admitting this applicant in conformity with what so many other Southern state universities have done for so many years, a peaceable and sensible solution would have been possible without any federal intervention.

The nation is proud of the many instances in which governors, educators and everyday citizens from the South have shown to the world the gains that can be made by persuasion and good will in a society ruled by law. Specifically I would like to take this occasion to express the thanks of the nation to those Southerners who have contributed to the progress of our democratic development in the entrance of students regardless of race to such great institutions as the state-supported Universities of Virginia, North Carolina, Georgia, Florida, Texas, Louisiana, Tennessee, Arkansas and Kentucky.

I recognize that the present period of transition and adjustment in our nation's southland is a hard one for many people. Neither Mississippi nor any other Southern state deserves to be charged with all the accumulated wrongs of the last 100 years of race relations. To the extent that there has been failure the responsibility for that failure must be shared by us all, by every state, by every citizen. . . . I close . . . with this appeal to the students of the university, the people who are most concerned.

You have a great tradition to uphold, a tradition of honor and courage, won on the field of battle and on the gridiron as well as the university campus. You have a new opportunity to show that you are men of patriotism and integrity. For the most effective means of upholding the law is not the state policeman or the marshals or the National Guard. It is you. It lies in your courage to accept those laws with which you disagree as well as those with which you agree. The eyes of the nation and all the world are upon you and upon all of us, and the honor of your university and the state are in the balance. I am certain the great majority of the students will uphold that honor.

There is in short no reason why the books on this case cannot now be quickly and quietly closed in the manner directed by the court. Let us preserve both the law and the peace and then healing those wounds that are within we can turn to the greater crises that are without and stand united as one people in our pledge to man's freedom.

Thank you and good night.[89]

But the audience President Kennedy principally addressed was not listening. As he spoke, violence took over at Ole Miss; students, and others, assaulted the federal marshals; state and local police withdrew; at last, the marshals, greatly outnumbered, responded with tear gas. It was morning before the rioting ended: many, including a number of federal marshals, were injured; two persons—one a correspondent for a European newspaper—was killed. (Among those later arrested by federal authorities as instigators of the violence was a recently retired army officer, who had just fought a losing campaign for the Democratic nomination for the governorship of Texas. He was Edwin A. Walker, the major general in command at Little Rock. Several weeks later, a board of examining psychiatrists found General Walker competent to stand trial. Thereafter, a federal grand jury, which indicted others for their part in the Oxford riots, declined to return an indictment against General Walker.)

Thus, at enormous cost, federal court orders were at last enforced: James Meredith was enrolled in the University of Mississippi. He attended classes and lived in a college dormitory, but he was under round-the-clock federal protection. Even this protection could not, however, ward off continuous student harassment—nor could it serve to prevent reprisals against those few students who went out of their way to befriend Meredith. As Meredith's first term ended, it was freely surmised that he would withdraw from college; but in January of 1963 he announced that he would continue.[90]

A couple of days before Meredith announced that he would stay at Ole Miss, Harvey Gantt, a Negro architecture student, presented himself at the campus of Clemson University, a state college in South Carolina. The university officials, acting in compliance with federal court orders, duly registered Gantt without incident. Gantt's enrollment at Clemson meant that no state in the union could continue to boast total noncompliance with the constitutional mandate of desegregation.

(4). The Court warns against delay

In the spring of 1963, the Supreme Court served notice that, in addition to insisting on the rigorous enforcement of particular desegregation decrees as they were entered, it had come to look with less and less tolerance on excuses put forward by local authorities under the rubric of "all deliberate speed," in order to postpone the entry of such decrees or to build into them timetables of extended duration.

The Court's vehicle was a case arising in Memphis. The question presented was whether, as the lower federal courts had held, the Memphis Park Commission was entitled to adopt a policy of gradual desegregation of the city's parks, playgrounds, golf courses, and other recreational facilities. Under its proposed program of gradualism, the Commission would not have completed the desegregation of these extensive municipal facilities for several more years.

The Supreme Court reversed the lower courts: "The continued denial to petitioners of the use of city facilities solely because of their race is," the Court held, "without warrant."[91] The Court unanimously declared that the "all deliberate speed" formula, contained in the second opinion in Brown v. Board of Education, was addressed to the special exigencies and complexities of school desegregation and had very little relevance in cases requiring the desegregation of other sorts of public facilities. Moreover, the Court warned that even in the realm of school desegregation factors which would legitimately have justified delay eight years before might not pass judicial muster in 1963.

Although the Court made no mention of the statistics, there is little doubt that the Justices were well aware that on the ninth anniversary of the *School Segregation Cases* not more than 9 per cent of the Negro children in southern and border areas were attending integrated schools.

The Court was unanimous. The opinion in *Watson v. Memphis* was written by the then newest member of the Court, former Justice Arthur J. Goldberg. The key portions of the opinion follow:

It is important at the outset to note the chronological context in which the city makes its claim to entitlement to additional time within which to work out complete elimination of racial barriers to use of the public facilities here involved. It is now more than nine years since this Court held in the first Brown *decision,* Brown v. Board of Education, 347 U.S. 483, *that racial segregation in state public schools violates the Equal Protection Clause of the Fourteenth Amendment. And it was almost eight years ago—in 1955, the year after the decision on the merits in* Brown—*that the constitutional proscription of state enforced racial segregation was found to apply to public recreational facilities. See* Dawson v. Mayor and City Council of Baltimore, 220 F. 2d 386, aff'd, 350 U.S. 877; *see also* Muir v. Louisville Park Theatrical Assn., 347 U.S. 971.

Thus, the applicability here of the factors and reasoning relied on in framing the 1955 decree in the second Brown *decision,* supra, *which contemplated the possible need of some limited delay in effecting total desegregation of public schools, must be considered not only in the context of factual similarities, if any, between that case and this one, but also in light of the significant fact that the governing constitutional principles no longer bear the imprint of newly enunciated doctrine. In considering the appropriateness of the equitable decree entered below inviting a plan calling for an even longer delay in effecting desegregation, we cannot ignore the passage of a substantial period of time since the original declaration of the manifest unconstitutionality of racial practices such as are here challenged, the repeated and numerous decisions giving notice of such illegality, and the many intervening opportunities heretofore available to attain the equality of treatment which the Fourteenth Amendment commands the States to achieve. These factors must inevitably and substantially temper the present import of such broad policy considerations as may have underlain, even in part, the form of decree ultimately framed in the Brown case. Given the extended time which has elapsed, it is far from clear that the mandate of the second Brown decision requiring that desegregation proceed with "all deliberate speed" would today be fully satisfied by types of plans or programs for desegregation of public educational facilities which eight years ago might have been deemed sufficient. Brown never contemplated that the concept of "deliberate speed" would countenance indefinite delay in elimination of racial barriers in schools, let alone other public facilities not involving the same physical problems or comparable conditions.*

When, in 1954, in the first Brown decision, this Court declared the constitutional impermissibility of racial segregation in public schools, it did not immediately frame a decree, but instead invited and heard further argument on the question of relief. In its subsequent opinion, the Court noted that "[f]ull implementation of these [applicable] constitutional principles may require solution of varied local school problems" and indicated an appropriate scope for the application of equitable principles consistent with both public and private need and for "exercise of [the] . . . traditional attributes of equity power." 349 U.S., at 299–300. The District Courts to which the cases there under consideration were remanded were invested with a discretion appropriate to ultimate fashioning of detailed relief consonant with properly cognizable local conditions. This did not mean, however, that the discretion was even then unfettered or exercisable without restraint. Basic to the remand was the concept that desegregation must proceed with "all deliberate speed," and the problems which might be considered and which might justify a decree requiring something less than immediate and total desegregation were severely delimited. Hostility to the constitutional precepts underlying the original decision was expressly and firmly pretermitted as such an operative factor. Id., at 300.

The nature of the ultimate resolution effected in the second Brown decision largely reflected no more than a recognition of the unusual and particular problems inhering in desegregating large numbers of schools throughout the country. The careful specification of factors relevant to a determination whether any delay in complying fully and completely with the constitutional mandate would be warranted demonstrated a concern that delay not be conditioned upon insufficient reasons or, in any event, tolerated unless it imperatively and compellingly appeared unavoidable.

This case presents no obvious occasion for the application of Brown. We are not here confronted with attempted desegregation of a local school system with any or all of the perhaps uniquely attendant problems, administrative and other, specified in the second Brown decision as proper considerations in weighing the need for further delay in vindicating the Fourteenth Amendment rights of petitioners. Desegregation of parks and other recreational facilities does not present the same kinds of cognizable difficulties inhering in elimination of racial classification in schools, at which attendance is compulsory, the adequacy of teachers and facilities crucial, and questions of geographic assignment often of major significance.

Most importantly, of course, it must be recognized that even the delay countenanced by Brown was a necessary, albeit significant, adaptation of the usual principle that any deprivation of constitutional rights calls for prompt rectification. The rights here asserted are, like all such rights, present rights; they are not merely hopes to some future enjoyment of some formalistic constitutional promise. The basic guarantees of our Constitution are warrants for the here and now and, unless there is an overwhelmingly compelling reason, they are to be promptly fulfilled. The second Brown decision is but a narrowly drawn, and carefully limited, qualification upon usual precepts of constitutional adjudication and is not to be unnecessarily expanded in application.

. . . . .

The existing and commendable goodwill between the races in Memphis, to which both the District Court and some of the witnesses at trial made express and emphatic reference as in some inexplicable fashion supporting the need for further delay, can best be preserved and extended by the observance and protection, not the denial, of the basic constitutional rights here asserted. The best guarantee of civil peace is adherence to, and respect for, the law.[92]

(5). *Tuscaloosa in 1963: a third governor defies
the federal courts*

"The best guarantee of civil peace is adherence to, and respect
for, the law." So the Supreme Court said on May 27, 1963
(*Watson v. Memphis*). But just over two weeks later the Governor of Alabama, George C. Wallace, redeemed a campaign
pledge by standing in the doorway of the University of Alabama
to bar the enrollment of two Negro students whose admission had
been directed by an Alabama federal court. Governor Wallace
had been personally enjoined from interfering with enforcement
of the court order. Nevertheless, he confronted the then Deputy
Attorney General of the United States, Nicholas deB. Katzenbach
(who was there to see that the court's orders were carried out),
with an assertion of the illegality of the supreme federal law:

Mr. Katzenbach:

*I take it from that statement that you are going to stand in
the door and that you are not going to carry out the orders of
the court, and that you are going to resist us from doing so. Is
that correct?*

Governor Wallace:

I stand according to my statement.

Mr. Katzenbach:

*Governor, I am not interested in a show. I don't know what
the purpose of this show is. I am interested in the orders of these
courts being enforced. I would ask you once again to responsibly
step aside. If you do not, I'm going to assure you that the orders
of these courts will be enforced.*[93]

And the two students were enrolled.

(6). *Eleven years after the decision*

The *School Segregation Cases* were decided on May 17, 1954.
In the narrowest legal sense the decisions affected only the
five school systems before the Court: Topeka, Kansas; New
Castle County, Delaware; Prince Edward County, Virginia;
Clarendon County, South Carolina; and the District of Columbia.
But the doctrines laid down quite obviously applied to every
American public school system in which, by operation of law,

Negro and white children were assigned to separate schools. And under the terms of the 1955 sequel to the 1954 decision, every such public school was required to desegregate "with all deliberate speed."

By the close of 1963, with the tenth anniversary of the decision near at hand, "all deliberate speed" had accomplished the following:

Of the five school systems before the Court in 1954, three had been desegregated: Topeka (the only segregated school system in Kansas); the District of Columbia; and New Castle County, Delaware. In Clarendon County, South Carolina, all Negro school children still attended separate and grossly inferior public schools. And in Prince Edward County, Virginia, all public schools had been closed since 1959. White children in the county had continued to go to school, attending a nominally private institution which (until the federal district court intervened in 1961) was publicly subsidized by a system of tax credits and tuition grants. But from 1959 to 1963 no Negro child in Prince Edward County attended any school. In 1963 a privately financed school system was organized—largely at the instance of Attorney General Robert F. Kennedy—for the education of the Negro children. Meanwhile, litigation testing the county's power to close its public schools wound its tortuous way toward the Supreme Court.

The region-wide desegregation picture was this: In the border areas—Delaware, Kentucky, Maryland, Missouri, Oklahoma, West Virginia, and the District of Columbia—56.2 per cent of the Negro school children attended schools with white school children. Farther south—in Alabama, Arkansas, Florida, Georgia, Louisiana, Mississippi, North Carolina, South Carolina, Tennessee, Texas, and Virginia—1.06 per cent of the Negro school children attended school with white school children. In the region as a whole, nine and a half years of "deliberate speed" had integrated 9.3 per cent of the Negro school children.[94]

The Supreme Court was not unaware of desegregation's magnolia pace. In the spring of 1963, in *Watson v. Memphis,* the Court had begun to make its impatience manifest: "*Brown* [the *School Segregation* opinion] never contemplated that the concept of 'deliberate speed' would countenance indefinite delay in elimination of racial barriers in schools. . . ." And it was against this background that the Court, in March of 1964, heard argument in two school cases: One of these raised the question of whether the Atlanta school authorities, who appeared to be desegregating on a grade-a-year basis from the twelfth grade down, were proceeding fast enough. The other case was that from Prince Edward County, where the response to the 1954 decision had been to close the county's public schools.

On May 25, 1964, ten years and eight days after the 1954 decision, the Supreme Court decided both cases. The Atlanta case (*Calhoun v. Latimer*) was returned to the trial court to consider plans announced by the Atlanta school board *following the argument in the Supreme Court* to accelerate the pace of desegregation.[94a] In the Prince Edward County case (*Griffin v. Prince Edward School Board*), the Court, speaking through Justice Black, took note of the fact that this was one of the five cases passed upon a decade before: "There has been entirely too much deliberation and not enough speed in enforcing the constitutional rights which we held . . . had been denied Prince Edward County Negro children." With this as his point of departure, Justice Black went on to consider two issues: The first was whether Virginia could permit one of its counties to abandon public education, for the purpose of avoiding desegregated schooling, where the balance of the state continued to maintain public schools; the Court unanimously concluded that this course of action denied the Negro school children of Prince Edward County the equal protection of the laws. The second issue was whether a federal court had power to compel a county to reopen its schools; on this issue seven Justices felt that the necessary power existed, but Justices Clark and Harlan disagreed. The heart of Justice Black's opinion for the Court was as follows:

> *Since 1959, all Virginia counties have had the benefits of public schools but one: Prince Edward. However, there is no rule that counties, as counties, must be treated alike; the Equal Protection Clause relates to equal protection of the laws "between persons as such rather than between areas."* Salsburg v. Maryland, *346 U.S. 545, 551 (1954). Indeed, showing that different persons are treated differently is not enough, without more, to show a denial of equal protection.* Kotch v. Board of River Port

Pilot Comm'rs, *330 U.S. 552, 556 (1947). It is the circumstances of each case which govern.* Skinner v. Oklahoma ex rel. Williamson, *316 U.S. 535, 539–540 (1942).*

Virginia law, as here applied, unquestionably treats the school children of Prince Edward differently from the way it treats the school children of all other Virginia counties. Prince Edward children must go to a private school or none at all; all other Virginia children can go to public schools. Closing Prince Edward's schools bears more heavily on Negro children in Prince Edward County since white children there have accredited private schools which they can attend, while colored children until very recently have had no available private schools, and even the school they now attend is a temporary expedient. Apart from this expedient, the result is that Prince Edward County school children, if they go to school in their own county, must go to racially segregated schools which, although designated as private, are beneficiaries of county and state support.

A State, of course, has a wide discretion in deciding whether laws shall operate statewide or shall operate only in certain counties, the legislature "having in mind the needs and desires of each." Salsburg v. Maryland, supra, *346 U.S., at 552. A State may wish to suggest, as Maryland did in* Salsburg, *that there are reasons why one county ought not to be treated like another. 346 U.S., at 553–554. But the record in the present case could not be clearer that Prince Edward's public schools were closed and private schools operated in their place with state and county assistance, for one reason, and one reason only: to ensure, through measures taken by the county and the State, that white and colored children in Prince Edward County would not, under any circumstances, go to the same school. Whatever nonracial grounds might support a State's allowing a county to abandon public schools, the object must be a constitutional one, and grounds of race and opposition to desegregation do not qualify as constitutional.*

.   .   .   .   .

We come now to the question of the kind of decree necessary and appropriate to put an end to the racial discrimination practiced against these petitioners under authority of the Virginia laws. That relief needs to be quick and effective. . . . The District Court enjoined the county officials from paying county tuition grants or giving tax exemptions and from processing applications for state tuition grants so long as the county's public schools remained closed. We have no doubt of the power of the court to give this relief to enforce the discontinuance of the county's racially discriminatory practices. . . . The injunction against paying tuition grants and giving tax credits while public schools remain closed is appropriate and necessary since those grants and tax credits have been essential parts of the county's program, successful thus far, to deprive petitioners of the same advantages of a public school education enjoyed by children in every other part of Virginia. For the same reasons the District Court may, if necessary to prevent further racial discrimination, require the Supervisors to exercise the power that is theirs to levy taxes to raise funds adequate to reopen, operate, and maintain without racial discrimination a public school system in Prince Edward County like that operated in other counties in Virginia.[95]

Justice Black's opinion was plainly one of major implication. For the people of Prince Edward County, the opinion foreshadowed the end of the nightmare of no public schools. In the fall of 1964 Prince Edward County's public schools reopened, at long last. But the schools were almost entirely black, since virtually all the white school children were attending the "private" schools financed by county funds. But in December of 1964 the Court of Appeals for the Fourth Circuit held that the continued government subvention of "whites-only" schools—whether denominated "private" or "public"—was itself unconstitutional.[96] Plainly, however, Justice Black's opinion in the *Prince Edward County* case had a significance which radiated far beyond the county's boundaries. For in upholding the power of a federal district court to go to the extraordinary length of directing the levying of taxes to finance the operation of a public school system, seven Justices of the Supreme Court were serving notice, if any were needed, that the second decade of school desegregation in the South would proceed more rapidly than the first.

With the beginning of the second decade—at the opening of school in the fall of 1964—the region-wide desegregation picture[97] was as follows:

SEGREGATION-DESEGREGATION STATUS

	School Districts			Enrollment		In Desegregated Districts		Negroes in Schools with Whites	
	Total	with Negroes & Whites	Deseg.	White	Negro	White	Negro	No	% †
Alabama	118	118	8	549,543**	293,476**	152,486**	88,952**	94	.032
Arkansas	412	228	24	333,630**	114,651**	93,072	23,943	930	.811
Florida	67	67	21	1,001,611*	246,215	812,268*	174,522*	6,524	2.65
Georgia	196	180	11	752,620	354,850	195,598	133,888	1,337	.377
Louisiana	67	67	3	489,000*	321,000*	61,885	86,248	3,581	1.12
Mississippi	150	150	4	308,409**	295,962**	34,620**	21,929**	58	.020
North Carolina	171	171	84	828,638	349,282	548,705	201,394	4,918	1.41
South Carolina	108	108	16	371,921	260,667	156,346	83,608	260	.100
Tennessee	152	141	61	724,327*	173,673*	459,162*	135,001	9,265*	5.33
Texas	1,380	862	291	2,086,752*	344,312*	1,500,000*	225,000*	25,000*	7.26
Virginia	130	128	81	733,524**	234,176**	585,491	189,046	11,883	5.07
SOUTH	2,951	2,220	604	8,179,975	2,988,264	4,599,633	1,368,531	63,850	2.14
Delaware	78	43	43	83,325	19,497	78,346	14,484	11,267	57.8
District of Columbia	1	1	1	17,487	123,906	17,487	123,906	106,578	86.0
Kentucky	204	165	164	620,000*	56,000*	540,000*	55,900*	35,000*	62.5
Maryland	24	23	23	565,434	166,861	560,359	166,861	86,203	51.7
Missouri	1,542	212*	203*	818,000*	102,000*	NA	94,000*	44,000*	44.1
Oklahoma	1,118	242	200	542,103*	43,954	324,981*	37,026*	13,923*	31.7
West Virginia	55	44	44	426,821*	21,000	389,921*	21,000*	18,500*	88.1
BORDER	3,022	730	678	3,073,170	533,218	1,911,094††	513,177	315,471	59.2
REGION	5,973	2,950	1,282	11,253,145	3,521,482	6,510,727††	1,881,708	379,321	10.8

* Estimated
** 1963–64
† Number of Negroes in schools with whites, compared to state's total Negro enrollment.
†† Missouri not included

Southern Education Reporting Service, December, 1964

As the second decade got under way, the Supreme Court had not yet addressed itself to what may in the long run turn out to be the even more perplexing problems presented by the "de facto" segregated schools which abound in the great urban centers of the North, Midwest and Far West. These are schools which are segregated not by virtue of legislative or school board mandates but because the residential neighborhoods which the schools are zoned to serve are overwhelmingly white or black.[98] Except where (as seems to have happened in New Rochelle) ostensibly objective school district lines have actually been so drawn as to create or perpetuate a segregated situation, it would appear that a public school system is not constitutionally required to take affirmative action to redistrict its schools or to reassign its pupils in order to overcome a "de facto" segregated pattern.[99] On the other hand, a school board desiring to promote integration apparently is not constitutionally precluded from taking racial considerations into account in rezoning schools or reassigning pupils.[100]

In the summer of 1965, eleven years after the decision, several hundred theretofore intransigently segregated southern school districts announced plans to desegregate at least some classrooms for the next academic year. A powerful new weapon—the threat of suspension of federal funds in aid of education for school systems which made no moves toward compliance with the 1954 decision— had come into play with enactment of Title VI of the Civil Rights Act of 1964. Ironically, the faintly quickening pace of southern school desegregation was jeopardizing the jobs of thousands of southern Negro teachers in systems which would accept some integration of students but little or none of teachers.[101]

d. The death of a President and the birth of a law

On the evening of June 11, 1963, President Kennedy spoke to the nation on civil rights. He took note of what had happened at the University of Alabama earlier that day, when Governor Wallace had made an abortive attempt to block the enrollment of two Negro students whose admission had been directed by a federal court. President Kennedy also took note of the massive challenge to discrimination spearheaded by Rev. Martin Luther King, Jr., in Birmingham a month before—a challenge which had in the intervening weeks triggered similar movements throughout the South and in many northern urban centers. The President said that "we face . . . a moral crisis as a country and a people. . . . It cannot be quieted by token moves or talk. It is a time to act. . . ." The text of his speech follows:

Good evening my fellow citizens.

This afternoon, following a series of threats and defiant statements, the presence of Alabama National Guardsmen was required on the University of Alabama to carry out the final and unequivocal order of the United States District Court of the Northern District of Alabama.

That order called for the admission of two clearly qualified young Alabama residents who happened to have been born Negro.

That they were admitted peacefully on the campus is due in good measure to the conduct of the students of the University of Alabama who met their responsibilities in a constructive way.

I hope that every American, regardless of where he lives, will stop and examine his conscience about this and other related incidents.

This nation was founded by men of many nations and backgrounds. It was founded on the principle that all men are created equal, and that the rights of every man are diminished when the rights of one man are threatened.

Today we are committed to a worldwide struggle to promote and protect the rights of all who wish to be free. And when Americans are sent to Vietnam or West Berlin we do not ask for whites only.

It ought to be possible, therefore, for American students of any color to attend any public institution they select without having to be backed up by troops. It ought to be possible for American consumers of any color to receive equal service in places of public accommodation, such as hotels and restaurants, and theaters and retail stores without being forced to resort to demonstrations in the street.

And it ought to be possible for American citizens of any color to register and to vote in a free election without interference or fear of reprisal.

It ought to be possible, in short, for every American to

enjoy the privileges of being American without regard to his race or his color.

In short, every American ought to have the right to be treated as he would wish to be treated, as one would wish his children to be treated. But this is not the case.

The Negro baby born in America today, regardless of the section or the state in which he is born, has about one-half as much chance of completing a high school as a white baby, born in the same place, on the same day; one-third as much chance of completing college; one-third as much chance of becoming a professional man; twice as much chance of becoming unemployed; about one-seventh as much chance of earning $10,000 a year; a life expectancy which is seven years shorter and the prospects of earning only half as much.

This is not a sectional issue. Difficulties over segregation and discrimination exist in every city, in every state of the Union, producing in many cities a rising tide of discontent that threatens the public safety.

Nor is this a partisan issue. In a time of domestic crisis, men of goodwill and generosity should be able to unite regardless of party or politics.

This is not even a legal or legislative issue alone. It is better to settle these matters in the courts than on the streets, and new laws are needed at every level. But law alone cannot make men see right.

We are confronted primarily with a moral issue. It is as clear as the American Constitution. The heart of the question is whether all Americans are to be afforded equal rights and equal opportunities; whether we are going to treat our fellow Americans as we want to be treated.

If an American, because his skin is dark, cannot eat lunch in a restaurant open to the public; if he cannot send his children to the best public school available; if he cannot vote for the public officials who represent him; if, in short, he cannot enjoy the full and free life which all of us want, then who among us would be content to have the color of his skin changed and stand in his place?

Who among us would then be content with the counsels of patience and delay. One hundred years of delay have passed since President Lincoln freed the slaves, yet their heirs, their grandsons, are not fully free. They are not yet freed from the bonds of injustice; they are not yet freed from social and economic oppression.

And this nation, for all its hopes and all its boasts, will not be fully free until all its citizens are free.

We preach freedom around the world, and we mean it. And we cherish our freedom here at home. But are we to say to the world—and much more importantly to each other—that this is the land of the free, except for the Negroes; that we have no second-class citizens, except Negroes; that we have no class or caste system, no ghettos, no master race, except with respect to Negroes.

Now the time has come for this nation to fulfill its promise. The events in Birmingham and elsewhere have so increased the cries for equality that no city or state . . . legislative body can prudently choose to ignore them.

The fires of frustration and discord are burning in every city, North and South. Where legal remedies are not at hand, redress is sought in the streets in demonstrations, parades and protests, which create tensions and threaten violence—and threaten lives.

We face, therefore, a moral crisis as a country and a people. It cannot be met by repressive police action. It cannot be left to increased demonstrations in the streets. It cannot be quieted by token moves or talk. It is a time to act in the Congress, in your state and local legislative body, and, above all, in all of our daily lives.

It is not enough to pin the blame on others, to say this is a problem of one section of the country or another, or deplore the facts that we face. A great change is at hand, and our task, our obligation is to make that revolution, that change peaceful and constructive for all.

Those who do nothing are inviting shame as well as violence. Those who act boldly are recognizing right as well as reality.

Next week I shall ask the Congress of the United States to act, to make a commitment it has not fully made in this century to the proposition that race has no place in American life or law.

The Federal judiciary has upheld that proposition in a series of forthright cases. The Executive Branch has adopted that proposition in the conduct of its affairs, including the employment of Federal personnel, and the use of Federal facilities, and the sale of Federally financed housing.

But there are other necessary measures which only the Congress can provide, and they must be provided at this session.

The old code of equity law under which we live commands for every wrong a remedy. But in too many communities, in too many parts of the country wrongs are inflicted on Negro citizens and there are no remedies in law.

Unless the Congress acts their only remedy is the street.

I am, therefore, asking the Congress to enact legislation giving all Americans the right to be served in facilities which are open to the public—hotels, restaurants and theaters, retail stores and similar establishments. This seems to me to be an elementary right.

Its denial is an arbitrary indignity that no American in 1963 should have to endure, but many do.

I have recently met with scores of business leaders, urging them to take voluntary action to end this discrimination. And I've been encouraged by their response. And in the last two weeks over 75 cities have seen progress made in desegregating these kinds of facilities.

But many are unwilling to act alone. And for this reason nationwide legislation is needed, if we are to move this problem from the streets to the courts.

I'm also asking Congress to authorize the Federal Government to participate more fully in lawsuits designed to end segregation in public education. We have succeeded in persuading many districts to desegregate voluntarily. Dozens have admitted Negroes without violence.

Today a Negro is attending a state-supported institution in every one of our 50 states. But the pace is very slow.

Too many Negro children entering segregated grade schools at the time of the Supreme Court's decision nine years ago will enter segregated high schools this fall, having suffered a loss which can never be restored.

The lack of an adequate education denies the Negro a chance to get a decent job. The orderly implementation of the Supreme Court decision therefore, cannot be left solely to those who may not have the economic resources to carry their legal action or who may be subject to harassment.

Other features will be also requested, including greater protection for the right to vote.

But legislation, I repeat, cannot solve this problem alone. It must be solved in the homes of every American in every community across our country.

In this respect, I want to pay tribute to those citizens, North and South, who've been working in their communities to make life better for all.

They are acting not out of a sense of legal duty but out of a sense of human decency. Like our soldiers and sailors in all parts of the world, they are meeting freedom's challenge on the firing line and I salute them for their honor—their courage.

My fellow Americans, this is a problem which faces us all, in every city of the North as well as the South. . . .

It seems to me that these are matters which concern us all—not merely Presidents, or Congressmen, or Governors, but every citizen of the United States.

This is one country. It has become one country because all of us and all the people who came here had an equal chance to develop their talents.

We cannot say to 10 per cent of the population that "you can't have that right. Your children can't have the chance to develop whatever talents they have, that the only way that they're going to get their rights is to go in the street and demonstrate."

I think we owe them and we owe ourselves a better country than that.

Therefore, I'm asking for your help in making it easier for us to move ahead and provide the kind of equality of treatment which we would want ourselves—to give a chance for every child to be educated to the limit of his talent.

As I've said before, not every child has an equal talent or an equal ability or equal motivation. But they should have the equal right to develop their talent and their ability and their motivation to make something of themselves.

We have a right to expect that the Negro community will be responsible, will uphold the law. But they have a right to expect the law will be fair, that the Constitution will be color blind, as Justice Harlan said at the turn of the century.

This is what we're talking about. This is a matter which concerns this country and what it stands for, and in meeting it I ask the support of all of our citizens.

Thank you very much.[102]

On June 19, 1963, the President's civil rights program was submitted to Congress. In the ensuing weeks there was a steady rise in popular support for the administration's legislative proposals. This culminated, on August 28, 1963, in a March on Washington: One of the largest assemblages in the city's history—more than 200,000 whites and Negroes from all parts of the country—gathered at the Lincoln Memorial to demand "jobs and freedom now" and to ask Congress to move quickly on the pending civil rights legislation.

On a Sunday morning three weeks later—as if in grim reply to the marchers' demands—a bomb tore apart the Sixteenth Street Baptist Church in Birmingham. Four little Negro girls were killed. The next day Charles Morgan, a white lawyer then still practicing in Birmingham, spoke about the bombing to the Birmingham Young Men's Business Club:

We are ten years of lawless preachments, ten years of criticism of law, of the courts, of our fellow men, a decade of telling school children the opposite of what the civics books say. We are a mass of intolerance and bigotry and shouted indictments before our young. We are cursed by the failure of each of us to accept responsibility, by our defense of an already dead institution.

.   .   .   .   .

Those four little Negro girls were human beings. They have lived their years in a leaderless city, a city where no one accepts responsibility. . . .

.   .   .   .   .

. . . It is a city where four little Negro girls can be born into a second-class school system, live a segregated life, ghettoed into their own little neighborhoods, restricted to Negro churches, destined to ride in Negro ambulances to Negro wards of hospitals, and from there to a Negro cemetery. Local papers, on their front and editorial pages, call for order and then exclude their names from obituary columns.

And who is really guilty? Each of us. Each citizen who has not consciously attempted to bring about peaceful compliance with the decisions of the Supreme Court of the United States; each citizen who has ever said, "They ought to kill that nigger";

*every citizen who votes for the candidate with the bloody flag;
every citizen and every school board member and school teacher
and principal and businessman and judge and lawyer who has
corrupted the minds of our youth; every person in this community who has, in any way, contributed during the past several
years to the popularity of hatred is at least as guilty, or more so,
than the demented fool who threw that bomb.*[103]

Violence begets violence. Two months later, on November
22, 1963, another "demented fool" picked up a rifle and killed the
President of the United States.

Two days after John F. Kennedy was buried, President
Lyndon B. Johnson spoke in sad and measured tones to the
Congress of the United States. In the name of his fallen friend, he
called upon Congress to act on the Kennedy legislative program,
including the civil rights program, without delay:

*We have talked long enough in this country about equal
rights. We have talked for one hundred years or more. It is time
now to write the next chapter—and to write it in the books of
law.*[104]

It took more than two months for the House of Representatives to respond to President Johnson's urgent plea. But when the
vote came, in February, a bipartisan coalition passed H.R. 7152
with an enormous majority: 290 (153 Democrats and 137 Republicans) in favor, and 130 (96 Democrats and 34 Republicans)
opposed. Moreover, the bill that emerged from the House was
stronger than that proposed by the administration in June of
1963. Its most widely discussed provisions were those creating a
federal right to service in most places of public accommodation
throughout the country. Other provisions of the bill reinforced
the authority of the Justice Department to protect voting rights;
authorized the Justice Department to intervene in school desegregation suits and empowered the federal Commissioner of
Education to assist school districts in the process of desegregation; authorized selective cutoffs of federal grant-in-aid funds
utilized by state and local officials to support discriminatory
programs; established a new federal agency to police discrimination in employment in industries affecting interstate commerce;

created a Community Relations Service which could perform mediating functions in local racial controversies; and continued the life of the federal Civil Rights Commission.

When the scene shifted to the Senate, the bill ran into the heavy weather of a Southern Democratic filibuster. The filibuster was finally broken by an overwhelming bipartisan vote of cloture, the first time that the Senate had ever voted to terminate an anti-civil-rights filibuster. The chief architect of the cloture vote was the Senate's minority leader, Everett McKinley Dirksen of Illinois. Thereafter debate resumed on a host of delaying amendments. But the bipartisan leadership (Senator Dirksen; Senate majority leader Mike Mansfield of Montana; Senator Hubert Humphrey, Democrat of Minnesota; and Senator Thomas Kuchel, Republican of California) was in full control, and the ultimate issue was no longer in doubt.

On June 18, Senator Barry Goldwater of Arizona, the leading contender for the Republican nomination for the Presidency, rose to explain his opposition to H.R. 7152:

> *Mr. President, there have been few, if any, occasions when the searching of my conscience and the reexamination of my views of our constitutional system have played a greater part in the determination of my vote than they have on this occasion.*
>
> .   .   .   .   .
>
> *I realize fully that the Federal Government has a responsibility in the field of civil rights. I supported the civil rights bills which were enacted in 1957 and 1960, and my public utterances during the debates on those measures and since reveal clearly the areas in which I feel that Federal responsibility lies and Federal legislation on this subject can be both effective and appropriate. Many of those areas are encompassed in this bill and to that extent, I favor it.*
>
> *I wish to make myself perfectly clear. The two portions of this bill to which I have constantly and consistently voiced objections, and which are of such overriding significance that they are determinative of my vote on the entire measure, are those which would embark the Federal Government on a regulatory course of action with regard to private enterprise in the area of so-called public accommodations and in the area of employment —to be more specific, titles II and VII of the bill. I find no consti-*

tutional basis for the exercise of Federal regulatory authority in either of these areas; and I believe the attempted usurpation of such powers to be a grave threat to the very essence of our basic system of government; namely, that of a constitutional republic in which 50 sovereign States have reserved to themselves and to the people those powers not specifically granted to the Central or Federal Government.

If it is the wish of the American people that the Federal Government should be granted the power to regulate in these two areas and in the manner contemplated by this bill, then I say that the Constitution should be so amended by the people as to authorize such action in accordance with the procedures for amending the Constitution which that great document itself prescribes. I say further that for this great legislative body to ignore the Constitution and the fundamental concepts of our governmental system is to act in a manner which could ultimately destroy the freedom of all American citizens, including the freedoms of the very persons whose feelings and whose liberties are the major subject of this legislation.

My basic objection to this measure is, therefore, constitutional. But, in addition, I would like to point out to my colleagues in the Senate and to the people of America, regardless of their race, color, or creed, the implications involved in the enforcement of regulatory legislation of this sort. To give genuine effect to the prohibitions of this bill will require the creation of a Federal police force of mammoth proportions. It also bids fair to result in the development of an "informer" psychology in great areas of our national life—neighbors spying on neighbors, workers spying on workers, businessmen spying on businessmen, where those who would harass their fellow citizens for selfish and narrow purposes will have ample inducement to do so. These, the Federal police force and an "informer" psychology, are the hallmarks of the police state and landmarks in the destruction of a free society.

I repeat again: I am unalterably opposed to discrimination of any sort and I believe that though the problem is fundamentally one of the heart, some law can help—but not law that embodies features like these, provisions which fly in the face of the Constitution and which require for their effective execution the creation of a police state. And so, because I am unalterably opposed to any threats to our great system of government and the loss of our God-given liberties, I shall vote "no" on this bill.

This vote will be reluctantly cast, because I had hoped to be able to vote "yea" on this measure as I have on the civil rights bills which have preceded it; but I cannot in good conscience to the oath that I took when assuming office, cast my vote in the affirmative. With the exception of titles II and VII, I could wholeheartedly support this bill; but with their inclusion, not measurably improved by the compromise version we have been working on, my vote must be "no."

If my vote is misconstrued, let it be, and let me suffer its consequences. Just let me be judged in this by the real concern I have voiced here and not by words that others may speak or by what others may say about what I think.

My concern extends beyond this single legislative moment. My concern extends beyond any single group in our society. My concern is for the entire Nation, for the freedom of all who live in it and for all who will be born into it.

It is the general welfare that must be considered now, not just the special appeals for special welfare. This is the time to attend to the liberties of all.[105]

The next day, June 19, was the day the Senate was scheduled to vote on H.R. 7152. It was also, as Senator Mansfield noted,[106] exactly one year after President Kennedy's civil rights program had been submitted to Congress. The last day of Senate debate began with a response by Senator Jacob Javits, Republican of New York, to Senator Goldwater's attack on the bill:

Mr. President, yesterday my distinguished colleague, Senator Goldwater, to whose every word the country now properly gives its attention, announced that he would vote "no" on this bill. I regret very much his decision and wish very much he had decided the other way.

.   .   .   .   .   .

Senator Goldwater made two points with respect to this bill which I believe urgently command reply in view of his important position in the Nation today. Both points have been raised many times before and answered many times, but since they come from so important a source, they must be answered again.

First, he stated that there is "no constitutional basis for the exercise of regulatory authority in" titles II and VII of the bill, dealing with public accommodations and equal employment opportunity, but that such action required a constitutional amendment; and, second, he stated that "to give genuine effect to the prohibitions of this bill will require the creation of a Federal police force of mammoth proportions" and will, in addition, he said, result "in the development of an informer psychology."

I rise to state my disagreement with both conclusions.

The always missing element in the arguments against this bill has been recognition that as to constitutional rights, we are a nation, not a collection of States; that there are national rights and national responsibilities just as sacred, just as vital as States' rights and just as fully entitled to protection by all the people.

The constitutional basis for both titles II and VII is sound; as a distinguished national panel of attorneys and law school deans and professors has confirmed, with ample citation of legal authorities, in a letter to the managers of this bill which has been referred to many times in this debate.

The public accommodations provision, title II, is squarely based on both the commerce clause and the 14th amendment to the Constitution. The equal employment opportunities provision, title VII, is squarely based on the commerce clause. The 14th amendment basis for the public accommodations provision was reaffirmed by the Supreme Court as recently as last year, in the sit-in decisions which struck down State-enforced discrimination in restaurants and lunch counters.

To challenge the commerce clause basis for either title II or title VII at the same time necessarily challenges the constitutionality of the entire range of existing Federal statutes based on that clause, such as the child labor and minimum wage laws, the pure food and drug laws, the labor-management laws, including the recent Landrum-Griffin Act and the Equal Pay for Women Act, the false labeling acts, and the antitrust laws, all of which also regulate the economic activities of individuals and private enterprise in their relations to other individuals and all of which also are deeply founded upon public morality.

All have been repeatedly upheld by the Supreme Court against constitutional attack. In addition to these, we have the *wide range of existing State legislation covering both the subject matter of title II and the subject matter of title VII, public accommodations and fair employment practices. All these have been upheld by State courts, under State constitutional provisions paralleling the Federal constitutional provisions, and have been upheld by the Supreme Court of the United States, under the applicable provisions of the Federal Constitution.*

The State public accommodations laws now number 32, and go back to 1865. It should be noted that 18 of the 32 were enacted before World War II; and 16 of the first 18 were enacted by Republican State governments. Nineteen of the State fair employment practices laws were enacted under Republican governors or by Republican legislatures; and the first four were enacted when Republicans controlled both houses of the legislature as well as the governorship.

I point out that in New York, under Governor Dewey and a Republican-controlled State legislature, the first fair employment practices law in the Nation was passed in 1945. It has worked splendidly in that very important and very heavily populated industrial State.

The fears of the Senator from Arizona [Mr. Goldwater] of a "Federal police force and an informer psychology" are equally unfounded. Those fears are rebutted by the long experience to the contrary of a majority of the States with their existing public accommodations and fair employment practices laws, many of which carry criminal penalties and are otherwise considerably more stringent and more far-reaching than the pending bill. . . .

. . . .

Mr. President, those fears are also rebutted by the Federal experience to the contrary under the Civil Rights Acts of 1957 and 1960, which dealt with voting, and of which the Senator from Arizona [Mr. Goldwater] says he approves. They are also rebutted by the experience under the many other Federal regulatory statutes to which I have referred. Our Nation's economy has grown and prospered because of, not in spite of, enforcement of these laws. Before the enactment of all these laws—State and Federal—the same bugaboos about Federal policing and enforcement were raised; but the experience of many years has proved that such fears were imaginary and groundless.

I conclude, therefore, that neither on constitutional grounds nor on the basis of fears about enforcement policy are the fears and the objections of the Senator from Arizona to title II and title VII tenable.[107]

The debate ended with a speech by Senator Dirksen, in the course of which he read to his colleagues a telegram supporting the bill signed by the governors of thirty-nine states and of the Virgin Islands.[108] The missing governors were those of the eleven states of the old Confederacy. And then the Senate voted approval for H.R. 7152, by a margin of seventy-three to twenty-seven.[109]

Because of minor Senate amendments, the bill moved back to the House for acquiescence in the changes. The House vote on the final bill (289 to 136) came on July 2, 1964. Just before the vote, Congressman Charles L. Weltner, of Atlanta, rose to explain to his colleagues why he was going to support a bill which he had voted against in February:

Manifestly, the issue is already decided, and approval is assured. By the time my name is called, votes sufficient for passage will have been recorded.

What, then, is the proper course? Is it to vote "no," with tradition, safety—and futility?

I believe a greater cause can be served. Change, swift and certain, is upon us, and we in the South face some difficult decisions.

We can offer resistance and defiance, with their harvest of strife and tumult. We can suffer continued demonstrations, with their wake of violence and disorder.

Or, we can acknowledge this measure as the law of the land. We can accept the verdict of the nation.

Already, the responsible elements of my community are counseling this latter course. And, most assuredly, moderation, tranquility, and orderly processes combine as a cause greater than conformity.

Mr. Speaker, I shall cast my lot with the leadership of my community. I shall cast my vote with the greater cause they serve. I will add my voice to those who seek reasoned and conciliatory adjustment to a new reality.

And finally, I would urge that we at home now move on to

the unfinished task of building a new South. We must not remain forever bound to another lost cause.[110]

That evening President Lyndon B. Johnson, a Democrat from Texas, signed into law the Civil Rights Act of 1964. Before the signing, he addressed his fellow citizens:

My fellow Americans.

I am about to sign into law the Civil Rights Act of 1964. I want to take this occasion to talk to you about what that law means to every American.

One hundred and eighty years ago this week a small band of valiant men began a long struggle for freedom.

They pledged their lives, their fortunes and their sacred honor not only to found a nation but to forge an ideal of freedom, not only for political independence but for personal liberty, not only to eliminate foreign rule but to establish the rule of justice in the affairs of men.

That struggle was a turning point in our history.

Today in far corners of distant continents the ideals of those American patriots still shape the struggles of men who hunger for freedom.

This is a proud triumph. Yet those who founded our country knew that freedom would be secure only if each generation thought to renew and enlarge its meaning.

From the Minutemen at Concord to the soldiers in Vietnam, each generation has been equal to that trust.

Americans of every race and color have died in battle to protect our freedom.

Americans of every race and color have worked to build a nation of widening opportunities.

Now, our generation of Americans, has been called on to continue the unending search for justice within our own borders.

We believe that all men are created equal—yet many are denied equal treatment.

We believe that all men have certain unalienable rights—yet many Americans do not enjoy those rights.

We believe that all men are entitled to the blessings of liberty—yet millions are being deprived of those blessings, not because of their own failures but because of the color of their skin.

The reasons are deeply imbedded in history and tradition and the nature of man. We can understand without rancor or hatred how this all happened. But it cannot continue.

Our Constitution, the foundation of our Republic forbids it. The principles of our freedom forbid it. Morality forbids it. And the law I will sign tonight forbids it. That law is the product of months of the most careful debate and discussion. It was proposed more than one year ago by our late and beloved President, John F. Kennedy. It received the bipartisan support of more than two-thirds of the members of both the House and the Senate. An overwhelming majority of Republicans as well as Democrats voted for it.

It has received the thoughtful support of tens of thousands of civic and religious leaders in all parts of this nation, and it is supported by the great majority of the American people.

The purpose of this law is simple. It does not restrict the freedom of any American so long as he respects the rights of others. It does not give special treatment to any citizen. It does say the only limit to a man's hope for happiness and for the future of his children shall be his own ability.

It does say that . . . those who are equal before God shall now also be equal in the polling booths, in the classrooms, in the factories and in hotels and restaurants, and movie theatres, and other places that provide service to the public.

.   .   .   .   .

This Civil Rights Act is a challenge to all of us to go to work in our communities and our states, in our homes and in our hearts to eliminate the last vestiges of injustice in our beloved country.

So, tonight I urge every public official, every religious leader, every business and professional man, every working man, every housewife—I urge every American to join in this effort to bring justice and hope to all our people and to bring peace to our land.

My fellow citizens, we have come now to a time of testing. We must not fail.

Let us close the springs of racial poison. Let us pray for wise and understanding hearts. Let us lay aside irrelevant differences and make our nation whole.

Let us hasten that day when our unmeasured strength and

*our unbounded spirit will be free to do the great works ordained
to this nation by the just and wise God who is the father of
us all.*[111]

Confident that some form of civil rights legislation would
emerge from Congress, President Johnson and his then Attorney
General, Robert F. Kennedy, had, together with certain private
groups, been hard at work during the spring and early summer of
1964 trying to create a favorable climate for the new legislation
prior to the day when it would be signed into law. Partly because
of this effort, there appeared to be, in the days following July 2,
1964, a substantial amount of prompt southern compliance with
the heatedly controversial public accommodations provisions of
the new law. This was particularly true in the border states, and
also in parts of Texas and Florida. Predictably enough, compliance was at a minimum in Alabama and Mississippi. But even in
these states the picture was not entirely bleak. Thus, although in
rural Mississippi civil rights workers were being killed and Negro
churches set on fire, in the State Capitol the Mayor and the
Chamber of Commerce both publicly stressed the importance of
compliance with the new law. Mayor Thompson of Jackson
stated his position this way:

*I don't like [the new law]. I don't believe in it. I think it is
taking away some of the freedoms of our people. But that's not
the question. It's the law and it must be obeyed until it is struck
down.*[112]

In part, the position voiced by Mayor Thompson, with the
evident acquiescence of substantial business groups, reflected "the
apparent willingness of white Southerners to bow to the will of
Congress more readily than to that of the courts."[113] And in part,
doubtless, compliance—where prevalent—stemmed from a sound
business instinct for larger sales and a more tranquil atmosphere: Unquestionably many of the affected restaurants, motels,
theaters, etc., were more than ready to give service on a nondiscriminatory basis the moment they had a law to "blame" compliance on.

The stand taken by Mayor Thompson and like-minded public officials and businessmen of course assumed that southern
places of public accommodation would again embrace segrega-

tion with enthusiasm the moment the new law was "struck down." A judicial challenge to the public accommodations provisions of the law was, of course, inevitable. As things turned out, the first challenge arose not in Mississippi or in Alabama but in Georgia—and, indeed, not in rural Georgia but in the cosmopolitan city of Atlanta. Atlanta's Mayor, Ivan Allen, Jr., had, in 1963, testified in support of a federal public accommodations law. And an Atlanta Congressman, Charles L. Weltner, had voted for the 1964 Act. But Lester Maddox was an Atlantan of a different stripe—a restaurant owner who seemed ready to sacrifice his stable business on the altar of high political principle. On July 3, 1964, Maddox refused service to three Negro divinity students. To make his refusal emphatic, he brandished a pistol and armed some of his staff with axe handles. A lawsuit to compel Maddox to conform to the requirements of the new law was begun almost immediately. His attorney argued to the three-judge federal court:

> The question is whether we will give the federal government control over our lives. The Constitution was designed to preserve the freedom of every man to discriminate.[114]

But the federal court was unpersuaded. The three judges found that the restaurant operated by Maddox was meaningfully related to interstate commerce: "Congress has the power to go this far."[115] Simultaneously the same federal court sustained the new law as applied to another place of public accommodations, in Atlanta, which served interstate travelers on a "whites-only" basis—the Heart of Atlanta Motel.

A few weeks after the decision of the Atlanta federal court sustaining the public accommodations sections of the 1964 Civil Rights Act, a federal court in Birmingham reached a contrary conclusion. The Birmingham case was initiated by an eating place called Ollie's Barbecue, which sought to enjoin the then Acting Attorney General, Nicholas deB. Katzenbach, from seeking to compel Ollie's Barbecue to comply with the provisions of the new federal statute. In one apparently significant respect, the Birmingham litigation was not like the Atlanta litigation—namely, neither before nor after the initiation of the Birmingham lawsuit had the federal government indicated any intention to compel Ollie's Barbecue, a relatively small establishment some distance from interstate highways, to comply with the statute's nondiscrimination requirements. Presumably this raised some real doubt as to whether the Birmingham litigation presented a "case" or "controversy" in the constitutional sense at all. Nevertheless, the Birmingham federal court proceeded to the merits and came to the conclusion that the asserted relationship of Ollie's Barbecue to interstate commerce (namely, to use the language of the statute, that a "substantial portion"—some 46%, or $70,000 worth annually—"of the food which it serves . . . has moved in commerce") was so attenuated that the federal commerce power could not constitutionally support federal regulation of its selection of customers. Otherwise, so the federal court indicated, the federal commerce power would seem to be without limit. Said the court:

> If Congress has the naked power to do what it has attempted in title II of this Act, there is no facet of human behavior which it may not control by mere legislative ipse dixit that conduct "affect[s] commerce" when in fact it does not do so at all, and rights of the individual to liberty and property are in dire peril.[116]

Recognizing the urgent need for a prompt review of these apparently conflicting decisions of the Birmingham and Atlanta federal district courts, the Supreme Court scheduled a special session of argument on October 5, 1964, one week in advance of the first session of regularly scheduled arguments for the 1964–65 Court Term. By virtue of a procedural error, one of the two Atlanta cases—the one involving Mr. Maddox's restaurant—was not ready for review. So the two cases heard by the Court were the Atlanta motel case (*Heart of Atlanta Motel v. United States*) and the Birmingham barbecue case (*Katzenbach v. McClung*). The approaches taken by counsel—and the responsive attitudes of some of the Justices—are apparent from the following excerpts from the argument in the *Heart of Atlanta Motel* case. The first lawyer to speak was Morton Rolleston, Jr., president of the Heart of Atlanta Motel, who was in effect representing himself:

MR. ROLLESTON: There are five theories of law that we rely on in this case.

No. 1, that the law of the land—and any lawyer is delighted to have a White Horse case that says what the law of the land is—is the decision of the civil rights cases by this Court in 1883.

The second proposition—

JUSTICE GOLDBERG—I notice in the discussions below about what a White Horse case is. Would you explain that to us?

MR. ROLLESTON—A White Horse case is one that just fits your case exactly. He doesn't have a red head or black tail. He is all white and fits our case precisely.

JUSTICE STEWART—We used to call that a bluebottle case.

MR. ROLLESTON—We know what we are talking about. The second proposition is that neither the 14th Amendment nor the Constitution prohibit racial discrimination by an individual.

The third proposition: We contend that the Civil Rights Act is an unlawful extension of the power of Congress under the commerce clause.

No. 4, we contend that the act, the Civil Rights Act, violates the Fifth Amendment to the Constitution. And last, that it violates the 13th Amendment to the Constitution.

And we submit, gentlemen, that if we can prevail on any theory, any one of those five theories, then this act has got to fail.

The fundamental question I submit is whether or not Congress has the power to take away the liberty of an individual to run his business as he sees fit in the selection and choice of his customers. This is the real important issue. And the fact of alleged civil rights of the Negroes involved is purely incidental, because if Congress can exercise these controls over the rights of individuals it is plausible that there is no limit to Congressional power to appropriate private property and liberty.

Theory Number 1: The Congress passed an act in 1875 which is almost identical with the public accommodations section of this act and, in 1883, this Supreme Court held that that act was unconstitutional upon the limited decision that the 14th Amendment did not prohibit racial discrimination by an individual where there was no state action involved, and let me hasten to say that there is no state action in any way involved in this case.

JUSTICE WHITE—Didn't the Court put the commerce clause expressly aside on the part of one of the defendants in that case?

MR. ROLLESTON—Your honor, I think all they said was

*this was not raised in that case as to whether they applied to put
it aside in the case of one of the defendants, I don't know.*

*JUSTICE HARLAN—It is not very germane [to argue about
the 14th Amendment]. There is no doubt about it that whatever
Congress intended to do beyond the commerce clause, it certainly intended to exercise its commerce clause power.*

*MR. ROLLESTON—In the [sit-in] case that was decided in
this court, handed down on June 22 of this year, Bell versus
Maryland, Mr. Justice Black's decision that was joined in by Mr.
Justice White and Mr. Justice Harlan, you three Justices said in
substance that the Constitution, including the 14th Amendment,
did not prohibit an individual from practicing racial discrimination unsupported by any state action.*

JUSTICE BLACK—In and of itself did not.

*MR. ROLLESTON—Of itself, and that is this case exactly; a
private individual elected to refuse to serve and refuse to participate or obey Civil Rights Act in order to bring the declaratory
judgment.*

*JUSTICE HARLAN—With one difference. That is, that since
that case was decided, Congress has passed this statute.*

MR. ROLLESTON—I realize that, sir.

*JUSTICE HARLAN—The rights of private property are cer-
tainly protected, in my judgment, by the Constitution, but it is
subject to an exercise of state police power and a valid exercise
of the commerce power of Congress. The question here is
whether this attempt to affect private property rights through the
exercise of Federal power under the commerce clause is a valid
exercise of that power.*

MR. ROLLESTON—That is right.

*JUSTICE HARLAN—So that it seems to me if you could
devote yourself to the question of whether this is a valid exercise of the commerce power by Congress, we would make more
progress.*

*MR. ROLLESTON—May it please the court, I am really
planning in the last half hour to talk about the commerce clause.
I want to try to cover these other theories which I contend, any
one of them, is good. The act will fail on those as well as the
commerce clause.*

*THE CHIEF JUSTICE—Mr. Rolleston, you have indicated
that you don't intend to get to your argument on the commerce*

clause until rebuttal. Don't you think that inasmuch as you both agree that the thrust of this case is under the commerce clause and inasmuch as you are on the top side of the case, we ought to hear your argument on the commerce clause before we hear from the Solicitor General?

MR. ROLLESTON—*Mr. Chief Justice, I would be glad to accede to the wishes of the Court. If I may comment on the 13th Amendment briefly, I will cover my brief theory of the theory of this commerce clause and come back for rebuttal.*

THE CHIEF JUSTICE—*Of course.*

MR. ROLLESTON—*The 13th Amendment simply says that neither slavery nor involuntary servitude shall exist within the United States. And 50 years ago this Court in the case of Hodges versus United States held that involuntary servitude was denounced by the 13th Amendment as a means of condition of enforcement of compulsory service of one to another. There have been other cases which have held that if a person is forced to serve another in business ways, that that involves an involuntary servitude prohibited by the 13th Amendment.*

Now may it please the Court, as to the commerce clause, Mr. Justice Goldberg made probably one of the most profound statements about the Constitution that I have ever read, in which I am not sure that a whole lot of lawyers in this country would agree with me or with the Justice at this time. I think it is still true, in the Maryland case, to quote Mr. Justice Goldberg:

"Our sworn duty to construe the Constitution requires, however, that we read it to effectuate the intent and purpose of the framers."

Not the framers, as if they were sitting in this room today passing judgment on what the Constitution is supposed to be, but what the framers intended the Constitution to be at the time it was adopted in 1787. If that theory is not so, then the Constitution is just like any other law. It can be changed from day to day by the Congress and by the courts.

The differences between our Government and any other government in this world is that we have a Constitution that stays a Constitution in the words that are there, unless it is amended in the way the Constitution provides. Our Constitution is still the same Constitution it was in 1787 except the amend-

ments that the people, the people have decided should be added to it.

When the Constitution was adopted, the United States was broke. We were in the middle of a depression as we know it, of financial chaos.

We say that the framers of the Constitution intended to cover commerce as commerce is known in business fields, and that it was intended to cover the transportation and movement and production of articles from agriculture, products of industry, methods of transportation, tariffs between states, which we don't have now thank goodness, and anything else that had to do with commerce. But as the Birmingham Justice in this case recently said, "unlike Tennyson's brook, commerce has got to come to an end somewhere and end sooner or later in a state. It can't go on forever."

And commerce means as the framers of the Constitution intended it to mean. The only thing they thought about at that time was actual goods in commerce and the transportation thereof.

JUSTICE DOUGLAS—We are talking here, aren't we, about the person moving in interstate commerce?

MR. ROLLESTON—Yes sir.

JUSTICE DOUGLAS—Driving from Virginia to Atlanta and asking for accommodations for the night? That is in interstate commerce, that person is moving in interstate commerce. You don't treat with it in your brief on that point precisely as I read your brief.

JUSTICE GOLDBERG—Mr. Rolleston, what do you do with Wickard versus Filburn?

If the court were to decide in your favor in this case, would we have to overrule that case?

MR. ROLLESTON—I don't think so, may it please the court. I say this is my reason for it. Of course in that case they said just because a man raised wheat in a field, he is just one man, he doesn't affect commerce by himself, but if you take all the rest of the farmers who raise wheat they will materially affect commerce. I think that is the substance [of] what it says.

JUSTICE GOLDBERG—Hasn't Congress in effect said that in this case, all the motels and all the hotels. . . .

MR. ROLLESTON—If you carry it to the extreme, then Con-

gress could cover every activity, every facet of life, because if you take any particular facet of life, even the manufacturer of pencils that a lawyer has to use, and say that because every lawyer has got to use a pencil if he doesn't do so and so he is subject to that act, to the power of Congress under the commerce clause, it gets to a ridiculous situation where Congress then can do anything.

If this Court will let Congress do anything it wants to under the commerce clause, and that is what that argument means, if this Court will let them do anything, then this Court has abdicated and there is no reason for the existence of the Supreme Court to adjust and maintain the balance of powers between the various governments in this country. That is the function of the Supreme Court. That is the very reason for its setup in the Constitution, to balance those powers between the two by declaring the act of a state unconstitutional or declaring an act of Congress unconstitutional.

And if you abdicate from that power there will be no reason for the Supreme Court because Congress then can do anything it wants in any facet of our lives.

JUSTICE BLACK—*You haven't discussed at all the thing that it seems to me is most important on both sides, that is, the Shreveport case. There it was stated that Congress has not only the right to regulate local activities, wholly local within the state, if Congress concludes that those activities adversely affect interstate commerce.*

It seems to me that you have not touched on that yet, that, to me, is a very important part of this case.

MR. ROLLESTON—*I recognize, your honor, that there are a large line of cases that the Congress can regulate, under the commerce power, intrastate activities, purely local activities, if Congress thinks that they place a burden on interstate commerce. I will try to hit that in rebuttal.*[117]

Mr. Rolleston was followed by the then Solicitor General, Archibald Cox, representing the United States:

MR. COX—*The Civil Rights Act of 1964 is surely the most important legislation enacted in recent decades. It is one of the half-dozen most important laws, I think, enacted in the last century. No legislation within my memory has been debated as widely, as long, or as thoroughly. Certainly none has been considered more conscientiously.*

Title 2, as I shall show, is addressed to a commercial problem of grave national significance.

JUSTICE GOLDBERG—*Only commercial, Mr. Solicitor General? Isn't there a moral problem, also?*

MR. COX—*I wish to emphasize and will emphasize repeatedly in my argument that Title 2 is addressed to a grave commercial problem, grave at the time the act was enacted and plainly growing.*

Nor should we forget, Mr. Justice Goldberg, that Congress in addressing itself to that commercial problem, was also keeping faith with the [promise] declared by the Continental Congress that all men are created equal.

The failure to keep that promise lay heavy on the conscience of the entire nation, North as well as South, East as well as West.

Happily, the difficulty of the constitutional issues here is not equal to their importance. Title 2, as we see it, rests upon the powers delegated to Congress to regulate commerce among the several states and upon the power to enact laws that are necessary and proper to effectuate the commerce power.

The constitutionality of Title 2 under those provisions is sustained by principles that are so familiar because they have been enacted over and over again, applied indeed throughout our entire history going back, as Mr. Justice Black pointed out a moment ago, to the opinion of Chief Justice Marshall in Gibbons versus Ogden and others. We do not seek the extension of any existing principles here. A fortiori, we invoke no new doctrine.

JUSTICE GOLDBERG—*Mr. Solicitor General, where does that leave the court? Does that mean that the Government loses the day in this court if the Court decides that your position on commerce is not to be sustained?*

MR. COX—*Frankly, I find that alternative so unlikely that if we were to lose on that ground, I might despair of persuading the Court on the other ground, because I think that one is so much stronger.*

JUSTICE GOLDBERG—*Well, for the purpose of this case therefore you are really saying to us that we stand or fall by the commerce clause?*

MR. COX—*That is correct.*

JUSTICE HARLAN—You have said that specifically in your brief.

MR. COX—I hope the point is clear.

JUSTICE HARLAN—"We stake our case" is your language, "we stake our case on the commerce clause."

MR. COX—On the commerce clause.

The major premise of our argument is the familiar rule that the powers delegated to Congress by the commerce and necessary-and-proper clauses authorize Congress to regulate local activities, at least activities that are local but separately considered, even though they are not themselves interstate commerce, if they have such a close and substantial relation to commerce that their regulation may be deemed appropriate or useful to foster or promote such commerce, or to relieve it of burdens and obstructions.

The minor premise of our argument is that Congress, to which the economic question thus raised is primarily committed, had ample basis upon which to find that racial discrimination does in fact constitute a source of burden or obstruction to interstate commerce. And, of course, from those premises the conclusion would follow that this is a legitimate exercise of the power under the commerce clause.

Here the record was made, and we do cite it, and we think that we show that there was ample basis for concluding that this segregation in all these kinds of establishments did create, was creating a grave national problem.

Congress heard evidence, for example, for about two months in the spring and early summer of 1963, and there were 634 demonstrations in 174 cities and 32 states and the District of Columbia. About a third of those were concerned solely with discrimination in places of public accommodation.

The effect of those demonstrations, picketing, boycotts, other forms of protest, upon business conditions and therefore upon interstate commerce, was tremendous.

Now it is evident that any general downturn in business, in retail business, will, if left unchecked, result in serious disruption of the flow of goods across state lines. If the retailers don't sell they won't buy, and if they won't buy then the demand for goods flowing in from other states of course, if unchecked the flow of goods will be dammed up.

The Secretary of Labor, who had a study made before testifying before Congress, summarized the results of the studies made by his department.

This general evidence shows that the impact of these disturbances arising out of racial discrimination was not merely social and moral. Nobody denies that aspect of it. But that it was national and commercial.

The testimony before Congress provided literally the overwhelming evidence that discrimination by hotels and motels impedes interstate travel. Suffice it to say, because it epitomizes the point, that on a motor trip between Washington, D.C., and Miami, Fla., the average distance it was found between accommodations of reasonable quality open to Negroes was 141 miles.

Simply to summarize we think there was ample evidence on which Congress could conclude that the racial practices in hotels and motels and like places did have a very substantial effect upon the movement of people in interstate commerce, and that therefore this statute applied to them is a measure adopted to freeing interstate commerce from restraints and burdens.

Now of course once that conclusion is reached, the other arguments presented by the appellant collapse of their own weight. The size of the establishment is obviously irrelevant.

Appellant also argues that the act violates the 13th Amendment. It is enough to point out that the motel is a corporation. But surely it would turn the world upside down for anyone to seriously suggest that the 13th Amendment was intended to prohibit either Congress or the state governments from guaranteeing Negroes equality of treatment in places of public accommodation.

And Alice, I think, even at the end of her long journey through wonderland, would have been surprised to be told that the restaurants and other places of public accommodation in 33 states in the year 1964 are held in involuntary servitude and that the Anglo-American common law for centuries has subjected to slavery innkeepers, hackmen, carriers, wharfage men, ferriers, all kinds of other people holding themselves out to serve the public.[118]

At very nearly the beginning of his argument the Solicitor General had said: "Happily, the difficulty of the constitutional issues here is not equal to their importance." He was echoing what John Marshall had said in *Marbury v. Madison:* "The question, whether an act, repugnant to the constitution, can become the law of the land, is a question deeply interesting to the United States; but, happily, not of an intricacy proportioned to its interest."[119]

The echo was an apt one. In few instances since John Marshall's time had the Supreme Court dealt with constitutional issues which were so central to the predominant political controversies currently dividing the nation. The Supreme Court arguments in *Heart of Atlanta Motel* and *McClung* took place just one month before the 1964 presidential election. In the closing weeks of the campaign the chief questions besetting those—professional politicians, pollsters, and ordinary voters—who sought to forecast the result were these: How massive was the much-talked-about "white blacklash"? Would Lyndon B. Johnson lose the allegiance of millions of normally Democratic white voters—voters who felt threatened by the Kennedy-Johnson civil rights program and sought solace under the banner of Barry Goldwater, who, defying the majority of his Republican congressional colleagues, had voted against the Civil Rights Act of 1964 and branded it unconstitutional?

Those who foresaw a "white blacklash" of huge dimension were chiefly influenced by the strong showing made by Alabama's Governor Wallace when, earlier in the summer of 1964, he had ventured into Democratic preferential primaries in Maryland, Indiana, and Wisconsin. Other political observers felt that Senator Goldwater's announced views on civil rights and on other issues (e.g., foreign policy and social security) would lose him far more votes among regular Republicans and crucial blocs of independent voters than he would gain from white Democratic disaffection. Among those who felt this way were such important Republican leaders as Governor Nelson Rockefeller of New York, Governor William Scranton of Pennsylvania, Governor George Romney of Michigan, Senator Kenneth Keating of New York, and Congressman John Lindsay of New York (the last three being candidates for re-election). Another astute observer who shared this view was President Johnson: In August, at the Democratic Convention, he predicted that he and his running-mate, Senator

Hubert H. Humphrey, would be the beneficiaries of a massive "frontlash."

It was against this background that the Justices heard the arguments in *Heart of Atlanta Motel* and *McClung*—and then, reserving decision, retired behind the red velvet draperies that insulate the process of decision from public view.

October moved on apace. "Opinion Mondays" came and went and the Court said not a word about the pending cases. Then Mr. Rolleston, as counsel for the Heart of Atlanta Motel, filed a motion requesting the Court to expedite its decision: Specifically, Mr. Rolleston called on the Court to decide his case in advance of Election Day, in view of the prevailing national interest in the constitutionality of the new law. Perhaps Mr. Rolleston did not fully understand the ways in which the Court has, with rare and highly regrettable exceptions, steadfastly maintained its vital separation from the partisan political process. Perhaps, in the alternative, Mr. Rolleston understood that vital separation all too well. At all events, by Monday, November 2, 1964, the Court had not ruled on the merits of the pending cases. Nor had it ruled on Mr. Rolleston's motion to expedite.

On Tuesday, November 3, the nation went to the polls. President Johnson overwhelmed Senator Goldwater. His popular majority was 41 million to 26 million. The only states Senator Goldwater carried were his own state of Arizona plus the deepest heart of the old Confederacy: Alabama, Georgia, Louisiana, Mississippi, South Carolina. Moreover, in Arkansas, Florida, Tennessee, Virginia, and probably North Carolina, the Democratic voters who carried the day for President Johnson were Negroes.[120]

Six days later the Supreme Court denied, without opinion, Mr. Rolleston's motion to expedite the decision of the *Heart of Atlanta Motel* case.

Throughout November the Court kept its peace. Meanwhile, President Johnson, vindicated in his sense of the new national climate, went forward with his administration's plans to implement the 1964 law. On December 10 the President addressed a gathering of the National Urban League, an organization long engaged in seeking to widen the field of employment opportunities for Negroes. The following is a portion of the President's remarks:

It is more than a hundred years since Abraham Lincoln charged the living to dedicate themselves to the unfinished work of the dead at Gettysburg.

Even Lincoln, with his deep sense of man's imperfections, could not know that a century later we would still be striving to abolish racial injustice.

No task is more deeply rooted in the complexities of American life. Poverty and tradition, fear and ignorance, the structure of our society and the workings of our economy, all converge on this enormous wrong which has troubled the American conscience from the beginning. Its just solution is essential, not only to give the full blessings of freedom to Negroes, but to liberate all of us.

There are those who say: It has taken us a century to move this far. It will take another hundred years to finish the job.

I do not agree.

Great social change tends to come rapidly, in periods of intense activity and progress before the impulse slows. I believe we are in the midst of such a period of change.

It is our task to carry forward nothing less than the full assimilation of more than 20,000,000 Negroes into American life. This is not to be assimilation of bland conformity. Our object is not to make all people alike. It is, as it has always been, to allow ready access to every blessing of liberty, while permitting each to keep his sense of identity with a culture and tradition. In this way we enlarge our freedom and enrich our nation.

We have just passed a milestone in this task.

The Civil Rights bill of 1964 extends the protection of law to many of the demands of justice.

This bill, of course, is not the whole answer. But I ask each of you to think what an enormous setback failure to pass it would have been.

Now your Government must, and will, move rapidly to carry out that legislation.[121]

On the following Monday, December 14, 1964, the Supreme Court, in two unanimous opinions (one being *Heart of Atlanta Motel*, the other being *McClung*), sustained the constitutionality of the public accommodations sections of the 1964 Civil Rights Act. Both opinions were written by Justice Tom Clark, the Texan elevated to the Court from the Attorney Generalship by President Truman. Justice Clark's rationale rested solely on the power of Congress pursuant to the commerce clause—a rationale which was, in essence, the one urged on the Court by Solicitor General Cox. Justices Douglas and Goldberg filed separate concurring opinions making the added point that the challenged public accommodations sections of the 1964 statute could also be sustained through reliance on congressional power to implement the equal protection clause of the Fourteenth Amendment.

There follows the major portion of Justice Clark's opinion in *Heart of Atlanta Motel v. United States:*

The [1964 Civil Rights] Act as finally adopted was most comprehensive, undertaking to prevent through peaceful and voluntary settlement discrimination in voting, as well as in places of accommodation and public facilities, federally secured programs and in employment. Since Title II is the only portion under attack here, we confine our consideration to those public accommodation provisions.

3. Title II of the Act.

This Title is divided into seven sections beginning with § 201 (a) which provides that:

All persons shall be entitled to the full and equal enjoyment of the goods, services, facilities, privileges, advantages, and accommodations of any place of public accommodation, as defined in this section, without discrimination or segregation on the ground of race, color, religion, or national origin.

There are listed in § 201 (b) four classes of business establishments, each of which "serves the public" and "is a place of public accommodation" within the meaning of § 201 (a) "if its operations affect commerce, or if discrimination or segregation by it is supported by State action." The covered establishments are:

(1) any inn, hotel, motel, or other establishment which provides lodging to transient guests, other than an establishment located within a building which contains not more than five rooms for rent or hire and which is actually occupied by the proprietor of such establishment as his residence;

(2) any restaurant, cafeteria . . . [not here involved];

(3) any motion picture house . . . [not here involved];

(4) any establishment . . . which is physically located

within the premises of any establishment otherwise covered by this subsection, or . . . within the premises of which is physically located any such covered establishment . . . [not here involved].

Section 201 (c) defines the phrase "affect commerce" as applied to the above establishments. It first declares that "any inn, hotel, motel, or other establishment which provides lodging to transient guests" affects commerce per se. Restaurants, cafeterias, etc., in the second class affect commerce only if they serve or offer to serve interstate travelers or if a substantial portion of the food which they serve or products which they sell have "moved in commerce." Motion picture houses and other places listed in class three affect commerce if they customarily present films, performances, etc., "which move in commerce." And the establishments listed in class four affect commerce if they are within, or include within their own premises, an establishment "the operations of which affect commerce." Private clubs are excepted under certain conditions. See § 201 (e).

Section 201 (d) declares that "discrimination or segregation" is supported by state action when carried on under color of any law, statute, ordinance, regulation or any custom or usage required or enforced by officials of the State or any of its subdivisions.

In addition, § 202 affirmatively declares that all persons "shall be entitled to be free, at any establishment or place, from discrimination or segregation of any kind on the ground of race, color, religion, or national origin, if such discrimination or segregation is or purports to be required by any law, statute, ordinance, regulation, rule, or order of a State or any agency or political subdivision thereof."

Finally § 203 prohibits the withholding or denial, etc., of any right or privilege secured by § 201 and § 202 or the intimidation, threatening or coercion of any person with the purpose of interfering with any such right or the punishing, etc., of any person for exercising or attempting to exercise any such right.

The remaining sections of the Title are remedial ones for violations of any of the previous sections. Remedies are limited to civil actions for preventive relief. The Attorney General may bring suit where he has "reasonable cause to believe that any person or group of persons is engaged in a pattern or practice of *resistance to the full enjoyment of any of the rights secured by this title, and that the pattern or practice is of such a nature and is intended to deny the full exercise of the rights herein described . . . ." § 206 (a). Thirty days written notice before filing any such action must be given to the appropriate authorities of a State or subdivision the law of which prohibits the act complained of and which has established an authority which may grant relief therefrom. § 204 (c). In States where such condition does not exist the court after a case is filed may refer it to the Community Relations Service which is established under Title X of the Act. § 204 (d). This Title establishes such service in the Department of Commerce, provides for a Director to be appointed by the President with the advice and consent of the Senate and grants it certain powers, including the power to hold hearings, with reference to matters coming to its attention by reference from the court or between communities and persons involved in disputes arising under the Act.*

4. Application of Title II to Heart of Atlanta Motel.

It is admitted that the operation of the motel brings it within the provisions of § 201 (a) of the Act and that appellant refused to provide lodging for transient Negroes because of their race or color and that it intends to continue that policy unless restrained.

The sole question posed is, therefore, the constitutionality of the Civil Rights Act of 1964 as applied to these facts. The legislative history of the Act indicates that Congress based the Act on § 5 and the Equal Protection Clause of the Fourteenth Amendment as well as its power to regulate interstate commerce under Art. I, § 8, cl. 3 of the Constitution.

The Senate Commerce Committee made it quite clear that the fundamental object of Title II was to vindicate "the deprivation of personal dignity that surely accompanies denials of equal access to public establishments." At the same time, however, it noted that such an objective has been and could be readily achieved "by congressional action based on the commerce power of the Constitution." S. Rep. No. 872, at 16–17. Our study of the legislative record, made in the light of prior cases, has brought us to the conclusion that Congress possessed ample power in this regard, and we have therefore not considered the other grounds relied upon. This is not to say that the remaining authority upon which it acted was not adequate, a question upon which we do not pass, but merely that since the commerce power is sufficient for our decision here we have considered it alone. Nor is § 201 (d) or § 202, having to do with state action, involved here and we do not pass upon those sections.

5. The Civil Rights Cases, 109 U.S. 3 (1883), and their Application.

In light of our ground for decision, it might be well at the outset to discuss the Civil Rights Cases, *supra, which declared provisions of the Civil Rights Act of 1875 unconstitutional. 18 Stat. 335, 336. We think that decision inapposite, and without precedential value in determining the constitutionality of the present Act. Unlike Title II of the present legislation, the 1875 Act broadly proscribed discrimination in "inns, public conveyances on land or water, theaters, and other public places of amusement," without limiting the categories of affected businesses to those impinging upon interstate commerce. In contrast, the applicability of Title II is carefully limited to enterprises having a direct and substantial relation to the interstate flow of goods and people, except where state action is involved. Further, the fact that certain kinds of businesses may not in 1875 have been sufficiently involved in interstate commerce to warrant bringing them within the ambit of the commerce power is not necessarily dispositive of the same question today. Our populace had not reached its present mobility, nor were facilities, goods and services circulating as readily in interstate commerce as they are today. Although the principles which we apply today are those first formulated by Chief Justice Marshall in* Gibbons v. Ogden, *9 Wheat. 1 (1824), the conditions of transportation and commerce have changed dramatically, and we must apply those principles to the present state of commerce. The sheer increase in volume of interstate traffic alone would give discriminatory practices which inhibit travel a far larger impact upon the nation's commerce than such practices had in the economy of another day. Finally, there is language in the* Civil Rights Cases *which indicates that the Court did not fully consider whether the 1875 Act could be sustained as an exercise of the commerce power. Though the Court observed that "no one will contend that the power to pass it was contained in the Constitution before adoption of the last three amendments (Thirteenth, Four-*

teenth, and Fifteenth)," the Court went on specifically to note that the Act was not "conceived" in terms of the commerce power and expressly pointed out:

> *Of course, these remarks [as to lack of congressional power] do not apply to those cases in which Congress is clothed with direct and plenary powers of legislation over the whole subject, accompanied with an express or implied denial of such power to the States, as in the regulation of commerce with foreign nations, among the several States, and with the Indian tribes . . . . In these cases Congress has power to pass laws for regulating the subjects specified in every detail, and the conduct and transactions of individuals in respect thereof. [At 18.]*

Since the commerce power was not relied on by the Government and was without support in the record it is understandable that the Court narrowed its inquiry and excluded the Commerce Clause as a possible source of power. In any event, it is clear that such a limitation renders the opinion devoid of authority for the proposition that the Commerce Clause gives no power to Congress to regulate discriminatory practices now found substantially to affect interstate commerce. We, therefore, conclude that the Civil Rights Cases have no relevance to the basis of decision here where the Act not only explicitly relies upon the commerce power, but the record is filled with testimony of obstructions and restraints resulting from the discriminations found to be existing. We now pass to that phase of the case.

6. The Basis of Congressional Action.

While the Act as adopted carried no congressional findings the record of its passage through each house is replete with evidence of the burdens that discrimination by race or color places upon interstate commerce. See Hearings before Senate Committee on Commerce on S. 1732, 88th Cong., 1st Sess.; S. Rep. No. 872, supra; Hearings before Senate Committee on the Judiciary on S. 1731, 88th Cong., 1st Sess.; Hearings before House Subcommittee No. 5 on miscellaneous proposals regarding Civil Rights, 88th Cong., 1st Sess., ser. 4; H. R. Rep. No. 914, supra. This testimony included the fact that our people have become increasingly mobile with millions of all races traveling from State to State; that Negroes in particular have been the subject of discrimination in transient accommodations, having to travel great distances to secure the same; that often they have been unable to obtain accommodations and have had to call upon friends to put them up overnight, S. Rep. No. 872, at 14–22; and that these conditions had become so acute as to require the listing of available lodging for Negroes in a special guidebook which was itself "dramatic testimony of the difficulties" Negroes encounter in travel, Senate Commerce Hearings, at 692–694. These exclusionary practices were found to be nationwide, the Under Secretary of Commerce testifying that there is "no question that this discrimination in the North still exists to a large degree" and in the West and Midwest as well. Senate Commerce Hearings, at 735, 744. This testimony indicated a qualitative as well as quantitive effect on interstate travel by Negroes. The former was the obvious impairment of the Negro traveler's pleasure and convenience that resulted when he continually was uncertain of finding lodging. As for the latter, there was evidence that this uncertainty stemming from racial discrimination had the effect of discouraging travel on the part of a substantial portion of the Negro community. Senate Commerce Hearings, at 744. This was the conclusion not only of the Under Secretary of Commerce but also of the Administrator of the Federal Aviation Agency who wrote the Chairman of the Senate Commerce Committee that it was his "belief that air commerce is adversely affected by the denial to a substantial segment of the traveling public of adequate and desegregated public accommodations." Senate Commerce Hearings, at 12–13. We shall not burden this opinion with further details since the voluminous testimony presents overwhelming evidence that discrimination by hotels and motels impedes interstate travel.

7. The Power of Congress Over Interstate Travel.

The power of Congress to deal with these obstructions depends on the meaning of the Commerce Clause. Its meaning was first enunciated 140 years ago by the great Chief Justice John Marshall in Gibbons v. Ogden, *9 Wheat. 1 (1824), in these words:*

> *The subject to be regulated is commerce; and . . . to ascertain the extent of the power, it becomes necessary to settle the meaning of the word. The counsel for the appellee would limit it to traffic, to buying and selling, or the interchange of commodities . . . but it is something more: it is intercourse . . . between nations, and parts of nations, in*

all its branches, and is regulated by prescribing rules for carrying on that intercourse. [*At 189–190.*]

.   .   .   .   .

To what commerce does this power extend? The constitution informs us, to commerce "with foreign nations, and among the several States, and with the Indian tribes."

It has, we believe, been universally admitted, that these words comprehend every species of commercial intercourse. . . . No sort of trade can be carried on . . . to which this power does not extend. [*At 193–194.*]

.   .   .   .   .

The subject to which the power is next applied, is to commerce "among the several States." The word "among" means intermingled. . . .

.   .   .   .   .

[I]t may very properly be restricted to that commerce which concerns more States than one. . . . The genius and character of the whole government seems to be, that its action is to be applied to all the . . . internal concerns [of the nation] which affect the States generally; but not to those which are completely within a particular State, which do not affect other States, and with which it is not necessary to interfere, for the purpose of executing some of the general powers of the government. [*At 194–195.*]

.   .   .   .   .

We are now arrived at the inquiry—What is this power?

It is the power to regulate; that is, to prescribe the rule by which commerce is to be governed. This power, like all others vested in Congress, is complete in itself, may be exercised to its utmost extent, and acknowledges no limitations, other than are prescribed in the constitution. . . . If, as has always been understood, the sovereignty of Congress . . . is plenary as to those objects [specified in the Constitution], the power over commerce . . . is vested in Congress as absolutely as it would be in a single government, having in its constitution the same restrictions on the exercise of the power as are found in the constitution of the United States. The wisdom and the discretion of Congress, their identity with the people, and the influence which their constituents possess at elections, are, in this, as in many other instances, as that, for example, of declaring war, the sole restraints on which they have relied, to secure them from its abuse. They are the restraints on which the people must often rely solely, in all representative governments. [*At 196–197.*]

In short, the determinative test of the exercise of power by the Congress under the Commerce Clause is simply whether the activity sought to be regulated is "commerce which concerns more than one state" and has a real and substantial relation to the national interest. Let us now turn to this facet of the problem.

That the "intercourse" of which the Chief Justice spoke included the movement of persons through more States than one was settled as early as 1849, in the Passenger Cases, 7 How. 283, where Mr. Justice McLean stated: "That the transportation of passengers is a part of commerce is not now an open question." At 401. Again in 1913 Mr. Justice McKenna, speaking for the Court, said: "Commerce among the States, as we have said, consists of intercourse and traffic between their citizens, and includes the transportation of persons and property." Hoke v. United States, 227 U.S. 308, 320. And only four years later in 1916 in Caminetti v. United States, 242 U.S. 470, Mr. Justice Day held for the Court:

> The transportation of passengers in interstate commerce, it has long been settled, is within the regulatory power of Congress, under the commerce clause of the Constitution, and the authority of Congress to keep the channels of interstate commerce free from immoral and injurious uses has been frequently sustained, and is no longer open to question. [*At 491.*]

Nor does it make any difference whether the transportation is commercial in character. Id., at 484–486. In Morgan v. Virginia, 328 U.S. 373 (1946), Mr. Justice Reed observed as to the modern movement of persons among the States:

> The recent changes in transportation brought about by the coming of automobiles does not seem of great significance in the problem. People of all races travel today more extensively than in 1878 when this Court first passed upon state regulation of racial segregation in commerce. [It but] emphasizes the soundness of this Court's early conclusion in Hall v. DeCuir, 95 U.S. 485. [*At 383.*]

The same interest in protecting interstate commerce which led Congress to deal with segregation in interstate carriers and the white slave traffic has prompted it to extend the exercise of *its power to gambling,* Lottery Case, *188 U.S. 321 (1903); to criminal enterprises,* Brooks v. United States, *267 U.S. 432 (1925); to deceptive practices in the sale of products,* Federal Trade Comm'n v. Mandel Bros., Inc., *359 U.S. 385 (1959); to fraudulent security transactions,* Securities & Exchange Comm'n v. Ralston Purina Co., *346 U.S. 119 (1953); to misbranding of drugs,* Weeks v. United States, *245 U.S. 618 (1918); to wages and hours,* United States v. Darby, *312 U.S. 100 (1941); to members of labor unions,* Labor Board v. Jones & Laughlin Steel Corp., *301 U.S. 1 (1937); to crop control.* Wickard v. Filburn, *317 U.S. 111 (1942); to discrimination against shippers,* United States v. Baltimore & Ohio R. Co., *333 U.S. 169 (1948); to the protection of small business from injurious price cutting,* Moore v. Mead's Fine Bread Co., *348 U.S. 115 (1954); to resale price maintenance,* Hudson Distributors, Inc. v. Eli Lilly & Co., *377 U.S. 386 (1964);* Schwegmann v. Calvert Distillers Corp., *341 U.S. 384 (1951); to professional football,* Radovich v. National Football League, *352 U.S. 445 (1957); and to racial discrimination by owners and managers of terminal restaurants,* Boynton v. Virginia, *364 U.S. 454 (1960).*

That Congress was legislating against moral wrongs in many of these areas rendered its enactments no less valid. In framing Title II of this Act Congress was also dealing with what it considered a moral problem. But that fact does not detract from the overwhelming evidence of the disruptive effect that racial discrimination has had on commercial intercourse. It was this burden which empowered Congress to enact appropriate legislation, and, given this basis for the exercise of its power, Congress was not restricted by the fact that the particular obstruction to interstate commerce with which it was dealing was also deemed a moral and social wrong.

It is said that the operation of the motel here is of a purely local character. But, assuming this to be true, "if it is interstate commerce that feels the pinch, it does not matter how local the operation that applies the squeeze." United States v. Women's Sportswear Mfrs. Assn., *336 U.S. 460, 464 (1949). See* Labor Board v. Jones & Laughlin Steel Corp., *supra. As Chief Justice Stone put it in* United States v. Darby, *supra:*

> *The power of Congress over interstate commerce is not confined to the regulation of commerce among the states. It extends to those activities intrastate which so affect inter-*

state commerce or the exercise of the power of Congress over it as to make regulation of them appropriate means to the attainment of a legitimate end, the exercise of the granted power of Congress to regulate interstate commerce. See McCulloch v. Maryland, 4 Wheat. 316, 421. [At 118.]

Thus the power of Congress to promote interstate commerce also includes the power to regulate the local incidents thereof, including local activities in both the States of origin and destination, which might have a substantial and harmful effect upon that commerce. One need only examine the evidence which we have discussed above to see that Congress may—as it has—prohibit racial discrimination by motels serving travelers, however "local" their operations may appear.

Nor does the Act deprive appellant of liberty or property under the Fifth Amendment. The commerce power invoked here by the Congress is a specific and plenary one authorized by the Constitution itself. The only questions are: (1) whether Congress had a rational basis for finding that racial discrimination by motels affected commerce, and (2) if it had such a basis, whether the means it selected to eliminate that evil are reasonable and appropriate. If they are, appellant has no "right" to select its guests as it sees fit, free from governmental regulation.

There is nothing novel about such legislation. Thirty-two States now have it on their books either by statute or executive order and many cities provide such regulation. Some of these Acts go back four-score years. It has been repeatedly held by this Court that such laws do not violate the Due Process Clause of the Fourteenth Amendment. Perhaps the first such holding was in the Civil Rights Cases, themselves, where Mr. Justice Bradley for the Court inferentially found that innkeepers, "by the laws of all of the States, so far as we are aware, are bound, to the extent of their facilities, to furnish proper accommodation to all unobjectionable persons who in good faith apply for them." At 25.

As we have pointed out, 32 States now have such statutes and no case has been cited to us where the attack on a state statute has been successful, either in federal or state courts. Indeed, in some cases the Due Process and Equal Protection Clause objections have been specifically discarded in this Court. Bob-Lo Excursion Co. v. Michigan, 333 U.S. 28, 34, n. 12 (1948). As a result the constitutionality of such state statutes stands unquestioned. *"The authority of the Federal Government over interstate commerce does not differ,"* it was held in United States v. Rock Royal Co-op., Inc., 307 U.S. 533 (1939), *"in extent or character from that retained by the states over intrastate commerce."* At 569–570. See also Bowles v. Willingham, 321 U.S. 503 (1944).

It is doubtful if in the long run appellant will suffer economic loss as a result of the Act. Experience is to the contrary where discrimination is completely obliterated as to all public accommodations. But whether this be true or not is of no consequence since this Court has specifically held that the fact that a "member of the class which is regulated may suffer economic losses not shared by others . . . has never been a barrier" to such legislation. Bowles v. Willingham, supra, at 518. *Likewise in a long line of cases this Court has rejected the claim that the prohibition of racial discrimination in public accommodations interferes with personal liberty. See* District of Columbia v. John R. Thompson Co., 346 U.S. 100 (1953), *and cases there cited, where we concluded that Congress had delegated law-making power to the District of Columbia "as broad as the police power of a state" which included the power to adopt "a law prohibiting discriminations against Negroes by the owners and managers of restaurants in the District of Columbia." At 110. Neither do we find any merit in the claim that the Act is a taking of property without just compensation. The cases are to the contrary. See* Legal Tender Cases, 12 Wall. 457, 551 (1870); Omnia Commercial Co. v. United States, 261 U.S. 502 (1923); United States v. Central Eureka Mining Co., 357 U.S. 155 (1958).

We find no merit in the remainder of appellant's contentions, including that of "involuntary servitude." As we have seen, 32 States prohibit racial discrimination in public accommodations. These laws but codify the common-law innkeeper rule which long predated the Thirteenth Amendment. It is difficult to believe that the Amendment was intended to abrogate this principle. Indeed, the opinion of the Court in The Civil Rights Cases *is to the contrary as we have seen, it having noted with approval the laws of "all of the states" prohibiting discrimination. We could not say that the requirements of the Act in this regard are in any way "akin to African slavery."* Butler v. Perry, 240 U.S. 328, 332 (1916).

We, therefore, conclude that the action of the Congress in

the adoption of the Act as applied here to a motel which con-
cededly serves interstate travelers is within the power granted it
by the Commerce Clause of the Constitution, as interpreted by
this Court for 140 years. It may be argued that Congress could
have pursued other methods to eliminate the obstructions it found
in interstate commerce caused by racial discrimination. But this
is a matter of policy that rests entirely with the Congress not
with the courts. How obstructions in commerce may be removed
—what means are to be employed—is within the sound and exclu-
sive discretion of the Congress. It is subject only to one caveat
—that the means chosen by it must be reasonably adapted to the
end permitted by the Constitution. We cannot say that its choice
here was not so adapted. The Constitution requires no more.[122]

Justice Clark documented that portion of his opinion which
argued that "There is nothing novel about such legislation" with
the following footnote:

The following States have enacted public accommodation
laws: Alaska Stats. §§ 11.60.230–11.60.240 (1962); Calif. Civil Code
§§ 51–54 (1954); Colo. Rev. Stats. §§ 25-1-1 to 25-2-5 (1953);
Conn. Gen. Stats. Ann. § 53.35 (1961); Del. Code Ann. Tit. 6. c. 45
(1963); Idaho Code §§ 18–7301 through 18–7303 (1961); Ill. Ann.
Stats. (Smith-Hurd ed.) c. 38 §§ 13–1 to 13–4 (1961)c. 43 § 133
(1944); Ind. Stats. Ann. (Burns ed.) §§ 10–901 to 10–914 (1961);
Iowa Code Ann. §§ 735.1–735.2 (1950); Kan. Gen. Stats. Ann. § 21–
2424 (Supp. 1962); Maine Rev. Stats. C. 137 § 50 (1954); Md. Ann.
Code § 49 B § 11 (1964); Mass. Ann. Laws C. 140 §§ 5 and 8
(1957), c. 272 §§ 92A, 9B (1963); Mich. Stats. Ann. §§ 28.343 and
28.344 (1962); Minn. Stats. Ann. § 327.09 (1947); Mont. Rev.
Codes, Tit. 64, § 211 (1962); Neb. Rev. Stats. C. 20 §§ 101 and
102 (1954); N. H. Rev. Stats. Ann. C. 354 §§ 1, 2, 4 and 5 (1963);
N. J. Stats. Ann., Tit. 10, §§ 1–2 to 1–7; Tit. 18, §§ 25–1 to 25.6
(1963); N. M. Stats. Ann. §§ 49–8–1 to 49–8–6 (1963); N. Y. Civil
Rights Law (McKinney's ed.) Art. 4, §§ 40, 41 (1946); Exec. Law
Art. 15, § 2901 (1964); Penal Law Art. 46, §§ 513–515 (1944);
N. Dak. Cent. Code § 12–22–30 (1963); Ohio Rev. Code (Page's
ed.) §§ 2901–35 and 2901–36 (1954); Oreg. Rev. Stats. §§ 30–670,
30–675, 30–680; (1963); Penn. Stats. Ann., Tit. 18, § 4654
(1963); R. I. Gen. Laws §§ 11–24–1 to 11–24–6 (1956); S. Dak.
Sess. Laws C. 58 (1963); Vt. Stats. Ann., Tit. 13, §§ 1451, 1452

(1958); Wash. Rev. Code Ann. §§ 49.60.010 to 49.60–170, 9.91.010 (1962); Wis. Stats. Ann. § 942–04 (1958); Wyo. Stats. Ann. § 6–83.1, 6–83.2 (1963).

In 1963 the Governor of Kentucky issued an executive order requiring all governmental agencies involved in the supervision or licensing of businesses to take all lawful action necessary to prevent racial discrimination.[123]

On the afternoon of the decision, President Johnson issued the following statement:

The Civil Rights Act of 1964 was proposed by two Presidents. It was overwhelmingly approved by Congress and now the constitutionality of the public accommodations section has been upheld by unanimous vote of the Supreme Court. The nation has spoken with a single voice on the question of equal rights and equal opportunity.

I have been heartened by the spirit with which the people of the South have accepted this act even though many of them were opposed to its passage. There already has been encouraging and widespread compliance with the act during the five months it has been law. Now that the Supreme Court has also ruled, I think we all join in the hope and the resolution that this kind of reasonable and responsible acceptance of law will continue and increase.[124]

On the same day the Supreme Court reversed two trespass convictions—one arising in South Carolina and the other in Arkansas—of persons who had "sat in" at, respectively, a lunch counter and a tea-room, where they had been denied service because they were Negroes. Both the lunch counter and the tearoom were located in large department stores, in other portions of which Negro patronage was welcomed. It was reasonably clear that the lunch counter and the tea-room were both "places of public accommodation," within the meaning of the 1964 Civil Rights Act. Moreover, in both instances, petitioners' demonstrations had been entirely peaceful. Accordingly, petitioners' behavior—remaining on the premises after having been denied service and having been requested to leave—was precisely the kind of behavior the 1964 Civil Rights Act sought to insulate from state prosecutions. The only difficulty presented by the two cases was that in each instance the "sit-ins" had taken place long before the enactment of the 1964 Act. And so the question confronting the Supreme Court was whether the 1964 Act required the discontinuance of prosecutions which had arisen prior to the Act for peaceful attempts to secure nondiscriminatory service which plainly would have been protected had they taken place after the Act went into effect.

As Anthony Lewis said of the *Hamm* and *Lupper* cases:[125]

> *What the Court did was apply to the sit-in cases an old common-law doctrine called abatement. The doctrine is that pending criminal prosecutions abate, or die, when the law that was allegedly violated is repealed or superseded.*
>
> *Justice Tom C. Clark, for the majority of five, held that the Civil Rights Act of 1964 required abatement of all pending state prosecutions of peaceful sit-in demonstrators for seeking service at places that now are covered by the act.*
>
> *There was no discussion of the act's effect on pending prosecutions during the long Congressional debate. But Justice Clark said the normal rule was to presume an intention to abate, and he saw no problem in extending this Federal rule, as he found it, to a Federal requirement that state cases be dismissed.*
>
> *The dissenters, on the other hand, found the skip from Federal to state most difficult. Justices Hugo L. Black and John Marshall Harlan said they had "grave" constitutional doubts. They and Justices White and Potter Stewart thought abatement should not be presumed, in any event, on the record of this statute.*
>
> *The opinions reflect the differing philosophical attitudes toward civil disobedience as well as the differences over the proper rule of abatement.*
>
> *Justice Clark emphasized that "the peaceful conduct for which petitioners were prosecuted was on behalf of a principle since embodied in the law of the land." Justice Black more than once spoke of the protesters' "lawless conduct" and wish "to take the law into their own hands."*
>
> *Critics were quick to attack the majority, and its opinion was certainly vulnerable on grounds of novelty. But from a practical point of view, the decision was doubtless a healthy one. More than 3,000 sit-in prosecutions are pending, and most will be*

wiped out as a result. This will remove a final irritant from a situation that Congress was trying to calm in the 1964 act. And it will relieve the great pressure on the Supreme Court from this large number of often morally compelling cases.[126]

The Court's abatement formula had what at least some of the Justices must have regarded as a further beneficial by-product. This method of disposing of the two cases before the Court—and, it was hoped, the vast bulk of the 3,000-odd cases pending in lower courts—meant that the Court was able again to avoid flatly confronting very difficult Fourteenth Amendment questions: namely, whether state trespass prosecutions of those "sitting-in" to secure nondiscriminatory service in public places contravene the equal protection clause. As of December of 1964, Justices Black, Harlan, and White had announced that such prosecutions were compatible with equal protection, while Chief Justice Warren and Justices Douglas and Goldberg had announced a contrary view. But no majority of the Justices was on record in either direction. The uncommitted Justices were able, through the abatement formula, to postpone—very likely, for some time to come—the hardening of doctrinal lines with respect to these extremely difficult constitutional issues. And such postponement, however irksome to those who cherish the idea that the Court's job is to resolve all major constitutional abstractions within reach, was probably a salutary thing. The Court's job is to decide cases, not ideas. Generally speaking, it is proper for the Court to eschew handing out the gold star of constitutionality to one idea or the red star of unconstitutionality to another, except in the course of deciding that case whose resolution inescapably calls for the formal ranking of competitive ideas.

After the decision of *Hamm* and *Lupper*, Jack Greenberg (who had, as General Counsel of the NAACP Legal Defense Fund, argued *Hamm*) observed: "The circle is finally closed. The young people whose 'sit ins' woke the nation's conscience and led to the enactment of the 1964 law have now been brought within the protection of the law they helped to make."[127]

On July 2, 1965, one year after enactment of the Civil Rights Act of 1964, Title VII of the Act went into effect. That title established a federal Equal Opportunities Commission to police discrimination on grounds of race, religion, or sex in employment affecting interstate commerce. By late July of 1965, nearly two hundred complaints had been filed with the Commission; most were directed at employers, but some alleged discrimination by labor unions and by employment agencies.[128]

D. THE COURT STRENGTHENS
THE FRANCHISE

FOR THE PAST GENERATION, the Supreme Court's principal job has been the vindication of the constitutional rights, both substantive and procedural, of the dispossessed—the rights of friendless individuals like Clarence Gideon (for whose story see p. 142), and also the rights of members of unpopular religious, racial, and political groups. In performing this job, the Court acts as a countervailing force against the occasional tyrannies of majorities. And this is a necessary and proper judicial role, precisely because the Constitution contemplates that our pervasive democratic commitment to majority rule is matched by an equally vigorous commitment to the preservation of each person's fundamental liberties against all odds.

Of course, in reviewing the constitutitionality of legislative enactments, the Court must bear in mind the great lesson which Holmes frequently found such difficulty in impressing upon his colleagues, "that legislatures are ultimate guardians of the liberties and welfare of the people in quite as great a degree as the courts."[1] As Justice Frankfurter put it, dissenting in the 1943 flag-salute case:

Jefferson's opposition to judicial review has not been accepted by history, but it still serves as an admonition against confusion between judicial and political functions. . . . For those who pass laws not only are under duty to pass laws. They are also under duty to observe the Constitution. And even though legislation relates to civil liberties, our duty of deference to those who have the responsibility for making the laws is no less relevant or less exacting. . . .[2]

But the judicial "duty of deference to those who have the responsibility for making the laws" is markedly less emphatic when there is reason to believe that the legislature, far from being the forum for achievement of widespread consensus which Madison envisaged, has degenerated into an instrument for the effectuation of particular parochial interests. For example, as the Court noted in a famous footnote in 1938 (*United States v. Carolene Products Co.*), when judges review

statutes directed at particular religious . . . or national . . . or racial minorities . . . prejudice against discrete and insular minorities may be a special condition, which tends seriously to curtail the operation of those political processes ordinarily to be relied upon to protect minorities, and which may call for a correspondingly more searching judicial inquiry.[3]

1. Enfranchising the Negro

Southern legislative discrimination against Negroes has surely been the most blatant example of corruption of the American legislative process. And the Supreme Court has candidly acknowledged that, because Negroes have been kept out of southern politics, judicial review of hostile southern legislation is, in most instances, the only even minimally effective method of political redress. Thus, in 1963, the Court decided, in *NAACP v. Button,* that certain Virginia statutes designed to restrict the NAACP's litigation efforts were unconstitutional. And the chief reason they were unconstitutional was that, in violation of the First and Fourteenth Amendments, they interfered with a form of *political* activity:

. . . In the context of NAACP objectives, litigation is not a technique of resolving private differences; it is a means for achieving the lawful objectives of equality of treatment by all government, federal, state, and local, for the members of the Negro community in this country. It is thus a form of political expression. Groups which find themselves unable to achieve their objectives through the ballot frequently turn to the courts. Just as it was true of the opponents of New Deal legislation during the 1930's, for example, no less is it true of the Negro minority today. And

under the conditions of modern government, litigation may well be the sole practicable avenue open to a minority to petition for redress of grievances.

.   .   .   .   .

The NAACP is not a conventional political party; but the litigation it assists, while serving to vindicate the legal rights of members of the American Negro community, at the same time and perhaps more importantly makes possible the distinctive contribution of a minority group to the ideas and beliefs of our society. For such a group, association for litigation may be the most effective form of political association.[4]

But the political victories won in court are purely defensive in character. Judges cannot clear slums or build public hospitals and public schools or alter the tax structure. Democratic theory and democratic practice alike dictate that, in the long term, the political interests of southern Negroes can be safeguarded only in proportion as southern Negroes become effective participants in the conventional political processes. Therefore, a significant chapter of judicial activity, beginning in the late 1920s and extending into the 1950s, was devoted to widening Negro participation in the southern franchise.

The doctrinal story is spelled out in a series of cases which established the right of Negroes to participate in the only election which is meaningful in the Deep South—the democratic "white primary."[5] Building on these decisions, Congress, in the Civil Rights Act of 1957—the first federal civil rights law since 1875—conferred on the Department of Justice and on the newly created Civil Rights Commission authority to inquire into and attempt to remedy denials of voting rights. This federal role was strengthened in the Civil Rights Acts of 1960 and 1964, both of which laws gave the Department of Justice added powers to seek federal court orders enjoining local voting officials from continuing to pursue the various discriminatory devices (such as fraudulently administered literacy tests) by which Negroes have been traditionally barred from registration. And in 1963 the Twenty-fourth Amendment to the Constitution put a permanent end to the use of the poll tax as a disenfranchisement device in federal elections.

It is one thing to get courts to declare the legal right to be a registered voter and to enjoin interference with that right. It is quite another to get hundreds of thousands of the disenfranchised to queue up at registration places and seek to exercise that right. This latter task—the proof of the legal pudding—calls for massive private initiatives. From 1958 on, a number of civil rights groups (whose efforts were ultimately coordinated under the Voter Education Project of the Southern Regional Council) have made a major assault upon the problem.

A generation ago, when the Supreme Court first became seized of the problem, Negro disenfranchisement was the rule in twelve southern states: Alabama, Arkansas, Florida, Georgia, Louisiana, Mississippi, North Carolina, Oklahoma, South Carolina, Tennessee, Texas, and Virginia. As of 1932, Negroes in these twelve states "were so effectively disfranchised, regardless of the 14th and 15th amendments to the Constitution, that considerably fewer than a hundred thousand were able to vote in general election[s], and virtually none was permitted to vote in the primary election[s]."[6] In fifteen years, by 1947, the number of registered Negroes had jumped to 645,000 (out of a voting-age Negro population of some five million).[7] By 1961, with the total Negro population in the twelve states remaining approximately constant, the number of registered Negroes had risen to 1,361,944.[8] Between 1962 and 1964, intensive voter registration drives conducted in all the listed states except Oklahoma (which no longer presents any major problem of discriminatory disenfranchisement) had made further substantial changes in the regional picture. By the spring of 1964, almost two million of the five million Negroes of voting age in those eleven states were registered.[9] By way of contrast, some twelve and a half million out of twenty million whites of voting age were registered.[10]

Although, as of 1964, almost 40 per cent of the voting-age Negroes in the eleven states were registered, the percentage was by no means a constant average throughout the region. In large areas of Mississippi, and in substantial segments of rural Alabama, Louisiana and Georgia, there continued to be only handfuls of registered Negroes. On the other hand, in a few places the percentage of Negro voters was large enough to constitute a potentially formidable base of political strength. Thus, in 1962, Atlanta elected a Negro state senator—the first Negro member of the Georgia legislature in over fifty years; since then, other Negroes have been elected to the Georgia legislature. But in other parts of the Deep South, emerging Negro voting strength was not treated so tolerantly.

In 1957, the small town of Tuskegee, Alabama—home of the famed university which bears the town's name—had 5,400 Negroes, 400 of whom were registered, and 1,300 whites, 600 of whom were registered. The Alabama legislature responded to this situation by redrawing the town boundaries of Tuskegee in such a way as to remove as many Tuskegee Negroes as possible from the town and transfer them to the larger voting pool of surrounding Macon County, where, although the population was five-to-one Negro, the registered voters were three-to-one white.[11] The Alabama statute was immediately challenged in an Alabama federal court. The federal judge noted that, pursuant to the legislative redesign of the theretofore rectangular town:

Tuskegee resembles a "sea dragon." The effect of the Act is to remove from the municipality of Tuskegee all but four or five of the qualified Negro voters and none of the qualified white voters. Plaintiffs state that said Act is but another device in a continuing attempt to disenfranchise Negro citizens not only of their right to vote in municipal elections and participate in municipal affairs, but also of their right of free speech and press, on account of their race and color.[12]

But the district court found itself powerless to interfere with Alabama's sovereign authority to redraw municipal boundaries. And the court of appeals, with one judge dissenting, affirmed.

The Supreme Court reversed unanimously. The prevailing opinion in *Gomillion v. Lightfoot* was written by the late Justice Frankfurter. There were brief concurrences by Justice Douglas and former Justice Charles E. Whittaker. The opinions follow:

. . . The complaint, charging that Act 140 is a device to disenfranchise Negro citizens, alleges the following facts: Prior to Act 140 the City of Tuskegee was square in shape; the Act transformed it into a strangely irregular twenty-eight-sided figure as indicated in the diagram appended to this opinion. The essential inevitable effect of this redefinition of Tuskegee's boundaries is to remove from the city all save only four or five of its 400 Negro voters while not removing a single white voter or resident. The

*result of the Act is to deprive the Negro petitioners discrimina-
torily of the benefits of residence in Tuskegee, including,* inter
alia, *the right to vote in municipal elections.*

*These allegations, if proven, would abundantly establish
that Act 140 was not an ordinary geographic redistricting measure
even within familiar abuses of gerrymandering. If these allegations upon a trial remained uncontradicted or unqualified, the
conclusion would be irresistible, tantamount for all practical
purposes to a mathematical demonstration, that the legislation is
solely concerned with segregating white and colored voters by
fencing Negro citizens out of town so as to deprive them of their
pre-existing municipal vote.*

*It is difficult to appreciate what stands in the way of ad-
judging a statute having this inevitable effect invalid in light of
the principles by which this Court must judge, and uniformly
has judged, statutes that, howsoever speciously defined, obviously
discriminate against colored citizens. "The [Fifteenth] Amendment nullifies sophisticated as well as simple-minded modes of
discrimination."* Lane v. Wilson, 307 *U.S. 268, 275.*

*The complaint amply alleges a claim of racial discrimination.
Against this claim the respondents have never suggested, either
in their brief or in oral argument, any countervailing municipal
function which Act 140 is designed to serve. The respondents
invoke generalities expressing the State's unrestricted power—unlimited, that is, by the United States Constitution—to establish,
destroy, or reorganize by contraction or expansion its political
subdivisions, to wit, cities, counties, and other local units. We
freely recognize the breadth and importance of this aspect of
the State's political power. To exalt this power into an absolute
is to misconceive the reach and rule of this Court's decisions. . . .*

. . . *[T]he Court has never acknowledged that the States
have power to do as they will with municipal corporations regardless of consequences. Legislative control of municipalities, no
less than other state power, lies within the scope of relevant
limitations imposed by the United States Constitution. . . .*

*The respondents find another barrier to the trial of this case
in* Colegrove v. Green, 328 *U.S. 549. In that case the Court passed*

on an *Illinois law governing the arrangement of congressional districts within that State. The complaint rested upon the disparity of population between the different districts which rendered the effectiveness of each individual's vote in some districts far less than in others. This disparity came to pass solely through shifts in population between 1901, when Illinois organized its congressional districts, and 1946, when the complaint was lodged. During this entire period elections were held under the districting scheme devised in 1901. The Court affirmed the dismissal of the complaint on the ground that it presented a subject not meet for adjudication. The decisive facts in this case, which at this stage must be taken as proved, are wholly different from the considerations found controlling in* Colegrove.

That case involved a complaint of discriminatory apportionment of congressional districts. The appellants in Colegrove *complained only of a dilution of the strength of their votes as a result of legislative inaction over a course of many years. The petitioners here complain that affirmative legislative action deprives them of their votes and the consequent advantages that the ballot affords. When a legislature thus singles out a readily isolated segment of a racial minority for special discriminatory treatment, it violates the Fifteenth Amendment. In no case involving unequal weight in voting distribution that has come before the Court did the decision sanction a differentiation on racial lines whereby approval was given to unequivocal withdrawal of the vote solely from colored citizens. Apart from all else, these considerations lift this controversy out of the so-called "political" arena and into the conventional sphere of constitutional litigation.*

In sum, as Mr. Justice Holmes remarked, when dealing with a related situation, in Nixon v. Herndon, *273 U.S. 536, 540, "Of course the petition concerns political action," but "The objection that the subject matter of the suit is political is little more than a play upon words." A statute which is alleged to have worked unconstitutional deprivations of petitioners' rights is not immune to attack simply because the mechanism employed by the legislature is a redefinition of municipal boundaries. According to the allegations here made, the Alabama Legislature has not merely redrawn the Tuskegee city limits with incidental inconvenience to the petitioners; it is more accurate to say that it has deprived the petitioners of the municipal franchise and consequent rights and to that end it has incidentally changed the city's boundaries. While in form this is merely an act redefining metes and bounds, if the allegations are established, the inescapable human effect of this essay in geometry and geography is to despoil colored citizens, and only colored citizens, of their theretofore enjoyed voting rights. That was not* Colegrove v. Green.

When a State exercises power wholly within the domain of state interest, it is insulated from federal judicial review. But such insulation is not carried over when state power is used as an instrument for circumventing a federally protected right. This principle has had many applications. It has long been recognized in cases which have prohibited a State from exploiting a power acknowledged to be absolute in an isolated context to justify the imposition of an "unconstitutional condition." What the Court has said in those cases is equally applicable here, viz., that "Acts generally lawful may become unlawful when done to accomplish an unlawful end, United States v. Reading Co., 226 U.S. 324, 357, *and a constitutional power cannot be used by way of condition to attain an unconstitutional result."* Western Union Telegraph Co. v. Foster, 247 U.S. 105, 114. *The petitioners are entitled to prove their allegations at trial.*

For these reasons, the principal conclusions of the District Court and the Court of Appeals are clearly erroneous and the decision below must be

Reversed.

MR. JUSTICE DOUGLAS, *while joining the opinion of the Court, adheres to the dissents in* Colegrove v. Green, 328 U.S. 549, *and* South v. Peters, 339 U.S. 276.

MR. JUSTICE WHITTAKER, *concurring.*

I concur in the Court's judgment, but not in the whole of its opinion. It seems to me that the decision should be rested not on the Fifteenth Amendment, but rather on the Equal Protection Clause of the Fourteenth Amendment to the Constitution. I am doubtful that the averments of the complaint, taken for present purposes to be true, show a purpose by Act No. 140 to abridge petitioners' "right . . . to vote," in the Fifteenth Amendment sense. It seems to me that the "right . . . to vote" that is guaranteed by the Fifteenth Amendment is but the same right to vote as is enjoyed by all others within the same election precinct, ward or other political division. And, inasmuch as no one has the right to vote in a political division, or in a local election concerning only an area in which he does not reside, it would seem to follow that one's right to vote in Division A is not abridged by a redistricting that places his residence in Division B if he there enjoys the same voting privileges as all others in that Division, even though the redistricting was done by the State for the purpose of placing a racial group of citizens in Division B rather than A.

But it does seem clear to me that accomplishment of a State's purpose—to use the Court's phrase—of "fencing Negro citizens out of" Division A and into Division B is an unlawful segregation of races of citizens, in violation of the Equal Protection Clause of the Fourteenth Amendment, Brown v. Board of Education, 347 U.S. 483; Cooper v. Aaron, 358 U.S. 1; *and, as stated, I would think the decision should be rested on that ground —which, incidentally, clearly would not involve, just as the cited cases do not involve, the* Colegrove *problem.*[13]

And so Alabama failed in its heavy-footed effort to make a sow's ear out of a silk purse, all for discrimination's sake. (For the full story of the lawsuit and what underlay it, see the excellent study by Bernard Taper.[14]) But, just as Alabama could not destroy the town of Tuskegee, so too it could not for long forestall the enfranchisement of Negroes throughout Macon County.[15] In the spring of 1964 Claude Sitton, one of the ablest journalists reporting on the contemporary South, filed a story about Macon County:

One of the chief reasons given for maintaining white supremacy in the South has been the fear that in some areas Negroes would outvote whites.

That point has now been reached in Macon County, a political entity that contains, among other things, several hundred acres of worn-out cotton land, Tuskegee Institute and a large Veterans' Administration hospital. But so far Negroes have refrained from seizing political control.

They appear to be attempting to use their new power for the general welfare of the county's 26,000 citizens, and thus to dispel the fear that has haunted whites since Reconstruction.

Moreover, there are indications that, in the long run, a large

Negro vote may improve race relations by eliminating extremists from office and establishing communication between whites and Negroes.[16]

But not too far from Tuskegee the white southern conspiracy to keep Negroes from the polls continued unabated. The issue came to a head in the opening months of 1965 in the middle-sized town of Selma, the county seat of a rural Alabama county in which few Negroes had ever been permitted to vote. Martin Luther King, Jr., recent recipient of the Nobel Peace Prize, had chosen Selma as the place to launch a massive voter registration drive. Although some local officials sought to pursue a course of moderation, a policy of brutal official reprisal quickly gained the upper hand. And official brutality triggered private brutality, finally culminating in the senseless murder of a Boston minister, one of hundreds of clergymen who had gone to Selma to lend their assistance to Dr. King. The murder of the minister—like the Mississippi murder of three civil rights workers in the summer of 1964—awoke the nation's conscience to what was going on in Selma. And in late March of 1965 the nation watched as Dr. King led a protest march of thousands (protected by federal court order and federalized national guard troops) along fifty miles of rural highway from Selma to Montgomery—"the cradle of the Confederacy" and Governor Wallace's official seat of power.

On March 15, a week before Dr. King's march, President Johnson sent to Congress a message outlining the insufficiency of existing federal protections of voting rights, including those embodied in the 1964 Civil Rights Act. The President and his new Attorney General, Nicholas deB. Katzenbach, had concluded that enforcing voting rights by litigation alone was an endless task; and they therefore sought legislative authority for executive appointment, in areas of hard-core southern resistance, of federal registrars empowered to register would-be voters in state and national elections. A portion of the President's message follows:

TO THE CONGRESS OF THE UNITED STATES:

In this same month ninety-five years ago—on March 30, 1870—the Constitution of the United States was amended for the fifteenth time to guarantee that no citizen of our land should be denied the right to vote because of race or color.

The command of the Fifteenth Amendment is unequivocal

and its equal force upon State Governments and the Federal Government is unarguable.

Section 1 of this Amendment provides:

> *The right of citizens of the United States to vote shall not be denied or abridged by the United States or by any State on account of race, color, or previous condition of servitude.*

By the oath I have taken "to preserve, protect and defend the Constitution of the United States," duty directs—and strong personal conviction impels—that I advise the Congress that action is necessary, and necessary now, if the Constitution is to be upheld and the rights of all citizens are not to be mocked, abused and denied.

I must regretfully report to the Congress the following facts:
1. That the Fifteenth Amendment of our Constitution is today being systematically and willfully circumvented in certain State and local jurisdictions of our Nation.
2. That representatives of such State and local governments acting "under the color of law," are denying American citizens the right to vote on the sole basis of race or color.
3. That, as a result of these practices in some areas of our country today no significant number of American citizens of the Negro race can be registered to vote except upon the intervention and order of a Federal Court.
4. That the remedies available under law to citizens thus denied their Constitutional rights—and the authority presently available to the Federal Government to act in their behalf—are clearly inadequate.
5. That the denial of these rights and the frustration of efforts to obtain meaningful relief from such denial without undue delay is contributing to the creation of conditions which are both inimical to our domestic order and tranquillity and incompatible with the standards of equal justice and individual dignity on which our society stands.

I am, therefore, calling upon the Congress to discharge the duty authorized in Section 2 of the Fifteenth Amendment "to enforce this Article by appropriate legislation."

It could never be a welcome duty for any President to place before Congress such a report of the willful failure and refusal of public officials to honor, respect and abide by any provision of the Constitution of the United States. It is especially repugnant to report such disregard directed against the Fifteenth Amendment by officials at the State and local levels.

The essence of our American tradition of State and local governments is the belief expressed by Thomas Jefferson that Government is best which is closest to the people. Yet that belief is betrayed by those State and local officials who engage in denying the right of citizens to vote. Their actions serve only to assure that their State governments and local governments shall be remote from the people, least representative of the people's will and least responsive to the people's wishes. . . .

The problem of discriminatory denial of the right to vote has been with us ever since colonial times.

The test of real property ownership was universal among the colonies and religious qualifications were numerous. Race, color, sex, age, employment and residence were all used as the basis for qualifying voters. Such restrictions continued to flourish among the States even after formation of the Union.

The first literacy tests were legislated in Northern States in an effort to exclude immigrants—especially Irish—from the franchise. When the Fifteenth Amendment was adopted, there were only six States which had never discriminated against voting by Negroes.

If discrimination has been a prevalent practice in our history of voting rights, the struggle against discrimination has been our consistent purpose generation after generation.

Since the adoption of the Bill of Rights, no other right has been strengthened and fortified so often by Constitutional Amendment as the right to vote. As early as 1804—and as recently as 1964—the Constitution of the United States has been amended on at least six occasions to prohibit discrimination against the right to vote, to enlarge the franchise, and to assure the expression of the people's will as registered by them at the polls.

The challenge facing us today is not a challenge of what the Constitution of the United States shall say—but of what it shall mean. . . .

For the life of this Republic, our people have zealously guarded their liberty against abuses of power by their governments. The one weapon they have used is the mightiest weapon in the arsenal of democracy—the vote. This has been enough, for *as Woodrow Wilson said, "The instrument of all reform in America is the ballot."*

Yet today, in areas of America, segments of our populace must live in just that involuntary condition—policed by forces they have no voice in choosing and forced to abide by laws they have no vote in adopting.

A people divided over the right to vote can never build a Nation united.

I am determined that these years shall be devoted to perfecting our unity so that we may pursue more successfully the fulfillment of our high purposes at home and in the world. While I have proposed to you other measures to serve the strengthening of our free society and the happiness of our free people, I regard action on the measures proposed in this Message to be first in priority. We cannot have government for all the people until we first make certain it is government of and by all the people.[17]

On the same day that he sent his message on voting rights, President Johnson addressed a joint session of Congress. This is what he said:

Mr. Speaker, Mr. President, Members of the Congress:

I speak tonight for the dignity of man and the destiny of democracy.

I urge every member of both parties, Americans of all religions and of all colors, from every section of this country, to join me in that cause.

At times history and fate meet at a single time in a single place to shape a turning point in man's unending search for freedom. So it was at Lexington and Concord. So it was a century ago at Appomattox. So it was last week in Selma, Alabama.

There, long-suffering men and women peacefully protested the denial of their rights as Americans. Many were brutally assaulted. One good man, a man of God, was killed.

There is no cause for pride in what has happened in Selma. There is no cause for self-satisfaction in the long denial of equal rights of millions of Americans.

But there is cause for hope and for faith in our democracy in what is happening here tonight.

For the cries of pain and the hymns and protests of op-

*pressed people, have summoned into convocation all the majesty
of this great government of the greatest nation on earth.*

Our mission is at once the oldest and the most basic of this
country: to right wrong, to do justice, to serve man.

In our time we have come to live with the moments of great
crisis. Our lives have been marked with debate about great
issues, issues of war and peace, issues of prosperity and depression. But rarely in any time does an issue lay bare the secret
heart of America itself. Rarely are we met with a challenge, not
to our growth or abundance, or our welfare or our security, but
rather to the values and the purposes and the meaning of our
beloved nation.

The issue of equal rights for American Negroes is such an
issue. And should we defeat every enemy, and should we
double our wealth and conquer the stars and still be unequal to
this issue, then we will have failed as a people and as a nation. . . .

Many of the issues of civil rights are very complex and most
difficult. But about this there can and should be no argument.
Every American citizen must have an equal right to vote. There
is no reason which can excuse the denial of that right. There is
no duty which weighs more heavily on us than the duty we have
to ensure that right.

Yet the harsh fact is that in many places in this country men
and women are kept from voting simply because they are
Negroes.

Every device of which human ingenuity is capable has been
used to deny this right. The Negro citizen may go to register
only to be told that the day is wrong, or the hour is late, or the
official in charge is absent. And if he persists and if he manages
to present himself to the registrar, he may be disqualified because
he did not spell out his middle name or because he abbreviated
a word on the application. And if he manages to fill out an
application he is given a test. The registrar is the sole judge of
whether he passes this test. He may be asked to recite the entire
constitution, or explain the most complex provisions of state laws.
And even a college degree cannot be used to prove that he can
read and write.

For the fact is that the only way to pass these barriers is to
show a white skin.

Experience has clearly shown that the existing process of law cannot overcome systematic and ingenious discrimination. No law that we now have on the books—and I have helped to put three of them there—can ensure the right to vote when local officials are determined to deny it. . . .

This time, on this issue, there must be no delay, or no hesitation or no compromise with our purpose.

We cannot, we must not refuse to protect the right of every American to vote in every election that he may desire to participate in. And we ought not, we must not wait another eight months before we get a bill. We have already waited a hundred years and more and the time for waiting is gone. . . .

But even if we pass this bill, the battle will not be over. What happened in Selma is part of a far larger movement which reaches into every section and state of America. It is the effort of American Negroes to secure for themselves the full blessings of American life.

Their cause must be our cause too. Because it is not just Negroes, but really it is all of us, who must overcome the crippling legacy of bigotry and injustice. And we shall overcome.

As a man whose roots go deeply into Southern soil I know how agonizing racial feelings are. I know how difficult it is to reshape the attitudes and the structure of our society.

But a century has passed, more than a hundred years, since the Negro was freed. And he is not fully free tonight.

It was more than a hundred years ago that Abraham Lincoln, the great President of the Northern party, signed the Emancipation Proclamation, but emancipation is a proclamation and not a fact.

A century has passed, more than a hundred years since equality was promised. And yet the Negro is not equal.

A century has passed since the day of promise. And the promise is unkept.

The time of justice has now come. I tell you that I believe sincerely that no force can hold it back. It is right in the eyes of man and God that it should come. And when it does, I think that day will brighten the lives of every American.

For Negroes are not the only victims. How many white children have gone uneducated, how many white families have lived in stark poverty, how many white lives have been scarred

*by fear because we wasted our energy and our substance to main-
tain the barriers of hatred and terror.*

*So I say to all of you here and to all in the nation tonight,
that those who appeal to you to hold on to the past do so at the
cost of denying you your future.*

*This great, rich, restless country can offer opportunity and
education and hope to all—all black and white, all North and
South, sharecropper, and city dweller. These are the enemies—
poverty, ignorance, disease. They are enemies, not our fellow
man, not our neighbor, and these enemies, too, poverty, disease
and ignorance, we shall overcome.*

*Now let none of us in any section look with prideful right-
eousness on the troubles in another section or the problems of
our neighbors. There is really no part of America where the
promise of equality has been fully kept. In Buffalo as well as
in Birmingham, in Philadelphia as well as in Selma, Americans
are struggling for the fruits of freedom. . . .*

*The real hero of this struggle is the American Negro. His
actions and protests, his courage to risk safety and even to risk
his life, have awakened the conscience of this nation. His demonstrations have been designed to call attention to injustice, designed to provoke change, designed to stir reform. He has called
upon us to make good the promise of America. And who among
us can say that we would have made the same progress were it
not for his persistent bravery, and his faith in American democracy.*

*For at the real heart of the battle for equality is a deep seated
belief in the democratic process. Equality depends not on the
force of arms or tear gas but depends upon the force of moral
right—not on recourse to violence but on respect for law and
order. . . .*

*We must preserve the right of free speech and the right of
free assembly. But the right of free speech does not carry with
it as has been said, the right to holler fire in a crowded theater.
We must preserve the right to free assembly but free assembly
does not carry with it the right to block public thoroughfares to
traffic.*

*We do have a right to protest, and a right to march under
conditions that do not infringe the Constitutional rights of our*

neighbors. I intend to protect all those rights as long as I am permitted to serve in this Office.

We will guard against violence, knowing it strikes from our hands the very weapons with which we seek progress—obedience to law, and belief in American values.

In Selma as elsewhere we seek and pray for peace. We seek order. We seek unity. But we will not accept the peace of stifled rights, or the order imposed by fear, or the unity that stifles protest. For peace cannot be purchased at the cost of liberty. . . .

The bill that I am presenting to you will be known as a civil rights bill. But, in a larger sense, most of the program I am recommending is a civil rights program. Its object is to open the city of hope to all people of all races, because all Americans just must have the right to vote. And we are going to give them that right.

All Americans must have the privileges of citizenship regardless of race. And they are going to have those privileges of citizenship regardless of race.

But I would like to caution you and remind you that to exercise these privileges takes much more than just legal right. It requires a trained mind and a healthy body. It requires a decent home, and the chance to find a job, and the opportunity to escape from the clutches of poverty.

Of course people cannot contribute to the nation if they are never taught to read or write, if their bodies are stunted from hunger, if their sickness goes untended, if their life is spent in hopeless poverty just drawing a welfare check.

So we want to open the gates to opportunity. But we are also going to give all our people, black and white, the help that they need to walk through those gates.

My first job after college was as a teacher in Cotulla, Texas, in a small Mexican-American school. Few of them could speak English and I couldn't speak much Spanish. My students were poor and they often came to class without breakfast, hungry, and they knew even in their youth that pain of prejudice. They never seemed to know why people disliked them. But they knew it was so. Because I saw it in their eyes. I often walked home late in the afternoon after the classes were finished, wishing there was more that I could do. But all I knew was to teach them the little that I knew, hoping that it might help them against the hardships that lay ahead.

Somehow you never forget what poverty and hatred can do when you see its scars on the hopeful face of a young child.

I never thought then in 1928 that I would be standing here in 1965. It never even occurred to me in my fondest dreams that I might have the chance to help the sons and daughters of those students and to help people like them all over this country. But now I do have the chance and I let you in on a secret, I mean to use it. And I hope that you will use it with me.

This is the richest and most powerful country which ever occupied this globe. The might of past empires is little compared to ours.

But I do not want to be the President who built empires, or sought grandeur, or extended dominion. I want to be the President who educated young children to the wonders of their world. I want to be the President who helped to feed the hungry and to prepare them to be taxpayers instead of taxeaters. I want to be the President who helped the poor to find their own way and who protected the right of every citizen to vote in every election. I want to be the President who helped to end hatred among his fellow men and who prompted love among the people of all races and all regions and all parties. I want to be the President who helped to end war among the brothers of this earth. . . .

Beyond this great chamber, out yonder, in the fifty states are the people we serve. Who can tell what deep and unspoken hopes are in their hearts tonight as they sit there and listen. We all can guess, from our own lives, how difficult they often find their own pursuit of happiness. How many problems each little family has. They look most of all to themselves for their futures. But I think that they also look to each of us.

Above the pyramid on the great seal of the United States it says—in Latin—"God has favored our undertaking."

God will not favor everything that we do. It is rather our duty to divine His will. But I cannot help believing that He truly understands and that He really favors the undertaking that we begin here tonight.[18]

Just under five months later, on August 6, 1965, President Johnson signed the Voting Rights Act of 1965. The law authorized the appointment of federal officials empowered to register voters in states and counties in which fewer than half of the eligible electorate were actually registered: Mississippi, Alabama, Georgia, Louisiana, South Carolina, and parts of Virginia and North Carolina; and also, anachronistically, Alaska, and isolated counties in Maine, Idaho, and Arizona. The law also (1) directed the Attorney General to seek a judicial declaration that state poll taxes are racially discriminatory and hence unconstitutional, and (2) enfranchised scores of thousands of New Yorkers (of Puerto Rican origin) who are literate in Spanish but not English.

2. The Court seeks to restructure American legislatures

In *Gomillion v. Lightfoot*,[19] the Court was unanimous in setting aside a state statute which, through the simple device of redrawing local political boundaries, sought to deny Negro voters the opportunity to exercise their franchise effectively with respect to local issues touching their everyday lives. On the face of the opinions, the only division within the Court was with respect to the decision's constitutional rationale: eight of the Justices, led by Justice Frankfurter, thought that the Alabama statute offended the Fifteenth Amendment. Justice Whittaker thought that the problem was more properly cognizable under the equal protection clause of the Fourteenth Amendment.

Lurking just below the surface of *Gomillion v. Lightfoot* there was, however, an explosive constitutional issue of far greater moment than that which separated Justice Whittaker from his colleagues. The existence of the issue was pinpointed by Justice Douglas' laconic notation of concurrence, that "while joining the opinion of the Court," he "adhere[d] to the dissents in *Colegrove v. Green*, 328 U.S. 549, and *South v. Peters*, 339 U.S. 276."[20] What Justice Douglas was saying, in judicial shorthand, amounted to this: Justice Douglas of course agreed that federal courts had power to strike down the sort of patently racist disenfranchisement exemplified by *Gomillion v. Lightfoot*. But in Justice Douglas' view (to which Justice Black had subscribed, in the two cases cited by Justice Douglas), federal courts also had power to address themselves to a far more pervasive form of disenfranchisement—the malady of malapportionment, which was undermining the vitality and integrity of virtually every legislature in the nation.

In recent years an ever-increasing number of observers of, and participants in, the American governmental process have voiced the view that our legislative arrangements are in a state of fundamental disarray. Perhaps the most sharply worded contemporary indictment was framed by Joseph Clark, Democratic Senator from Pennsylvania, in a book published in 1964:

It is the third branch of government, the legislative, where things have gone awry. Whether we look at city councils, the state legislatures or the Congress of the United States, we react to what we see with scarcely concealed contempt. This is the area where democratic government is breaking down. This is where the vested-interest lobbies tend to run riot, where conflict of interest is concealed from the public, where demagoguery, sophisticated or primitive, knows few bounds, where political lag keeps needed action often a generation behind the times, where the nineteenth century sometimes reigns supreme in committees, where ignorance can be at a premium and wisdom at a discount, where the evil influence of arrogant and corrupt political machines, at the local and state level, ignores most successfully the general welfare, where the lust for patronage and favors for the faithful do the greatest damage to the public interest.

As a former chief executive of a large American city, as a member of the United States Senate, as a public servant who, in both capacities, has been obliged to know a good deal about the workings of state government, I have no hesitation in stating my deep conviction that the legislatures of America, local, state and national, are presently the greatest menace in our country to the successful operation of the democratic process.[21]

Obviously, the symptoms described by Senator Clark are traceable to a host of maladies. But one malady which ranks high up on the agenda of almost every concerned observer is that of malapportionment—a condition which mocks the concept of majority rule and, by the same token, distorts the intended functioning of a two-party system.

Concretely, what has happened in almost every state is that

more and more people have been crowded into metropolitan centers, without any meaningful correlative redistribution of legislative representation in state legislatures or in the House of Representatives. This has meant that the rural voter frequently has ten, or even a hundred, times the voting strength of his urban or suburban fellow-citizen. Legislatures apportioned in such a way hardly seem harmonious with the American precept that "all men are created equal"—a precept given content in the area of voting rights by the Fourteenth, Fifteenth, Nineteenth, and Twenty-fourth Amendments.

Furthermore, it is plain that such situations are unlikely to be corrected by appeals to legislatures to reapportion themselves. ". . .[T]he very heart of the problem is that the incumbent elective officials who have the power to make or block remedial laws are themselves not 'the people's representatives.' They are the faithful servants of muscular minorities whose continued control over state—and (though to a lesser extent) national—policy depends upon and will insure eternal vigilance against encircling majorities and eternal frustration of their attempted reforms."[22]

Confronted with this failure of the democratic political process—a failure which goes to its very structural integrity—those who sought remedies to malapportionment concluded, in the years following World War II, that the only potentially effective avenues of redress would be appeals to the federal courts for judicial directives requiring equitable reapportionment. For it seemed not unreasonable to argue that a malapportionment which made one man's vote ten times more valuable than his fellow-citizen's was a denial of equal protection of a peculiarly virulent kind. Nevertheless, the Supreme Court, under the leadership of Justice Frankfurter, declined to let federal courts entertain cases seeking judicial redress of malapportionment. A challenge to legislative apportionment, so the Court held, presented a "political," and hence not a justiciable, question.[23] Justices Black, Douglas, and Murphy (and, to a degree, Justice Rutledge) dissented from the Court's view that the federal judiciary was powerless to intervene. And thus it was that in 1960, when *Gomillion v. Lightfoot* was decided, Justice Douglas felt it appropriate to note his continued adherence to the proposition that federal courts could cope not only with racist disenfranchisment but also with some aspects of what Justice Frankfurter, in *Gomillion*, characterized as "familiar abuses of gerrymandering."[24]

In 1960, when *Gomillion* was decided, a new malapportionment case was moving toward the Supreme Court. And when it reached the Court—a Court whose composition had changed markedly in the previous several years—a new judicial response was forthcoming. The case was *Baker v. Carr*.[25] The nature of the case, and some speculation as to what it portended, were succinctly set forth in the fall of 1962, a few months after the decision, by Professor Robert G. McCloskey, a political scientist who is a perceptive student of the Court:

> *The case involved an action under the Civil Rights Acts brought by certain Tennessee voters on their own behalf and on behalf of others similarly situated and alleging that the present apportionment of the state legislature deprived them of their federal constitutional rights to equal protection of the laws. A district court was asked for a declaratory judgment invalidating the 1901 state legislation on which the apportionment was based, for an injunction restraining the defendant election officials from holding an election under the existing system, and for a decree reapportioning the legislature, or in the alternative, for an order that the next election be held at large. The argument as ultimately presented by the complainants and by the United States, appearing as amicus curiae, was in essence that, although the Tennessee constitution provided for decennial apportionment of representatives and senators among counties and districts according to their respective numbers, the legislature had failed to make such a reapportionment since 1901; that because of population changes in the past sixty years the votes of the appellants had been unconstitutionally debased, since the equal protection clause forbids arbitrary and unreasonable apportionment of legislative seats. The starting point, it was said, for measuring an apportionment against this prohibition is "per capita equality of representation," and departures from that standard must rest on a rational foundation. The action had been dismissed by the district court on the grounds that the court lacked jurisdiction of the subject matter and that the complaint failed to state a claim upon which relief could be granted. These stated grounds reflected the district court's understanding of the "federal rule, as enunciated*

. . . *by the Supreme Court . . . that the federal courts, whether from a lack of jurisdiction or from the inappropriateness of the subject matter for judicial consideration, will not intervene in cases of this type to compel legislative reapportionment.*"

The Supreme Court held that the dismissal was error. The federal courts do possess jurisdiction of the subject matter; the appellants have stated a justiciable cause of action upon which they "would be entitled to appropriate relief"; and they do have standing to challenge the statute. The issue presented is not, as the district court thought, a "political question" immune from judicial control. Colegrove v. Green *and other supposed precedents have been misread on that point. And the claim does not involve any of the characteristics that have caused the Court in the past to label a question "political" and deny jurisdiction. The cause was therefore remanded for trial and decision. It is perhaps worth emphasizing at this point that the Supreme Court offered the lower court no standards by which the decision should be reached and no hints about the remedy that might be appropriate if the plaintiffs prevailed. "Judicial standards under the Equal Protection clause," Justice Brennan said, "are well developed and familiar" and it would be "improper now to consider what remedy would be most appropriate. . . ."*

History can be an intractable wench, going her own way without regard to the paths we have envisioned for her, and one who writes contemporaneously about a Supreme Court term is uneasily aware of her capriciousness. There is no assurance that posterity will see the term as the present sees it, will concur with us in singling out the events that are noteworthy. Some little-observed horseshoe nail may have dropped by the way in the spring of 1962, and the future, with its advantage of hindsight, may decide that this was the really consequential incident of the season.

But with these concessions to an uncertain world duly registered, it must still be guessed that 1962 will appear to historians of the Supreme Court as the Year of the Reapportionment Case. *By almost any criterion for assaying such matters this seems a fair conjecture. For one thing, no development since the* Segregation Cases *has so focused the public eye on the doings of the Court. The publicity and popular interest evoked by a court decision may be among the less dependable of indices for eval-*

uating its importance, but they cannot be left altogether out of the account. Those who will wear the boot are not perhaps the only judges of whether it will pinch when it is broken in, but their judgment commands our attention. Especially does this seem so when we reflect that a court decision can become, in a sense, what the public thinks it is. The public version of the Chief Justice's opinion in Dred Scott *was a very different thing from the opinion that he wrote, but it was the public version that helped to kindle the Civil War.*

For another thing, it is hard to recall a decision in modern history which has had such an immediate and significant effect on the practical course of events, or—again excepting the Segregation Cases—which seems to contain such a potential for influencing that course in the future. The short-term response has been nothing short of astonishing. It has been as if the decision catalyzed a new political synthesis that was already straining, so to speak, to come into being. Not only federal judges, but state judges as well, have taken the inch or so of encouragement offered by the Supreme Court and stretched it out to a mile. Legislatures all over the country have been bidden to redistrict or to face the prospect of having the judiciary do the job for them. Under this spur, and sometimes in anticipation of it, a number of them have set going their laborious machinery of conflict and compromise. The shape of the apportionment plans that will emerge from this strange confluence of judicial and legislative power remains to be seen, but there can be no doubt that the American political world is stirring.

The long-term results are, of course, even more speculative, but the immediate reaction just described may cast a few shadows ahead. As we know, court decisions have not always generated such a ready—almost over-ready—spirit of compliance. When a decision fails to strike a responsive chord in the public breast, the tendency is at best to abide by its minimum compulsions grudgingly interpreted. The tendency suggested by early reactions to the reapportionment decision seems very different from this, and it may warrant the conjecture that the Court here happened to hit upon what the students of public opinion might call a latent consensus. It is quite true, as Justice Frankfurter reminds us, that neither our past nor our present political institutions have treated numbers as the "basic" principle of representa-

tion. But institutions sometimes lag behind opinion, and it may be that most Americans have come to think of some version of the majority principle as at least the presumptive democratic standard. If so, the implied ratification of the standard in the Reapportionment Case *may have struck them, in Jefferson's terms, as "the common sense of the subject," commanding their assent as "an expression of the American mind." And the decision, even without further adumbration, may precipitate a train of events that will alter profoundly the nature of representation in American politics.*

But this is speculation, not premonition, much less confident prophecy. For the present, there is no way of being sure about these and other possibly enduring effects—which political party will gain and which lose; whether the increment of electoral strength will be greater for suburbia or for central cities; whether the vitality of state government will be augmented or diminished; whether the cause of racial equality will be significantly advanced. The nature and scale of such repercussions will depend on imponderables and unforeseeables—including the substantial question whether and how the Supreme Court itself will elaborate the jurisdictional potential this decision created. The one thing that seems fairly certain is that seismic events will be continuing for some years to come.[26]

Technically speaking, the decision in *Baker v. Carr* merely announced that the judiciary was open for business to entertain challenges to unequally apportioned legislatures. The decision did not purport to declare at just what point inequality in apportionment offended the equal protection clause. This, presumably, was to be clarified by further litigation. And the Court plainly supposed that a considerable volume of litigation would ensue. As Professor McCloskey's commentary indicates, however, the volume and pace of reapportionment cases initiated after *Baker v. Carr* exceeded all expectations. By November of 1962, "at least 30 state legislatures had been challenged in state and federal courts. . . ."[27]

Curiously enough, the first inequality-in-voting case to reach the Supreme Court after *Baker v. Carr* did not present issues of legislative malapportionment. But it was a case of the same genre. *Gray v. Sanders* was a test of Georgia's so-called county unit system, as that system operated to maintain rural domination in Democratic primaries to select candidates for state-wide office. Under the county unit system, each county was assigned a number of "units," all of which were counted for the candidate who won a popular majority in that county. But the units were allocated to the various counties in such a way as to give the sparsely populated rural counties overwhelmingly greater voting strength than such urban centers as Fulton County, in which the great metropolis of Atlanta is situated. Under this arrangement it was relatively easy for a candidate supported by a popular minority of voting Democrats to be nominated—and, in the virtually one-party state of Georgia, elected.

In *Gray v. Sanders,* the Supreme Court, by a margin of eight to one, struck down the county unit system. (Justice Harlan, who had dissented in *Baker v. Carr,* was the lone dissenter in *Gray v. Sanders.* Justice Frankfurter, who also dissented in *Baker v. Carr,* had retired in the summer of 1962; his successor, Justice Arthur Goldberg, was with the majority in *Gray v. Sanders.*) Justice Douglas, speaking for the Court in *Gray v. Sanders,* said that the problem presented by the county unit system was different from that involved in the reapportionment cases, of which *Baker v. Carr* was the prototype. There the question is whether a state can structure its state legislative districts (or its congressional districts) so that some legislators can represent significantly smaller constituencies than others, with the result that one voter in one district has a markedly greater voice in the totality of the legislature than another voter in another district. In the county unit litigation, as the Supreme Court viewed it, the question was whether the election of a single official could be so structured that one voting member of the constituency could cast a far weightier vote, in the selection of that official, than another voting member of the same constituency.

The argument had been made, in support of the county unit system, that this sort of inequality is constitutionally sanctioned in our electoral college method of selecting a President and Vice President. That method not only gives all of a state's electoral vote to the candidate winning the popular vote of that state, but markedly overweights the votes of small states, since the electoral delegation of a particular state is measured by its total representation in Congress—representatives and senators added together —and all states have the same number of senators. But the Court found the "federal analogy" unpersuasive. "The electoral college was designed by men who did not want the election of the President to be left to the people," and stems from a "conception of political equality [which] belongs to a bygone day. . . ."[28]

Having rejected the "federal analogy," the Supreme Court found the governing standard elsewhere:

The conception of political equality from the Declaration of Independence, to Lincoln's Gettysburg Address, to the Fifteenth, Seventeenth, and Nineteenth Amendments can mean only one thing—one person, one vote.[29]

Accordingly, so the Court held:

Once the geographical unit for which a representative is to be chosen is designated, all who participate in the election are to have an equal vote—whatever their race, whatever their sex, whatever their occupation, whatever their income, and wherever their home may be in that geographical unit. This is required by the Equal Protection Clause of the Fourteenth Amendment. . . .[30]

Although Justice Douglas expressly divorced the county unit problem from the malapportionment problem, and although Justices Stewart and Clark emphasized that disjuncture in a brief concurring opinion, Justice Harlan in his dissent appeared to see in the majority's "one person, one vote" principle a foretaste of what the majority would find constitutionally required in the malapportionment context. Whether Justice Harlan read his brethren's leanings correctly would only be discoverable when the Court turned to cases dealing directly with malapportionment. Meanwhile it seemed fair to say that the Court's opinion in *Gray v. Sanders* was full of language readily transferable from the county unit context to the malapportionment context. Moreover, the short shrift given the electoral college analogy in *Gray v. Sanders* strongly suggested that reliance on the Senate as an example of constitutionally anointed legislative inequality would do little to persuade a majority of the Supreme Court that the districts represented in a *state* legislative chamber can likewise be geared to political subgroupings rather than to population.

In early 1964, the Court gave further evidence of its commitment to the "one person, one vote" formula. The case was *Wesberry v. Sanders*, which held Georgia's congressional districts to be improperly designed because of the gross population discrepancies among the districts: the largest district (which included the South's biggest city, Atlanta) had over 800,000 people, which was more than twice the average size of Georgia's ten districts and more than three times the size of the smallest district.

More surprising than the Court's holding ("as nearly as is practicable one man's vote in a congressional election is to be worth as much as another's") was its rationale. Six members of the Court, speaking through Justice Black, found that substantial equality of population in congressional districts (or else the election of congressmen-at-large) was constitutionally compelled— *not* by virtue of the Fourteenth Amendment's equal protection clause, whose applicability they did not pass upon—but by virtue of the directives in Article I, Section 2, of the Constitution: "The House of Representatives shall be composed of Members chosen . . . by the People of the several States. . . ." and "Representatives . . . shall be apportioned among the several States which may be included within this Union, according to their respective Numbers. . . ."

The constitutional provisions, on their face, govern the mode of allocation of representatives *among* the states. So read, these provisions are, of course, the *quid pro quo* of the Connecticut Compromise which—giving the states equal voting power in the Senate, and representation by population in the House— made it possible for the Constitutional Convention to reconcile the conflicting wishes of the large and the small states with respect to the design of the national legislature. But in the view of the *Wesberry* majority, the quoted constitutional provisions have a momentum not apparent on their face:

It would defeat the principle solemnly embodied in the Great Compromise—equal representation in the House for equal numbers of people—for us to hold that, within the States, legislatures may draw the lines of congressional districts in such a way as to give some voters a greater voice in choosing a Congressman than others. . . .[31]

Justice Harlan—joined on this issue (but not on the issue of justiciability) by Justices Clark and Stewart—flatly disagreed:

> *The upshot of all this is that the language of Art. I, §§ 2 and 4, the surrounding text, and the relevant history are all in strong and consistent direct contradiction of the Court's holding. The constitutional scheme vests in the States plenary power to regulate the conduct of elections for Representatives, and, in order to protect the Federal Government, provides for congressional supervision of the States' exercise of their power. Within this scheme, the appellants do not have the right which they assert, in the absence of provision for equal districts by the Georgia Legislature or the Congress. The constitutional right which the Court creates is manufactured out of whole cloth.*[32]

What was not readily apparent was just why the majority preferred to approach the *Wesberry* case on Article I grounds, rather than—as Justice Clark urged—on the equal protection theory adumbrated by *Baker v. Carr.* One possible explanation was that the members of the majority felt that to read the equal protection clause as requiring adherence to a "one person, one vote" principle in congressional apportionment would compel the same result at the state level *and for both branches of a bicameral state legislature*—conclusions that the six Justices were perhaps not yet of one mind about.[33]

Whatever the rationale for the decision in *Wesberry,* there was no blinking the enormity of its potential impact on the future structure of the House of Representatives. As Justice Harlan observed:

> *. . . The Court's holding that the Constitution requires States to select Representatives either by elections at large or by elections in districts composed "as nearly as is practicable" of equal population places in jeopardy the seats of almost all the members of the present House of Representatives.*
>
> *In the last congressional election, in 1962, Representatives from 42 States were elected from congressional districts. In all but five of those States, the difference between the populations of the largest and smallest districts exceeded 100,000 persons. A*

difference of this magnitude in the size of districts the average population of which in each State is less than 500,000 is presumably not equality among districts "as nearly as is practicable," although the Court does not reveal its definition of that phrase. Thus, today's decision impugns the validity of the election of 398 Representatives from 37 States, leaving a "constitutional" House of 37 members now sitting.[34]

A tabulation of the population gap between the largest and smallest congressional districts in every districted state appears as an appendix to Justice Harlan's dissent.[35] Within three months after the *Wesberry* decision, one of the states with a particularly gross deviation from equal districts reformed itself: Connecticut's legislature, anticpating an adverse federal court decree, approved a redistribution of the state's six districts and thereby mooted the federal law suit. The episode illustrates what may well become a substantial pattern of political behavior: That political solutions to malapportionment problems, both at the state and the federal level, which could not have emerged prior to *Baker v. Carr,* will now be facilitated precisely because political leaders will decide that they cannot afford to remit the problems to the judicial initiatives which will inevitably come into play if the political mechanisms remain stalled.

In June of 1964 the Supreme Court decided the first group of state reapportionment cases to come before the Court since *Baker v. Carr* had opened the doors of the federal courts to such lawsuits. The chief cases in the group were *Reynolds v. Sims* and *Lucas v. Colorado General Assembly,* which challenged the alleged structural inequities of the Alabama and Colorado legislatures. Chief Justice Warren spoke for the Court in both cases, and aligned with him were the other five members of the *Wesberry* majority.

The Chief Justice's principal opinion was rendered in *Reynolds v. Sims.* First, the Chief Justice articulated the general rationale underlying the Court's insistence that "one person, one vote" is the only safe principle for organizing state legislatures:

Legislators represent people, not trees or acres. Legislators are elected by voters, not farms or cities or economic interests. As long as ours is a representative form of government, and our legislatures are those instruments of government elected directly by and directly representative of the people, the right to elect legislators in a free and unimpaired fashion is a bedrock of our political system. It could hardly be gainsaid that a constitutional claim had been asserted by an allegation that certain otherwise qualified voters had been entirely prohibited from voting for members of their state legislature. And, if a State should provide that the votes of citizens in one part of the State should be given two times, or five times, or 10 times the weight of votes of citizens in another part of the State, it could hardly be contended that the right to vote of those residing in the disfavored areas had not been effectively diluted. It would appear extraordinary to suggest that a state could be constitutionally permitted to enact a law providing that certain of the state's voters could vote two, five or 10 times for their legislative representatives, while voters living elsewhere could vote only once. And it is inconceivable that a state law to the effect that, in counting votes for legislators, the votes of citizens in one part of the State would be multiplied by two, five, or 10, while the votes of persons in another area would be counted only at face value, could be constitutionally sustainable. Of course, the effect of state legislative districting schemes which give the same number of representatives to unequal numbers of constituents is identical. Overweighting and overvaluation of the votes of those living here has the certain effect of dilution and undervaluation of the votes of those living there. The resulting discrimination against those individual voters living in disfavored areas is easily demonstrable mathematically. Their right to vote is simply not the same right to vote as that of those living in a favored part of the State. Two, five, or 10 of them must vote before the effect of their voting is equivalent to that of their favored neighbor. Weighting the votes of citizens differently, by any method or means, merely because of where they happen to reside, hardly seems justifiable. One must be ever aware that the Constitution forbids "sophisticated as well as simple-minded modes of discrimination." Lane v. Wilson, 307 U.S. 268, 275, Gomillion v. Lightfoot, 364 U.S. 339, 342. As we stated in Wesberry v. Sanders, *supra:*

> *We do not believe that the Framers of the Constitution intended to permit the same vote-diluting discrimination to be accomplished through the device of districts containing widely varied numbers of inhabitants. To say that a vote is*

worth more in one district than in another would . . . run counter to our fundamental ideas of democratic government. . . .

State legislatures are, historically, the fountainhead of representative government in this country. A number of them have their roots in colonial times, and substantially antedate the creation of our Nation and our Federal Government. In fact, the first formal stirrings of American political independence are to be found, in large part, in the views and actions of several of the colonial legislative bodies. With the birth of our National Government, and the adoption and ratification of the Federal Constitution, state legislatures retained a most important place in our Nation's governmental structure. But representative government is in essence self-government through the medium of elected representatives of the people, and each and every citizen has an inalienable right to full and effective participation in the political processes of his State's legislative bodies. Most citizens can achieve this participation only as qualified voters through the election of legislators to represent them. Full and effective participation by all citizens in state government requires, therefore, that each citizen has an equally effective voice in the election of members of his state legislature. Modern and viable state government needs, and the Constitution demands, no less.

Logically, in a society ostensibly grounded on representative government, it would seem reasonable that a majority of the people of a State could elect a majority of that State's legislators. To conclude differently, and to sanction minority control of state legislative bodies, would appear to deny majority rights in a way that far surpasses any possible denial of minority rights that might otherwise be thought to result. Since legislatures are responsible for enacting laws by which all citizens are to be governed, they should be bodies which are collectively responsive to the popular will. And the concept of equal protection has been traditionally viewed as requiring the uniform treatment of persons standing in the same relation to the governmental action questioned or challenged. With respect to the allocation of legislative representation, all voters, as citizens of a State, stand in the same relation regardless of where they live. Any suggested criteria for the differentiation of citizens are insufficient to justify any discrimination, as to the weight of their votes, unless relevant to the permissible purposes of legislative apportionment. Since the achieving of fair and effective representation for all citizens is concededly the basic aim of legislative apportionment, we conclude that the Equal Protection Clause guarantees the opportunity for equal participation by all voters in the election of state legislators. Diluting the weight of votes because of place of residence impairs basic constitutional rights under the Fourteenth Amendment just as much as invidious discriminations based upon factors such as race, Brown v. Board of Education, 347 U.S. 483, or economic status, Griffin v. Illinois, 351 U.S. 12, Douglas v. California, 372 U.S. 353. Our constitutional system amply provides for the protection of minorities by means other than giving them majority control of state legislatures. And the democratic ideals of equality and majority rule, which have served this Nation so well in the past, are hardly of any less significance for the present and the future.

We are told that the matter of apportioning representation in a state legislature is a complex and many-faceted one. We are advised that States can rationally consider factors other than population in apportioning legislative representation. We are admonished not to restrict the power of the States to impose differing views as to political philosophy on their citizens. We are cautioned about the dangers of entering into political thickets and mathematical quagmires. Our answer is this: a denial of constitutionally protected rights demands judicial protection; our oath and our office require no less of us. As stated in Gomillion v. Lightfoot, supra:

> When a State exercises power wholly within the domain of state interest, it is insulated from federal judicial review. But such insulation is not carried over when state power is used as an instrument for circumventing a federally protected right.

To the extent that a citizen's right to vote is debased, he is that much less a citizen. The fact that an individual lives here or there is not a legitimate reason for overweighting or diluting the efficacy of his vote. The complexions of societies and civilizations change, often with amazing rapidity. A nation once primarily rural in character becomes predominantly urban. Representation schemes once fair and equitable become archaic and outdated. But the basic principle of representative government remains,

*and must remain, unchanged—the weight of a citizen's vote can-
not be made to depend on where he lives. Population is, of
necessity, the starting point for consideration and the controlling
criterion for judgment in legislative apportionment controversies.
A citizen, a qualified voter, is no more nor no less so because he
lives in the city or on the farm. This is the clear and strong command of our Constitution's Equal Protection Clause. This is an
essential part of the concept of a government of laws and not
men. This is at the heart of Lincoln's vision of "government of the
people, by the people, [and] for the people." The Equal Protection Clause demands no less than substantially equal state legislative representation for all citizens, of all places as well as of all
races.*[36]

Next, Chief Justice Warren developed the proposition "that,
as a basic constitutional standard, the Equal Protection Clause
requires that the seats in both houses of a bicameral state legislature must be apportioned on a population basis."[37] And, in
developing this proposition, the Chief Justice sought to show why
the so-called "federal analogy" was not a constitutionally apt
model for state legislatures to emulate:

*We hold that, as a basic constitutional standard, the Equal
Protection Clause requires that the seats in both houses of a
bicameral state legislature must be apportioned on a population
basis. . . .*

*Since neither of the houses of the Alabama Legislature, un-
der any of the three plans considered by the District Court, was
apportioned on a population basis, we would be justified in
proceeding no further. However, one of the proposed plans, that
contained in the so-called 67-Senator Amendment, at least super-
ficially resembles the scheme of legislative representation followed in the Federal Congress. Under this plan, each of Alabama's 67 counties is allotted one senator, and no counties are
given more than one Senate seat. Arguably, this is analogous to
the allocation of two Senate seats, in the Federal Congress, to
each of the 50 States, regardless of population. Seats in the Alabama House, under the proposed constitutional amendment, are
distributed by giving each of the 67 counties at least one, with
the remaining 39 seats being allotted among the more populous
counties on a population basis. This scheme, at least at first*

glance, appears to resemble that prescribed for the Federal House of Representatives, where the 435 seats are distributed among the States on a population basis, although each State, regardless of its population, is given at least one Congressman. Thus, although there are substantial differences in underlying rationale and result, the 67-Senator Amendment, as proposed by the Alabama Legislature, at least arguably presents for consideration a scheme analogous to that used for apportioning seats in Congress.

Much has been written since our decision in Baker v. Carr *about the applicability of the so-called federal analogy to state legislative apportionment arrangements. After considering the matter, the court below concluded that no conceivable analogy could be drawn between the federal scheme and the apportionment of seats in the Alabama Legislature under the proposed constitutional amendment. We agree with the District Court, and find the federal analogy inapposite and irrelevant to state legislative districting schemes. Attempted reliance on the federal analogy appears often to be little more than an after-the-fact rationalization offered in defense of maladjusted state apportionment arrangements. The original constitutions of 36 of our States provided that representation in both houses of the state legislatures would be based completely, or predominantly, on population. And the Founding Fathers clearly had no intention of establishing a pattern or model for the apportionment of seats in state legislatures when the system of representation in the Federal Congress was adopted. Demonstrative of this is the fact that the Northwest Ordinance, adopted in the same year, 1787, as the Federal Constitution, provided for the apportionment of seats in territorial legislatures solely on the basis of population.*

The system of representation in the two Houses of the Federal Congress is one ingrained in our Constitution, as part of the law of the land. It is one conceived out of compromise and concession indispensable to the establishment of our federal republic. Arising from unique historical circumstances, it is based on the consideration that in establishing our type of federalism a group of formerly independent States bound themselves together under one national government. Admittedly, the original 13 States surrendered some of their sovereignty in agreeing to join together "to form a more perfect Union." But at the heart of our constitutional system remains the concept of separate and distinct governmental entities which have delegated some, but not all, of their formerly held powers to the single national government. The fact that almost three-fourths of our present States were never in fact independently sovereign does not detract from our view that the so-called federal analogy is inapplicable as a sustaining precedent for state legislative apportionments. The developing history and growth of our republic cannot cloud the fact that, at the time of the inception of the system of representation in the Federal Congress, a compromise between the larger and smaller States on this matter averted a deadlock in the constitutional convention which had threatened to abort the birth of our Nation. In rejecting an asserted analogy to the federal electoral college in Gray v. Sanders, supra, we stated:

> *We think the analogies to the electoral college, to districting and redistricting, and to other phases of the problems of representation in state or federal legislatures or conventions are inapposite. The inclusion of the electoral college in the Constitution, as the result of specific historical concerns, validated the collegiate principle despite its inherent numerical inequality, but implied nothing about the use of an analogous system by a State in a statewide election. No such specific accommodation of the latter was ever undertaken, and therefore no validation of its numerical inequality ensued.*

> *Political subdivisions of States—counties, cities, or whatever —never were and never have been considered as sovereign entities. Rather, they have been traditionally regarded as subordinate governmental instrumentalities created by the State to assist in the carrying out of state governmental functions. As stated by the Court in Hunter v. City of Pittsburgh, 207 U.S. 161, 178, these governmental units are "created as convenient agencies for exercising such of the governmental powers of the State as may be entrusted to them," and the "number, nature and duration of the powers conferred upon [them] . . . and the territory over which they shall be exercised rests in the absolute discretion of the State." The relationship of the States to the Federal Government could hardly be less analogous.*

> *Thus, we conclude that the plan contained in the 67-Senator Amendment for apportioning seats in the Alabama Legislature*

cannot be sustained by recourse to the so-called federal analogy. Nor can any other inequitable state legislative apportionment scheme be justified on such an asserted basis. This does not necessarily mean that such a plan is irrational or involves something other than a "republican form of government." We conclude simply that such a plan is impermissible for the States under the Equal Protection Clause, since perforce resulting, in virtually every case, in submergence of the equal-population principle in at least one house of a state legislature.

Since we find the so-called federal analogy inapposite to a consideration of the constitutional validity of state legislative apportionment schemes, we necessarily hold that the Equal Protection Clause requires both houses of a state legislature to be apportioned on a population basis. The right of a citizen to equal representation and to have his vote weighted equally with those of all other citizens in the election of members of one house of a bicameral state legislature would amount to little if States could effectively submerge the equal-population principle in the apportionment of seats in the other house. If such a scheme were permissible, an individual citizen's ability to exercise an effective voice in the only instrument of state government directly representative of the people might be almost as effectively thwarted as if neither house were apportioned on a population basis. Deadlock between the two bodies might result in compromise and concession on some issues. But in all too many cases the more probable result would be frustration of the majority will through minority veto in the house not apportioned on a population basis, stemming directly from the failure to accord adequate overall legislative representation to all of the State's citizens on a nondiscriminatory basis. In summary, we can perceive no constitutional difference, with respect to the geographical distribution of state legislative representation, between the two houses of a bicameral state legislature.[38]

Finally, the Chief Justice argued that, even under a "one person, one vote" principle, the valid purposes of bicameralism could be fulfilled. Moreover, he indicated that the Court was disposed to apply the "one person, one vote" principle with more flexibility at the state legislative level than at the congressional level. Indeed, the Chief Justice said that "some deviations from the equal-population principle are constitutionally permissible," provided "the divergencies from a strict population standard are based on legitimate considerations incident to the effectuation of a rational state policy."[39] In the portion of the Chief Justice's opinion which follows, it is apparent that the Court might look with favor on some representation of "political subdivisions"— towns and counties, for example—as a "legitimate consideration" permitting escape from a strict population standard, but that the Court would frown on representation of "economic or other sorts of group interests." This last portion of the opinion does not fully distinguish the "legitimate" from the "nonlegitimate considera- tion"; but the opinion acknowledges that here, as in other phases of constitutional law, "case-by-case" adjudication is the process that will give content to the Court's generalizations:

We do not believe that the concept of bicameralism is ren- dered anachronistic and meaningless when the predominant basis of representation in the two state legislative bodies is re- quired to be the same—population. A prime reason for bicameral- ism, modernly considered, is to insure mature and deliberate consideration of, and to prevent precipitate action on, proposed legislative measures. Simply because the controlling criterion for apportioning representation is required to be the same in both houses does not mean that there will be no differences in the composition and complexion of the two bodies. Different constit- uencies can be represented in the two houses. One body could be composed of single-member districts while the other could have at least some multimember districts. The length of terms of the legislators in the separate bodies could differ. The numerical size of the two bodies could be made to differ, even significantly, and the geographical size of districts from which legislators are elected could also be made to differ. And apportionment in one house could be arranged so as to balance off minor inequities in the representation of certain areas in the other house. In sum- mary, these and other factors could be, and are presently in many States, utilized to engender differing complexions and collective attitudes in the two bodies of a state legislature, although both are apportioned substantially on a population basis.

By holding that as a federal constitutional requisite both houses of a state legislature must be apportioned on a population basis, we mean that the Equal Protection Clause requires that a State make an honest and good faith effort to construct districts, in both houses of its legislature, as nearly of equal population as is practicable. We realize that it is a practical impossibility to arrange legislative districts so that each one has an identical number of residents, or citizens, or voters. Mathematical exactness or precision is hardly a workable constitutional requirement.

In Wesberry v. Sanders, supra, *the Court stated that congressional representation must be based on population as nearly as is practicable. In implementing the basic constitutional principle of representative government as enunciated by the Court in* Wesberry—*equality of population among districts—some distinctions may well be made between congressional and state legislative representation. Since, almost invariably, there is a significantly larger number of seats in state legislative bodies to be distributed within a State than congressional seats, it may be feasible to use political subdivision lines to a greater extent in establishing state legislative districts than in congressional districting while still affording adequate representation to all parts of the State. To do so would be constitutionally valid, so long as the resulting apportionment was one based substantially on population and the equal population principle was not diluted in any significant way. Somewhat more flexibility may therefore be constitutionally permissible with respect to state legislative apportionment than in congressional districting. Lower courts can and assuredly will work out more concrete and specific standards for evaluating state legislative apportionment schemes in the context of actual litigation. For the present, we deem it expedient not to attempt to spell out any precise constitutional tests. What is marginally permissible in one State may be unsatisfactory in another, depending on the particular circumstances of the case. Developing a body of doctrine on a case-by-case basis appears to us to provide the most satisfactory means of arriving at detailed constitutional requirements in the area of state legislative apportionment. Cf. Slaughter-House Cases, 16 Wall. 36, 78–79. Thus, we proceed to state here only a few rather general considerations which appear to us to be relevant.*

A State may legitimately desire to maintain the integrity of various political subdivisions, insofar as possible, and provide for compact districts of contiguous territory in designing a legislative apportionment scheme. Valid considerations may underlie such aims. Indiscriminate districting, without any regard for political subdivision or natural or historical boundary lines, may be little more than an open invitation to partisan gerrymandering. Single-member districts may be the rule in one State, while another State might desire to achieve some flexibility by creating multimember or floterial districts. Whatever the means of accomplishment, the overriding objective must be substantial equality of population among the various districts, so that the vote of any citizen is approximately equal in weight to that of any other citizen in the State.

History indicates, however, that many States have deviated, to a greater or lesser degree, from the equal-population principle in the apportionment of seats in at least one house of their legislatures. So long as the divergencies from a strict population standard are based on legitimate considerations incident to the effectuation of a rational state policy, some deviations from the equal-population principle are constitutionally permissible with respect to the apportionment of seats in either or both of the two houses of a bicameral state legislature. But neither history alone nor economic or other sorts of group interests, are permissible factors in attempting to justify disparities from population-based representation. Citizens, not history or economic interests, cast votes. Considerations of area alone provide an insufficient justification for deviations from the equal-population principle. Again, people, not land or trees or pastures, vote. Modern developments and improvements in transportation and communications make rather hollow, in the mid-1960's, most claims that deviations from population-based representation can validly be based solely on geographical considerations. Arguments for allowing such deviations in order to insure effective representation for sparsely settled areas and to prevent legislative districts from becoming so large that the availability of access of citizens to their representatives is impaired are today, for the most part, unconvincing.

A consideration that appears to be of more substance in justifying some deviations from population-based representation in state legislatures is that of insuring some voice to political subdivisions, as political subdivisions. Several factors make more than insubstantial claims that a State can rationally consider ac-

cording political subdivisions some independent representation in at least one body of the state legislature, as long as the basic standard of equality of population among districts is maintained. Local governmental entities are frequently charged with various responsibilities incident to the operation of state government. In many States much of the legislature's activity involves the enactment of so-called local legislation, directed only to the concerns of particular political subdivisions. And a State may legitimately desire to construct districts along political subdivision lines to deter the possibilities of gerrymandering. However, permitting deviations from population-based representation does not mean that each local governmental unit or political subdivision can be given separate representation, regardless of population. Carried too far, a scheme of giving at least one seat in one house to each political subdivision (for example, to each county) could easily result, in many States, in a total subversion of the equal-population principle in that legislative body. This would be especially true in a State where the number of counties is large and many of them are sparsely populated, and the number of seats in the legislative body being apportioned does not significantly exceed the number of counties. Such a result, we conclude, would be constitutionally impermissible. And careful judicial scrutiny must of course be given, in evaluating state apportionment schemes, to the character as well as the degree of deviations from a strict population basis. But if, even as a result of a clearly rational state policy of according some legislative representation to political subdivisions, population is submerged as the controlling consideration in the apportionment of seats in the particular legislative body, then the right of all of the State's citizens to cast an effective and adequately weighted vote would be unconstitutionally impaired.[40]

Three Justices strongly dissented from the basic propositions announced by the majority. One of them, Justice Harlan, had been in dissent in *Baker v. Carr*, and, as a result, he has been at odds with every judicial step since. But the new Court mandate, foreshadowing the compulsory reapportionment of virtually every chamber of every state legislature, drew renewed fire from the Justice:

It is difficult to imagine a more intolerable and inappropriate interference by the judiciary with the independent legislatures of the States.[41]

Justices Clark and Stewart had agreed with the result reached by the Court in *Baker v. Carr*. And they agreed with the result reached by the Court in *Reynolds v. Sims*, but only in the limited sense that they felt that the composition of the Alabama legislature—last reorganized over sixty years ago—was wholly irrational. But they, like Justice Harlan, could find no constitutional warrant for the conclusion that both chambers of a bicameral legislature had to be geared to districts of equal population. In the dissenting opinion in *Lucas v. Colorado General Assembly*, Justice Stewart, speaking for himself and Justice Clark, put the matter this way:

> *It is important to make clear at the outset what these cases are not about. They have nothing to do with the denial or impairment of any person's right to vote. Nobody's right to vote has been denied. Nobody's right to vote has been restricted. Nobody has been deprived of the right to have his vote counted. The voting right cases which the Court cites are, therefore, completely wide of the mark. Secondly, these cases have nothing to do with the "weighting" or "diluting" of votes cast within any electoral unit. The rule of* Gray v. Sanders, 372 U.S. 368 *is, therefore, completely without relevance here. Thirdly, these cases are not concerned with the election of members of the Congress of the United States, governed by Article I of the Constitution. Consequently, the Court's decision in* Wesberry v. Sanders, 376 U.S. 1, *throws no light at all on the basic issue now before us.*
>
> *The question involved in these cases is quite a different one. Simply stated, the question is to what degree, if at all, the Equal Protection Clause of the Fourteenth Amendment limits each sovereign State's freedom to establish appropriate electoral constituencies from which representatives to the State's bicameral legislative assembly are to be chosen. The Court's answer is a blunt one, and, I think, woefully wrong. The Equal Protection Clause, says the Court, "requires that the seats in both houses of a bicameral state legislature must be apportioned on a population basis."*

After searching carefully through the Court's opinions in these and their companion cases, I have been able to find but two reasons offered in support of this rule. First, says the Court, it is "established that the fundamental principle of representative government in this country is one of equal representation for equal numbers of people. . . ." With all respect, I think that this is not correct, simply as a matter of fact. It has been unanswerably demonstrated before now that this "was not the colonial system, it was not the system chosen for the national government by the Constitution, it was not the system exclusively or even predominantly practiced by the States at the time of adoption of the Fourteenth Amendment, it is not predominantly practiced by the States today." Secondly, says the Court, unless legislative districts are equal in population, voters in the more populous districts will suffer a "debasement" amounting to a constitutional injury. As the Court explains it, "To the extent that a citizen's right to vote is debased, he is that much less a citizen." We are not told how or why the vote of a person in a more populated legislative district is "debased," or how or why he is less a citizen, nor is the proposition self-evident. I find it impossible to understand how or why a voter in California, for instance, either feels or is less a citizen than a voter in Nevada, simply because, despite their population disparities, each of those States is represented by two United States Senators.

To put the matter plainly, there is nothing in all the history of this Court's decisions which supports this constitutional rule. The Court's draconian pronouncement, which makes unconstitutional the legislatures of most of the 50 States, finds no support in the words of the Constitution, in any prior decision of this Court, or in the 175-year political history of our Federal Union. With all respect, I am convinced these decisions mark a long step backward into that unhappy era when a majority of the members of this Court were thought by many to have convinced themselves and each other that the demands of the Constitution were to be measured not by what it says, but by their own notions of wise political theory. The rule announced today is at odds with long-established principles of constitutional adjudication under the Equal Protection Clause, and it stifles values of local individuality and initiative vital to the character of the Federal Union which it was the genius of our Constitution to create.

What the Court has done is to convert a particular political philosophy into a constitutional rule, binding upon each of the 50 States, from Maine to Hawaii, from Alaska to Texas, without regard and without respect for the many individualized and differentiated characteristics of each State, characteristics stemming from each State's distinct history, distinct geography, distinct distribution of population, and distinct political heritage. My own understanding of the various theories of representative government is that no one theory has ever commanded unanimous assent among political scientists, historians, or others who have considered the problem. But even if it were thought that the rule announced today by the Court is, as a matter of political theory, the most desirable general rule which can be devised as a basis for the make-up of the representative assembly of a typical State, I could not join in the fabrication of a constitutional mandate which imports and forever freezes one theory of political thought into our Constitution, and forever denies to every State any opportunity for enlightened and progressive innovation in the design of its democratic institutions, so as to accommodate within a system of representative government the interests and aspirations of diverse groups of people, without subjecting any group or class to absolute domination by a geographically concentrated or highly organized majority.

Representative government is a process of accommodating group interests through democratic institutional arrangements. Its function is to channel the numerous opinions, interests, and abilities of the people of a State into the making of the State's public policy. Appropriate legislative apportionment, therefore, should ideally be designed to insure effective representation in the State's legislature, in cooperation with other organs of political power, of the various groups and interests making up the electorate. In practice, of course, this ideal is approximated in the particular apportionment system of any State by a realistic accommodation of the diverse and often conflicting political forces operating within the State.

I do not pretend to any specialized knowledge of the myriad of individual characteristics of the several States, beyond the records in the cases before us today. But I do know enough to be aware that a system of legislative apportionment which might be best for South Dakota, might be unwise for Hawaii with its many islands, or Michigan with its Northern Peninsula. I do know enough to realize that Montana with its vast distances is not Rhode Island with its heavy concentrations of people. I do know enough to be aware of the great variations among the several States in their historic manner of distributing legislative power—of the Governors' Councils in New England, of the broad powers of initiative and referendum retained in some States by the people, of the legislative power which some States give to their Governors, by the right of veto or otherwise, of the widely autonomous home rule which many States give to their cities. The Court today declines to give any recognition to these considerations and countless others, tangible and intangible, in holding unconstitutional the particular systems of legislative apportionment which these States have chosen. Instead, the Court says that the requirements of the Equal Protection Clause can be met in any State only by the uncritical, simplistic, and heavy-handed application of sixth-grade arithmetic.

But legislators do not represent faceless numbers. They represent people, or, more accurately, a majority of the voters in their districts—people with identifiable needs and interests which require legislative representation, and which can often be related to the geographical areas in which these people live. The very fact of geographic districting, the constitutional validity of which the Court does not question, carries with it an acceptance of the idea of legislative representation of regional needs and interests. Yet if geographical residence is irrelevant, as the Court suggests, and the goal is solely that of equally "weighted" votes, I do not understand why the Court's constitutional rule does not require the abolition of districts and the holding of all elections at large.

The fact is, of course, that population factors must often to some degree be subordinated in devising a legislative apportionment plan which is to achieve the important goal of ensuring a fair, effective, and balanced representation of the regional, social, and economic interests within a State. And the further fact is that throughout our history the apportionments of State Legislatures have reflected the strongly felt American tradition that the public interest is composed of many diverse interests, and that in the long run it can better be expressed by a medley of component voices than by the majority's monolithic command. What consti-

tutes a rational plan reasonably designed to achieve this objective will vary from State to State, since each State is unique, in terms of topography, geography, demography, history, heterogeneity and concentration of population, variety of social and economic interests, and in the operation and interrelation of its political institutions. But so long as a State's apportionment plan reasonably achieves, in the light of the State's own characteristics, effective and balanced representation of all substantial interests, without sacrificing the principle of effective majority rule, that plan cannot be considered irrational.[42]

The reapportionment decisions of June 15, 1964, provoked anguished outcries from many quarters of the country. In most instances, the criticism was from those whose political power seemed threatened by the decisions. But some of the criticism clearly reflected doubt that the Court was on firm jurisprudential ground in insisting that both chambers of all state legislatures should be based on the "one person, one vote" principle.

In the weeks following the decisions, opposition to the decisions crystallized in an attempt (1) to overrule the Supreme Court by amending the Constitution, and (2) pending completion of the lengthy amendment process, to enact federal legislation requiring federal courts to stay implementation of any reapportionment decrees for from two to four years. The second proposal, introduced as a rider to the 1964 foreign aid legislation by Senate minority leader Everett M. Dirksen, was viewed with deep concern by lawyers who perceived it as an impermissible legislative interference with the judicial process. Fifteen law school deans and professors expressed this concern in the following terms:

We object to this and similar proposals, entirely apart from the merits of the recent Supreme Court decisions on apportionment, because the legislative approach unwisely and indeed dangerously threatens the integrity of our judicial process.

The effect of these proposals is not, as has sometimes been said, merely to limit the jurisdiction of the Federal courts. It is to declare by statute, without constitutional amendment, that for a period of time certain constitutional rights may not be vindicated in any court, state or Federal.

Although the language is not altogether clear, it appears to require that the United States Supreme Court issue stays of state court apportionment decisions brought to the Supreme Court for review. This would be a drastic interference with the power and duty of the state courts to enforce the Federal Constitution, and of the Supreme Court to insure uniformity of interpretation.

Once in our history Congress acted to prevent a constitutional decision which it anticipated. That was in 1868, when a statute was passed to prevent the Supreme Court from holding unconstitutional the military trial of a Mississippi editor, McCardle, for his editorial criticism of those who were occupying the South during Reconstruction.

Most historians and legal analysts have regarded the McCardle affair as an unfortunate episode in our history. It ought not to be repeated in this even more drastic form.

For the foregoing reasons the proposed statute raises the most serious questions for our basic constitutional scheme. It should be considered only after full hearings and discussion.[43]

Senator Dirksen's 1964 attempt to halt reapportionment litigation came to naught. So, too, a year later, did his proposed constitutional amendment, under which states would have been permitted to organize one house of a state legislature on the basis of factors other than population: On August 4, 1965, the Senate voted fifty-seven to thirty-nine for the proposed amendment, but this margin was seven votes shy of the necessary two-thirds which would have taken the proposal to the House and, if endorsed there, to the states for ratification. Curiously enough, the Senate, led by Senator Dirksen and by majority leader Mike Mansfield, on the very same day approved and sent to President Johnson the Voting Rights Act of 1965.[44]

Meanwhile, reapportionment litigation multiplied. The stresses these novel cases can impose on the courts were illustrated by a remarkable episode in judicial history which took place in New York in the summer of 1965. The highest state court (the New York Court of Appeals) and the federal appellate court which embraces New York (the Court of Appeals for the Second Circuit) came to diametrically opposed views on the validity of an interim reapportionment plan adopted by the New York legislature. On the basis of their conflicting views, the two courts issued inconsistent judicial directives to the state officials responsible for conducting New York's 1965 elections. Because the Supreme Court was not in session, the conflict of courts was remitted to and resolved by the Circuit Justice who has supervisory authority over the Second Circuit. There was special irony in the fact that the Circuit Justice was the only remaining member of the Court who had steadfastly dissented from *Baker v. Carr* and each of its judicial progeny—Justice Harlan. The Justice's memorandum opinion, resolving the extraordinary conflict, follows:

These are two applications for stays, before me as Circuit Justice. Oral argument has been requested, but in view of the fact that the basic factors underlying these applications have earlier been argued before me, I consider this course unnecessary.

On May 24, 1965, a three-judge Federal District Court ordered New York to hold a special legislative election on Nov. 2, 1965, over objections that the reapportionment plan under which the election was to be conducted had been held by the New York Court of Appeals to violate provisions of the New York Constitution. On June 1 this court, over my dissent, refused to stay the District Court's order pending appeal. Travia v. Lomenzo, 381 U.S. 431.

On July 9 the New York Court of Appeals, by a divided vote, enjoined the holding of the election, considering that no "final and binding" order requiring the election had yet been issued by the Federal courts. Glinski v. Lomenzo, . . . N.Y. 2d. . . . There ensued further proceedings before the district court, resulting in an order dated July 13 which enjoins all persons from in any way interfering with the holding of such election.

Petitioners Travia et al have reapplied for a stay of the order of the district court entered on May 24, and have also, joined by certain New York City officials, applied for a stay of the order of the district court entered on July 13. Appeals are being taken to this court from both orders, and appeals are pending in this court from the judgment of the New York Court of Appeals holding unconstitutional under the State Constitution the reapportionment plan under which the district court has ordered the election to be held. In re orans [sic], 15 N.Y. 2d 339, appeal pending, Rockefeller v. Orans, No. 319, 1965 term.

Were this court in session I would have referred both of these applications to it for disposition, as was done with the earlier application for a stay of the district court's order of May 24. Travia v. Lomenzo, supra. I consider it, however, my duty in the circumstances to act on these applications myself, deeming that I would not be justified in asking the Chief Justice to take steps to convene the court in special session. Given what has already transpired, I am left in no doubt as to what the decision on these applications must be.

While I have heretofore expressed my strong disagreement both with this court's basic state reapportionment decisions (see my dissenting opinion in Reynolds v. Sims, 377 U.S. 533, 589) and with the court's subsequent refusal, at least so far, to give plenary consideration to any of the challenges that have been made to the particular kinds of relief granted by district courts (see my opinions in Hughes v. WMCA, Inc., 379 U.S. 694; Fortson v. Toombs, 379 U.S. 621, 623; Travia v. Lomenzo, supra; cf. Parsons v. Buckley, 379 U.S. 359, 364), nevertheless I can only conclude that the denial of these applications is compelled by this court's earlier summary denial of a stay pending appeal of the district court's order of May 24 directing the election in question.

That denial surely signified this court's unwillingness to interfere with the district court's direction of the election, even though the election was to be held under a plan of apportionment which violated the New York Constitution. See my dissenting opinion in Travia v. Lomenzo, supra, at 434–435. That being so, the supremacy clause of the Federal Constitution requires the state courts to give recognition to the district court's order. See Marbury v. Madison, 1 Cranch. 137; United States v. Peters, 5 Cranch. 115; Ableman v. Booth, 21 How. 506; Sterling v. Constantin, 287 U.S. 378.

This is not meant to suggest that, following the District Court's order of May 24, the New York courts could take no action whatever with reference to these electoral matters. This court has repeatedly encouraged the state courts to fashion appropriate relief in reapportionment cases, even after a federal court has itself entered an order. Scranton v. Drew, 379 U.S. 40; Scott v. Germano, 381 U.S. 407; see Maryland Committee v. Tawes, 377 U.S. 656, 674.

Whether the Federal Court will then defer to the state court depends not on the supremacy clause, but on the exercise of discretion by the Federal court pursuant to considerations of comity inherent in federalism. However, the solution reached by the state Court of Appeals on July 9—to hold no election this fall—had already been rejected by the District Court in its order of May 24, and, by necessary implication, had also been rejected by this court in denying a stay of that order. It is clear in such circumstances that an exercise of discretion refusing to defer to the state courts cannot be deemed inappropriate.

The Federal District Court has entered an injunction which bars any further action in the New York courts. But for this injunction, it is conceivable that the New York courts (putting aside any questions of state law limitations) could yet fashion a remedy which would permit an election in 1965 under a form of "Plan A" modified so as to be more compatible with the State Constitution. However, the likelihood of such action (or any other which might be appropriate) is obviously slight, and the possibility cannot be ignored that at this late date any further proceedings in the state courts might well serve simply to compound the confusion already engendered by this matter.

In these circumstances I cannot say that the district court's injunction against any further actions was improper. I am accordingly constrained to leave it in full effect.

In conclusion, I think it pertinent to observe that these applications illustrate how important it is for this court to act in a sensitive and not heavy-handed manner in this novel and delicate constitutional field. It is manifest from the majority opinion of the New York Court of Appeals that the present unfortunate situation would not have arisen had this court explicated its reasons for refusing to stay the district court's order of May 24.

Orders will issue denying stays of both the May 24 and July 13 orders of the district court.[45]

V

Amending the Constitution

T HE CONSTITUTION OF THE UNITED STATES defines the structure of the national government; distributes the power to govern within that national government and between the nation and the states; and, as the prime means of maintaining a democratic society, limits the scope of governmental power over the individual and superintends the manner of its exercise, at every level of American governmental authority. By and large, the authority to determine the limits set by the Constitution is committed, on a case-by-case basis, to the judiciary—and, particularly, to the Supreme Court. There is some leeway in these judicial determinations, for the reason that no two cases are ever identical—and also for the reason that constitutional pronouncements arrived at in one case are, precisely because of their ultimate character, always subject to reconsideration in a later case. "Happily," as Justice Douglas has recently observed, "all constitutional questions are always open."[1]

Basic changes in constitutional structure can, however, be accomplished only by amending the Constitution. Ten amendments (proposed by two thirds of the two Houses of Congress and ratified by three-fourths of the states) were added in the first three years of Washington's first term. But since then only fourteen further changes (all of them proposed and ratified in the same way) have been made.

Except for the proviso in Article V that no state shall lose its equal representation in the Senate without its consent, the Constitution sets no limit on what changes can be accomplished by amendment. But the American people, presumably because they are essentially satisfied with the form and the functioning of their political institutions, have made few major changes in the structure of the American enterprise. Indeed, if one considers the Bill of Rights as essentially a clarification, rather than an alteration, of the Constitution proper, the only amendments that have altered the system in fundamental ways are those which immediately followed the Civil War.

In 1962 and 1963 considerable quiet momentum developed behind three newly proposed amendments. One amendment would have overturned *Baker v. Carr,* the 1962 reapportionment decision. A cognate proposal to amend the Constitution was advanced in 1964 to overrule the "one person, one vote" cases, *Reynolds v. Sims* and *Lucas v. Colorado General Assembly.*[2] A second amendment would have subordinated the Supreme Court to a so-called Court of the Union, composed of the chief justices of the fifty states. (The notion of a court supremer than the Supreme Court traces its lineage back at least a century and a half, to an idea put forward by the Pennsylvania legislature and rejected by the Virginia legislature in 1809–10;[3] but there was contemporary innovative genius in the concept of an appellate court so populous that it could double in brass as an infantry platoon or a professional football squad.) But the third of the trio of proposed amendments was far more radical than the other two. And the odd thing was that on casual inspection the third proposal looked harmless enough, for it was a proposal that would not of its own force have made any change whatsoever in our existing governmental institutions. All the proposal purported to do was to abolish the alternate method of constitutional amendment (the method under which two thirds of the states ask Congress to convene a constitutional convention, a method that has never heretofore been utilized) and substitute another in its place.

On close inspection, however, it turned out that if the proposed substitute process of amendment were adopted, a *minority* of the American people would thereafter have power to amend the Constitution. Moreover, under the substituted process, consideration of proposed amendments would, apparently, be wholly confined to the isolated state legislatures: the current prerequisite to achieve constitutional change—a national consensus fashioned in a national forum such as Congress or a national constitutional convention—could be wholly circumvented.

Fortunately, some students of the constitutional scene perceived the real thrust of the proposal; in the spring of 1963, they began to sound the alarm. Perhaps the most influential critique of the proposal was one written by Professor Charles L. Black, Jr. After its publication had alerted the bar and the press to the implications of the proposal, the curiously covert campaign on behalf of the amendment began to lose momentum. The *coup de grâce* was administered in May of 1963, when the Board of

Governors of the highly conservative American Bar Association expressed disapproval.[4] So, for the present, the threat seems to be pretty much ended. However, Professor Black's trenchant exposure of that deeply ominous assault on the Constitution will remain a document of permanent importance in American annals. Nor is it a document for the archivist alone. The proponents of this particular proposal have fallen back in disarray. But it is not inconceivable that others might, at a future time, seek to revive it or pursue a variant tack. Therefore, it seems appropriate to read Professor Black's critique with care, the better to understand the existing mechanisms of amendment which make it possible—but, happily, not easy—to alter the fundamental structure and functions of our federal republic: Professor Black's article follows:

Three proposals for amending the Constitution have recently come from the Council of State Governments, and are being propelled down the never before used alternative route of article V— the route via state applications to Congress for the calling of a convention. Of the three, one (which would establish a Court of the Union, composed of the state Chief Justices in all their multitude, to meet on extraordinary occasions to review judgments of the Supreme Court) is so patently absurd that it will probably sink without trace. Another, eradicating Baker v. Carr *concerns a special subject, and hence does not generally affect the federal power or the whole shape of the Union. The third is of supreme interest to students of constitutional law. Its adoption would effect a constitutional change of a higher order of importance than any since 1787—if one excepts (and that only doubtfully) the* de facto *change implicit in the result of the Civil War.*

It is wonderful that this proposal—which has already commended itself to a number of state legislatures—has been so little noticed. This is doubtless because the proposed change is in procedure. But a change in the procedure of constitutional amendment—unless it is purely formal, and this one is not—is a change in the distribution of ultimate power. The proposed article V, if adopted, would make it easily possible for a proportion of the American people no greater than that which supported Landon in 1936 to impose on the rest of the country any alteration what-

*ever in the Constitution. The people who could do this would
be, by and large, those inhabitants of the less populous states
who reside in the districts that are over-represented in their own
state legislatures. "Unto him that hath it shall be given." This
component of the population—to which we are all accustomed to
conceding a veto power on constitutional amendment, as on many
other matters—would under the proposed plan have something
very different from a veto power. It would have the affirmative
power of forcing its will on the majority, as to anything which
may be the subject of constitutional amendment—that is to say,
as to everything. Such a proposal ought to be scrutinized with
the very greatest care, and the same careful scrutiny should be
given to the method by which its proponents hope to coerce its
submission to the state legislatures for ratification as an amendment.*

*If this proposal were to win its way through, article V would
read as follows:*

The Congress, whenever two-thirds of both Houses shall
deem it necessary, or, on the application of the Legislatures
of two-thirds of the several states, shall propose amendments
to this Constitution, which shall be valid to all intents and
purposes, as part of this Constitution, when ratified by the
Legislatures of three-fourths of the several states. Whenever
applications from the Legislatures of two-thirds of the total
number of states of the United States shall contain identical
texts of an amendment to be proposed, the President of the
Senate and the Speaker of the House of Representatives
shall so certify, and the amendment as contained in the application shall be deemed to have been proposed, without
further action by Congress. No State, without its consent,
shall be deprived of its equal suffrage in the Senate.

*It may be convenient to the reader to have set out the text of
the present article V:*

The Congress, whenever two thirds of both Houses shall
deem it necessary, shall propose Amendments to this Constitution, or, on the Application of the Legislatures of two
thirds of the several States, shall call a Convention for proposing Amendments, which, in either Case, shall be valid to
all Intents and Purposes, as Part of this Constitution, when
ratified by the Legislatures of three fourths of the several
States, or by Conventions in three fourths thereof, as the one

or the other Mode of Ratification may be proposed by the
Congress; Provided that no Amendment which may be made
prior to the Year One thousand eight hundred and eight shall
in any Manner affect the first and fourth Clauses in the
Ninth Section of the first Article; and that no State, without
its Consent, shall be deprived of its equal Suffrage in the
Senate.

The proposed plan, it will be seen, abolishes the (never used)
"convention" way of amendment, and puts in its place a method
wholly under the control, as to substance and procedure, of the
state legislatures. It does this by making it mandatory that Congress submit for ratification any amendment called for by the
legislatures of two-thirds of the states, and by simultaneously
taking away Congress' power to elect the state convention mode
of ratification.

At present, an amendment may be passed (and all have actually passed in this way) if two-thirds of each national house wants
it, and if it is ratified by three-fourths of the states in the manner
chosen by Congress. One might also pass if (on proper application of two-thirds of the states) a convention, summoned by Congress and having such structure as Congress thought wise to
give it, proposed the amendment, and if it were then ratified in
the manner chosen by Congress.

Along the new route opened by the proposed article V,
Congress would control neither substance nor procedure. Three-
fourths of the state legislatures, without the consent of any other
body, could change the presidency to a committee of three,
hobble the treaty power, make the federal judiciary elective,
repeal the fourth amendment, make Catholics ineligible for public office, and move the national capital to Topeka. These are (in
part at least) cartoon illustrations. But the cartoon accurately
renders the de jure picture, and seems exaggerated only because
we now conceive that at least some of these actions have no
appeal to anybody. Some amendments—e.g., something like the
Bricker Amendment—would be very likely of early passage. At
present the main dangers would be to civil and political rights, to
national conduct of foreign relations, and to the federal taxing
power. But (particularly since the proposed change would be
absolutely irreversible, thirteen states being enough to block its
reversal) the cartoon does not exaggerate the possibilities of the

long future. A country in which the large majority would have to dread and sometimes submit to constitutional innovations appealing only to a minority could not call itself, even poetically, a democracy, and the possible tensions between consensus and Constitution would be dangerous in the extreme.

At present, when an amendment passes the House and the Senate by two-thirds, there is fair ground for the inference that there is national consensus upon it; at least the means of ascertaining that crucial fact, though rough, are fairly well adapted to the end. If the national convention method, under the present article V, were ever to be used, Congress, in setting up the convention, could ensure that it be so representative as to be likely to express a national consensus. Congress even retains control over the ratification process; if the state legislatures were in its view to come to be dangerously unrepresentative, Congress could provide for ratification by state conventions so chosen as accurately to reflect the views of each state's people. Properly used, the present article V can ensure that no constitutional change be effected which is disliked, deplored, or detested by a distinct majority of the American people.

What is the situation under the proposed new article V? Here one must talk numbers—even statistics of a rough kind. Let us note first that the thirty-eight least populous states, whose legislatures could under the proposed article V repeal the full faith and credit clause, contain about 40 per cent of the country's population. That really ought to be enough. That these particular people should, in the name of federalism, have a veto power, is acceptable; at least it is accepted beyond change. What rational ground could there be for giving them, in addition, the power affirmatively to govern the rest of the people?

But of course one cannot stop there. The power given by the new article V is not in the states but in their legislatures. It cannot be too strongly stressed that one need not approve of Baker v. Carr *in order to accept the fact, as a fact, that the state legislatures do not accurately represent the people of their states—that a majority in each house of most state legislatures can be made up of votes representing a distinct minority of the state's people. This situation may have a certain romantic appeal; even if one does not appreciate its beauty, one may not think the remedying of it a fit job for the federal courts. But neither of these judg-*

ments supports the conclusion that the uncontrolled power of federal constitutional amendment should be turned over to bodies so constituted.

So back to numbers: In the best table accessible [N.Y. Times, Mar. 28, 1962, p. 22, col. 3.], relevant data are given for thirty-four of the thirty-eight least populous states of the Union. On the average, it takes 38 per cent of the people in one of these states to form the constituencies of enough state senators or representatives to pass a measure through the more accurately representative house of the state legislature. Taking this figure as good enough for present purposes, if the proposed article V were in force, the income tax could be abolished, by repeal of the sixteenth amendment, if about 15 per cent of the American people were represented by legislators who desired that result.

Now of course it can be replied that such a coalition cannot be formed without the implication that a good many other people are like-minded with it. Granted. But the margin is enormous. If the right 30 per cent of the people favored some amendment, its chance of passage would be very great indeed, whatever the other 70 per cent might think. And it is very important that the distortion is not random but systematic—it is a distortion operating steadily in favor of rural districts and small towns. It is not too much to say that the proposed article V would enable the inhabitants of such districts to effect any change they persistently wanted in the Constitution of the United States. They may be better and wiser than the rest of us; perceptive fiction and the exacter sociology are not clear on this, but let us assume it is so. Does that justify turning the Constitution over to them, affirmatively and negatively, to keep or to change as they will?

Reference was made above to the result of the Civil War. The proposed article V rests on the theory, at least in part, that the result ought to be revised. The several states now have a crucial part in the process of constitutional amendment; the new proposal would (as far as one alternative method is concerned) give it entirely into their hands, setting at nothing the concept of national consensus among the American people considered as a whole people. It is a proposal for state rule only, on the basis of state-by-state count only, and through state institutions only, with the popular and national principles altogether submerged.

If history has any lessons, our history teaches that such a location of ultimate power would put us in mortal danger.

It should only be added that this proposal, as a corollary to its discard of the concept of national consensus as a prerequisite to amendment, does away with national consideration and debate as a part of the amendment process. Under the present article V, any amendment must be examined and considered in a fully national forum—whether Congress or Convention—before it goes out to the several states. Such debate focusses national attention on something which is above all of national concern. Under the proposal, the only public debate would be in fifty separate state legislatures; the rest of the process would be ministerial only. This short-circuiting of national deliberation is actually one of the most offensive features of the plan.[5]

As Professor Black has demonstrated, the effect of the proposal, if adopted, would have been to deliver the ultimate power to govern the United States into the hands of a minority of the American people. The proposal put at stake nothing less than our survival as a *federal republic*, as a *democracy*, and as a *united nation*.

In a way, the basic insolence of the idea is best revealed by the method through which it was sought to be fastened on the American people: *not*, as every amendment heretofore had been achieved, through a proposal which Congress debates, finds wise, and then submits to state legislatures or conventions; *but rather* through a proposal initiated by the several state legislatures and then siphoned through a constitutional convention and back to the states for ratification. Moreover, the proposal itself sought to jettison the convention method of amendment. The constitutional convention sought by the proponents of the proposal would not, assuming the convention approved the proposal, merely complete its own limited agenda and then dissolve. Such a convention would insure that no further national deliberation of fundamental national issues need ever take place. The adjournment of such a constitutional convention might well adjourn American constitutional history, *sine die*.

VI

Perspectives

VI

Perspectives

Thomas Jefferson (1816)

THE EXCERPT THAT FOLLOWS is taken from a letter to Samuel Kercheval, written on July 12, 1816, seven years after Mr. Jefferson had left the presidency, almost thirty years after the Constitutional Convention, and forty years after the Declaration of Independence:

Some men look at constitutions with sanctimonious reverence and deem them like the ark of the covenant, too sacred to be touched. They ascribe to the men of the preceding age a wisdom more than human, and suppose what they did to be beyond amendment. I knew that age well; I belonged to it, and labored with it. It deserved well of its country. It was very like the present, but without the experience of the present; and forty years of experience in government is worth a century of book-reading; and this they would say themselves, were they to rise from the dead. I am certainly not an advocate for frequent and untried changes in laws and constitutions. I think moderate imperfections had better be borne with; because, when once known, we accommodate ourselves to them, and find practical means of correcting their ill effects. But I know also that laws and institutions must go hand in hand with the progress of the human mind. As that becomes more developed, more enlightened, as new discoveries are made, new truths disclosed, and manners and opinions change with the change of circumstances, institutions must advance also, and keep pace with the times. We might as well require a man to wear still the coat which fitted him when a boy, as civilized society to remain ever under the regimen of their barbarous ancestors. . . .[1]

Finley Peter Dunne (1901)

Finley Peter Dunne was a Chicago newspaperman, and one of the handful of great American humorists. The plainest evidence of Dunne's brilliance is his anonymity: he was all but swallowed up in his magnificent creation, "Mr. Dooley." In the classic colloquy that follows, Mr. Dooley and his friend Mr. Hennessy are discussing *Downes v. Bidwell*,[2] in which the Supreme Court first wrestled with the applicability of the Constitution's protective provisions to the far-flung overseas possessions acquired by the United States at the close of the Spanish-American War. Concretely, the question was whether Congress could impose a duty on oranges grown in Puerto Rico and shipped to New York, a policy that Congress had not, and presumably could not have, pursued with respect to Florida or California oranges shipped to New York or any other state of the union. By a vote of five to four, the Court sustained the government's position that Congress, in establishing the new tariff policy for territories, was not inhibited by the constitutional limitations that protect the several states. However, the five members of the majority could not agree on a common opinion, so the rationale of the decision remained obscure. The view that commended itself to four members of the majority was that the Constitution did not apply to newly acquired possessions until Congress chose to "incorporate" them within the constitutional scheme. Justice Brown, the fifth member of the majority, seemed to feel that the Constitution was divisible—those of its provisions which guaranteed "natural rights" could be made to leap oceans, but others did not have to. The confusion engendered by the divided majority was compounded by the spate of dissenting opinions.

As Mr. Dooley perceives, in the following colloquy, the real significance of the decision was that it harmonized closely with the spirit of "manifest destiny" that dominated American politics at the turn of the century. In effect, the Supreme Court was giving Congress and the President a green light to expand our imperial domain without feeling that the Constitution would compel the immediate duplication, overseas, of all our domestic political institutions:

"I see," said Mr. Dooley, "Th' supreme coort has decided th' constitution don't follow th' flag."

"Who said it did?" asked Mr. Hennessy.

"Some wan," said Mr. Dooley. "It happened a long time ago an' I don't raymimber clearly how it come up, but some fellow said that ivrywhere th' constitution wint, th' flag was sure to go. 'I don't believe wan wurrud iv it,' says th' other fellow. 'Ye can't

make me think th' constitution is goin' thrapezin' around ivrywhere a young liftnant in th' ar-rmy takes it into his head to
stick a flag pole. It's too old. It's a home-stayin' constitution with
a blue coat with brass buttons onto it, an' it walks with a goold-
headed cane. It's old an' it's feeble an' it prefers to set on th' front
stoop an' amuse th' childher. It wudden't last a minyit in thim
thropical climes. 'T wud get a pain in th' fourteenth amindmint
an' die befure th' doctors cud get ar-round to cut it out. No, sir,
we'll keep it with us, an' threat it tenderly without too much
hard wurruk, an' whin it plays out entirely we'll give it dacint
buryal an' incorp'rate oursilves under th' laws iv Noo Jarsey.
That's what we'll do,' says he. 'But,' says th' other, 'if it wants to
thravel, why not lave it?' 'But it don't want to.' 'I say it does.'
'How'll we find out?' 'We'll ask th' supreme coort. They'll know
what's good fr it.' "

"So it wint up to th' supreme coort. They'se wan thing about
th' supreme coort, if ye lave annything to thim, ye lave it to
thim. Ye don't get a check that entitles ye to call fr it in an hour.
The supreme coort iv th' United States ain't in anny hurry about
catchin' th' mails. It don't have to make th' las' car. I'd back th'
Aujitoroom again it anny day fr a foot race. If ye're lookin' fr a
game iv quick decisions an' base hits, ye've got to hire another
empire. It niver gives a decision till th' crowd has dispersed an'
th' players have packed their bats in th' bags an' started fr home.

"Fr awhile ivrybody watched to see what th' supreme coort
wud do. I knew mesilf I felt I cudden't make another move in
th' game till I heerd fr'm thim. Buildin' op'rations was suspinded
an' we sthud wringin' our hands outside th' dure waitin' fr information fr'm th' bedside. 'What're they doin' now?' 'They just
put th' argymints iv larned counsel in th' ice box an' th' chief
justice is in a corner writin' a pome. Brown J. an' Harlan J. is
discussin' th' condition iv th' Roman Empire befure th' fire. Th'
r-rest iv th' coort is considherin' th' question iv whether they
ought or ought not to wear ruchin' on their skirts an' hopin' crino-
line won't come in again. No decision to-day?' An' so it wint fr
days, an' weeks an' months. Th' men that had argyied that th'
constitution ought to shadow th' flag to all th' tough resorts on th'
Passyfic coast an' th' men that argyied that th' flag was so lively
that no constitution cud follow it an' survive, they died or lost
their jobs or wint back to Salem an' were frgotten. Expansionists

contracted an' anti-expansionists blew up an' little childher was born into th' wurruld an' grew to manhood an' niver heerd iv Porther Ricky except whin some won get a job there. I'd about made up me mind to thry an' put th' thing out iv me thoughts an' go back to wurruk when I woke up wan mornin' an' see be th' pa-aper that th' Supreme Coort had warned th' constitution to lave th' flag alone an' tind to its own business.

"That's what th' pa-aper says, but I've r-read over th' decision an' I don't see annything iv th' kind there. They'se not a wurrud about th' flag an' not enough to tire ye about th' constitution. 'T is a matther iv limons, Hinnissy, that th' Supreme Coort has been settin' on f'r this gineration—a cargo iv limons sint fr'm Porther Ricky to some Eyetalian in Philydelphy. Th' decision was r-read be Brown J., him bein' th' las' justice to make up his mind, an' ex-officio, as Hogan says, th' first to speak, afther a crool an' bitther contest. Says Brown J.: 'Th' question here is wan iv such gr-reat importance that we've been sthrugglin' over it iver since ye see us las' an' on'y come to a decision (Fuller C. J., Gray J., Harlan J., Shiras J., McKenna J., White J., Brewer J., an' Peckham J. dissentin' fr'm me an' each other) because iv th' hot weather comin' on. Wash'n'ton is a dhreadful place in summer (Fuller C. J. dissentin'). Th' whole fabric iv our government is threatened, th' lives iv our people an' th' pro-gress iv civilization put to th' bad. Men ar-re excited. But why? We ar-re not. (Harlan J., "I am." Fuller C. J. dissentin', but not f'r th' same reason.) This thing must be settled wan way or th' other undher that dear ol' constitution be varchue iv which we are here an' ye ar-re there an' Congress is out West practicin' law. Now what does th' constitution say? We'll look it up thoroughly whin we get through with this case (th' rest iv th' coort dissentin'). In th' manetime we must be governed be th' ordnances iv th' Khan iv Beloochistan, th' laws iv Hinnery th' Eighth, th' opinyon iv Justice iv th' Peace Oscar Larson in th' case iv th' township iv Red Wing varsus Petersen, an' th' Dhred Scott decision. What do they say about limons? Nawthin' at all. Again we take th' Dhred Scott decision. This is wan iv th' worst I iver r-read. If I cudden't write a betther wan with blindhers on, I'd leap off th' bench. This horrible fluke iv a decision throws a gr-reat, an almost dazzlin' light on th' case. I will turn it off. (McKenna J. concurs,

but thinks it ought to be blowed out.) But where was I? I must put on me specs. Oh, about th' limons. Well, th' decision iv th' Coort (th' others dissentin') is as follows: First, that th' Disthrict iv Columbya is a state; second, that it is not; third, that New York is a state; fourth, that it is a crown colony; fifth, that all states ar-re states an' all territories ar-re territories in th' eyes iv other powers, but Gawd knows what they ar-re at home. In th' case iv Hogan varsus Mullins, th' decision is he must paper th' barn. (Hinnery VIII, sixteen, six, four, eleven.) In Wiggins varsus et al. th' cow belonged. (Louis XIV, 90 in rem.) In E. P. Vigore varsus Ad Lib., the custody iv th' childher. I'll now fall back a furlong or two in me chair, while me larned but misguided collagues r-read th' Histhry iv Iceland to show ye how wrong I am. But mind ye, what I've said goes. I let thim talk because it exercises their throats, but ye've heard all th' decision on this limon case that'll get into th' fourth reader.' A voice fr'm th' audjeence, 'Do I get me money back?' Brown J.: 'Who ar-re ye?' Th' Voice: 'Th' man that ownded th' limons.' Brown J.: 'I don't know.' (Gray J., White J., dissentin' an' th' r-rest iv th' birds concurrin' but fr entirely diff'rent reasons.)

"*An' there ye have th' decision, Hinnissy, that's shaken th' intellicts iv th' nation to their very foundations, or will if they thry to read it. 'T is all r-right. Look it over some time. 'T is fine spoort if ye don't care fr checkers. Some say it laves th' flag up in th' air an' some say that's where it laves th' constitution. Annyhow, something's in th' air. But there's wan thing I'm sure about.*"

"*What's that?*" asked Mr. Hennessy.

"*That is,*" said Mr. Dooley, "*no matther whether th' constitution follows th' flag or not, th' supreme coort follows th' iliction returns.*"[3]

James Bradley Thayer (1901)

In 1893 Professor James B. Thayer of the Harvard Law School published in the *Harvard Law Review* an essay entitled "The Origin and Scope of the American Doctrine of Constitutional Law," a pioneering and vastly influential study of the principles underlying American judicial review of legislative action. Professor Thayer argued persuasively that the exercise of the power of judicial review must be reserved for the most egregious legislative trespasses on manifest constitutional limitations: ". . . having regard to the great, complex, ever-unfolding exigencies of government, much which will seem unconstitutional to one man, or body of men, may reasonably not seem so to another. . . . [T]he constitution often admits of different interpretations. . . . [T]here is often a range of choice and judgment. . . . [I]n such cases the constitution does not impose upon the legislature any one specific opinion, but leaves open this range of choice; and . . . whatever choice is rational is constitutional."[4] Professor Thayer's fear of excessive judicial zeal in policing the legislature has been iterated from the bench, for the past seventy years, by Justices Holmes, Brandeis, and Frankfurter, and by Judge Learned Hand. What underlay that fear was articulated by Professor Thayer, in 1901, in a book on Chief Justice Marshall:

. . . When one reflects upon the multitude, variety, and complexity of the questions relating to the regulation of interstate commerce, upon the portentous and ever increasing flood of litigation to which the Fourteenth Amendment has given rise; upon the new problems in business, government, and police which have come in with steam and electricity, and their ten thousand applications; upon the growth of corporations and of wealth, the changes of opinion on social questions, such as the relation of capital and labor, and upon the recent expansions of our control over great and distant islands,—we seem to be living in a different world from Marshall's.

Under these new circumstances, what is happening in the region of constitutional law? Very serious things, indeed.

The people of the States, when making new constitutions, have long been adding more and more prohibitions and restraints upon their legislatures. The courts, meantime, in many places, enter into the harvest thus provided for them with a light heart, and too promptly and easily proceed to set aside legislative acts. The legislatures are growing accustomed to this distrust, and more and more readily incline to justify it, and to shed the consideration of constitutional restraints,—certainly as concerning the exact extent of these restrictions,—turning that subject over to

*the courts; and, what is worse, they insensibly fall into a habit of
assuming that whatever they can constitutionally do they may
do,—as if honor and fair dealing and common honesty were not
relevant to their inquiries.*

*The people, all this while, become careless as to whom they
send to the legislature; too often they cheerfully vote for men
whom they would not trust with an important private affair, and
when these unfit persons are found to pass foolish and bad laws,
and the courts step in and disregard them, the people are glad
that these few wiser gentlemen on the bench are so ready to protect them against their more immediate representatives.*

*From these causes there has developed a vast and growing
increase of judicial interference with legislation. This is a very
different state of things from what our fathers contemplated, a
century and more ago, in framing the new system. Seldom, indeed, as they imagined, under our system, would this great,
novel, tremendous power of the courts be exerted,—would this
sacred ark of the covenant be taken from within the veil. Marshall himself expressed truly one aspect of the matter, when he
said in one of the later years of his life: "No questions can be
brought before a judicial tribunal of greater delicacy than those
which involve the constitutionality of legislative acts. If they become indispensably necessary to the case, the court must meet
and decide them; but if the case may be determined on other
grounds, a just respect for the legislature requires that the obligation of its laws should not be unnecessarily and wantonly assailed." And again, a little earlier than this, he laid down the one
true rule of duty for the courts. When he went to Philadelphia at
the end of September, in 1831, . . . in answering a cordial
tribute from the bar of that city he remarked that if he might be
permitted to claim for himself and his associates any part of the
kind things they had said, it would be this, that they had "never
sought to enlarge the judicial power beyond its proper bounds,
nor feared to carry it to the fullest extent that duty required."*

*That is the safe twofold rule; nor is the first part of it any
whit less important than the second; nay, more; today it is the
part which most requires to be emphasized. For just here comes
in a consideration of very great weight. Great and, indeed, in-
estimable as are the advantages in a popular government of this
conservative influence,—the power of the judiciary to disregard*

unconstitutional legislation,—it should be remembered that the exercise of it, even when unavoidable, is always attended with a serious evil, namely, that the correction of legislative mistakes comes from the outside, and the people thus lose the political experience, and the moral education and stimulus that come from fighting the question out in the ordinary way, and correcting their own errors. . . .

The tendency of a common and easy resort to this great function, now lamentably too common, is to dwarf the political capacity of the people, and to deaden its sense of moral responsibility. It is no light thing to do that.

What can be done? It is the courts that can do most to cure the evil; and the opportunity is a very great one. Let them resolutely adhere to first principles. Let them consider how narrow is the function which the constitutions have conferred on them,— the office merely of deciding litigated cases; how large, therefore, is the duty intrusted to others, and above all to the legislature. It is that body which is charged, primarily, with the duty of judging of the constitutionality of its work. The constitutions generally give them no authority to call upon a court for advice; they must decide for themselves, and the courts may never be able to say a word. Such a body, charged, in every State, with almost all the legislative power of the people, is entitled to the most entire and real respect; is entitled, as among all rationally permissible opinions as to what the constitution allows, to its own choice. Courts, as has often been said, are not to think of the legislators, but of the legislature,—the great, continuous body itself, abstracted from all the transitory individuals who may happen to hold its power. It is this majestic representative of the people whose action is in question, a coordinate department of the government, charged with the greatest functions, and invested, in contemplation of law, with whatsoever wisdom, virtue, and knowledge the exercise of such functions requires.

To set aside the acts of such a body, representing in its own field, which is the very highest of all, the ultimate sovereign, should be a solemn, unusual, and painful act. Something is wrong when it can ever be other than that. And if it be true that the holders of legislative power are careless or evil, yet the constitutional duty of the court remains untouched; it cannot rightly attempt to protect the people, by undertaking a function not its own. On the other hand, by adhering rigidly to its own duty, the court will help, as nothing else can, to fix the spot where responsibility lies, and to bring down on that precise locality the thunderbolt of popular condemnation. The judiciary, to-day, in dealing with the acts of their coordinate legislators, owe to the country no greater or clearer duty than that of keeping their hands off these acts wherever it is possible to do it. For that course—the true course of judicial duty always—will powerfully help to bring the people and their representatives to a sense of their own responsibility. There will still remain to the judiciary an ample field for the determinations of this remarkable jurisdiction, of which our American law has so much reason to be proud; a jurisdiction which has had some of its chief illustrations and its greatest triumphs, as in Marshall's time, so in ours, while the courts were refusing to exercise it.[5]

Thomas Reed Powell (1925)

The late T. R. Powell, who taught law first at Columbia and later at Harvard, was for decades a wise and witty student of the Constitution. "Constitutional Metaphors," which follows, appeared in *The New Republic* in 1925; it was a review of a book on the Constitution written by the then Solicitor General of the United States, James M. Beck:

Even before the Eighteenth Amendment books about the United States Constitution were apt to be pretty dry. They usually tell what the Supreme Court says in a lot of cases and try to show how what it says in one case will jibe all right with what it says in the other cases. After the writers tell what happens in each case, then they try to forget it and to put all the cases together and make up a set of rules to show what the Supreme Court has been up to and what it is going to do next. This is a very hard thing to do and it is very hard to read after it has been done. You have to think very hard all the time and even then you get all mixed up. This kind of book makes you tired because you have to try so hard to think, and so you usually stop trying to read it.

The new book [The Constitution of the United States, *by for-*

mer Solicitor General James M. Beck] which Mr. Beck has written
about the Constitution is a very different kind of book. You can
read it without thinking. If you have got tired trying to read the
other kind of books, you will be glad of the nice restful book
that Mr. Beck has written. It runs along like a story in a very interesting way. Most of the story is about how the Constitution got
made. This is really history, but it is written in a very lively way
like a novel, with a great many characters, almost all male, and
plenty of conversation and a very exciting plot. Many of the
chapters have names like those in a novel, such as The Opening
of the Battle, The Crisis, The Dawn, Nearing the End, The
Curtain Falls, and others. Besides the story there are many quotations from Shakespeare, Beethoven, Horace, Isaiah, Euripides,
Beard and other famous men. Many of these quotations are quite
old, but some of them seem fairly new. They help to make the
book a really high class book. There is not much more to say
about the part of the book that tells how the Constitution got
made, except that it is fun and easy to read and seems pretty
true to life.

The rest of the book is about what a good Constitution it is
and how bad it is to make changes in it. The main reason why it
is so good is because it was made by such good men. Mr. Beck
says very nice things about them. He calls them "a group of
gentlemen of substance and honor" and he thinks that "all apparently were inspired by a fine spirit of self-effacement." They
kept their ears a good ways from the ground as gentlemen of
substance and honor should, for Mr. Beck says that "they represented the spirit of representative government at its best in avoiding the cowardice of time-servers and the low cunning of dema-
gogues." This means that they were the kind of men who would
do what they thought was best for all the people without trying
to find out what the people thought was best for themselves.
Some of the people in those days who were not gentlemen of
substance and honor had been trying to do very foolish things
and it was partly to stop such foolishness that these good men
came together to make the Constitution.

It was this foolishness of the men who didn't make the Constitution that made the men who made it make it such a good
Constitution. This was the second main reason why it is so
good. It is what Mr. Beck has in his mind when he speaks of

"the anterior necessity of those who had property interests to protect themselves against that spirit of social revolt which we today call 'bolshevism.' " If these men who made the Constitution had not been so full of their *"fine spirit of self-effacement,"* they might not have seen so clearly what was the best thing to do. But they did. Mr. Beck says that it was because of the hard times that we got such a good constitution. This was the third main reason. Of course the hard times couldn't give us a good Constitution all by themselves, but you can see how much they helped when you read Mr. Beck's book where it says:

> It is therefore true that the Constitution was born of an economic travail, and that its merits were largely determined by the commercial necessities of the American people. It was largely the work of men of affairs; for most of the members of the Convention were influential, and, for the times, well-to-do professional and business men, who felt that, if their property interests were to be safeguarded and prosperity were to return after the panic of 1785, there must be, not merely freer commercial intercourse between the States, but also greater security to the rights of property against the disintegrating social tendencies, due to the distress among the masses, which, then, as now, inevitably follows a depreciated currency.

I never knew what the Constitution really is until I read Mr. Beck's book. He says that *"it is something more than a written formula of government—it is a great spirit. It is a high and noble assertion, and, indeed, vindication, of the morality of government."* It is splendid to have a Constitution like that and to know, as Mr. Beck tells us, that *"to the succeeding ages, the Constitution will be a flaming beacon."* This is not all that it is, for Mr. Beck says also:

> I have elsewhere likened the Constitution to a Gothic cathedral, like that of Rheims. Its foundations seem secure, even though some of its buttresses may be weakened and its statuary mutilated. Nevertheless it remains a noble and serviceable temple of Liberty and Justice. Let us hope that, with the present indifference of the masses to the Constitution and the spirit of innovation of this restless and impatient age, that the time will not come that the Constitution will be as the Cathedral of Rheims when the author

saw it in the summer of 1916. Rheims was a noble but pitiful ruin. Its high altar had been overthrown, and its glorious rose windows hopelessly shattered.

The high altar of the Constitution is the self-restraint which the American people of 1787 were wise enough to impose upon themselves, and their posterity, and the rose windows are those great traditions of Liberty which we have gained at an infinite sacrifice of treasure and life from our English-speaking ancestry.

It helps us to know what the Constitution is if we know what it is not. It is a beacon and a Gothic cathedral, but it is not a rock and it is not a beach. Instead of these things, it is a floating dock. Mr. Beck puts it very beautifully when he says:

The Constitution is neither, on the one hand, a Gibraltar rock, which wholly resists the ceaseless washing of time and circumstance, nor is it, on the other hand, a sandy beach, which is slowly destroyed by the erosion of the waves. It is rather to be likened to a floating dock, which, while firmly attached to its moorings, and not therefore at the caprice of the waves, yet rises and falls with the tide of time and circumstance.

You might think that a Constitution which is all these wonderful things would be sure to last forever without any help from anything else. But this is not so. Mr. Beck says that it would not have lasted so long as it has if it had not been for the Supreme Court which he says is "the balance wheel of the Constitution." He has a whole chapter which he calls The Balance Wheel and this chapter ends up by saying:

But always the Supreme Court stands as a great lighthouse, and even when the waves beat upon it with terrific violence (as in the Civil War, when it was shaken to its very foundation), yet after they have spent their fury, the great lamp of the Constitution—as that of another Pharos—illumines the troubled face of the waters with the benignant rays of those immutable principles of liberty and justice, which alone can make a nation free as well as strong.

It makes you see how marvelous the Supreme Court really is when it can be a balance wheel at the beginning of a chapter and a lighthouse at the end.

Even if you are not interested in the Constitution for its own sake, you will like to read what Mr. Beck says about it because he is such a lovely writer. He is the kind of writer who likes to write just for the sake of writing. He shows how he loves his work. He is not one of those writers who have to stop in their writing while they are making up their minds what to say. You can read him right along because he is so simple in his thoughts. He does not get you all mixed up the way so many writers do, but he brings up in your mind beautiful pictures of the Constitution as a temple and a beacon and a floating dock and he lets you see the Supreme Court shining and balancing in a very wonderful way. I have read a great many books about the Constitution, but there is no other book that has given me just the same kind of pleasure that this one has.

    You will have a very happy feeling while you are reading Mr. Beck's book, until you come to the last three chapters. Then you will begin to feel sad. The ending is not a happy ending. It tells of dangers that will hurt our country if we do not look out. It is not enough to have a Gothic cathedral with a balance wheel. We must all be wise and good men who will not make changes. This is like so many books that have a moral lesson at the end. On his very last page Mr. Beck tells us what we should do. He says that when the Constitution came out of the safe in the State Department a few years ago, "the ink, in which it had been engrossed nearly one hundred and thirty-seven years ago, was found to have faded." He hopes that this is not a bad sign. This is what he means when he says that "all who believe in constitutional government must hope that this is not a portentous symbol." Just hoping will not help any, and it would not do any good to put fresh ink on top of the ink that is fading. We must do something different from that. Mr. Beck tells us very plainly what we should do when he says that "the American people must write the compact, not with ink upon a parchment, but with 'letters of living light'—to use Webster's phrase—upon their hearts." That must be a very hard way to write, and I should think it would be a good thing to write the ink letters as well as the light letters, because the light might go out before the ink had all faded.[6]

James O. Eastland (1960)

"It is a mistake," said Justice David J. Brewer in 1898, "to suppose that the Supreme Court is either honored or helped by being spoken of as beyond criticism. On the contrary, the life and character of its justices should be the objects of constant watchfulness by all, and its judgments subject to the freest criticism. . . . True, many criticisms may be, like their authors, devoid of good taste, but better all sorts of criticism than no criticism at all."[7]

If the intensity with which the Court is criticized is a fair measure of the Court's vitality, that durable tribunal is today in the best of health. Beginning with the *School Segregation Cases* in 1954, a number of decisions in the areas of racial discrimination, church-state relations, procedural due process, and legislative reapportionment have stirred the ire of millions of Americans —and the admiration of other millions of Americans. But ire— reaching its crescendo in the cheerful chorus, "Impeach Earl Warren"—has generally out-shouted admiration. Throughout this period, one of the Court's most faithful antagonists has been James O. Eastland of Mississippi, the Chairman of the Senate Judiciary Committee. The following excerpt from *The New York Times* describes a speech made by Senator Eastland in the course of the Senate debate on the Civil Rights Act of 1960. The speech seems to belong to that genre of criticism characterized by Justice Brewer as "devoid of good taste":

Twice during his pre-midnight stand on the floor, the Mississippi Democrat referred to a Supreme Court decision upholding the constitutionality of the 1957 civil rights act as "crap." In the Congressional Record, the word was changed in one case to "claptrap" and, in the other, to "useless material."[8]

Charles L. Black, Jr. (1961)

Professor Black, formerly on the faculty of the Columbia Law School and now a teacher both of law and of political science at Yale, has written widely on the Supreme Court. The paragraphs that follow are taken from an article by Professor Black entitled "The Supreme Court and Democracy":

> *Democracy . . . has many and various means of realizing itself. None of these means is perfect; all are heavily marked by the accidents of history. Even as to the sheerly ideal, there is no single infallible scripture. These facts make it impossible to isolate pure and geometrically precise premises of democracy. But some formulations would enjoy, I should think, a fairly wide acceptance. One of these is that democracy rests on respect for human beings collectively, just as the willingness to accord freedom to individuals rests on respect for single human beings. Democracy respects people enough to insist that they are fit to conduct their own affairs, and do not need to have their affairs conducted for them under some species of degrading tutelage.*
>
> *But the classic difficulty felt with democracy arises, as all know, from the fact that democracy can never express the will of the whole people, because there never exists any such monolithic will (at least in any society that can call itself democratic). The concept of government of the whole people by the whole people must be looked on as in the poetry rather than in the prose of democracy; the fact of prose is that real democracy means government by some kind of dominant majority.*
>
> *And the ever-present danger, repeatedly realized in fact, is that this dominant majority may behave toward those who are not of the majority in such a manner as to undercut the moral basis of democracy itself—respect for human beings, for the right of people, because they are people, to have some important say in the setting of their own course and in the use of their own faculties. Other forms of government may similarly fail to respect human independence. But there is at least no contradiction in that; the underlying assumption of every kind of government by wisers and betters is that people on the whole are not fit to manage their own affairs, but must have someone else do it for them, and there is no paradox when such a government treats its subjects without respect, or deals with them on the basis of their having no rights the government must take into account. But democracy affirms that people are fit to control themselves, and it cannot live in the same air with the theory that there is no*

limit to the extent to which public power—even the power of a majority—can interfere with the lives of people.

Rational limitation on power is therefore not a contradiction to democracy, but is of the very essence of democracy as such. Other sorts of government may impose such limitations on themselves as an act of grace, of noblesse oblige. Democracy is under the moral duty of limiting itself, because such limitation is an essential to the survival of that respect for human persons which is in the foundations of democracy. Respect for the freedom of all people cannot of course be the only guide, for there would then be no government. Delicate ongoing compromise is what must be looked for. But democracy, unless it is to deny its own moral basis, must accept the necessity for making this compromise, and for giving real weight to the claims of those without the presently effective political power to make their claims prevail in elections.

Beyond doubt, more ways than one could be and have been devised for bringing it about, in the working of real democratic governments, that the dominant majority exert its power within the channels of rational definition and of decent respect for all people. The distinctively American institution devoted to this end is the institution of judicial review. We have committed ourselves to the noble idea that the dominant majority of today, like that of yesterday and tomorrow, is to be subjected to law, with regard to the definition of its power and with respect to its obligations of deference to the rights of all people, whether in the majority or not.

If democracy means very simply that the majority is to have whatever it presently hankers after, then judicial review is an intrusive body in democracy. If democracy means that the majority is generally to have its way because human beings are to be respected and their conception of their own interests not disregarded, then the commitment of the majority to limits set by law is of the essence of democracy. It is a device on which we can pin the hope that democracy will not defeat the very values that underlie itself.

This commitment to law would of course be wholly undemocratic if it were imposed ab extra—*if some benevolent dictator had set up a game of limited popular rule, indulging the people just so far and no further, and ordaining the Supreme*

Court as umpire to keep the rules. But we have already seen that judicial review neither grew up nor is kept going in that way. The submission of our democracy to the law of its own Constitution, expounded by courts of its own creation, is the work of democracy itself, a work of democratic self-limitation.

A commitment to law is a commitment to the processes of law as well as to the idea of law. And the process of law as we know it is exactly the process represented by judicial review—initial authoritative adoption of stated norms, followed by professionally skilled and disinterested expounding and application. Of course the Supreme Court has never attained to its ideal working, and has often fallen far short. Can anything else be said for any institution ever devised? Who will say that our Supreme Court has more sharply disappointed ideal expectations than has been true of our Congresses on the whole, or of the occupants, on the whole, of our Presidency?

The power of the Supreme Court, to summarize, is utterly incompatible with a simplistic pseudo-logical view of democracy. But that view is itself worthless, for it has no application to any major institution of our government, or to that government as a whole. Proceeding to real issues. . . . First, judicial review has not been imposed on an unwilling and helpless people, but has on the contrary been accepted by the people in a most decided way, when they might have rejected it. Secondly, judicial review is not now fastened on the people by a fatal ancestral inadvertence or folly, but may be done away with by them when they want to do away with it. Thirdly, and by far most important, judicial review, I have tried to suggest, contradicts democracy only as the edge of a curved steel track contradicts the flange of the locomotive wheel; it is a device which our democracy has selected for assuring life to the very values out of which democracy grows.

The prevailing academic mood in regard to the power of the Court has, for the last quarter-century, been one of cynical deploring. I suggest to you, as we stand perhaps thirty years away from the beginning of our third life, from the day when no one is left who was alive when someone still lived who was born before our Constitution came into being, that this power may be on its way to greater usefulness, to a more nearly perfect fulfillment of the promise of these early years of our history.[9]

Lyndon B. Johnson (1965)

. . . [F]ree speech, free press, free religion, the right of free assembly, yes, the right of petition, the right to buy ads and to have teach-ins, and sit-ins, and parades and marches and demonstrations—well, they're still radical ideas. And so are secret ballots, and so are free elections, and so is the principle of equal dignity, and so is the principle of equal rights for all the sons and daughters of man. But all of these things are what America stands for. . . .[10]

The Court: ". . . our always unfinished work" (1965)

The Senate of the United States prides itself on being a continuing body. The Supreme Court of the United States *is* a continuing body. The nine incumbent Justices are linked with the nearly ninety retired and dead Justices in a long, black-robed line stretching back to the beginnings of the Republic.

The Court is also a collegial body. The Justices call themselves "brethren." The word is fitting. The Justices are brothers: brothers in the passion of their philosophic disagreements; and brothers in their abiding affection and respect for one another, and for the institution which unites them in a common enterprise.

Because the Court is so small and closely knit a partnership, the departure of one of the Justices is likely to work important changes in the institution. The principal changes may not, however, be those which are most widely advertised—that a "conservative" has been replaced by a "liberal," or vice versa. The principal changes may flow from the Court's loss of a Justice of massive intellectual attainment; or one who is singularly familiar with certain specialized fields of federal law; or one who has a matchless sense of the Court's institutional capacities and limitations; or one blessed with an aptitude for leading divided colleagues along a middle path. The retirement or death of a Justice, and his replacement by another, do not ordinarily usher in a "new

Court"; but these events may well mean that the continuing Court, however subtly regrouped, enters a new phase.

And so it was, pre-eminently, with Justice Frankfurter's departure from the Court. Of all the men who have ever sat upon the Court, it is a fair appraisal that "a dozen—no more—have made their mark, so that their distinctive work is part of the American Constitution. Among the moderns, excluding any still sitting, one counts Brandeis, Holmes, perhaps Hughes, perhaps Stone, possibly Cardozo, and certainly Felix Frankfurter. His voice will be heard, and he will influence political thoughts so long as there is a Supreme Court and so long as men are concerned to make their actions fit the American constitutional tradition."[11]

On August 28, 1962, Justice Frankfurter wrote a letter advising President Kennedy that he was retiring forthwith from active membership on the Court:

My Dear Mr. President:

Pursuant to the provisions of 28 U.S.C. Section 371(b), 68 Stat. 12, I hereby retire at the close of this day from regular active service as an Associate Justice of the Supreme Court of the United States.

The occasion for my retirement arises from the affliction which I unexpectedly suffered last April. Since then I have undergone substantial improvement. High expectations were earlier expressed by my doctors that I would be able to resume my judicial duties with the beginning of the next Term of the Court, commencing October 1. However, they now advise me that the stepped-up therapy essential to that end involves hazards which might jeopardize the useful years they anticipate still lie ahead of me.

The Court should not enter its new Term with uncertainty as to whether I might later be able to return to unrestricted duty. To retain my seat on the basis of a diminished work schedule would not comport with my own philosophy or with the demands of the business of the Court. I am thus left with no choice but to regard my period of active service on the Court as having run its course.

I need hardly tell you, Mr. President, of the reluctance with which I leave the institution whose concerns have been the absorbing interest of my life. May I again convey to you my gratitude for your call upon me during the summer and for the solicitude you were kind enough to express.

    With high respect and esteem,

            Faithfully yours,

               FELIX FRANKFURTER

The President,
The White House,
Washington, D.C.[12]

President Kennedy replied in the following terms:

            The White House,
        Washington, August 28, 1962.

My Dear Mr. Justice Frankfurter:

    Your retirement from regular active service on the Supreme Court ends a long and illustrious chapter in your life and I understand well how hard a choice you have made. Along with all your host of friends I have followed with admiration your gallant and determined recovery, and I have shared the general hope that you would return soon to the Court's labors. From my own visit I know of your undiminished spirit and your still contagious zest for life. That you now take the judgment of the doctors and set it sternly against your own demanding standard of judicial effectiveness is characteristic, but it comes as an immediate disappointment.

    Still, if you will allow it, I will say that there is also consolation in your decision. I believe it good for you as well as for the rest of us that you should now be free, in reflective leisure, for activities that are impossible in the demanding life of a Justice of the Supreme Court. You have been part of American public life for well over half a century. What you have learned of the meaning of our country is reflected, of course, in many hundreds of opinions, in thousands of your students, and in dozens of books and articles. But you have a very great deal still to tell us, and therefore I am glad to know that the doctors are telling you, in effect, not to retire, but only to turn to a new line of work, with new promise of service to the nation.

    Meanwhile, I should like to offer to Mrs. Frankfurter and to you, for myself and for all Americans, our respectful gratitude for the character, courage, learning and judicial dedication with which you have served your country over the last twenty-three years.

Sincerely,

JOHN KENNEDY

The Honorable Felix Frankfurter,
Associate Justice,
Supreme Court of the United States,
Washington, D.C.[13]

On September 27, 1962, the Justices wrote to their colleague:

Supreme Court of the United States,
Chambers of The Chief Justice,
Washington 25, D.C., September 27, 1962.

Honorable Felix Frankfurter,
Associate Justice of the Supreme Court, Retired,
Washington, D.C.

Dear Justice Frankfurter:
As the opening day of our 1962 Term approaches, it becomes increasingly difficult for all of us to realize that you will not be in your accustomed chair, which you filled with such distinction and in such good fellowship with your colleagues for almost a quarter of a century.

All of us, except Mr. Justice White, our newest member, have served with you for years and we, more than any others, will feel the loss that comes from your retirement. We regret the necessity for it, but we reluctantly accept your decision because your doctor has told you and us that if this course is pursued there will be opened to you new avenues of usefulness to the profession to which you dedicated yourself 60 years ago.

Every one of those years was an eventful year for you as you strained every fiber of your mind and body to the administration of justice and to the welfare of the Court. Few men in the life of the Supreme Court have made contributions to its jurisprudence equal to your own. As a scholar, teacher, critic, public servant, and a member of the Court for 24 Terms, you have woven your philosophy of law and your conception of our institutions into its annals where all may read them and profit thereby.

Your retirement does not end our association. It merely

changes the form of it. You will always be one of us, and after rest and relaxation from the rigors of the Court work restore you to health, we look forward to years of continued happy association with you. In the meantime, our best wishes for a rapid recovery will always be with you.

Sincerely,

EARL WARREN

HUGO L. BLACK

WM. O. DOUGLAS

TOM C. CLARK

JOHN M. HARLAN

WM. J. BRENNAN, JR.

POTTER STEWART

BYRON R. WHITE[14]

The next day Justice Frankfurter replied:

Supreme Court of the United States,
Chambers of Justice Felix Frankfurter,
Washington, D.C., September 28, 1962.

My Dear Brethren:

It would be unnatural for me not to address you thus, although you have been apprised that I have advised the President of my decision to retire as of August 28th, under the appropriate provisions of law, as an active member of the Court. I still address you as I do, for the endeavors which the business of the Court entails in the daily intimacy of our association have forged bonds of fellowship which cannot be abruptly severed. The final manifestation of your fraternal feelings toward me, your letter of September 27th, your generous words of farewell, are a cheering close to our uniformly happy curial relations over the years, and I shall enduringly cherish your moving letter. Retiring from active membership on the Court of itself would involve a wrench in my life, but the fact is that I have served the Court in one professional way or another almost from the day that I ceased to be a law student, not merely during the years that I have actually been on the Bench.

My years on the Court have only deepened my conviction that its existence and functioning according to its best historic traditions are indispensable for the well-being of the nation. The nature of the issues which are involved in the legal controversies that are inevitable under our constitutional system does not warrant the nation to expect identity of views among the members of the Court regarding such issues, nor even agreement on the routes of thought by which decisions are reached. The nation is merely warranted in expecting harmony of aims among those who have been called to the Court. This means pertinacious pursuit of the processes of Reason in the disposition of the controversies that come before the Court. This presupposes intellectual disinterestedness in the analysis of the factors involved in the issues that call for decision. This in turn requires rigorous self-scrutiny to discover, with a view to curbing, every influence that may deflect from such disinterestedness.

I have spent happy years in my fellowship with you and I carry away the abiding memory of years of comradeship in grappling with problems worthy of the best in fallible men.

My best wishes for happy, long years for each of you and continued satisfying labors, and every good wish that the Court may continue its indispensable role in the evolution of our beloved nation.

With the happiest memories, I am
Sincerely and faithfully yours,
FELIX FRANKFURTER[15]

Justice Frankfurter never fully regained his health. He died on February 23, 1965. The following Monday, March 1, Chief Justice Warren began the Court's proceedings with these words:

It is on a note of sadness that we open this session of the court because, since we last met, our friend and brother, Felix Frankfurter, has passed away.

It was 26 years ago on Jan. 30 that Mr. Felix Frankfurter took his seat on this court. One week ago, he died after a gallant fight for the restoration of the health which he had lost three years ago. In more than 23 years of service here, he had one of the longest and, without doubt, one of the most brilliant careers in the history of the court.

He was one of the most knowledgeable of men. He came to his high position with a combination of scholarship and public experience rarely equalled. As a scholar, teacher, public servant, man of letters, patron of the arts, and the confidant of Presidents, he had already made great contributions to the life of our nation.

But notwithstanding his manifold activities, the law was always his preoccupation. He caught its spirit early in life, and to his very last day devoted himself fervently to its development under the Constitution which he revered.

His death leaves a great void in the communities of scholars and jurists, but fortunately his written words, so pregnant with meaning, will be a heritage for all who love the law and believe in it as the sheet anchor of our civilization.

We of the Supreme Court who knew him so well mourn his passing, both as our associate and friend, but we also know that his ebullient spirit would want us to get on with our always unfinished work.[16]

NOTES

IV. Democratic Restraints on the Power to Govern

THE FIRST AMENDMENT

[1] *Palko v. Connecticut,* 302 U.S. 319, 326–27 (1937).

[2] Milton Sanford Mayer, ed., *The Tradition of Freedom: Selections from the Writers Who Shaped the Traditional Concepts of Freedom and Justice in America* (New York: Oceana Publications, 1957), pp. 10–11.

[3] Thomas Jefferson, *Writings,* Paul L. Ford, ed., 10 vols. (New York: Putnam's Sons, 1892–99), X, 140.

[4] Saul K. Padover, ed., *The Complete Jefferson* (New York: distributed by Duell, Sloan & Pearce, 1943), pp. 384–85.

[5] James Parker Hall, "Free Speech in War Time," 21 *Columbia Law Review* 526, 527–28 (1921).

[6] *Schenck v. United States,* 249 U.S. 47, 51–52 (1919).

[7] *Abrams v. United States,* 250 U.S. 616, 627–31 (1919).

[8] Hall, 21 *Columbia Law Review* 528.

[9] Zechariah Chafee, Jr., *Free Speech in the United States* (Cambridge: Harvard University Press, 1946), p. 51.

[10] *Gitlow v. New York,* 268 U.S. 652, 659–60 (1925).

[11] See *Barron v. Baltimore,* 7 Pet. 243 (1833).

[12] 268 U.S. 666.

[13] Ibid., pp. 668–69.

[14] Ibid., pp. 672–73.

[14a] Gitlow, while still in prison, was the Communist Party vice-presidential candidate in 1924, as he was again in 1928. He enlivened the 1924 campaign by promising that he and his running mate, William Z. Foster, would, if elected, "use one room in the White House and turn the rest of the mansion into apartments for the workers and poor farmers." The Foster-Gitlow ticket did not prevail. In 1929, Gitlow and other leaders of the American Communist Party were expelled from the Communist International by Stalin. Gitlow died in 1965. *The New York Times,* July 20, 1965, p. 33C.

[14b] In *Lamont v. Postmaster General,* 381 U.S. 301 (1965), the Court invalidated a 1962 law empowering the Secretary of the Treasury to intercept, and hold until notice was given to the addressee and delivery requested by him, mail found by the Secretary to be "communist political propaganda."

[15] *Whitney v. California,* 274 U.S. 380 (1927).

[16] Felix Frankfurter, *Law and Politics: Occasional Papers of Felix Frankfurter, 1913–1938,* Archibald MacLeish and E. F. Prichard, Jr., eds. (New York: Harcourt, Brace & Co., 1939), p. 120.

[17] 274 U.S. 373–77.

[18] *Dunne v. United States,* 138 F.2d 137 (C.A.8, 1943), *cert. denied,* 320 U.S. 790 (1943).

[19] See *United States v. McWilliams,* 163 F.2d 695 (C.A. D.C., 1947).

[20] *Dennis v. United States,* 341 U.S. 494 (1951). But see *Yates v. United States,* 354 U.S. 298 (1957), which imposed on the government so rigorous a burden of proving defendants' knowledge of the party's unlawful purposes as, for a time, to impede widespread application of the Smith Act; but cf. *Scales v. United States,* 367 U.S. 203 (1961).

[20a] See, e.g., as to: picketing—*International Brotherhood of Teamsters v. Vogt,* 354 U.S. 284 (1957); legislative investigations—*Gibson v. Florida Legislative Investigation Committee,* 372 U.S. 539 (1963), and *Barenblatt v. United States,* 360 U.S. 109; loyalty programs—Ralph S. Brown, Jr., *Loyalty and Security* (New Haven: Yale University Press, 1958); obscene books and motion pictures—*Roth v. United States,* 354 U.S. 476 (1957), *Kingsley Books v. Brown,* 354 U.S. 436 (1957) and *Freedman v. Maryland,* 380 U.S. 51 (1965); contempt of court—*Wood v. Georgia,* 370 U.S. 375 (1962); deportation—*Harisiades v. Shaughnessy,* 342 U.S. 580 (1952) and *Rowoldt v. Perfetto,* 355 U.S. 115 (1957); libel—*New York Times Co. v. Sullivan,* 376 U.S. 254 (1964) (in this pioneering decision, the Court held that a public official may not recover damages for false criticism of his official conduct unless the defendant can be shown to have spoken or written with reckless or malicious disregard of the truth).

[21] Learned Hand, *The Spirit of Liberty: Papers and Addresses;* collected, and with an introduction and notes, by Irving Dilliard, 3d ed., enl. (New York: Knopf, 1960), p. 189.

[22] See volume 1, p. 122.

[23] *The New York Times,* June 23, 1960, p. 1.

[24] *Rockwell v. Morris,* 211 N.Y.S.2d 25, 35–36 (1961).

[25] Ibid., pp. 50–51.

[26] *The New York Times,* Feb. 1, 1962, p. 30.

[27] *Feiner v. New York,* 340 U.S. 315 (1951).

[28] Ibid., p. 317.

[29] Ibid., p. 330.

[30] Ibid., p. 275.

[31] Ibid., p. 314.

[32] *Edwards v. South Carolina,* 372 U.S. 229 (1963).

[33] *Fields v. City of Fairfield,* 143 So. 2d 177, 178 (1962); reversed *per curiam* 375 U.S. 248 (1963).

[34] 143 So. 2d 178.

[35] 330 U.S. 258 (1947).

[36] *Fields v. Fairfield,* 375 U.S. 248 (1963).

[37] 362 U.S. 199 (1960), considered below, pp. 179–83.

[38] 368 U.S. 157 (1961).

[39] *The New York Times,* Aug. 6, 1964, p. 18.

[40] 268 U.S. 652 (1925), set forth above, p. 11.

[41] *Marsh v. Alabama,* 326 U.S. 501 (1946).

[42] 325 U.S. 761 (1945).

[43] 354 U.S. 234, 256 (1957).

[44] Paul A. Freund, *On Understanding the Supreme Court* (Boston: Little, Brown & Co., 1951), p. 42.

[45] Hugo L. Black, "The Bill of Rights," 35 *New York University Law Review* 865 (1960).

[46] *Barenblatt v. United States,* 360 U.S. 109, 140 (1959), dissenting opinion.

[47] See ibid., p. 143.

[48] Cf. Alexander M. Bickel, "Mr. Justice Black," *The New Republic,* March 14, 1960; Louis H. Pollak, "Language and Its Interpreters," *The New Republic,* May 23, 1960; Charles L. Black, Jr., "Mr. Justice Black, the Supreme Court, and the Bill of Rights," *Harper's,* Feb. 1961; Charles A. Reich, "Mr. Justice Black and the Living Constitution," 76 *Harvard Law Review* 673 (1963).

[49] Thomas I. Emerson, "Toward a General Theory of the First Amendment," 72 *Yale Law Journal* 877, 893–95 (1963).

[50] *Everson v. Board of Education,* 330 U.S. 1, 33 (1947), dissenting opinion.

[51] Theodore H. White, *The Making of the President 1960* (New York: Atheneum Publishers, 1961), pp. 237–38.

[52] Leo Pfeffer, *Church, State and Freedom* (Boston: Beacon Press, 1953), p. 95.

[53] Henry Steele Commager, ed., *Documents of American History,* 4th ed. (New York: Appleton-Century-Crofts, 1948), p. 104. The paragraph quoted is variously attributed to Patrick Henry and to Madison and George Mason. Pfeffer, *Church, State and Freedom,* p. 95; Justice Rutledge dissenting in *Everson v. Board of Education,* 330 U.S. 1, 34 (1947).

[54] 330 U.S. 1, 72–73.

[55] Ibid., p. 72.

[56] Reprinted as Appendix to dissenting opinion of Justice Rutledge, in *Everson v. Board of Education,* 330 U.S. 1, 63–71.

[57] Commager, *Documents,* pp. 125–26.

[58] Padover, *The Complete Jefferson,* pp. 518–19.

[59] *McCollum v. Board of Education,* 333 U.S. 203 (1948).

[60] Ibid., p. 246, dissenting opinion.

[61] Samuel E. Morison, ed., *Sources and Documents Illustrating the American Revolution* (Oxford: Clarendon Press, 1923), p. xl.

[62] See volume 1, p. 43.

[63] John Courtney Murray, "Law or Prepossessions?," 14 *Law and Contemporary Problems* 23, 41 (1949).

64 Alexis de Tocqueville, *Democracy in America,* 2 vols. (New York: J. and H. G. Langley, 1841), I, 337.

65 *McGowan v. Maryland,* 366 U.S. 420 (1961).

66 *Torcaso v. Watkins,* 367 U.S. 488 (1961).

67 *McCollum v. Board of Education,* 333 U.S. 203, 214–16.

68 22 *Catholic World* 433, 434–35 (1876).

69 Pfeffer, *Church, State and Freedom,* pp. 429, 513.

70 *Pierce v. Society of Sisters,* 268 U.S. 535 (1925).

71 *Hamilton v. Regents,* 293 U.S. 245 (1934).

72 *Minersville School Dist. v. Gobitis,* 310 U.S. 586 (1940).

73 *Board of Education v. Barnette,* 319 U.S. 642 (1943).

74 Ibid., pp. 659–61.

75 *Everson v. Board of Education,* 330 U.S. 1, 16 (1947).

76 Ibid., p. 17.

77 Ibid., pp. 44–46.

78 Ibid., p. 63.

79 *McCollum v. Board of Education,* 333 U.S. 203, 205 (1948).

80 Ibid., pp. 209–210.

81 See, for example, the symposium "Religion and the State," in *Law and Contemporary Problems,* winter, 1949.

82 *Zorach v. Clauson,* 343 U.S. 306 (1952).

83 *Engel v. Vitale,* 370 U.S. 421 (1962).

84 Ibid., p. 442.

85 Ibid.

86 Ibid., p. 443.

87 See Louis H. Pollak, "W.B.R.: Some Reflections," 71 *Yale Law Journal* 1451, 1455–58 (1962).

88 370 U.S. 444.

89 Ibid., p. 435 n. 21.

90 *The New York Times,* June 27, 1962, p. 1.

91 Leo Pfeffer, "Court, Constitution and Prayer," 16 *Rutgers Law Review,* 735 (1962).

92 *The New York Times,* June 27, 1962, p. 1.

93 Ibid.

94 *The New York Times,* June 28, 1962, p. 12.

95 *The New York Times,* June 26, 1962, p. 1.

96 *The New York Times,* July 11, 1962, p. 24.

97 *The New York Times,* June 26, 1962, p. 1.

98 *New Haven Register,* Dec. 12, 1962, p. 2.

99 *The New York Times,* June 26, 1962, p. 1.

100 See, for example, Philip B. Kurland, "The Regents Prayer Case, 'Full of Sound and Fury, Signifying . . . ,'" 1962 *Supreme Court Review* 1; Arthur E. Sutherland, "Establishment According to Engel," 76 *Harvard Law Review* 25 (1962); "The Supreme Court, the First Amendment, and Religion in the Public Schools," 63 *Columbia Law Review* 73 (1963).

101 Paul A. Freund, address before the American Jewish Committee, Boston, Nov. 11, 1962.

102 *The New York Times,* June 17, 1963, editorial page, col. 1.

103 *Abington Township School District v. Schempp,* 374 U.S. 203, 222–26 (1963).

104 Ibid., pp. 234–42.

105 Ibid., pp. 312–13.

106 Louis H. Pollak, "The Supreme Court 1962 Term Foreword: Public Prayers in Public Schools," 77 *Harvard Law Review* 62, 77 (1963).

107 *The New York Times,* June 18, 1963, p. 27.

108 *The New York Times,* Aug. 7, 1963, p. 35.

109 *The New York Times,* Aug. 6, 1963, p. 1.

110 See below, p. 290.

111 See, for example, "The Constitutionality of the Inclusion of Church-Related Schools in Federal Aid to Education," 50 *Georgetown Law Journal* 397 (1961).

112 See earlier, p. 90.

113 White, *The Making of the President 1960,* pp. 391–93.

114 *Griswold v. Connecticut,* 381 U.S. 479 (1965). To be sure, there was no formal insistence by the American Catholic bishops on the propriety of the Connecticut law; indeed, many influential Catholics, here and abroad, had long since challenged traditional church opposition to birth control mechanisms. See John Thomas Noonan, *Contraception—A History of Its Treatment* (Cambridge: Harvard University Press, 1965).

115 *The New York Times,* July 18, 1965, Sec. 6.

DUE PROCESS OF LAW IN CRIMINAL TRIALS

1 *Burdeau v. McDowell,* 256 U.S. 465, 477 (1921), dissenting opinion.

2 *People v. Gitlow,* 234 N.Y. 132, 158 (1922), dissenting opinion, *affirmed* 268 U.S. 652 (1925).

3 Felix Frankfurter, "Mr. Justice Brandeis and the Constitution," 45 *Harvard Law Review* 33, 94 (1931).

4 See Carl B. Swisher, *Roger B. Taney* (New York: Macmillan Co., 1935), pp. 550 ff.

5 *Ex parte Merryman,* 17 Fed. Cases 144 (1861).

6 See below, p. 209.

7 Robert H. Jackson, *The Struggle for Judicial Supremacy* (New York: Knopf, 1941), pp. 326–27.

8 James D. Richardson, comp., *A Compilation of the Messages and Papers of the Presidents,* 20 vols. (New York: Bureau of National Literature, Inc., 1897–1922), VII, 3225–26.

9 James Garfield Randall, *Constitutional Problems under Lincoln.* (New York: Appleton, 1926), p. 162 n. 43.

10 See below, p. 212.

11 Four Justices were unwilling to go so far, and perhaps they were prescient: see *Ex parte Quirin,* 317 U.S. 1 (1942) sustaining military trials of German saboteurs (one apparently an American citizen)

delivered by German submarines to Long Island and Florida and subsequently apprehended in New York and Chicago. But see, more recently, *Kinsella v. Singleton*, 361 U.S. 234 (1960), and *McElroy v. Guagliardo*, 361 U.S. 281 (1960) barring courts-martial at American bases abroad of (1) civilian dependents of military personnel and (2) civilian employees of the armed services.

[12] *Ex parte Milligan*, 4 Wall. 2, 120–21 (1866).

[13] See William Allen Jowitt, *The Strange Case of Alger Hiss* (Garden City: Doubleday & Co., 1953); Alistair Cooke, *A Generation on Trial: U.S.A. v. Alger Hiss* (New York: Knopf, 1952); Whittaker Chambers, *Witness* (New York: Random House, 1952); Alger Hiss, *In the Court of Public Opinion* (New York: Knopf, 1957).

[14] *Hiss v. United States*, 340 U.S. 948 (1951).

[15] *Rosenberg v. United States*, 346 U.S. 273 (1953).

[16] See *Chessman v. Teets*, 350 U.S. 3 (1955).

[17] See E. Barrett Prettyman, Jr., *Death and the Supreme Court* (New York: Harcourt, Brace & World, 1961); William Styron, "The Living Death of Benjamin Reid," *Esquire*, Feb. 1962.

[18] Zechariah Chafee, Jr., Walter H. Pollak, and Carl S. Stern, *Draft Mooney-Billings Report Submitted to the National Commission on Law Observance and Enforcement, Appendix A* (1931), p. 9.

[19] *Mooney v. Holohan*, 294 U.S. 103 (1935).

[20] Henry M. Hart, Jr., and Herbert Wechsler, *The Federal Courts and the Federal System* (Brooklyn: Foundation Press, 1953), p. 1256, n. 3.

[21] For example, Robert H. Montgomery, *Sacco-Vanzetti: The Murder and the Myth* (New York: Devin-Adair Co., 1960).

[22] See Felix Frankfurter, *The Case of Sacco and Vanzetti* (Boston: Little, Brown & Co., 1961); George L. Joughin and Edmund M. Morgan, *The Legacy of Sacco and Vanzetti* (New York: Harcourt, Brace & Co., 1948); *Hearings before Joint Judiciary Committee of Massachusetts Legislature on the Sacco-Vanzetti Case*, April 2, 1959 (published by the Committee for the Vindication of Sacco and Vanzetti, 1959); Herbert B. Ehrmann, *The Untried Case: The Sacco and Vanzetti Case and the Morelli Gang* (New York: Vanguard Press, 1960). One recent study (Francis Russell, *Tragedy in Dedham: The Story of the Sacco-Vanzetti Case*, [New York: McGraw Hill, 1962]) suggests that Sacco was guilty and Vanzetti innocent. But see Ben H. Bagdikian, "New Light on Sacco and Vanzetti," *The New Republic*, July 13, 1963.

[23] *Powell v. Alabama*, 287 U.S. 45 (1932).

[24] See *Norris v. Alabama*, 294 U.S. 587 (1935); cf. *Patterson v. Alabama*, 294 U.S. 600 (1935).

[25] See Paul A. Freund and others, *Constitutional Law: Cases and Other Problems*, 2d ed., 2 vols. (Boston: Little, Brown & Co., 1961), II, 1113–14.

[26] See Arthur Garfield Hays, *Trial by Prejudice* (New York: Covici-Friede, 1933); Quentin Reynolds, *Courtroom* (New York: Farrar, Straus and Co., 1950).

[27] See earlier, pp. 11–15.

[28] *Powell v. Alabama,* 287 U.S. 45 (1932).

[29] 316 U.S. 455 (1942).

[30] See Paul A. Freund, *On Understanding the Supreme Court* (Boston: Little, Brown & Co., 1951); Yale Kamisar, "The Right to Counsel and the Fourteenth Amendment," 30 *Univ. of Chicago Law Review* 1, 684 (1962).

[31] 332 U.S. 46, 71 (1947), considered below, pp. 156–59.

[32] Freund, *On Understanding the Supreme Court,* pp. 34–35.

[33] *Gideon v. Wainwright,* 372 U.S. 338 (1963).

[34] Ibid., p. 345.

[35] Ibid., p. 349.

[36] Ibid.

[37] Anthony Lewis, *Gideon's Trumpet* (New York: Random House, 1964), pp. 221–22.

[38] *Sweezy v. New Hampshire,* 354 U.S. 234, 267 (1957), concurring opinion.

[39] Lewis, *Gideon's Trumpet,* p. 238.

[40] *Hardy v. Mississippi,* No. 22005, Jan. 12, 1965. Cf. the decisions of the Appellate Division of the Connecticut Circuit Court in *State v. Krozel* and *State v. Lucas, Cases Argued and Determined in the Appellate Division of the Circuit Court, State of Connecticut* (1963), III, 104 and 62, respectively; discussed in Louis H. Pollak, Book Review, 38 *Connecticut Bar Journal* 720, 723–26 (1964).

[41] *Palko v. Connecticut,* 302 U.S. 319 (1937).

[42] 211 U.S. 78 (1908).

[43] See p. 141.

[44] *Adamson v. California,* 332 U.S. 46 (1947).

[45] Ibid., pp. 74–75.

[46] See volume 1, pp. 301–7.

[47] 332 U.S. 75.

[48] Ibid., pp. 67–68.

[49] *Francis v. Resweber,* 329 U.S. 459, 460, 472 (1947).

[50] Ibid., p. 480 n. 2.

[51] Charles Pelham Curtis, *Law as Large as Life* (New York: Simon and Schuster, 1959), pp. 31–32.

[52] *Sweezy v. New Hampshire,* 354 U.S. 234, 267, concurring opinion of Justice Frankfurter.

[53] *Francis v. Resweber,* 329 U.S. 459 (1947).

[54] Fowler V. Harper, *Justice Rutledge and the Bright Constellation* (Indianapolis: Bobbs-Merrill Co., 1965), p. 356.

[55] Felix Frankfurter, *Of Law and Men: Papers and Addresses, 1939–1956,* Philip Elman, ed. (New York: Harcourt, Brace, 1956), pp. 98–99.

[56] William J. Brennan, Jr., "The Bill of Rights and the States," 36 *New York University Law Review,* 761, 769 (1961).

[57] 367 U.S. 643 (1961), quoted below, p. 194.

[58] 372 U.S. 335 (1963), quoted above, p. 143.

⁵⁹ 378 U.S. 1 (1964). A year later the Court held that state court judges and prosecutors may not comment on a defendant's failure to take the witness stand. *Griffin v. California,* 380 U.S. 609 (1965).

⁶⁰ 378 U.S. 4–8.

⁶¹ Ibid., p. 15.

⁶² See Louis Henkin, "'Selective Incorporation' in the Fourteenth Amendment," 73 *Yale Law Journal* 74 (1963).

⁶³ *Rudolph v. Alabama,* 84 S. Ct. 155 (1963).

⁶⁴ Susanna McBee, "Edging Away from Capital Punishment," *The New Republic,* Jan. 30, 1965, pp. 11–12.

⁶⁵ *The New York Times,* Dec. 22, 1964, p. 14.

⁶⁶ Freund, *On Understanding the Supreme Court,* p. 43.

⁶⁷ *Thompson v. Louisville,* 362 U.S. 199 (1960).

⁶⁸ Zechariah Chafee, Jr., Walter H. Pollak, and Carl S. Stern, *Lawlessness in Law Enforcement* (National Commission on Law Observance and Enforcement, 1931), IV, 1.

⁶⁹ *Olmstead v. United States,* 277 U.S. 438 (1928); cf. *On Lee v. United States,* 343 U.S. 747 (1952); *Silverman v. United States,* 365 U.S. 505 (1961).

⁷⁰ See *Nardone v. United States,* 302 U.S. 379 (1937).

⁷¹ See *Benanti v. United States,* 355 U.S. 96 (1957); "Wiretapping, Eavesdropping and the Bill of Rights," *Hearings before the Subcommittee on Constitutional Rights of the Committee on the Judiciary,* United States Senate, 85th and 86th Cong. (1958 and 1959); Louis H. Pollak, "Wiretapping—Lawlessness in Law Enforcement," *The New Republic,* May 16, 1960, p. 13.

⁷² See *McDonald v. United States,* 355 U.S. 863 (1948); cf. *Abel v. United States,* 362 U.S. 217 (1960).

⁷³ See *Mapp v. Ohio,* 367 U.S. 643 (1961) and *Monroe v. Pape,* 365 U.S. 167 (1961).

⁷⁴ *Wolf v. Colorado,* 338 U.S. 25 (1949).

⁷⁵ See *Ashcraft v. Tennessee,* 322 U.S. 143 (1944).

⁷⁶ See *Leyra v. Denno,* 347 U.S. 556 (1954); and cf. *Lisenba v. California,* 314 U.S. 219, 239–40 (1941).

⁷⁷ See *Brown v. Mississippi,* 297 U.S. 278 (1936).

⁷⁸ See *Bram v. United States,* 168 U.S. 532 (1897); *Chambers v. Florida,* 309 U.S. 227 (1940).

⁷⁹ See *Mallory v. United States,* 354 U.S. 449 (1957); *McNabb v. United States,* 318 U.S. 332 (1943); "Confessions and Public Detention," *Hearings before the Subcommittee on Constitutional Rights of the Committee on the Judiciary,* United States Senate, 85th Cong., 2d Sess., March 7 and 11, 1958.

⁷⁹ᵃ "The Suspect Confesses—But Who Believes Him?" *The New York Times,* May 16, 1965, Sec. 6.

⁸⁰ *Nardone v. United States,* 302 U.S. 379 (1937), and 308 U.S. 338 (1939); *Benanti v. United States,* 355 U.S. 96 (1957).

⁸¹ *Schwartz v. Texas,* 344 U.S. 199 (1952); cf. *Pugach v. Dollinger,* 365 U.S. 458 (1961).

[82] 232 U.S. 383 (1914).

[83] *Wolf v. Colorado,* 338 U.S. 25, 27–28 (1949).

[84] Ibid., p. 31.

[85] See above, pp. 157–59.

[86] 338 U.S. 39–40.

[87] Ibid., pp. 47–48.

[88] *Rochin v. California,* 342 U.S. 172–74 (1952).

[89] Ibid., p. 174.

[90] *Irvine v. California,* 347 U.S. 128 (1954).

[91] Ibid., pp. 138–39.

[92] *Mapp v. Ohio,* 367 U.S. 643 (1961).

[93] Ibid., p. 668, concurring opinion.

[94] Ibid., p. 673, dissenting opinion.

[95] Ibid., p. 672.

[96] Ibid., pp. 644–45.

[97] Ibid., pp. 661–63, 666.

[98] See Edwin M. Borchard, *Convicting the Innocent* (New Haven: Yale University Press, 1932); Jerome Frank and Barbara Frank, *Not Guilty* (New York: Doubleday & Co., 1957).

[99] See the table of coerced-confession cases that appears in *U.S. Commission on Civil Rights—Report on Justice* (1961), pp. 256–62.

[100] *Olmstead v. United States,* 277 U.S. 438, 470 (1928).

[101] Ibid., p. 485.

[102] *The New York Times,* Aug. 11, 1964, p. 1.

[103] Brennan, 36 *New York University Law Review,* 761, 778 (1961).

[104] Cited in Arthur J. Goldberg, "Equality and Government," 39 *New York University Law Review* 205, 225 n. 97 (1964).

"ALL MEN ARE CREATED EQUAL"

[1] Set forth earlier, volume 1, pp. 230–47.

[2] 8 Fed. Cas. 493 (C.C.D. S.C., 1823).

[3] Donald G. Morgan, *Justice William Johnson, the First Dissenter* (Columbia: University of South Carolina Press, 1954), pp. 192–202.

[4] Charles Warren, *The Supreme Court in United States History,* 3 vols. (Boston: Little, Brown & Co., 1922), III, 17 n. 1.

[5] Ibid., p. 18.

[6] See Robert H. Jackson, *The Struggle for Judicial Supremacy* (New York: Knopf, 1941), pp. 326–27, quoted earlier, p. 122.

[7] *Scott v. Sandford,* 19 How. 393 (1857).

[8] Paul M. Angle, ed., *Created Equal? The Complete Lincoln-Douglas Debates of 1858* (Chicago: University of Chicago Press, 1958), pp. 77–79.

[9] Ibid., pp. 394–96.

[10] Harry V. Jaffa, *Crisis of the House Divided* (Garden City: Doubleday & Co., 1959), p. 10.

[11] "Emancipation Proclamation," *U.S. Statutes,* XII, 1268–69.

[12] See Thomas I. Emerson and Arthur E. Bonfield, "A Proposal for Enforcement of Section 2 of the Fourteenth Amendment," *The Nation,*

Jan. 21, 1960, p. 55. Subsequent litigation has not been fruitful.

[13] See *Smith v. Allwright,* 321 U.S. 649 (1944); *Terry v. Adams,* 345 U.S. 461 (1953).

[14] See volume 1, p. 276.

[15] 16 Wall. 81.

[16] *Strauder v. West Virginia,* 100 U.S. 303, 307 (1880).

[17] 100 U.S. 339 (1880).

[18] 18 U.S. 356 (1886).

[19] See, for example, the Supreme Court's decision in *Norris v. Alabama,* 294 U.S. 587 (1935), which was the Court's *second* reversal of the successive convictions in the *Scottsboro Cases;* cf. *Powell v. Alabama,* 287 U.S. 45 (1932), the Supreme Court's first decision in the *Scottsboro Cases,* set forth earlier, p. 130.

[20] 109 U.S. 3 (1883).

[21] Ibid., p. 19.

[22] 95 U.S. 485 (1878), set forth in volume 1, p. 260.

[23] 109 U.S. 24–25.

[24] See earlier, p. 38.

[25] *Dorsey v. Stuvyesant Town,* 299 N.Y. 512 (1949); *cert. denied,* 339 U.S. 981 (1950).

[26] Jack Greenberg, *Race Relations and American Law* (New York: Columbia University Press, 1959), p. 46.

[27] Cf. *Railway Mail Ass'n v. Corsi,* 326 U.S. 88 (1945).

[28] 109 U.S. 24–25, quoted earlier, p. 230.

[29] William O. Douglas, *The Rule of Law in World Affairs* (Santa Barbara, Cal.: Center for the Study of Democratic Institutions, 1961), p. 5.

[30] 334 U.S. 1 (1948).

[31] See *Barrows v. Jackson,* 346 U.S. 249 (1953); and cf. Louis Henkin, "*Shelley v. Kraemer:* Notes for a Revised Opinion," 110 *University of Pennsylvania Law Review* 473 (1962).

[32] 362 U.S. 199 (1960), quoted earlier, p. 194.

[33] *Garner v. Louisiana,* 368 U.S. 157 (1961).

[34] *Peterson v. Greenville,* 373 U.S. 244 (1963).

[35] *Bell v. Maryland,* 378 U.S. 226 (1964).

[36] Ibid., pp. 227–37.

[37] Ibid., p. 244.

[38] Ibid., pp. 322–23.

[39] Ibid., pp. 326–43.

[40] Ibid., p. 286.

[41] Ibid., pp. 290–311.

[42] See pp. 296–341.

[43] See volume 1, p. 260.

[44] See pp. 228–32.

[44a] *Plessy v. Ferguson,* 163 U.S. 537 (1896).

[45] See *Civil Rights Cases,* as reported in *Lawyers' Edition,* XXVII, 837.

[46] 163 U.S. 548 (1896).

⁴⁷ See *Travelers' Official Railway Guide,* Jan. 1896, Timetables, pp. 667–68; Maps, pp. 22, 686.

⁴⁸ 222 U.S. 20 (1911), set forth earlier, volume 1, p. 312.

⁴⁹ *State ex rel. Abbott v. Judge,* 44 La. Ann. 770 (1892).

⁵⁰ C. Vann Woodward, "The Case of the Louisiana Traveler," in John A. Garraty, ed., *Quarrels That Have Shaped the Constitution,* (New York: Harper & Row, 1964), p. 147.

⁵¹ *Ex parte Plessy,* 45 La. Ann. 80, 87.

⁵² Woodward, in Garraty, *Quarrels,* pp. 152–53.

⁵³ 163 U.S. 550–51.

⁵⁴ 100 U.S. 303, 307.

⁵⁵ See, for example, his dissent in *Lochner v. New York,* 198 U.S. 45 (1905), quoted earlier, volume 1, p. 295.

⁵⁶ See *Adair v. United States,* 208 U.S. 161 (1908); *Cumming v. Board of Education,* 175 U.S. 528 (1899).

⁵⁷ Paul A. Freund and others, *Constitutional Law: Cases and Other Problems,* 2d ed., 2 vols. (Boston: Little, Brown & Co., 1961), II, xl.

⁵⁸ 163 U.S. 559.

⁵⁹ *Plessy v. Ferguson,* 163 U.S. 537 (1896).

⁶⁰ C. Vann Woodward, *The Strange Career of Jim Crow* (New York: Oxford University Press, 1957), p. 93.

⁶¹ *Korematsu v. United States,* 323 U.S. 214 (1944).

⁶² Alexander M. Bickel, "The Original Understanding and the Segregation Decision," 69 *Harvard Law Review* 1, 64 (1955).

⁶³ Ibid., pp. 63–64, 65.

⁶⁴ *Brown v. Board of Education,* 347 U.S. 483 (1954).

⁶⁵ *Bolling v. Sharpe,* 347 U.S. 497 (1954).

⁶⁶ *Brown v. Board of Education,* 349 U.S. 294, 301 (1955).

⁶⁷ James Morton Smith and Paul L. Murphy, eds., *Liberty and Justice: A Historical Record of American Constitutional Development* (New York: Knopf, 1958), p. 562.

⁶⁸ *Board of Education v. Barnette,* 319 U.S. 624, 637 (1943).

⁶⁹ See *Ebony,* Dec. 1956, p. 12.

⁷⁰ Bickel, 69 *Harvard Law Review* 65.

⁷¹ Arnold M. Rose, "Sociological Factors in the Effectiveness of Projected Legal Remedies," 11 *Journal of Legal Education* 470 (1959).

⁷² *Brown v. Board of Education,* 347 U.S. 493.

⁷³ *McCollum v. Board of Education,* 333 U.S. 203, 231 (1948), concurring opinion.

⁷⁴ See Louis H. Pollak, "Ten Years after the Decision," 24 *Federal Bar Journal* 123 (1964); Alexander M. Bickel, "The Decade of School Desegregation: Progress and Prospects," 64 *Columbia Law Review* 193 (1964). And see below, pp. 290–96.

⁷⁵ See Hodding Carter, "Desegregation Does Not Mean Integration," *The New York Times,* Feb. 11, 1962, Sec. 6, p. 21.

⁷⁶ See *Civil Rights U.S.A.: Public Schools North and West 1962* (Staff Reports Submitted to and Published by U.S. Commission on Civil Rights).

[77] *Cooper v. Aaron*, 358 U.S. 1, 7 (1958).

[78] *The New York Times*, Sept. 26, 1957, p. 12.

[79] 358 U.S. 1. There was also a concurring opinion by Justice Frankfurter.

[80] See *The New Orleans School Crisis* (Report of the Louisiana State Advisory Committee to the U.S. Commission on Civil Rights).

[81] Reporter's Headnote, *Bush v. Orleans School Board*, 364 U.S. 500 (1960).

[82] Ibid.

[83] *Meredith v. Fair*, 306 F.2d 374 (1962).

[84] *Meredith v. Fair*, 83 S. Ct. 10, 11 (1962).

[85] Ibid.; and see *Fair v. Meredith*, 83 S. Ct. 49 (1962).

[86] *Southern School News*, Oct. 1962, p. 10.

[87] Ibid., p. 12.

[88] Ibid.

[89] Ibid.

[90] See James H. Meredith, "I Can't Fight Alone," *Look*, April 9, 1963, p. 70.

[91] *Watson v. Memphis*, 373 U.S. 526, 539 (1963).

[92] Ibid.

[93] *The New York Times*, June 12, 1963, p. 20.

[94] *Statistical Summary of School Segregation-Desegregation in the Southern and Border States, 1963–1964* (Southern Education Reporting Service), p. 2.

[94a] 377 U.S. 263 (1964).

[95] *Griffin v. Prince Edward School Board*, 377 U.S. 218 (1964).

[96] *Griffin v. Board of Supervisors*, 339 F. 2d 486 (1964).

[97] *Southern School News*, Dec. 1964, p. 1.

[98] See *Civil Rights U.S.A.*; John Kaplan, "Segregation Litigation and the Schools, 58 *Northwestern University Law Review*, 1, 157 (1963); and 59 *Northwestern University Law Review* 121 (1964).

[99] See *Bell v. School City of Gary*, 213 F. Supp. 819, aff'd 324 F. 2d 209 (7th Cir. 1963), *cert. den.* 32 U.S.L.W. 3385 (1964).

[100] See *Morean v. Board of Education*, 42 N.J. 237 (1964); *Balaban v. Rubin*, 14 N.Y.2d 193 (1964).

[101] See *The New York Times*, July 30, 1965, p. 23, and Aug. 3, 1965, p. 1.

[102] *The New York Times*, June 12, 1963, p. 1.

[103] *The New York Times*, Sept. 17, 1963, p. 24.

[104] *The New York Times*, Nov. 28, 1963, p. 1.

[105] 110 *Cong. Rec.*, pp. 13825–26.

[106] Ibid., p. 14010.

[107] Ibid., pp. 13943–44.

[108] Ibid., p. 14012.

[109] Ibid., p. 14013.

[110] *The New York Times*, July 3, 1964, p. 9.

[111] Ibid.

[112] *The New York Times*, July 19, 1964, Sec. 5, p. 10.

[113] *The New York Times,* July 12, 1964, Sec. 5, p. 7.
[114] *New Haven Register,* July 21, 1964, p. 1.
[115] *The New York Times,* July 23, 1964, p. 1.
[116] *McClung v. Katzenbach,* 33 U.S.L.W. 2151, 2152, Sept. 17, 1964.
[117] *The New York Times,* Oct. 6, 1964, p. 28.
[118] Ibid.
[119] See volume 1, p. 181.
[120] *Newsweek,* Nov. 23, 1964, p. 36.
[121] *The New York Times,* Dec. 11, 1964, p. 31.
[122] *Heart of Atlanta Motel v. United States,* 33 U.S.L.W. 4059, 4061–65 (1964).
[123] Ibid., p. 4064.
[124] *The New York Times,* Dec. 15, 1964, p. 50.
[125] *Hamm v. Rock Hill* and *Lupper v. Arkansas,* 379 U.S. 306 (1964).
[126] *The New York Times,* Dec. 20, 1964, Sec. 4, p. 7.
[127] Jack Greenberg, conversation with L. H. Pollak, Dec. 14, 1964.
[128] *The New York Times,* July 30, 1965, p. 23.

THE COURT STRENGTHENS THE FRANCHISE

[1] *Missouri, Kansas & Texas R. Co. v. May,* 194 U.S. 267, 270 (1904).
[2] *Board of Education v. Barnette,* 319 U.S. 624, 667 (1943).
[3] *United States v. Carolene Products Co.,* 304 U.S. 144, 152–53 n. 4 (1938).
[4] *NAACP v. Button,* 371 U.S. 429–31 (1963).
[5] See *Nixon v. Herndon,* 273 U.S. 536 (1927); *Nixon v. Condon,* 286 U.S. 73 (1932); *Grovey v. Townsend,* 295 U.S. 45 (1935); *Smith v. Allwright,* 321 U.S. 649 (1944) (overruling *Grovey v. Townsend); Terry v. Adams,* 345 U.S. 461 (1953).
[6] See U.S. Department of Justice, *Protection of the Rights of Individuals* (1952), p. 4.
[7] *U.S. Commission on Civil Rights—Report on Voting* (1961), p. 22.
[8] Ibid.
[9] *The New York Times,* Aug. 3, 1964.
[10] *The New York Times,* Feb. 17, 1964.
[11] See *United States v. Alabama,* 267 F.2d 808 n. 3 (C.A. 5, 1959).
[12] *Gomillion v. Lightfoot,* 167 F. Supp. 405, 407 (D.C. M.D. Ala., 1958).
[13] *Gomillion v. Lightfoot,* 364 U.S. 339 (1960).
[14] Bernard Taper, *Gomillion v. Lightfoot: The Tuskegee Gerrymander Case* (New York: McGraw-Hill Publishing Co., 1962).
[15] See *Alabama v. United States,* 304 F.2d 583 (C.A. 5, 1962).
[16] *The New York Times,* May 24, 1964, p. 66.
[17] 23 *Cong. Quarterly,* pp. 447–49.
[18] Ibid., pp. 445–47.
[19] 364 U.S. 339 (1960). See above, p. 346.
[20] 364 U.S. 348.

[21] Joseph S. Clark, *Congress: The Sapless Branch* (New York: Harper & Row, 1964), pp. 22–23.

[22] Louis H. Pollak, "Judicial Power and 'The Politics of the People,'" 72 *Yale Law Journal* 81, 88 (1962).

[23] *Colegrove v. Green*, 328 U.S. 549 (1946); *MacDougall v. Green*, 335 U.S. 281 (1948); *South v. Peters*, 339 U.S. 276 (1950). See Anthony Lewis, "Legislative Apportionment and the Federal Courts," 71 *Harvard Law Review* 1057 (1958).

[24] 364 U.S. 341.

[25] 369 U.S. 186 (1962). For a variety of responses to *Baker v. Carr*, see "Symposium," 72 *Yale Law Journal* 8 (1962).

[26] Robert G. McCloskey, "The Reapportionment Case," 76 *Harvard Law Review* 54–59 (1962).

[27] *Gray v. Sanders*, 372 U.S. 368, 382 (1963), dissenting opinion.

[28] Ibid., p. 376 n. 8.

[29] Ibid., p. 381.

[30] Ibid., p. 379.

[31] *Wesberry v. Sanders*, 376 U.S. 1, 14 (1964).

[32] Ibid., pp. 41–42.

[33] Cf. *Wright v. Rockefeller*, 376 U.S. 52 (1964).

[34] 376 U.S. 20–21.

[35] Ibid., p. 49.

[36] *Reynolds v. Sims*, 377 U.S. 533, 562–68 (1964).

[37] Ibid., p. 568.

[38] Ibid., pp. 568–76.

[39] Ibid., p. 579.

[40] Ibid., pp. 576–81.

[41] Ibid., p. 615.

[42] *Lucas v. Colorado General Assembly*, 377 U.S. 744–51 (1964), dissenting opinion.

[43] *The New York Times*, Aug. 10, 1964, p. 36.

[44] *The New York Times*, Aug. 5, 1965, pp. 1, 13.

[45] *The New York Times*, July 17, 1965, p. 9.

V. Amending the Constitution

[1] *Gideon v. Wainwright*, 372 U.S. 335, 345 (1963), concurring opinion.

[2] See earlier, p. 371.

[3] See volume 1, p. 162.

[4] *The New York Times*, May 23, 1963, p. 23.

[5] Charles L. Black, Jr., "The Proposed Amendment of Article V: A Threatened Disaster," 72 *Yale Law Journal* 957 (1963).

VI. Perspectives

[1] Thomas Jefferson, *Writings*, Paul L. Ford, ed., 10 vols. (New York: Putnam's Sons, 1892–99), X, 42–43.

[2] 182 U.S. 244 (1901).

3 Finley Peter Dunne, *Mr. Dooley: Now and Forever;* selected, with commentary and introduction by Louis Filler. (Stanford: Academic Reprints, 1954), pp. 157–62.

4 James B. Thayer, "The Origin and Scope of the American Doctrine of Constitutional Law," *Harvard Law Review* (1893).

5 James B. Thayer, *John Marshall* (Boston: Houghton, Mifflin & Co., 1901), pp. 102–10.

6 Thomas Reed Powell, "Constitutional Metaphors [a review of *The Constitution of the United States,* by James M. Beck]," *The New Republic,* Feb. 11, 1925.

7 David J. Brewer, "Government by Injunction," 15 *Nat. Corp. Rep.* 849 (1898).

8 *The New York Times,* March 3, 1960, p. 14.

9 Charles L. Black, Jr., "The Supreme Court and Democracy," 50 *Yale Review* 188, 198–201 (winter, 1961).

10 *The New York Herald-Tribune,* Aug. 4, 1965, p. 1.

11 Alexander M. Bickel, "Felix Frankfurter 1882–1965," *The New Republic,* March 6, 1965, p. 7.

12 371 U.S. XI.

13 371 U.S. XII.

14 371 U.S. VIII.

15 371 U.S. IX.

16 *The New York Times,* March 2, 1965, p. 43.

APPENDIX

The Birth Control Case
Griswold v. Connecticut (1965)

These two volumes devote much attention to the limitations imposed by the Constitution upon the authority of the several states. And throughout these volumes the editor has frequently advanced the view that on the whole—albeit with a few huge failures—the Supreme Court's policing of these limitations, especially in the last three decades, has been conspicuously successful. These volumes would not be complete if they failed to include an extremely recent instance of this aspect of the Court's work: *Griswold v. Connecticut*, 381 U.S. 479 (1965), involves the validity of a Connecticut statute prohibiting the use of contraceptive devices—a statute the Court had twice before declined to come to grips with. The doctrinal lines pursued by the majority of the Court in striking down the statute (as applied to married couples) take the case out of the doctrinal organization followed by the editor in putting these volumes together. Hence, the case appears here, as an appendix. Collectively the opinions in *Griswold* constitute summaries of, and pointed commentaries upon, many of the major themes developed earlier in these volumes.

The multiplicity and contrariety of the opinions strongly suggest that here (as in *Francis v. Resweber, supra*, pp. 159–171) the Court was unequal to the unique issues it faced. In the editor's view, the Court reached the right result, but the rationales advanced, for five members of the Court, by Justices Douglas and Goldberg, are signally less persuasive than those of their concurring brethren, Justices Harlan and White.

The *Griswold* case (like *Poe v. Ullman*, 367 U.S. 497 [1961], in which a majority of the Court found a challenge to the Connecticut statute not to be justiciable) was planned and developed by the late Fowler V. Harper. Professor Harper died a few short weeks before the Supreme Court argument; in the last days of his illness, he asked his friend and colleague Thomas I. Emerson to carry the case forward.

The opinions follow:

MR. JUSTICE DOUGLAS *delivered the opinion of the Court.*

Appellant Griswold is Executive Director of the Planned Parenthood League of Connecticut. Appellant Buxton is a licensed physician and a professor at the Yale Medical School who served as Medical Director for the League at its Center in New Haven—a center open and operating from November 1 to November 10, 1961, when appellants were arrested.

They gave information, instruction, and medical advice to married persons as to the means of preventing conception. They examined the wife and prescribed the best contraceptive device or material for her use. Fees were usually charged, although some couples were serviced free.

The statutes whose constitutionality is involved in this appeal are §§ 53–32 and 54–196 of the General Statutes of Connecticut (1958 rev.). The former provides:

> *Any person who uses any drug, medicinal article or instrument for the purpose of preventing conception shall be fined not less than fifty dollars or imprisoned not less than sixty days nor more than one year or be both fined and imprisoned.*

Section 54–196 provides:

> *Any person who assists, abets, counsels, causes, hires or commands another to commit any offense may be prosecuted and punished as if he were the principal offender.*

The appellants were found guilty as accessories and fined $100 each, against the claim that the accessory statute as so applied violated the Fourteenth Amendment. The Appellate Division of the Circuit Court affirmed. The Supreme Court of Errors affirmed that judgment. 151 Conn. 544, 200 A. 2d 479. We noted probable jurisdiction. 379 U.S. 926.

We think that appellants have standing to raise the constitutional rights of the married people with whom they had a professional relationship. Tileston v. Ullman, 318 U.S. 44, is different, for there the plaintiff seeking to represent others asked for a declaratory judgment. In that situation we thought that the requirements of standing should be strict, lest the standards of "case or controversy" in Article III of the Constitution become blurred. Here those doubts are removed by reason of a criminal conviction for serving married couples in violation of an aiding-and-abetting statute. Certainly the accessory should have standing to assert that the offense which he is charged with assisting is not, or cannot constitutionally be, a crime.

This case is more akin to Truax v. Raich, 239 U.S. 33, where an employee was permitted to assert the rights of his employer; to Pierce v. Society of Sisters, 268 U.S. 510, where the owners of private schools were entitled to assert the rights of potential pupils and their parents; and to Barrows v. Jackson, 346 U.S. 249, where a white defendant, party to a racially restrictive covenant, who was being sued for damages by the covenantors because she had conveyed her property to Negroes, was allowed to raise the issue that enforcement of the covenant violated the rights of prospective Negro purchasers to equal protection, although no Negro was a party to the suit. And see Meyer v. Nebraska, 262 U.S. 390; Adler v. Board of Education, 342 U.S. 485; NAACP v. Alabama, 357 U.S. 449; NAACP v. Button, 371 U.S. 415. The rights of husband and wife, pressed here, are likely to be diluted or adversely affected unless those rights are considered in a suit involving those who have this kind of confidential relation to them.

Coming to the merits, we are met with a wide range of questions that implicate the Due Process Clause of the Fourteenth Amendment. Overtones of some arguments suggest that Lochner v. New York, 198 U.S. 45, should be our guide. But we decline that invitation. . . . We do not sit as a super-legislature to determine the wisdom, need, and propriety of laws that touch economic problems, business affairs, or social conditions. This law, however, operates directly on an intimate relation of husband and wife and their physician's role in one aspect of that relation.

The association of people is not mentioned in the Constitution nor in the Bill of Rights. The right to educate a child in a school of the parents' choice—whether public or private or parochial—is also not mentioned. Nor is the right to study any particular subject or any foreign language. Yet the First Amendment has been construed to include certain of those rights. . . . [A discussion of cases is omitted.]

Those cases involved more than the *"right of assembly"—a*

right that extends to all irrespective of their race or ideology. De Jonge v. Oregon, 299 U.S. 353. *The right of "association," like the right of belief* (Board of Education v. Barnette, 319 U.S. 624), *is more than the right to attend a meeting; it includes the right to express one's attitudes or philosophies by membership in a group or by affiliation with it or by other lawful means. Association in that context is a form of expression of opinion; and while it is not expressly included in the First Amendment its existence is necessary in making the express guarantees fully meaningful.*

The foregoing cases suggest that specific guarantees in the Bill of Rights have penumbras, formed by emanations from those guarantees that help give them life and substance. See Poe v. Ullman, 367 U.S. 497, 516–522 *(dissenting opinion). Various guarantees create zones of privacy. The right of association contained in the penumbra of the First Amendment is one, as we have seen. The Third Amendment in its prohibition against the quartering of soldiers "in any house" in time of peace without the consent of the owner is another facet of that privacy. The Fourth Amendment explicitly affirms the "right of the people to be secure in their persons, houses, papers, and effects, against unreasonable searches and seizures." The Fifth Amendment in its Self-Incrimination Clause enables the citizen to create a zone of privacy which government may not force him to surrender to his detriment. The Ninth Amendment provides: "The enumeration in the Constitution, of certain rights, shall not be construed to deny or disparage others retained by the people."*

The Fourth and Fifth Amendments were described in Boyd v. United States, 116 U.S. 616, 630, *as protection against all governmental invasions "of the sanctity of a man's home and the privacies of life." We recently referred in* Mapp v. Ohio, 367 U.S. 643, 656, *to the Fourth Amendment as creating a "right to privacy, no less important than any other right carefully and particularly reserved to the people." See* Beaney, *The Constitutional Right to Privacy,* 1962 Sup. Ct. Rev. 212; Griswold, *The Right to be Let Alone,* 55 Nw. U. L. Rev. 216 (1960). . . .

The present case, then, concerns a relationship lying within the zone of privacy created by several fundamental constitutional guarantees. And it concerns a law which, in forbidding the use of contraceptives rather than regulating their manufacture or sale, seeks to achieve its goals by means having a maximum destructive impact upon that relationship. Such a law cannot stand in light of the familiar principle, so often applied by this Court, that a "governmental purpose to control or prevent activities constitutionally subject to state regulation may not be achieved by means which sweep unnecessarily broadly and thereby invade the area of protected freedoms." NAACP v. Alabama, 377 U.S. 288, 307. Would we allow the police to search the sacred precincts of marital bedrooms for telltale signs of the use of contraceptives? The very idea is repulsive to the notions of privacy surrounding the marriage relationship.

We deal with a right of privacy older than the Bill of Rights—older than our political parties, older than our school system. Marriage is a coming together for better or for worse, hopefully enduring, and intimate to the degree of being sacred. It is an association that promotes a way of life, not causes; a harmony in living, not political faiths; a bilateral loyalty, not commercial or social projects. Yet it is an association for as noble a purpose as any involved in our prior decisions.

Reversed.

MR. JUSTICE GOLDBERG, *whom* THE CHIEF JUSTICE *and* MR. JUSTICE BRENNAN *join, concurring.*

I agree with the Court that Connecticut's birth-control law unconstitutionally intrudes upon the right of marital privacy, and I join in its opinion and judgment. Although I have not accepted the view that "due process" as used in the Fourteenth Amendment incorporates all of the first eight Amendments (see my concurring opinion in Pointer v. Texas, 380 U.S. 400, 410, *and the dissenting opinion of* MR. JUSTICE BRENNAN *in* Cohen v. Hurley, 366 U.S. 117, 154), *I do agree that the concept of liberty protects those personal rights that are fundamental, and is not confined to the specific terms of the Bill of Rights. My conclusion that the concept of liberty is not so restricted and that it embraces the right of marital privacy though that right is not mentioned explicitly in the Constitution is supported both by numerous decisions of this Court, referred to in the Court's opinion, and by the language and history of the Ninth Amendment. In reaching the conclusion that the right of marital privacy is protected, as being within the protected penumbra of specific guarantees of the Bill of Rights, the Court refers to the Ninth Amendment, ante, at 484. I add these words to emphasize the relevance of that Amendment to the Court's holding. . . .*

The Ninth Amendment reads, "The enumeration in the Constitution, of certain rights, shall not be construed to deny or disparage others retained by the people." The Amendment is almost entirely the work of James Madison. It was introduced in Congress by him and passed the House and Senate with little or no debate and virtually no change in language. It was proffered to quiet expressed fears that a bill of specifically enumerated rights could not be sufficiently broad to cover all essential rights and that the specific mention of certain rights would be interpreted as a denial that others were protected.

In presenting the proposed Amendment, Madison said:

> *It has been objected also against a bill of rights, that, by enumerating particular exceptions to the grant of power, it would disparage those rights which were not placed in that enumeration; and it might follow by implication, that those rights which were not singled out, were intended to be assigned into the hands of the General Government, and were consequently insecure. This is one of the most plausible arguments I have ever heard urged against the admission of a bill of rights into this system; but, I conceive, that it may be guarded against. I have attempted it, as gentlemen may see by turning to the last clause of the fourth resolution [the Ninth Amendment]. I Annals of Congress 439 (Gales and Seaton ed. 1834). . . .*

Nor am I turning somersaults with history in arguing that the Ninth Amendment is relevant in a case dealing with a State's infringement of a fundamental right. While the Ninth Amendment—and indeed the entire Bill of Rights—originally concerned restrictions upon federal power, the subsequently enacted Fourteenth Amendment prohibits the States as well from abridging fundamental personal liberties. And, the Ninth Amendment, in indicating that not all such liberties are specifically mentioned in the first eight amendments, is surely relevant in showing the existence of other fundamental personal rights, now protected from state, as well as federal, infringement. In sum, the Ninth Amendment simply lends strong support to the view that the "liberty" protected by the Fifth and Fourteenth Amendments from infringement by the Federal Government or the States is

*not restricted to rights specifically mentioned in the first eight
amendments.* . . .

Mr. Justice Harlan, *concurring in the judgment.*

*I fully agree with the judgment of reversal, but find myself
unable to join the Court's opinion. The reason is that it seems to
me to evince an approach to this case very much like that taken
by my Brothers* Black *and* Stewart *in dissent, namely: the Due
Process Clause of the Fourteenth Amendment does not touch this
Connecticut statute unless the enactment is found to violate some
right assured by the letter or penumbra of the Bill of Rights.*

*In other words, what I find implicit in the Court's opinion is
that the "incorporation" doctrine may be used to restrict the
reach of Fourteenth Amendment Due Process. For me this is just
as unacceptable constitutional doctrine as is the use of the "incorporation" approach to impose upon the States all the requirements of the Bill of Rights as found in the provisions of the first
eight amendments and in the decisions of this Court interpreting
them. See, e.g., my concurring opinions in* Pointer v. Texas, *380
U.S. 400, 408, and* Griffin v. California, *380 U.S. 609, 615, and my
dissenting opinion in* Poe v. Ullman, *367 U.S. 497, 522, at pp.
539–545.*

*In my view, the proper constitutional inquiry in this case is
whether this Connecticut statute infringes the Due Process
Clause of the Fourteenth Amendment because the enactment
violates basic values "implicit in the concept of ordered liberty,"*
Palko v. Connecticut, *302 U.S. 319, 325. For reasons stated at
length in my dissenting opinion in* Poe v. Ullman, *supra, I believe
that it does. While the relevant inquiry may be aided by resort
to one or more of the provisions of the Bill of Rights, it is not
dependent on them or any of their radiations. The Due Process
Clause of the Fourteenth Amendment stands, in my opinion, on
its own bottom.*

*A further observation seems in order respecting the justifica-
tion of my Brothers* Black *and* Stewart *for their "incorporation"
approach to this case. Their approach does not rest on historical
reasons, which are of course wholly lacking (see Fairman, Does
the Fourteenth Amendment Incorporate the Bill of Rights? The
Original Understanding, 2 Stan. L. Rev. 5 (1949)), but on the
thesis that by limiting the content of the Due Process Clause of*

the Fourteenth Amendment to the protection of rights which can be found elsewhere in the Constitution, in this instance in the Bill of Rights, judges will thus be confined to "interpretation" of specific constitutional provisions, and will thereby be restrained from introducing their own notions of constitutional right and wrong into the "vague contours of the Due Process Clause." Rochin v. California, 342 U.S. 165, 170.

While I could not more heartily agree that judicial "self restraint" is an indispensable ingredient of sound constitutional adjudication, I do submit that the formula suggested for achieving it is more hollow than real. "Specific" provisions of the Constitution, no less than "due process," lend themselves as readily to "personal" interpretations by judges whose constitutional outlook is simply to keep the Constitution in supposed "tune with the times" (post, p. 522). Need one go further than to recall last Term's reapportionment cases, Westbury v. Sanders, 376 U.S. 1, and Reynolds v. Sims, 377 U.S. 533, where a majority of the Court "interpreted" "by the People" (Art. I, § 2) and "equal protection" (Amdt. 14) to command "one person, one vote," an interpretation that was made in the face of irrefutable and still unanswered history to the contrary? See my dissenting opinions in those cases, 376 U.S., at 20; 377 U.S., at 589.

Judicial self-restraint will not, I suggest, be brought about in the "due process" area by the historically unfounded incorporation formula long advanced by my Brother BLACK, *and now in part espoused by my Brother* STEWART. *It will be achieved in this area, as in other constitutional areas, only by continual insistence upon respect for the teachings of history, solid recognition of the basic values that underlie our society, and wise appreciation of the great roles that the doctrines of federalism and separation of powers have played in establishing and preserving American freedoms. See Adamson v. California, 332 U.S. 46, 59 (Mr. Justice Frankfurter, concurring). Adherence to these principles will not, of course, obviate all constitutional differences of opinion among judges, nor should it. Their continued recognition will, however, go farther toward keeping most judges from roaming at large in the constitutional field than will the interpolation into the Constitution of an artificial and largely illusory restriction on the content of the Due Process Clause.*

MR. JUSTICE WHITE, *concurring in the judgment.*

In my view this Connecticut law as applied to married couples deprives them of "liberty" without due process of law, as that concept is used in the Fourteenth Amendment. I therefore concur in the judgment of the Court reversing these convictions under Connecticut's aiding and abetting statute. . . .

As I read the opinions of the Connecticut courts and the argument of Connecticut in this Court, the State claims but one justification for its anti-use statute. Cf. Allied Stores of Ohio v. Bowers, 358 U.S. 522, 530; Martin v. Walton, 368 U.S. 25, 28 (DOUGLAS, J., *dissenting). There is no serious contention that Connecticut thinks the use of artificial or external methods of contraception immoral or unwise in itself, or that the anti-use statute is founded upon any policy of promoting population expansion. Rather, the statute is said to serve the State's policy against all forms of promiscuous or illicit sexual relationships, be they premarital or extramarital, concededly a permissible and legitimate legislative goal.*

Without taking issue with the premise that the fear of conception operates as a deterrent to such relationships in addition to the criminal proscriptions Connecticut has against such conduct, I wholly fail to see how the ban on the use of contraceptives by married couples in any way reinforces the State's ban on illicit sexual relationships. See Schware v. Board of Bar Examiners, 353 U.S. 232, 239. *Connecticut does not bar the importation or possession of contraceptive devices; they are not considered contraband material under state law,* State v. Certain Contraceptive Materials, 126 Conn. 428, 11 A. 2d 863, *and their availability in that State is not seriously disputed. The only way Connecticut seeks to limit or control the availability of such devices is through its general aiding and abetting statute whose operation in this context has been quite obviously ineffective and whose most serious use has been against birth-control clinics rendering advice to married, rather than unmarried, persons. Cf.* Yick Wo v. Hopkins, 118 U.S. 356. *Indeed, after over 80 years of the State's anti-use proscription, the legality of the sale of such devices to prevent disease has never been expressly passed upon, although it appears that sales have long occurred and have only infrequently been challenged. This "undeviating policy . . .*

throughout all the long years . . . bespeaks more than prosecutorial paralysis." Poe v. Ullman, 367 U.S. 497, 502. *Moreover, it would appear that the sale of contraceptives to prevent disease is plainly legal under Connecticut law.*

In these circumstances one is rather hard pressed to explain how the ban on use by married persons in any way prevents use of such devices by persons engaging in illicit sexual relations and thereby contributes to the State's policy against such relationships. Neither the state courts nor the State before the bar of this Court has tendered such an explanation. It is purely fanciful to believe that the broad proscription on use facilitates discovery of use by persons engaging in a prohibited relationship or for some other reason makes such use more unlikely and thus can be supported by any sort of administrative consideration. Perhaps the theory is that the flat ban on use prevents married people from possessing contraceptives and without the ready availability of such devices for use in the marital relationship, there will be no or less temptation to use them in extramarital ones. This reasoning rests on the premise that married people will comply with the anti-use ban in regard to their marital relationship, notwithstanding total nonenforcement in this context and apparent nonenforcibility, but will not comply with criminal statutes prohibiting extramarital affairs and the anti-use statute in respect to illicit sexual relationships, a premise whose validity has not been demonstrated and whose intrinsic validity is not very evident. At most the broad ban is of marginal utility to the declared objective. A statute limiting its prohibition on use to persons engaging in the prohibited relationship would serve the end posited by Connecticut in the same way, and with the same effectiveness, or ineffectiveness, as the broad anti-use statute under attack in this case. I find nothing in this record justifying the sweeping scope of this statute, with its telling effect on the freedoms of married persons, and therefore conclude that it deprives such persons of liberty without due process of law.

MR. JUSTICE BLACK, *with whom* MR. JUSTICE STEWART *joins, dissenting.*

I agree with my Brother STEWART'S *dissenting opinion. And like him I do not to any extent whatever base my view that this Connecticut law is constitutional on a belief that the law is wise or that its policy is a good one. In order that there may be no room at all to doubt why I vote as I do, I feel constrained to add that the law is every bit as offensive to me as it is to my Brethren of the majority and my Brothers* HARLAN, WHITE *and* GOLDBERG *who, reciting reasons why it is offensive to them, hold it unconstitutional. There is no single one of the graphic and eloquent strictures and criticisms fired at the policy of this Connecticut law either by the Court's opinion or by those of my concurring Brethren to which I cannot subscribe—except their conclusion that the evil qualities they see in the law make it unconstitutional.*

Had the doctor defendant here, or even the nondoctor defendant, been convicted for doing nothing more than expressing opinions to persons coming to the clinic that certain contraceptive devices, medicines or practices would do them good and would be desirable, or for telling people how devices could be used, I can think of no reasons at this time why their expressions of views would not be protected by the First and Fourteenth Amendments, which guarantee freedom of speech. Cf. Brotherhood of Railroad Trainmen *v.* Virginia ex rel. Virginia State Bar, *377 U.S. 1;* NAACP *v.* Button, *371 U.S. 415. But speech is one thing; conduct and physical activities are quite another. See, e.g.,* Cox *v.* Louisiana, *379 U.S. 536, 554–555;* Cox *v.* Louisiana, *379 U.S. 559, 563–564; id., 575–584 (concurring opinion);* Giboney *v.* Empire Storage & Ice Co., *336 U.S. 490; cf.* Reynolds *v.* United States, *98 U.S. 145, 163–164. The two defendants here were active participants in an organization which gave physical examinations to women, advised them what kind of contraceptive devices or medicines would most likely be satisfactory for them, and then supplied the devices themselves, all for a graduated scale of fees, based on the family income. Thus these defendants admittedly engaged with others in a planned course of conduct to help people violate the Connecticut law. Merely because some speech was used in carrying on that conduct—just as in ordinary life some speech accompanies most kinds of conduct—we are not in my view any more justified in holding that the First Amendment forbids the State to punish their conduct. Strongly as I desire to protect all First Amendment freedoms, I am unable to stretch the Amendment so as to afford protection to the conduct of these defendants in violating the Connecticut law. What would be the constitutional fate of the law if hereafter applied to punish nothing but speech is, as I have said, quite another matter.*

The Court talks about a constitutional "right of privacy" as though there is some constitutional provision or provisions forbidding any law ever to be passed which might abridge the "privacy" of individuals. But there is not. There are, of course, guarantees in certain specific constitutional provisions which are designed in part to protect privacy at certain times and places with respect to certain activities. Such, for example, is the Fourth Amendment's guarantee against "unreasonable searches and seizures." But I think it belittles that Amendment to talk about it as though it protects nothing but "privacy." To treat it that way is to give it a niggardly interpretation, not the kind of liberal reading I think any Bill of Rights provision should be given. The average man would very likely not have his feelings soothed any more by having his property seized openly than by having it seized privately and by stealth. He simply wants his property left alone. And a person can be just as much, if not more, irritated, annoyed and injured by an unceremonious public arrest by a policeman as he is by a seizure in the privacy of his office or home.

One of the most effective ways of diluting or expanding a constitutionally guaranteed right is to substitute for the crucial word or words of a constitutional guarantee another word or words, more or less flexible and more or less restricted in meaning. This fact is well illustrated by the use of the term "right of privacy" as a comprehensive substitute for the Fourth Amendment's guarantee against "unreasonable searches and seizures." "Privacy" is a broad, abstract and ambiguous concept which can easily be shrunken in meaning but which can also, on the other hand, easily be interpreted as a constitutional ban against many things other than searches and seizures. I have expressed the view many times that First Amendment freedoms, for example, have suffered from a failure of the courts to stick to the simple language of the First Amendment in construing it, instead of invoking multitudes of words substituted for those the Framers used. See, e.g., New York Times Co. v. Sullivan, 376 U.S. 254, 293 *(concurring opinion); cases collected in* City of El Paso v. Simmons, 379 U.S. 497, 517, n. 1 *(dissenting opinion);* Black, The

Bill of Rights, 35 N.Y.U.L. Rev. 865. For these reasons I get nowhere in this case by talk about a constitutional "right of privacy" as an emanation from one or more constitutional provisions. I like my privacy as well as the next one, but I am nevertheless compelled to admit that government has a right to invade it unless prohibited by some specific constitutional provision. For these reasons I cannot agree with the Court's judgment and the reasons it gives for holding this Connecticut law unconstitutional.

This brings me to the arguments made by my Brothers HARLAN, WHITE *and* GOLDBERG *for invalidating the Connecticut law. Brothers* HARLAN *and* WHITE *would invalidate it by reliance on the Due Process Clause of the Fourteenth Amendment, but Brother* GOLDBERG, *while agreeing with Brother* HARLAN, *relies also on the Ninth Amendment. I have no doubt that the Connecticut law could be applied in such a way as to abridge freedom of speech and press and therefore violate the First and Fourteenth Amendments. My disagreement with the Court's opinion holding that there is such a violation here is a narrow one, relating to the application of the First Amendment to the facts and circumstances of this particular case. But my disagreement with Brothers* HARLAN, WHITE *and* GOLDBERG *is more basic. I think that if properly construed neither the Due Process Clause nor the Ninth Amendment, nor both together, could under any circumstances be a proper basis for invalidating the Connecticut law. I discuss the due process and Ninth Amendment arguments together because on analysis they turn out to be the same thing—merely using different words to claim for this Court and the federal judiciary power to invalidate any legislative act which the judges find irrational, unreasonable or offensive.*

The due process argument which my Brothers HARLAN *and* WHITE *adopt here is based, as their opinions indicate, on the premise that this Court is vested with power to invalidate all state laws that it considers to be arbitrary, capricious, unreasonable, or oppressive, or on this Court's belief that a particular state law under scrutiny has no "rational or justifying" purpose, or is offensive to a "sense of fairness and justice." If these formulas based on "natural justice," or others which mean the same thing, are to prevail, they require judges to determine what is or is not constitutional on the basis of their own appraisal of what laws are unwise or unecessary. The power to make such decisions is of course that of a legislative body. Surely it has to be admitted that no provision of the Constitution specifically gives such blanket power to courts to exercise such a supervisory veto over the wisdom and value of legislative policies and to hold unconstitutional those laws which they believe unwise or dangerous. I readily admit that no legislative body, state or national, should pass laws that can justly be given any of the invidious labels invoked as constitutional excuses to strike down state laws. But perhaps it is not too much to say that no legislative body ever does pass laws without believing that they will accomplish a sane, rational, wise and justifiable purpose. While I completely subscribe to the holding of* Marbury v. Madison, 1 Cranch 137, *and subsequent cases, that our Court has constitutional power to strike down statutes, state or federal, that violate commands of the Federal Constitution, I do not believe that we are granted power by the Due Process Clause or any other constitutional provision or provisions to measure constitutionality by our belief that legislation is arbitrary, capricious or unreasonable, or accomplishes no justifiable purpose, or is offensive to our own notions of "civilized standards of conduct." Such an appraisal of the wisdom of legislation is an attribute of the power to make laws, not of the power to interpret them. The use by federal courts of such a formula or doctrine or whatnot to veto federal or state laws simply takes away from Congress and States the power to make laws based on their own judgment of fairness and wisdom and transfers that power to this Court for ultimate determination—a power which was specifically denied to federal courts by the convention that framed the Constitution. . . .*

MR. JUSTICE STEWART, *whom* MR. JUSTICE BLACK *joins, dissenting.*

Since 1879 Connecticut has had on its books a law which forbids the use of contraceptives by anyone. I think this is an uncommonly silly law. As a practical matter, the law is obviously unenforceable, except in the oblique context of the present case. As a philosophical matter, I believe the use of contraceptives in the relationship of marriage should be left to personal and private choice, based upon each individual's moral, ethical, and religious beliefs. As a matter of social policy, I think professional counsel about methods of birth control should be available to all, so that each individual's choice can be meaningfully made. But we are not asked in this case to say whether we think this law is unwise, or even asinine. We are asked to hold that it violates the United States Constitution. And that I cannot do.

In the course of its opinion the Court refers to no less than six Amendments to the Constitution: the First, the Third, the Fourth, the Fifth, the Ninth, and the Fourteenth. But the Court does not say which of these Amendments, if any, it thinks is infringed by this Connecticut law.

We are told that the Due Process Clause of the Fourteenth Amendment is not, as such, the "guide" in this case. With that much I agree. There is no claim that this law, duly enacted by the Connecticut Legislature, is unconstitutionally vague. There is no claim that the appellants were denied any of the elements of procedural due process at their trial, so as to make their convictions constitutionally invalid. And, as the Court says, the day has long passed since the Due Process Clause was regarded as a proper instrument for determining "the wisdom, need, and propriety" of state laws. Compare Lochner v. New York, 198 U.S. 45, with Ferguson v. Skrupa, 372 U.S. 726. My Brothers HARLAN and WHITE to the contrary, "[w]e have returned to the original constitutional proposition that courts do not substitute their social and economic beliefs for the judgment of legislative bodies, who are elected to pass laws." Ferguson v. Skrupa, supra, at 730.

As to the First, Third, Fourth, and Fifth Amendments, I can find nothing in any of them to invalidate this Connecticut law, even assuming that all those Amendments are fully applicable against the States. It has not even been argued that this is a law "respecting an establishment of religion, or prohibiting the free exercise thereof." And surely, unless the solemn process of constitutional adjudication is to descend to the level of a play on words, there is not involved here any abridgment of "the freedom of speech, or of the press; or the right of the people peaceably to assemble, and to petition the Government for a redress of grievances." No soldier has been quartered in any house. There has been no search, and no seizure. Nobody has been compelled to be a witness against himself.

The Court also quotes the Ninth Amendment, and my Brother GOLDBERG's concurring opinion relies heavily upon it.

But to say that the Ninth Amendment has anything to do with this case is to turn somersaults with history. The Ninth Amendment, like its companion the Tenth, which this Court held "states but a truism that all is retained which has been surrendered," United States v. Darby, 312 U.S. 100, 124, was framed by James Madison and adopted by the States simply to make clear that the adoption of the Bill of Rights did not alter the plan that the Federal Government was to be a government of express and limited powers, and that all rights and powers not delegated to it were retained by the people and the individual States. Until today no member of this Court has ever suggested that the Ninth Amendment meant anything else, and the idea that a federal court could ever use the Ninth Amendment to annul a law passed by the elected representatives of the people of the State of Connecticut would have caused James Madison no little wonder.

What provision of the Constitution, then, does make this state law invalid? The Court says it is the right of privacy "created by several fundamental constitutional guarantees." With all deference, I can find no such general right of privacy in the Bill of Rights, in any other part of the Constitution, or in any case ever before decided by this Court.

At the oral argument in this case we were told that the Connecticut law does not "conform to current community standards." But it is not the function of this Court to decide cases on the basis of community standards. We are here to decide cases "agreeably to the Constitution and laws of the United States." It is the essence of judicial duty to subordinate our own personal views, our own ideas of what legislation is wise and what is not. If, as I should surely hope, the law before us does not reflect the standards of the people of Connecticut, the people of Connecticut can freely exercise their true Ninth and Tenth Amendment rights to persuade their elected representatives to repeal it. That is the constitutional way to take this law off the books.

TABLE OF CASES

INDEX